METAPHYSICS FOR A HUMANIST

METAPHYSICS FOR A HUMANIST

S.K. LEUNG

eMPIRICUS
BOOKS
London, England

First published in Great Britain 2001 by
Empiricus Books
76 Great Titchfield Street,
London W1P 7AF

www.januspublishing.co.uk

British Library Cataloguing-in-Publication Data
A catalogue record for this book
is available from the British Library

ISBN 1 902835 11 5

Typeset in 11pt Baskerville
By Chris Cowlin

Cover Design Lee Poole

Printed and bound in Great Britain

Nobody who devotes himself to science from other reasons than superficial ones, like ambition, money making, or the pleasure of brain-sport, can neglect the questions, what are the aims of science, how far are its general results true, what is essential and what based on accidental features of the development?

Concepts which have been proved to be useful in ordering things easily acquire such an authority over us that we forget their human origin and accept them as invariable. Then they become 'necessities of thought,' 'given *a priori*,' etc. The path of scientific progress is then, by such errors, barred for a long time. It is therefore no useless game if we are practising to analyse current notions and to point out on what conditions their justification and usefulness depends, how they have grown especially from the data of experience. In this way their exaggerated authority is broken. They are removed, if they cannot properly legitimate themselves; corrected, if their correspondence to the given things was too negligently established; replaced by others, if a new system can be developed that we prefer for good reasons.

Albert Einstein
From the obituary article on Ernst Mach
Phys. Zeitschr. 17, p.101 (1916)

CONTENTS

INTRODUCTION

Metaphysics seems to be far removed from everyday concerns; not all of us can always find satisfaction in the mere, daily chore of existence. Human spirit even in the firmest state of belief in materialism will pop up now and then, in hours of discontentment, to ask questions of, or try to understand, a reality to which human existence is inevitably bonded. What there is, and what reality is, are not always seen to be important unless and until a man has to search in his soul to understand his actions and those of others. It is in this connection that metaphysics is not just an item of knowledge or an insight, but a way for satisfaction in all things we do in this world.

In a way, to write about metaphysics is to write about the 'universe', not of its scientific details, but of a quest for the understanding of what the 'universe' is. But all that can be said of a universe is nothing but generality, that is universality. In this book, universals are seen as the content of humanity; thus the understanding of universals cannot be subjected to a limitation set by men, since the limitation in understanding comes as naturally the sun. It is the nature of men that sets its own limitation, and the imposition of a limit to our understanding is not only unnecessary, but futile. This limitation is self-prohibiting in that human knowledge will cease to progress when it reaches this limit. There is no need to shout aloud about this limitation or to preach such. The universe is necessarily a human universe otherwise it cannot be conceived at all. That the universe has a huge amount of human content is what human metaphysics is all about. The Greek and Cartesian rationalistic metaphysics are not humanistic metaphysics since their conceived universal content of necessity cannot explain human values, the acquisition of knowledge of this universe, together with human interactions imposed not by reasoning within universality and necessity. For reasoning, if it is just logical deduction, cannot allow men to get out of what is already contained in notions with which the universe is composed. A rational universe can only be a universe given, which man must find with his reason, and to which he must subserve. This is all very well if men do not see themselves as free in their nature with values that are not explicable by reason.

The explanation of the universe is the understanding of the universe in terms of human endeavours and in this sense, the universe is a reflection of human limitation as well as human excellence. To see the reason and purpose of the universe also reflects much of man's own values and nature; for a purpose can only make sense within man's nature, outside which a man cannot conceive of it. It is man who conceives of a purpose within his own conception of his nature. In this way, the purpose of the universe and man's purpose are one and the same. Each man sees the purpose of the universe from his own perspective, for if there is a universal purpose, men would not have disputed as he has among his contemporaries. Some think that the universal purpose conceived by them is a necessity because they can deduce it from their formal logic with such certainty without realizing its subjective content, and that they have imposed a subjective view upon others who may not have reasoned as vigorously as they do, perhaps. One of the purposes of this book is to set out the inevitable human content in a rational universe seen by them.

Since metaphysics is not remote from many human beliefs, the popular idea of personal identity that gives rise to many political concepts of nationhood or community, is considered a central point in humanity. There are two considered opinions for a person's identity. First, one may consider that a man has no identity unless he partakes in some objective existents outside himself. Carefully considering this, we shall see that this is a popular belief of how a human identity comes about with or without our being conscious of it. The second way, which I think must be the true way, is by the understanding of the substantive content of one's own being, extending it outside to the common, essential similarities among others. These similarities are not arbitrary since they constitute my own being and underline my understanding of others. Thus this book attempts to argue for the substantive content that constitutes the being of men.

Why is this metaphysics called humanist metaphysics? I consider the alternative metaphysics to this show themselves in two opposing camps. One is materialism, in all forms including scientific materialism, realism or physicalism. The other is the metaphysics of rationalism, of any kind. But humanism itself is very difficult to define since the very nature of humanity can be seen from any of these philosophical viewpoints. What kind of humanism one should believe depends on one's view of what human nature is. The title of this metaphysics by no means claims a universal doctrine on humanity. Human nature in my view is not totally materialistic or rationalistic. I say 'totally' because in this metaphysics there is an admission of a minimal dualistic nature in man's understanding. This minimal objectivity lies in human nature itself and perhaps something 'unspeakable' outside us. Hence this philosophy will continue to argue for what true humanism should be, as does another book.[1]

In the present volume, readers will not find detailed expositions of what other philosophers have said about the various topics in this book. Quotations of, and references to, others are kept to a minimum, used only to illustrate important points or to explain terms that are more eloquently put by others. In this book, I tend to get straight to the core problems to argue for the validity of alternative views of the problems. The validity of the conclusions is thus left to the strength of the arguments and I would not ask for more. I do believe that there are some new insights into various philosophical problems in this book; and if the arguments are not vigorous enough to convince, perhaps these insights may inspire others' effort.

PART I

EXISTENCE AND REALITY

1 The separation of epistemology from metaphysics

1.1 The problems in defining existence

Three ontological terms

The terms, 'existence', 'being' and 'reality' are unavoidably used in a manner interchangeable among themselves, especially between 'existence' and 'being'. It is not uncommon for us to say 'existence' is synonymous with 'being'. If there is anyone erudite enough to spell out philosophers' curious definitions of these terms, it should be Bertrand Russell. In his *The Problems of Philosophy*[14] (p51) he says with confidence and assurance to the readers,

> We shall find it convenient only to speak of things existing when they are in time, that is to say, when we can point to some time at which they exist (not excluding the possibility of their existing at all times). Thus thoughts and feelings, mind and the physical objects exist. But universals do not exist in this sense; we shall say that they subsist or have being, where 'being' is opposed to 'existence' as being timeless.[14]

Thus according to Russell, being is marked out from existence by being extra-sensual and extra-experiential; there are 'beings' over and above what can be perceived, sensed in space and time. If God is a being, God cannot exist according to this definition. Many proofs of God's existence rely on this notion of 'being', a timeless being. I hope we can see that the problem is with consistency in the use of terms.

In a sense, one may think that definitions of these terms do not matter that much so long as we recognize their application. However, definitions are important in order that they are applied consistently in explaining the world of existents, of beings and of reality. In this first part, I do not make a distinction between 'existence' and 'being' in the way Russell does. The distinction between being timeless and not timeless, in 'being' and 'existence' is brought out as a distinction between 'reality' and 'existence'.

It has been said that which there is, should be known to be. If so, is that which is known, always an existent? Or must that whichever exists be real? Is an existent a reality or must reality exist? These are curious questions not because they are difficult to answer, but because they have crossed the divide between epistemology and metaphysics and need some detailed analysis. Within these terms such as 'what there is'; 'what exists' and 'what is real', there lie some inevitable entailments. What exists must be known to exist, otherwise how do we know it existed? Whatever is a being, must exist, otherwise how can it be there? What exists must be real, otherwise how can it exist? Whatever that is there or whatever that is real, must be known to be so too. All these must have been accepted by many. For those who have doubts must be aware that we discuss, analyse, define and search for a meaning of, and say something about, these terms through nothing other than our understanding of them. This is in a way appealing to our knowledge to establish what there is, what exists and what is real. If we reverse the questions and ask if our knowledge of all existents, all reality and all things, depends on the beings, the existents or reality, then the real problem begins.

Of course, it is possible to say that speculative metaphysics is not about a metaphysical system expounding a reality, an existent or a being to us, but about how we can define reality, existence and being in our own particular way so as to fit our own respective metaphysical systems into a universe. One can say that something is real but does not exist or something can exist but is not real. One can say that existence is dependent while being is not. Hence within these criteria we strive to see the universe within the confines we place around it. That a thing can have a being, but is not real; or that a thing can be real, but is not a being; or that a thing can exist, but is not real nor a being; or that a thing can be, but does not exist, are all about different conceptions of the meanings of reality, existence and being. The history of philosophy tells us that men cannot formulate coherently to explain how it is that something can be of independent existence or a being and yet of no existence. But this is not to suggest that a definition of reality, existence or being is not sought after; for it is perfectly within human curiosity or desperation to yearn for, or to explore whether there are things whose being is quite independent of our conception of them. The case of 'God' is a good example. In that case, I would use the term 'dependent existence' or 'independent existence' without having to eliminate the notion of 'existence', or to replace it with another word, such as 'being'. We are not playing a word game here. 'Existence' has certainly more connotations than a mere 'dependence'. Nor would I dare venture to say that what is real may not exist; I would rather say that there is a concept of 'permanency' separating these two words about reality.

It is quite a curious thing because we rely on our knowledge to establish what there is, what is real and what exists, and yet when it comes to justifying our knowledge of the existence of these things, or to justifying our knowledge in turn by our knowledge, we are hesitant. We are staring at the chasm between knowledge and things. Somehow, those who say that a thing exists irrespectively of whatever we know about it or not, must have different notions of these terms. Or those who struggle to tell us what there is, what exists and what is real, must be wasting their time, if they cannot substantiate the knowledge of the thing and at the same time say that again its existential properties are firmly rooted to sayings and experience. Let me examine these existential notions one by one.

Existence distinguished from reality

If there is something there, do we have to say that we know it is there? Leaving out this problematic word 'know' which involves the concepts of truth, falsehood and belief, what can we put in its place? If we cannot, we have to say that if something is there, we have to be incorrigibly certain that it is there. One problem at present is not about how we can be so certain, but about the possibility that we are wrong about this thing being there. It is this possibility that enables us to have the contrasting terms, 'real' and 'exist'. But something which is not there is not real and does not exist. Again, why should something which is not there be real or unreal? Something which is not there is a void in all conceivable possibilities, including thoughts; the sense of 'real' is fatally indifferent to all these. For nothing can be asserted in a state of non-being and at the same time named. Is it true to say that we have this terms 'real' because of the possibility that we can be wrong about this reality? Otherwise what can we say of something not being there, with this concept of reality? One should draw attention to C. S. Lewis's 'nobody' in *Alice in Wonderland* to appreciate the absurdity in asserting a non-being and naming it at the same time.

'Reality' is epistemological

Again, we contrast the notion of 'something is there' with the notion of 'something is not there' and conclude that it is only in the face of these two contraries that we create this concept of 'real'. And we cannot say that something is not there, is unreal because this concept of 'unreal' asserts no entity and only applies to a contrary position of the original sense of 'something is there'. Something not there is neither real nor unreal. So, when we are talking about something unreal, or something real for the same reason, we are talking about epistemology alone and not metaphysics. When we say that something is there, it must not automatically be followed by saying that it is real. Readers must be immensely patient with me to see that I have not necessarily advocated that when I say that something is there, I do not naturally believe that it is the case. My conclusion is to bring about the chasm between what there is and what is real, or between metaphysics and epistemology.

If I apply this chasm to thoughts, I see that the argument is a lot clearer. If there is a thought of a thought, does it make sense for me to say if this thought is real or not real; for the possibility of this thought, in being thought of, being mistaken, is unimaginable? Why is it unimaginable? The existence of a thought cannot be doubted. Even when we forget something, its existence is not a question since it is not in our consciousness until it is supposedly recalled. If it is not recalled, it would not be and if it is recalled, then, it will exist. Therefore, the dilemma of whether there is a thought or not, will not exist at the same time in questioning such existence. It will be absurd for the dilemma to exist at the same time. I may say that I had a thought of such at an earlier time, but the existence of that thought depends on my awareness of the present and not my awareness at the earlier time. At an earlier time, I would not have had a notion that this particular thought did not exist, any more than I can at present claim that the thought is not with me. It is this temporal difficulty and our imagination that create our retrospective correction of our existential claims, and hence the two possibilities of being true or false, in the immediacy of reality. This in turn gives rise to these, the terms of 'real' and 'unreal' in our perception of things.

Existence not perceived

Examine the empirical idealists' 'infamous' proposition: things do not exist when not perceived. The argument that we know things through only our perceptual experience and nothing else, is very persuasive. If this premiss is accepted, anything lacking the measure of experience or sense-data (if they are seen too as human experience), derives no exposition of external existence over and above sensibility, and therefore does not exist without it. Its existence depends on it. How is it that such a logical conclusion can play havoc with our common sense which happily accepts the continuation of existence in things unperceived? This is the main point I would like to bring out clearly, if not forcefully.

How is reality different from existence?

The retrospective view of the whole perceptual experience at different times provides us with the possibility of falsehood in what we call an existence, but immediate instances of our perceptual experience cannot provide such. What we can know about something, is really about the instances in time, of the conception of knowledge, and not reality. To consider human knowledge as a whole in a personal history is to consider the relations among a person's instances in the conception of knowledge, and not about the nature of immediate knowledge itself. That is reality. When we attempt to justify reality by the instances of perception, we lack many facets collected at different times. A cup in front of me shows me its parts in its colours, shades and other properties, and in more than one instance; the reality of this cup, judged by me rightly or wrongly, is by the totality of many qualities of many instances, some of which may not be in the immediacy of perception, such as its bottom or its back.

Hence the question of metaphysics is the question of the totality of instances of our perceptual and conceptual experience. It is not to say that existence cannot be unrelated to the totality of our knowledge, but that, an instance of perceptual knowledge is only about existence alone. It is this difficulty in isolating instances from a totality that encourages the mixing of epistemological issues with metaphysical ones. This is my view that mixing these two questions creates many philosophical problems in metaphysics. The conclusion I draw from this is that a true proposition in epistemology may not necessarily be a true proposition in metaphysics, or that a false proposition in epistemology may not necessarily be false in metaphysics, which takes into account the totality of instances of experience and their relationship. Again, this is not to say that metaphysics can be studied without perceptual knowledge, but that knowledge of an instance can exclude metaphysical considerations of the totality of experience and relations within itself.

Existence is an instance of reality

Returning to the three notions of 'what there is', 'what exists' and 'what is real', I think that these notions all have their instances and totality. An assertion of something being 'there' has an instance of knowing 'what there is' and nothing more, like seeing a part of a cup in front of me. Knowing what this cup is, in its totality of all relational qualities, just as knowing the property of gold, is about a reality established by these relations in the totality of knowledge, past and present. That is metaphysic. As I have argued before, the notions of 'exist' and 'real' need a totality of knowledge of different instances to provide the possibility of a falsehood and, therefore of 'non-exist' and 'unreal'. In an instance of knowing what there is, we cannot necessarily make an inference from existence to reality.

Incorrigibility of existence (even if it is not reality)

What there is, is an instance of judgement, an epistemological judgement that can be indifferent to the notion of reality. This is not entirely without some historical insight in philosophical investigations. The two incorrigible sources of certainty, in the Cartesian thoughts, and in the given and immediate empirical sensibility, claimed by philosophers, lay down an incorrigibility of the instances of immediate knowledge. The incorrigibility of a thought's existence, as opposed to the existence of 'thought in general' (the distinction will be made later) together with the incorrigibility of immediate sense experience, are about instances and not about the totality. If my argument is correct, accepting this incorrigibility (epistemological) of an instance but not accepting a metaphysical conclusion (totality), may not be contradictory at all. Thus Berkeley's famous conclusion that things do not exist unperceived can be true as long as it is referring to the immediate instances of knowledge (epistemological) only, but not to the totality of perceptual experience. I am here using the words 'can be true' because I wish to emphasize that this conclusion may be extended into metaphysical investigation of reality for different reasons.

The notions of existence and reality may or may not be synonymous, and if they are not, then that which exists may not be real or vice versa. This will be discussed later (see p.50). However, if from 'what there is' we infer 'it is real' or 'it is not real', we must introduce clear terminology and content in our reasoning to jump this metaphysico-epistemological divide. What there is will always be what there is, a cold fact of nature devoid of human content of beliefs, not a candidate for doubts, therefore, truth neutral. Unless, of course, men look upon cold facts from a human angle and introduce relations for their own understanding. Later on, the 'that which is real must exist', and 'that which exists may not be real', will be considered (see p.50).

1.2 Metaphysical and epistemological priorities

Their separation

Having made a separation of epistemology from metaphysics, I now propose a notion of priority in respect of these two aspects of philosophy. A metaphysical priority is a temporal priority in events and movements. That something happens before something else is a priority of this nature. Normally, we perceive natural events in the temporal order given to us and there is no possibility that we see things in a reverse temporal order. Thus our knowledge of these events in this sequence is a normality conforming to the 'temporal order of nature'. That is to say, that we cannot know of events in advance of their happening, and we know of prior events before we know of posterior events that occur later. Thus, if this is the nature of things, an epistemological priority, i.e. knowing something before something else, is not at all different from a metaphysical priority.

However, there are times when we know of something first, which occurs in nature in posteriority to something else, before we know of this something else, then I shall say this is an epistemological priority, which is not the same as a metaphysical priority. This may be an odd notion, but this is not to tell readers that nature has two separate temporal 'orders'. An epistemological priority owes more to men's limitations than nature's inconsistency. This is not what we may call a logical priority. This will be explained later on. Sometimes, we know of two things at the same time even though we may think that they have a sequential order. Of course, the ideas of epistemological priority and simultaneity can only come about in philosophical deliberations. I can think of three types of concepts where an epistemological priority but not a metaphysical priority, is conceivable.

The first type is in the understanding of cause and effect. In understanding causality, we do not start with a premiss that every cause has an effect, but a premiss that every event must have a cause. The distinction here is the epistemological priority in knowing an effect first before knowing its cause. In another book of mine (*Causation and Causality*, Empiricus Books, London 2001) discussing causality, I have elaborated my arguments on this priority. The argument is simply that if something must have a cause, we must start from the knowledge of this something and proceed to argue for the existence of the other, a cause. This is the argument from the effect to a cause, and the effect is an ordinary event with an implication of causality. We cannot argue from a cause or any prior event, claiming that there will be an effect to follow, because such an argument is analytically circular in having the notion of causality readily contained in the concept attributed to the first event. Such an argument from an event to a cause is effectively an argument from a subsequently known effect to a cause that is temporally prior. As we know, nature's events have the temporal order from cause to effect and not the other way round, hence I say that in causality, effects are epistemologically prior but temporally posterior to their cause.

The second case refers to the conceptions of intention and action. The understanding of an intention is in the action itself. An intention to act without an action is nothing but a thought. A thought is not always followed by an action; therefore, a thought without an action is strictly not an intention. Hence, we say that we know of an intention through its action; and in order to know an intention we must know of an action first to which it is supposed to relate. However, in nature's scheme, we always conceive a thought (not yet an intention) first before we act upon it and in this sense a thought to act is temporally prior to its action. Yet, in terms of knowing a thought as an intention, an action has an epistemological priority to it; that is to say, we must know the act first. The introduction of this epistemological priority is not merely to argue whether the effect is known before its cause or an action is known before its intention, but to bring out the possibility of conceiving that the epistemological order (also temporal) of knowing events and their actual temporal priority (metaphysical) can be different. Perhaps, perceptual knowledge is one too.

The last case concerns the notions of essence and existence. In this connection, there is the same sense of confusion between metaphysical reality and epistemological reality, which I have discussed earlier. The question of whether essence precedes existence or existence precedes essence is quite contentious. The traditionalists will hold that essence precedes existence and they are so firm in their belief that the idea of existence preceding essence is regarded as irrational. From a metaphysical point of view, one can be convinced that without essence there can be no existence. But the revolt against this can hardly be seen to have started from the same metaphysical point. To answer this question from the epistemological point of view, one asks the question of whether we know of the essence or an existence first. If one holds, for whatever reasons, that we know of existence first before we know of the essence, one is hardly committing the sin of being irrational. In terms of knowing, it is certainly possible that we know of something with a minimal inference of an essence; but to say that essence precedes existence is to separate the existence from essence itself in order to create a precedence of one over another, temporal or otherwise. Thus, it is not rational to claim that we can have essence without existence, which is nonsense. If we accept that essence is existence without the separation of precedence, then they must coexist at the same time, either metaphysically or epistemologically.

Do we know of an essence before we know of its existence, or do we know of an existent before we know of its essence? These are not easy questions to answer. But if we wish to answer them, we must be aware whether this priority is metaphysical or epistemological. If we do not know of something, we cannot say that it exists, but it does not follow that it may not exist at all. But philosophy is not about things of which we cannot even conceive. Therefore, the first inference is an epistemological inference and the latter is a metaphysical inference. I think it is not irrational to say that I know of something without knowing what (essence) there is; for this may be an epistemological mistake but not a metaphysical mistake. An epistemological mistake cannot rule out a metaphysical existence or non-existence. This will not create a contradiction. That I may infer an existent without knowing what it is, can be wrong depending on how I make this inference. If there is no existent, it is not because of my error, and if there is an existent, it is not because of my inference. In my view, essence and existence are one and the same if we hold such a view and if they are not, they should coexist without any precedence and priority. We cannot say of one without the other and because of this indispensability, they must coexist. This difference should highlight the need to separate epistemological reality from metaphysical reality.

2 Existence

2.1 Knowledge and existence

Problems in describing an existence

Our experience is rich beyond what we can say of it. So too are our thoughts in the process of being conceived. When I open my eyes, I see a house, a tree, a garden, a road and some people. Are these all that I see? What is more that I have not seen? I can go on and on adding details to a house, inside and outside; to a tree with a size and its numerous leaves, colours and shades; to grass spread across the garden with what is lying under it; and to the people, who are of course more infinite for me to fathom. Not only the quantities of things, big and small, are beyond our finite descriptions, the actual qualities upon which we lay our existential question in these things, are impossible to describe in their fullness. Here, I am not only talking about an understanding of qualities shared by us, but also the direct identity of and the exact reference to, the shared (universal) data or qualities. This is an old philosophical problem. For example, redness as either a sensation in us, or a sense datum outside that cannot be described by words without the help of objects we can point to, even if we can say that their understanding is shared among us all.

An expression alone cannot always succeed in referring to an object that it sets about describing. For expressions can no more fulfil this function than the mind, and no more refer to the sensibility in a particular way than in a general way. This is not due to the shortcoming of our language, but due to a missing link between a language used and the users. The failure of a referential function in words leaves words only with meaning, which cannot be referential as regards identity. Hence, there is the question of how we can use words to introduce existents in space and time. Russell has his ingenious solution in saying that there are certain expressions with definite descriptions which, though being non-committal to any existent in particular, nevertheless may give finite descriptions pointing to particulars. This description sets a parameter for something to exist within but not without this parameter. To put a complex parameter in a simple example, an expression of 'The author of Waverley was a poet' will have a parameter in 'Something wrote Waverley and this something was a poet and nothing else wrote Waverley'. By breaking down a language into bits in order to show the constituents of meaning, one can assume too much and assume too little at different times. One can assume too much by using terms, as they are called by logicians 'bound variables' or 'variables of quantification', such as 'something', 'someone', 'everything', 'everyone' or 'nothing', in such a way as to assume that no ontological commitments can be inferred by these terms. One can assume too little by ignoring the connotative content in expressions in favour of ontological terms.

Failure of the ontological function in words

I do not think I can justify that using a term 'something' can give a proposition an ontological non-commitment, anymore than I can justify that it cannot. I see the problem not in terms of how clever we can be to find a definition through a maze of words, and to determine what there is. I see the problem in the divide between personal experience and the description of it. To say that expressions cannot denote and have no part in denoting objects, is the position of the anti-realists or idealists and the opposite is the position of the realists. Words and expressions are no doubt general in their nature in an ontological 'reference' (if there is such a thing), but it is the instances of experience that are particular. Therefore, the particularity of all things does not lie outside personal experience without implying that all personal experiences are particular.

Experience and awareness are indescribable in precision, unspeakable and also inaccessible to others. To this end, I have argued about this in detail. The gist of the idea is that our shared common reality is presupposed through the understanding of words by pointing to (invoking) these experiences, but is not a consequent of a common linguistic understanding. If this is so, descriptions, despite having interpersonal understanding, cannot be a direct translation of experience in perceptual aspects, and therefore cannot possibly be a definite referential tool independent of recalled experience. An expression that can successfully 'denote' or 'refer' to objects and existents, must be conditional to having an understanding of the particulars, since it is a person (the hearer) who agrees to and understands a reference proposed by an ontological expression. When there is a particular understanding, and if there is also a 'referential' content within, it is this understanding that provides a possible reference to anything particular. If so, words only serve as a pointer to a common, particular experience so presupposed. Thus an ontological reference is not in the words thought out to have such functions, but in the immediate experience or thoughts, which words can provoke. The expression, 'the present King of France' may succeed in referring to an individual if the circumstances of the personal experience will warrant such reference; it will not succeed if the circumstances of personal experience will not warrant such reference, and, above all, if its connotation is not understood. To understand this expression, one should not only know the connotations in 'the', 'present', 'king' and 'France', one must also know the history of France, the convention about kingdoms and kings. Words and expressions are contingent in this aspect of 'referring to objects', and have not a separate function set apart from connotation.

Existence is about the existence of particulars in space and time and that must be found in the immediacy of perceptual instances, not in words, not in reasoning and not in the relations and association with other things (which is reality). As regards the existence that is a reality through reasoning and 'objectivity', this will be discussed in the last two sections (see pp. 50-92). The sense of 'existence' through objectivity and independence is, some may call, the reality that exists not in space and time, but in the mind or reasons.

2.2 The limitation of 'existence'

Description beyond existence

In enquiring about the meaning of existence, we have stepped slightly away from a direct, immediate perceptual situation of seeing what there is. Here, the relational aspects of what there is and its understanding are called for. Perhaps, this stepping away is metaphorical in giving a wrong impression as if a temporal gap existed in between sensing and contemplating. The awareness of things and the contemplation of their relational aspects are two epistemological steps, not necessarily separated by a temporal instance. The earlier proposition, which argued for the difference between epistemological and metaphysical priority, will now serve this purpose.

A description of what there is, is an introduction of relational aspects to an existent. It is therefore an introduction to this existent of our knowledge and understanding in terms of our personal experience as a whole within a relational consistency. When it comes to descriptions, we have descriptions which confer no ontological status intended for objects in existence, if we allow that all existents are of a spatio-temporal type. Objects signified names, proper names that cannot be seen, such as a unicorn, moral standards, Venus (a god) or a squared circle are examples. How they may come to be regarded as being or reality, but not as existents is probably argued like this. Since whatever exists must be conceived by us to exist, therefore, as some have argued, whatever can be conceived by us must be capable of being (which does not follow unless we introduce a different meaning of existence (being) in terms of objectivity or independence). Or the conception of something that is clear and not self-contradictory must have its 'being' (more to the point: reality) through this conception. If we were to accept the reality of universals, this position must be taken seriously. Take mathematical entities for instance. Many abstract entities are deduced from hypothetical premisses in mathematics. In other words, they are conceived in our thoughts and are thought to have an objective being (existence) or reality. Thus there is created a separate reality of existents not of our normal spatio-temporal world, but of a world capable of being conceived through reasoning.

Rejection of the rational existence and 'being' in realism

The reality of such a conceptual world is best examined in chapters later on, but whether or not we can have problems in the inclusion of this world into reality, is analysed here. First, if the existence of anything can be conceived to be so, it does not follow that everything that is conceived as such will necessarily exist, especially those conceived in the relational context of a whole reality. Second, when we say a table exists, we do not only mean that the idea of a particular table exists, which may be true; but also that a table exists in a spatio-temporal reality, independent of our conceiving, which may not be true. Whether or not one of these alternative realities is true, is not the point here. The point is that there is a difference between saying an object in space and time exists and saying that the idea of this object exists. If reality is such that only the ideas of objects are the true existents, then the meaning of existence is laid firmly on the conception of ideas alone. What can distinguish the reality between a squared circle and any general concept? Even within this idealistic reality, there is a need to examine the nature of thoughts as related to perceptual experience so that conceptual coherency alone may not be relied upon to determine an objective reality. Something may exist because we can conceive of the possibility that it may exist, or indeed the possibility that it may not exist. We do so by implicitly marking a difference between saying there are things and justifying their existence, therefore existence must be substantiated, unless existence does not need contemplation. The existence of a unicorn as a conceived entity must be substantiated, otherwise, an idea of a unicorn will always remain an idea and its conceptual existence will not be for discussion. To substantiate the existence of a thought of a non-spatial entity, we cannot appeal to the spatial content of experience, and the conceptual, internal coherency is what is left for us. Readers are reminded of Lobachevsky's geometry or Riemann's system, which are totally coherent and consistent within themselves, but arguably truth neutral. Their failure lies not in the lack of internal coherency, but in the lack of an empirical criterion. The existence of the ideas of percepts is not justified by sight; one cannot say that a unicorn exist, if it cannot be seen. If one uses the correspondence or verification criterion to justify the existence of non-perceptual ideas or even their incorrigibility, one begs the question of what substantiates their ontological status in this conceptual reality. Are we then content with such a definition of existence?

The need to define 'existence'

There is another existential claim about possibilities. We can conceive of possibilities in the absence of or in contrast to their actualities. That possibilities not actualized can exist, at least in a different reality, is not appetizing to some people. If the possibility of something that can exist remains a possibility, it will not follow that the existence of a possibility will entail the existence of something. The urgency to formulate the concept of existence to satisfy all sundry claims is apparent.

Why do we question existence? When we see something, it is not that we have any trouble with what we are given in front of us, but that there are troubles in putting this understanding of whatever is seen in the context of a whole experience (a relational context). We see sense-data of a table and can more or less describe it, but this is only a description in terms of one aspect as regards its immediate sensibility. In another aspect, a table can be described as a conjoinment of several pieces of wood; of colours, shades and shapes; of functions shared by other objects. Such disparagingly different descriptions of what there is, must provoke a question as to which of these sets of descriptions is veridical, or what real thing there is? In this view, existence is not only an acknowledgement of the epistemological passivity of perception, but a demand for a description of what we think there is.

The perceptual passivity of awareness demands an attention and consideration within so-called non-perceptual thoughts and ideas. Those who claim that these categories are real will always argue that they are not man made, but discovered and given. They say that men did not invent curious mathematical 'entities', but discovered them by their reason. The justification of what there is brings out the content of existence or what others will call the essence of existence. The question now is: what essence does an existent have, truly? Whether a table is an external object of external colours and shades and an object of function too, is contentious, and because of this, raising the question of existence should be justified. As I have argued before, the questions of existence in 'there is' and 'what there is' are separate and yet the same. And the question of existence is not only a question of content, but a question of content in the context of reality.

Existence in thoughts lies not in generality

Let us turn to thoughts themselves to explore the concept of existence. We cannot say anything about anything without being aware of something. Whether or not thinking of something and being aware of this thinking are the same is not important here; nonetheless, I cannot say that I can think without knowing or being aware of that I am thinking. Therefore I think because I know that I think. In this way, there is a separation between 'I think' and 'I know that I think', where one is the act of thinking and the other is the content of the thought. It is extremely doubtful to me as to whether thinking can be an act without content, but if so, this separation must be accepted in order to give a content to a thought. A thought without content is nonsense. Thus in thoughts, there is an epistemological duality in the act of thinking and in its content, each of which are indispensable from each other. In thinking of thinking, we allow the act of thinking to be its content as well of its act; they are the same metaphysically speaking, but different, epistemologically. When I have a thought, what existential question can I ask of it or of its content? Is it whether the thought is mine? Is it whether the act exists? Is it whether the thought exists? Why should we ask an existential question on thoughts at all, if to doubt the existence of a thought is to doubt the existence of the thinking itself, which is impossible, and doubting this existence is itself a thought. If we do not, why do we have the need to consider if the content of a thought is an existent, such as a unicorn in a thought? So, in a conceptual reality, the question of existence is also about a particular instance of thinking and its content. For the reality of thinking generally, but not particularly, does not exist.

Defining existence without reality is a tautology

Again, without the call for a justification of existence in terms of perceptual reality as a whole, there can be no reason and no basis to raise any existential question on thoughts or their content. Thus if someone says that there is a unicorn in his thought, we shall agree that there is a unicorn in his thought and will always agree whenever he says so. If he says that his unicorn exists, we shall enquire: in what respect its existence is proposed? If he says that it exists in his mind, we shall say that all thoughts 'exist' in minds anyway. This kind of existence as regards a unicorn is an epistemological sense of existence, just as colours exist in perception. Whether a colour is out there or not out there is not about an existence concerning relations because whatever there is and whatever there is not, are self-proposing; and that whatever there is must exist is a simple tautology. It is when the question of substantiation is raised, there is a different sense of existence, an existence that involves reality. Since we have not proposed whether a colour is real or part of reality, therefore the question of existence as regards colours and relations does not arise. In this simple notion of existence, we cannot find any circumstance under which the further question of existence by justification is called for, except when truth, veridicality and relations with reality are tested. If a conceiver of a unicorn proceeds to climb mountains and cross rivers to find his unicorn to prove its existence, we can only remind him that the unicorn is his idea existed in his mind. Of course, if one applies the existential criterion of testing tables and chairs in reality, to the testing of ideas in thoughts, one should fail.

Existence of possibility

Returning to the existence of a possibility as opposed to that of an actuality, one must make a clear distinction between a possibility of an existence and the existence of a possibility. A possibility of existence not actualized remains a possibility forever, and never will an unactualized possibility be a part of reality. There is a sense that the possibility of the sun rising from the

West exists. But this possibility is not inconsistent with the whole reality, even if it may not happen in future. Such a use of the concept of existence will further encourage my idea that the only circumstance when a relational existential question arises is when we consider the relations between what there is and the totality of reality. When someone says that the present King of France exists as a possibility, he is being ambiguous. We must know whether he is saying about the possibility that there is a King of France or that there really exists at present the King of France. In the first case, that a possibility exists as an actuality in space is nonsense. If it is about whether 'possibility' itself can exist, it says no more than that there is a possibility. The existence of a possibility itself is an inference of existence by relational consistency. But a possibility is a relation that cannot be said to exist, unless it is said of something of which existence can bring about its conceptual realization. There are relations but not relations of relations. There can be a possibility of a happening, but there cannot be a possibility of a possibility of a happening. To say some existent is possible is to bring out a relation to other existents within a whole relational reality, and not to refer to a particular existence of a relation, a possibility. In this sense, existence, if it is conceived to be more than just what there is, is a relational thing brought on by the wholeness of reality. To say that a happening may be a fact is to say that there is an existential relation (possibility) of such a happening to the conception of another fact. Therefore, saying that a possibility (itself) of something exists is the same as saying that a particular relation 'exists' among other existents, but not that the thing itself exists. A possibility can be conceived to 'exist' in being considered as an existential relation or content to other things in a whole reality; it is not that a possibility can exist, but that something can exist as inferred by a relation. All things considered, there is one actualized world and there are infinitely many possible 'worlds'. If it is the possibility that all possible worlds exists, then only this possibility of all possibilities will exist, and this will follow that a relation of relations can exist. This we must reject. A possible world is conceivable because a relation points to this existential possibility, which implies no actuality without further evidence or relations. A possibility is not real in this sense, or all possible worlds exist. It is a game of words in saying that things can exist in a possibility. But a possibility is only conceived as a relation, which owes its existence to things or is contemporaneous with them.

Separating reality and existence

Consequently, the test of existence in thoughts, like the test of existence of sensible objects, has its basis connected to reality through relations, relations of consistency. This brings me to the following questions:

* Can something be real but not exist?
* Can something exist that is not real?
* Are existence and reality synonymous?

I would like to think that existence and reality are two different issues altogether, but not independent of each other. I wish to say that reality implies existence, but existence may not imply reality. Reality depends on existence because, as I have argued before, the very notion of existence in reality cannot come about without a reference to, or a test on, our conceived, whole reality. But it is not my idea that if the test of reality fails, the notion of existence formed from the judgement of reality should evaporate too. The call for a conception of existence in terms of a whole, relational reality to bring about a notion of justified existence (existence in reality), is an epistemological undertaking.

Existence is more than reality (not that reality is more than existence)

That something existing may not be real, is certainly not a self-contradictory statement. To see how this separation of existence from reality is brought about, readers may wait until I proceed to analyse the notion of reality. That something that exists is not real depends on the relations of the existent in order that an existence may not always have a reality. In this way, we can say that the content of our dreams exists, or did exist while we dreamt, but is not real. A note of caution here: it is similarly held by the rationalistic philosophies that universals are real but do not exist. This will be rejected later. There is a difference between saying that all things that existed are real and saying that all things real must exist. We uphold the latter and reject the former. If all things that existed may not be real, an illusion existed, but is not real in a retrospective measure with reality. The fact that something did occur to me is not to be denied insofar as its occurrence is concerned.

In our definitions, we define existence in terms of sensibility, sensing and conceiving, and we can add to this an element of relation to confine a part of existence within reality, so that, logically, reality may not consist of all things that exist, and all things real will be within the embrace of existence. Within all existents there can be things that are not real, therefore, within these definitions, it cannot be said that things real may not necessarily exist. Things real must exist.

Can there be reality without sensibility?

Conversely, the rationalistic metaphysics sees existence and reality this way. Instead of existence being defined as more than reality, it is reality that is more than all things that exist. In this case, logically, all things that exist must be real, but not all things real are existents. In addition, things real may not exist. The possible claim that universals are real, but not existents (sensibles), is based on this logical inclusion of existence within reality. In order for reality to consist of all things that exist or do not exist, we have to define reality first and bring out one common notion shared between existence and reality while maintaining a difference between them.

If reality is conceived by the criterion of reasoning, logic or coherency alone, and if existence is conceived by the criterion of sensibility, then reality and existence are logically distinct, since sensibility and reasoning may not be connected. If so, neither reality nor existence can imply the other. In this case, the claim that things real (i.e. universals) are not existents, will be quite acceptable. But this leaves the definition of reality as something conceived through reason.

However, if existence and reality share a common thing, this thing that shares the same notion will be both real and an existent. What is this common thing? If it is reason or logic, then are we saying that reasoning or logic is also necessary to conceive of existence (sensible)? For the claim that things real may not exist, this position may be the only alternative. If this common thing shared between existence and reality is sensibility, that existence is all inclusive of reality, must be the case; and it is not possible for things real not to exist. If we conceive reality by the criterion of reason or logic, and claim that there are things real that do not exist, then we must also accept that some things in existence can be conceived in reality by reason or logic without sensibility. But can there be reality without sensibility?

Though this method of defining reality paves a way for reality to exclude part of sensibility so that we can have real things that do not exist (sensibles), the philosophy of this kind does not say that entities conceived by reason and logic can reveal themselves without sensibility. Whether we should accept this way of defining reality, we must decide for ourselves. If we wish to reject this kind of philosophy, we must look at the reality of reason and logic to see if their origin lies anywhere other than our given sensibility. This is beyond the aim of this book. Rejecting this way of defining reality is merely a rejection of a definition.

Since the ontological claim to sustain the reality of the entities of reason, such as universals, is that they are real, but do not exist as sensibles, this ontological claim cannot be maintained within our formulation of the definitions of existence and reality. That is, existence embraces all reality but not vice versa. With this distinction, we can say of non-perceptual entities (such as unicorns or mathematical entities), that they cannot be real as well as existents for the lack of sensibility that sustain existence. If they do not exist, they are not real. If they are real, they must exist. When I say that something 'exists' in thoughts only, I am judging a relation in terms of reality with the content of existence being conceived, perceived or both within these thoughts. Again, this depends on a definition that all reality is inclusive within existence, or that reality cannot be conceived outside existence. Having satisfied myself that something can exist without being real, I find it less inhibitive to start thinking of the notion of existence from mere conception only, just as I can conceive of the existence of a unicorn in dreams or in thoughts with sensibility as its content.

2.3 The conception of existence

Existence is not in utterances

Since I hold that the unbridgeable gap between thoughts and experience or between experience and its linguistic descriptions has been the failure in philosophy to define many important concepts, such as 'existence', I shall not discuss 'existence' in terms of how words can bring about a fruitful conclusion by examining all the grammatical and logical constituents in expressions functioning as a reference to what there is. One may be persuaded to think that to accept a linguistic understanding and its 'reference' is to accept the facts of the world or vice versa, because it is how we use language to talk about reality. But our reality is not laid down in a scheme of logic or linguistic system. When I say that I see a table, I know exactly what I mean by paying attention to my awareness at that particular instant. Reality is presented to me in a silent way so that my ultimate 'language' is the silent awareness or consciousness that confers no words. Linguistic formation of existential expression relies on variables, and on the identity of indiscernibles in its analysis. When I see a table, I do not see or think of the situation to postulate: 'there is an X and this X is a table'. I do not know what this X is, nor do I conceive that there is an X besides (ontologically) a table, either in my thoughts or in my expressions learned over many years. It is amazing how any so-called ordinary language philosopher can reject universal terms and at the same time accept the reality of variables, whether or not they are linguistic or logical variables. Can there be such things as variables? Can things say nothing and everything, depending on your attribution of so-called 'values'? This ontological point lies in 'attributing' itself and nowhere else. Can variables shed light to help us in our ontological enquiry?

Nothingness cannot precede existence

Hegel thinks that the first step to existence is nothingness which is also identical with existence. I think he only means that there can be a conception of nothingness. Hegel, I believe, is the father of all philosophies that have the central theme of 'being' in their prime ideas. One may ask to what extent the conception of nothingness is possible; this will be examined at the end of this book (see pp. 419-19). Nothingness, in a sense, is a void and nothing should be said of a void, except thinking of the void (space) itself. In this case, the void is a concept that is the content of a thought, for, if not, there can be no thought of nothing and no conception of such. Here, the distinction between metaphysics and epistemology will highlight two conceptions of this idea. Epistemologically, there can be no thought without a content; if a void is metaphysically a nothingness it cannot be imagined and hence no thought will exist. In this way, the reality of nothingness is not an existent outside an unimaginable thought; and any metaphysics starting from this interpretation is only a metaphysics of the impossible. If we allow the possibility of the concept of a void, such existential investigation is of course an investigation of epistemological 'reality'. Further still, we cannot have a concept of the void without the concepts of being and fullness, and the latter may even precede the former, epistemologically speaking. So, far from being a starting point for the 'revelation' of being, conceiving nothingness is, at best, an inference from an ontological knowledge preceding it, and at worst an unreality itself and the inconceivable.

Existence before reality

To pronounce an existence, we must know of something first. But if we have known of something, why do we need to pronounce its existence? To what extent can we say that existence is independent of our knowledge or our awareness? Since I think that, that which there is has its reality firmly rooted to the understanding of existence, I shall therefore proceed from existence to argue for a reality, and let reality subserve existence. If we leave out reality, what can we say of any essence of existence and how do we begin? Then, is there an essence to be determined from that which there is, distinct from the thing itself? If an existent has an essence independent of us, how do we know of it? The notion of existence is therefore primarily an epistemological concept but reality seeking.

Simultaneity in essence and existence

Though it may not be necessary to say that something can exist without considering its relation to other things, we nevertheless often invoke such an existential question about things there are. If there is a cognitive stage prior to a judgement of essence, we cannot logically know anything at this stage. Therefore, if man's intellect can detect extra-experiential reality, it can help man to conjure dubious entities prior to knowing an essence. But, as soon as we can talk of an essence, our concern about our veridical judgement (judgement of existence) is immediate, for such a judgement has consequences in man's pursuits and actions within the world of things. Therefore, we can talk of these existential judgements, as if the comfort of reality is constantly in demand. The essence of existence (whatever we can say of an existence or whatever there is to substantiate an existence) must be known either before or at the same time as the conception of existence. Since speaking of knowing an essence before existence is nonsense, their simultaneity, allowing for a separation of these two epistemological processes without having to consider them as two temporal processes, must be the only alternative, since the other alternative is incredible. Since I think I can legitimately talk of conceiving existence and its essence separately without giving up this simultaneity, I shall start with my exploration of existence this way.

2.4 The minimal perceptual content of awareness

The Incorrigible minimum

What there is, calls for no further existential enquiry other than perceiving that something is there, unless and until such an occasion arises as to provide an inception to conceive of the possibility that what there is, may not be so. This existential question comes about when other aspects of our knowledge such as what is remembered, projected, deduced, induced, conjectured and related, are brought into consideration. A man dreams not of things that are unreal until he is awake. Nor do I nor can I question what I am perceiving at a particular moment is not what it really is, or only an appearance to me. A thought at the moment of conception has no existential concern except that it is there, in the awareness of a privileged kind. This is the situation in which direct knowledge or experience shows itself when an indubitability of knowledge has dawned. There is no real purpose to doubt what is given to us as perceptual sensibles, or as an actual content of awareness itself. Thus this sets out the difference between what there is, as the given (sensibles), and what can be said of it, over and above what is perceived or in awareness. The latter is the beginning of an ontology concerning metaphysical reality. How minimal is our given sensibility remains to be seen.

Ontological sensing, minimal conditions and their Existential Implication

In order to avoid postulating that something is there as a minimal sensibility, without having said what it is, I must draw on the immediacy of an instance of a perceptual occasion. At this moment, we have sense-data which can be taken as inside, outside us or both to avoid an immature diversion into the problems of perception. What all these alternative interpretations have in common, is that sense-data are given in perception. We are not concerned here with the generality of what is given in perception, but with a particular datum or groups of particular data of which we are said to be aware. Whatever is being aware has a minimum description of 'in-being'; and we do not have to commit ourselves to any ontological identity by using words. This is a relational connection with an ontological implication. What is minimally aware can be 'termed' in whatever way we wish, but cannot be 'nothing'. 'Nothing' here has both an epistemological and metaphysical sense. Whatever there is to stir up an awareness is the epistemological sense. We can only refer to it as the stirred-up awareness that cannot be denied. What can be said of this stirred-up awareness is that, that which is there is so metaphysically. That which is there stirs up our awareness in a passive perceptual experience, and has no metaphysical commitment and is therefore only epistemological without an existential question, and cannot call for an existential question. This is not a contradiction because of the separation of epistemology from metaphysics.

The first minimal content, of which I shall argue in Part II of this book, is brought forward here for current discussion. The mind cannot think, conceive, perceive and be aware of anything without an attention to a content that is limited, be it sense-data or thoughts. Hence the mind sets a parameter in conceiving all existents, as singularities with limits and as its content. So to determine a boundary or limit we must have a content first. This may pose difficulty for us to argue for the mind's power to limit a content as the first existential awareness, if this content is non-spatial. Empirical content has boundary in space. This rules out the first and minimal existential content as being purely conceptual (non-spatial). As I will argue later, the marking of boundary in nothingness or emptiness is possible, through space, which is in reality nothingness. Hence the first and minimal existential awareness is limitation, and in space. The mind sets its parameters for sensibles so that sensibles are perceived and conceived as particulars (with boundaries). In this way, sense-data are no longer indistinguishable in space, for, if it is not, there can be no comprehension of sensibility by the mind. The mind, even when it looks into a vast void, can readily conceive of its parts by its demarcation of regions within emptiness. But, this is done without content in the void. Hence it must be the case that setting parameters in space precedes the awareness of sensible content. Setting a limit for awareness must be setting a limit for a content. This is the minimal implication of content in awareness even if this content is emptiness marked out by the mind.

To be in a state of limited conceiving or perceiving, as opposed to knowing, is to be in an epistemological state of being, passive to possible perceptions. In this way, having an illusion, having a dream, having a phantom pain or hearing a voice in your own head, have the same acknowledgement of the passivity in perceptions. These illusion, dream, phantom pain and voice are only judged to be unreal in retrospection, introspection and reasoning with relational comparison instituted on other things in awareness. When I dream, I have no idea that I am in a dream state until I wake up; nor can I deny sensing something that may be judged not to have 'existed' later. All these, no doubt, are given in passive awareness; be they judged to be occurrences outside or inside our brains. Of course, there are times when the idea of existence and reality does arise. But until then, this is a minimal condition of conception and perception, and that is no more to say that awareness is now raised and aroused by limiting a content. Is it not that such passivity and minimal awareness must always be implicit in all contemplation of an external world? The minimal content in consciousness, that is a minimal condition for conceiving being or beings, exists simultaneously with conceiving being or beings. In the Cartesian sense, this minimal content is of course the awareness of thinking in which the self may or may not be an inevitable, simultaneous consequent. In the immediacy of perceptual arousal, any understanding of what there is, presupposes an inevitable condition in which the self is postulated as a metaphysical, minimal existent to supply those conditions.. This I have argued in another book.[2] These conditions and existential implication are necessary for all ontological awareness or 'sensing.'

'There is' and 'what is'

I ask myself: if I say 'there is', instead of 'there is ... whatever', does it make any sense? For different reasons, Hegel thinks that it is possible to get rid of all predicates in an expression, leaving us with an existential assertion of nothing in particular. But that is not what I have in mind, for I am not asserting an ontological entity through a verbal convenience. Let me explain what this 'there is' may mean.

Subjectively speaking can I refer to a happening in my awareness without an ontological commitment? Is awareness itself the content of existence, not a content of my own existence, but a content of something other than myself? If one can say that a thought can exist in one's consciousness, surely I can say of something, such as a tickle or an itch without having to say what tickles me or what makes me itch. I am not talking of causality here. The historical idea that the genesis of existence is in being conceived first is initially quite credible. The problem is: what is this thing being conceived? Can conceiving or thinking be an act itself without contents? Therefore an ontological 'sensing' without an ontological commitment is an occurrence in awareness that is passive. In saying that something is passive, I may be invoking the notion of relations, of which causality is one.

In other writings, I have argued that causation is the case of a cause and an effect being described or seen as one event. Thus, it was also argued that an effect can be known prior to a cause, and, until the whole event is understood, it will then be conceived retrospectively to be temporally prior. I hold that there is no necessity outside our conception of causality binding the cause and effect together, and that causality is only a conceived connection through our description of two events as one. Without having to apply causality to conceive of an existent or to make an expression like, 'there is', ontologically committed, I think the situation could not be dissimilar. Insofar as a reality is laden in every conception of existence, an ontological commitment in an expression like, 'there is', comes not from its linguistic content, but from the nature of man exemplified by such an expression. Every conception or thought has at least a minimal content of awareness, and this content is an ontological commitment to reality that says nothing in particular. Our nature demands a reality, or a relation to all things known. It is possible to say that I conceive that there is something without saying what it is, because such a conception is purely judgmental from my own awareness, which is metaphysically nothing but epistemologically a demand for relations and thus for reality. Whether I can be right or wrong about this judgement that there is something, is not important. The important point is that it can make sense, if I can convince myself to see all existents in terms of a relation to all things.

A minimal awareness and judgmental awareness of existence

When I say: I see a patch of colour, I am not saying that I have conceived that something exists and this something is coloured. I am saying that there is something in my awareness that makes my awareness possible, that demands an ontological understanding. And I conceive it necessarily in terms of the relations with other things known to serve my will. Hence I judge this to be a colour through a relation. Because of this judgement, I have committed to an existent and to the idea, an ontological assertion. The second minimal content in the conception of existence is an ontological reason for understanding through relations, to imply an outside existence. Such an ontological 'sensing' is a happening in awareness itself. Our nature craves for a reality so that our sensibility can rest on consistent relations with all else to serve our will. Even if there is a world full of colours independent of my conceiving them, these colours would not have been known as existents unless I conceive them to be so in my awareness. Without this, 'colours' are no more than mere happenings in awareness in a minimal existence in human cognition not committed. Existence in its minimal state is like something outside 'knocking at the door of consciousness'.

At the moment of conception of an existence, we have two epistemological judgements, simultaneously; one is ontologically non-committal (happenings) and the other is committal (cognitive). The minimal content of awareness is the non-committal judgement. The committal judgement is a judgement of relations and therefore of reality. These doubly guarantee that if an ontologically committed judgement is at fault, we would not be left with nothing in our awareness. We will still have a minimal content of existence, and will not be left empty of content so as to render awareness itself void and disappeared. In practice, a man cannot deny seeing something even if he cannot put it to words. Thus, existence is not an all-or-nothing affair depending on knowing an essence. Though it is still true that nothing (without essence) can exist without being conceived, the conception of a relational reality is simultaneous with this minimal awareness. This can be seen as a sympathetic argument for existentialism without having to pronounce that existence precedes essence. In this way, when I say that this chair exists or this object exists, there is a simultaneous commitment of the essence (chairness or objectness) to this existence as well as a non-committal, ontological awareness on which this understanding is related. This is a demand for a reality of existence. A sense of existence lies in every awareness, epistemologically independent of an essence. That existence precedes essence is epistemologically possible.

Existence is in being conceived. This is almost a truism, at least not faulted on epistemological grounds. Martin Heidegger, in his *Being and Time*[22] says, 'Its Being-what-it-is (essentia) must, so far as we can speak of it at all, be conceived in terms of its Being (existentia)'. He is not speaking of existence from the point of view of metaphysics, but of the view in terms of what we can and should know. To say that these philosophers who have existence at the centre of their philosophies, revolt against the empirical idealism of Berkeley and Hume, is to understate the power of Berkeley and Hume's reasoning. I do not see them to be in revolt against Berkeley and Hume, but to be reluctant heirs to these British empiricists. Reluctant, because they are not prepared to accept Berkeley's conclusion. Heirs, because they accept that nothing can be said of anything there is, except of things that have ontological origins in ourselves. Hence I see that phenomenalism is a conclusion from the Berkeleian philosophy in total disregard for the question: can things exist without being conceived (or perceived) by us? This will be discussed later on. With this in mind, I return to the notion of existence and ask the question: notwithstanding that this question of things-in-themselves is unanswerable, how do we make of our own existence, if every existent has its being in being conceived? Do I need to be conceived by a being for my own existence? If so, I can only exist in something that conceives my being and since I cannot be aware of other beings' conceptions, I would not know of my existence. This is of course absurd.

2.5 Being and in-being (existent and existence)

Thinking with a minimal content

Earlier on, I said that without content, thoughts are nothing. This is a very important point in my philosophical system. Thus the Cartesian thought has this weakness, as seen in being general without a content of particularity. As a thought can only exist with a content, the Cartesian cogito cannot be so without an implication of a content. We cannot deny that we think, because such denial is a thought-content itself. Thinking cannot be a general thinking. It cannot be thinking of anything not in particular, or of nothing. 'I think' must imply a minimal content of this thinking of thinking itself. It is a self-evident fact that we cannot think of nothing in particular or nothing at all, and still hold that there is thinking going on. I am not saying that we cannot think of 'not thinking' or 'thinking of nothing' because this will itself be taken as a content. I cannot say that I think without having at least this thought of 'I think', or without having to be aware of this thinking. Without this awareness, there is no thought. So, the minimal condition of a thought is awareness of a thought itself. If we can deduce anything from the *cogito* to the conclusion that I exist, we must deduce it from the secondary awareness of the thought of thinking, and not from a general thinking, since there is no such a thing. Having said this, we have no need to bring out another thought of a thought of thinking itself and tour the precipice of infinite regress.

In-being and essence

The content of conceiving existence, like that of any other thought, is peculiar in that it is not seen to be the content of an existent outside. We have a similar sentiment given by Heidegger in his '... so far as we can speak of it at all ...' (quoted earlier, see p.37) or in the empiricists' idea that everything we can say of anything is always the content of our sense-experience. Thus there is a contention of whether the content of conceiving an existence is the existent itself, or whether the existent and its existential conception are one and the same. Some may regard the essence as being in the thing that existed; and since it comes into existence through being conceived (by a being, I suppose), it is regarded as the in-beings, that is, existed in a being. But, how we can introduce this being is totally a different matter. Some may rely on the Cartesian *cogito* saying that the only being that cannot be denied is 'I'. Some are more sceptical.

Therefore, depending on your metaphysical views, if all physical objects are no more than sum totals of descriptive perceptual experience or thought-sustained reality, then all things existed are in-beings, in this sense.

That every thought needs a thinker, every percept needs a perceiver or every conception of being needs a being, says no more than what can be inferred respectively from 'thought', 'perceive' and 'being' and 'conceiving' originally. This is an analytical circularity. If in-beings owe their existence to beings, this relation is unfortunately construed as a one-sided dependence. In proposing an idea of interdependence, I cannot say that the being itself must also have its existence in conceiving itself. It may be true that we can deny the content or a being that conceives, but we cannot deny conceiving itself, but to hold that everything that can be said of any essence is inevitably a description of our own is to imply the existence of our selves. What is it for something to be existentially conceived without implying a conceiver?

Conceiving essence has no perceptual minimum, but cognitive understanding

There is nothing else left for us to grapple with, except the content of conception of an existent, that is, the content of whatever we can say about anything, or any essence. I have been talking about this 'essence' as if it is something that we can say of anything, and that is not something everyone will agree. There is an idea, dating back to Aristotle, that essence is in the thing that exists, and is what makes the thing what it is. This essence is not attributed by anything, but independent of any attribution. This essence, taken together with an underlining reality, cannot be a subjective creation of the mind. Or, in other words, essence is more than predications. How is this possible? Again, we stumble onto this gulf between metaphysics and epistemology. Anything that is beyond our attribution of qualities, is also beyond our knowledge and therefore not knowable. 'Nothing' that cannot be known or conceived, cannot therefore exist, for something to exit without anything said of it, it must remain only within the realm of possibility. A contrast should be made between the unknowable and the 'unspeakable' in a minimal awareness. A minimal awareness is perceptual whereas the unknowable is conceptual. The perceptual can be conceptual at the same time, but they are not necessarily the same. The perceptual cannot be eliminated by the absence of a conceptual content. But the conceptual is nothing if it is lacking a content.

Similarly, the interdependence between being and in-being, is in the self-revealing of both simultaneously. The awareness of the content (essence) not only says much of existence, but may require a metaphysical condition or necessity for it (the content) to be so understood. This condition may not be a logical, analytical or verbal entailment in an expression, such as thinking needs a thinker, or the like. A close examination of any content of understanding, or of existence, shall reveal a condition or conditions for their being so understood as an essence.

Let us see if all things that can be said of an existent, such as qualities, quantity, attributes, sense-data, thoughts, imagination or even 'substance', are permanent and outside ourselves. Is there anything that we can regard not as our own, or not as subjective sensation or thought? Of course it is not probable to make such a claim without positing that there is some existent outside, not because any property or whatever said of a thing is a composite of our experience and sense reporting, but because ultimately the epistemological gap will prevent us from making an identity out of existential essence and verbal or experiential content. If we can say anything about something at all, we can only say it from a repertoire of experience within us. This is not so much a logical consideration as it is an observation. Even if there is an objectivity in an essence, we are still far from identifying an essence with things in space. If there is anything outside, the hope of an existential confirmation lies within the so-called internal content.

The way to the permanency in essence

Many things we can say of existence are possible, not simply because they are so conceived clearly without doubts. I find the question of how things are so understood in the way they are understood, not very easy to answer, especially when we consider the difficulty in veridical judgements. Why is a chair a chair and not lumps of wood or metal? In fact, can we ever have something we can understand, as it is forever permanent? To think of something changing, is to think of the change in our conception of it all the same. Still we can think of it as having a sense of permanency, by looking for a fixed anchor point to which all changes are measured, so that these changes can be conceived as a variation with a permanent base. A patch of white seen at a different angle, on the red surface of a box does not create a sense of inconsistency in a claim that the box is both white and red. This is because this patch of whiteness has a relation conceived in conjunction with the rest of the red box, explainable by a fixed condition. This white patch is therefore not said to be the permanent colour of the red box. If a normal perceptual condition cannot be established as a permanent reference for all colour anomalies, we still have wavelengths of colour spectrums as a measure of constancy.

How the content or essence should stand on its own without a measure of, and relations to, other things is a very ancient problem. The old way of looking at this problem is to propose that since dependence is not a satisfactory affair for existence, conceptual essence has to be totally independent. A search for such independence will inevitably lead to disappointment for those passionate enough to pursue this end. I see that this search is not a cry for relations, but a hope to establish how the content or essence can be so understood to be what it is, without having an extra something in addition. If so, there is an epistemological reference and an 'anchor'-begging. This something is not only a relation, but something that is pivotal, upon which all qualities are measured in a necessary condition for they to be so understood. With this distinction, therefore, a percept is not said to be dependent on a perceiver, but impossible in being conceived to be what it is, without the postulation of a point of permanent anchor or reference. So too is an essence.

How can a thing be conceived of as a horse or indeed a thing at all? For if there are things outside us, they can never be 'horses' or 'cats', which are in reality our own conceptions. Things are the inconceived, and never conceived to be 'what they are' without a reason explaining why they are what they are (conceived). This reason is not about how a horse can have a horseness, or a cat, catness. It is not about whether we are right to call a horse a horse, or a cat a cat, but about how it is possible to conceive of 'anything' to be 'anything' at all. This is not about a horse not capable of being an independent existent, granted that there is such a thing as a horse conceivable in principle, but about why a thing is conceived of as a horse and not something else. It is not about the content of a conception not capable of standing on its own without being perceived, but about the content of a conception not capable of being understood at all and therefore conceived of at all.

Hot water is so conceived not because it depends on our sensation of hotness, but because 'hotness' and 'water' and their association (hot water) on their own cannot be understood even if there is a relation between them and with other things. Everything is related to everything only through a fixed evaluative reference. If hotness is measured by the movement of mercury within a thermometer and if we can only refer to the positions (high or low in a thermometer) as an indication of something being hot or not hot, it can never be understood in the way we understand hotness by experience. 'Hotness' by reference to the positional relation in a thermometer always remains a relation, and never becomes a 'sensible' understanding conceived through experience.

The anchor for relations and the understanding of essence

The proposal that things need being conceived in order to exist, relies on the premiss that things are conceived to be so. If we were to abandon all these premisses and start from an epistemological genesis to assume that there are first qualities, contents, or data, we will see that they must be understood, and therefore existentially conceived first. There is no point in asking for an epistemological dependence, if we cannot give the reason for their being so conceived in the first place. Saying that things exist in being known or understood, is not at all the same as saying that things exist in being conceived, if conceiving an existent does not include an understanding or determination. Perhaps conceiving something and understanding something are the same, but lacking an epistemological condition for this understanding is the same as lacking an epistemological condition for a conceived existence. Therefore something not capable of being understood can never be conceived of. If things are forever conceived in relations only, there can be no conception of existence in things in terms of definitive value. If a man is defined in a relation as a biped, a full existential identity can never be reached; for relations are forever infinite in numbers, and a satisfactory identity will be improbable to achieve. For reasons I shall give in later chapters, definite identity lies not in relational conception of an existent, but in human experience, which cannot be absolutely described. There are many entities that we habitually consider to be objects without realizing that they are in fact names for relations or sets of relations, the ontological status of which is erroneously compared to those of spatial objects. In this way, we may say that every quality substantiating an existence has two aspects of epistemological dependence, one is relational and the other is non-relational; and from this non-relational dependence we can introduce a pivotal point - something on which the understanding of all qualities are measured and depends. This epistemological support, which provides values to relations and makes hotness not just positional reference on a thermometer, is of course the self, with its nature.

Since we have rejected that the notion 'essence' is more than qualities, essence and qualities are taken as the same. Qualities, that is, what we can say of anything, are of two kinds, one spatial and the other non-spatial. Things that are seen in space cannot be conceived in space (since conceiving is spaceless) even if we can report this conception (in thoughts) with space reference. So when we say that things exist by being conceived, are we saying that things conceived without space can exist? Since normally reality is about things in space, things that have no spatial content are not real in this sense. Must existence be also real? This we have discussed before and concluded that some existents may not be real. If we do not accept such a distinction between existence and reality, perhaps there are two realities, one spatial and the other non-spatial. Since existence relies on the notion of conceiving, it will be hard to exclude spatial percepts completely. If we perceive a table in space, and conceive of it in our thoughts with an understanding, a table in space is too conceived as well as perceived to exist in spaceless thoughts as well as in spatial experience; how can we distinguish between the spatial reality of a table and that of a non-spatial one? The difference between the spatial and non-spatial conceptions of a thing comes from existence (space). An existence in merely being conceived of must lack a spatial reality. Therefore all entities conceived of alone without space must be in this limbo of reality. I shall return to this limbo later on.

It cannot be said that space content of things is not epistemological independent. Space, too, in its being understood and conceived of, albeit together with sense-data, needs a referential anchoring point for it to be determinable as to positions, regions, directions and distance, which are mere relational quantities without an anchoring point of reference. This anchoring point for the determination of space values, is again the self, being a permanent, perceptual point. As it is in space, time that enables the understanding of movements in space, on its own also lacks a referential point to anchor all temporal quantitative measures in the understanding of it. The space-related speed, the temporal perceptual rhythms, the past, the present and future are all quantitative measures, the values of which are epistemologically dependent on a fixed, anchoring point of being, the self. Thus when people say that things exist through being conceived, I would rather say that things can exist when their conceptual dependence has a support, making possible an ascription of value from a permanent, fixed reference.

The Aristotelian and Lockean sense of support for qualities is very much empty words. They conceive that because qualities are not in the things and therefore need a support, they are, by analogy, like a falling stone that needs something underneath to stop it falling. Nothing can be said about what this support might mean. A substratum or a substance is very much a meaningless word to introduce, to imply somehow something can occupy space giving a concreteness to a bundle of qualities. I believe the self is more substantial in content, in this respect. That every quality needs an epistemological support for them to be understood at all, even if this quality is supposed to be given to us, must be a more tangible ontological dependence. So, an existent given, in being conceived of, entails an 'arbiter' or a fixed point of evaluation to enable it to come to an epistemological existence. This fixed reference must be a real being on which all qualities depend for their epistemological in-being. If this arbiter can offer no epistemological content to all in-beings, it cannot support them in their epistemological needs to be understood. Therefore, if this being is a metaphysical being outside conception, like an Aristotelian substance, it cannot conceive other in-beings to fulfil their epistemological lacking, and therefore its existence will in turn be dependent on being conceived by something else. Thus a being that conceives of other in-beings is an epistemological source to conceive of all qualities, and support their epistemological dependence. This being is the self. When we talk about consciousness, we are talking about an epistemological source in conceiving everything that is conceivable, in reflecting, in understanding, and in reasoning that point always to a referential source of qualitative values, which in turn condition what are conceived to be what and how they are. Men are not aware of their being at birth until they have learned and known. If the awareness of things and conception of them are the essence of consciousness, the knowledge that gives our ability to make such conception must be the content of consciousness, a content of value. Thus the wiser we are, the more conscious we are of our beings. Consciousness is in the conception of things, and of their dependence of being in us; and philosophy is a game of consciousness.

A being will not reveal its epistemological support if no qualities or in-beings are conceived. The non-conception of qualities or their non-being will likewise not reveal a being on which their epistemological shortcomings depend. Therefore we can say that if there is nothing in this world to invoke this dependence, there is no being and there are no selves. We exist because we conceive of other beings in us (the in-beings) and we exist not, if there is nothing that depends on our conception, or if we lack the capacity to conceive of in-beings. In reality, we can hardly imagine that we do not conceive of things.

Independence and existence

Now, can I conclude that because I conceive of all things and sundries, and because all things conceived infer such dependence, all qualities conceived must exist 'outside' me through this separation? I think it may be difficult for me to make such a conclusion. For when we start to define existence, we set out to say that existents have their epistemological dependence on being conceived, we have not considered the metaphysical reality of these contents of our conception. If existence is about being conceived and epistemologically dependent, then such existence can only be an existence based on conception, that is, an epistemological existence or an idealistic existence. Whether there are things that exist quite independently of us or whether there is a sense to define existence without having to conceive of it, are two questions we have not answered. Perhaps, things can be conceived by others in their own repertoire of knowledge and are not conceived by us at all. But if we accept that if there are things outside, we cannot say that they exist unless we know that they exist, then the notion of existence must firmly be tied to our conceiving things. This must be a true position on existence. If the possibility that the existence of things depends not on being conceived is credible, we must treat our conclusion as an epistemological reality. But, then, the metaphysics discussed in this book is a human metaphysics and anything that is beyond human conception must be the unthinkable.

The dependence of thoughts

Thus, in existence, a duality of interdependency that gives rise to the being and its in-beings must allow me to say that 'I' supplies the standard for things to be so understood and conceived in the way they are conceived. This demands a metaphysical independence to be measured against these epistemological relations. 'I', therefore is such a reality that supplies a reference with permanency. If there is minimal content in a thought, the thinking of thinking is such a minimal content of a thought itself. This entails a metaphysical necessity in this particular content (as opposed to a general content) of a thought and in an epistemological dependence. Thinking of thinking cannot be understood without at least an act of thinking itself, therefore an act of thinking must reveal itself in a thought. If any thought in being understood to be a thought, an act of thinking must be such an epistemological dependence. Again, 'I' is this act of thinking, this metaphysical necessity.

'I' exists because there is a content in conceiving, and this content in many ways constructs a platform for existence through conception and through the appearance of trails of experience and values not found in things. This epistemological platform is the 'I'. Without content, there can be no conceiving, and thus an emptiness or void. In the same way, the act of thinking is not different from the minimal perceptual content in awareness or the unspeakable happenings in awareness. Qualities exist because I exist in conceiving them in the way they are conceived. Unicorns and mathematical notions exist conceptually too, but not spatially. These are things that exist but are not real, and not all things that exist are real. But I cannot say that something real does not exist. Existence can be an epistemological reality, and not a metaphysical reality. For some, the idea that something can exist but is not real, does not inspire a silent consent, it is only because existence is not taken as synonymous with reality. If one accepts that there is more to reality than existence, such a claim is not at all incomprehensible. With this, we shall make begin our excursion into the concept of reality.

3 Reality

3.1 Reality within existence

Knowing reality

One can hardly disagree with so many, that metaphysics or indeed the notion of reality has nothing remotely connected to the ordinary, daily livelihood of humanity. It is not as if such a question about reality can be at the forefront in our daily decisions, or as if individuals of immense importance in a society will seriously care about what the notion of reality can offer them. But the question of reality can creep up unnoticed all too often. Should an abandoned lover or a battered woman not try to reconcile the 'realities' of a lover being different 'persons' at different periods, so as to grieve at her choice made without hindsight? What a person is like is indeed a concern of reality in any sense. Would a woman not say that one of her conceptions of the character of her lover, at different times, is real while another is not? Knowledge acquired certainly transforms a previous judgement, and that includes a judgement about reality. To understand the notion of reality is to equip oneself with a tool for one's actions, which certainly are one's reactions and interactions with what there are. Perhaps the connection between philosophy and daily life is not easily brought to light at the flash of a moment when a decision is made.

When we change our belief about something being unreal, we seem to say not only that we did not know this thing well enough before, but we know more about it now. Hence the reality we conceived beforehand with less knowledge, in contrast to what we have now conceived with more knowledge, has an important bearing on how we choose to act upon this reality. So, this 'reality' is not just a term to signify permanent existents. In fact, the permanency of an existence seems to hinge on knowing more or less about it. The more we can say of something, the more we feel sure of its reality.

Existence may lack reality

The problem following this is not only about knowing more, but about knowing more of something, that is false. As falsehood cannot constitute a reality, therefore the existence based on mere conceptions is constantly checked against falsehood; what we can say of things cannot be the only measure of existence, if an existent is placed firmly in check with reality. Existence without reflections is an existence lacking a sense of reality and yet it should not be meaningless either; for such a denial would be a denial of the very essence of conceiving. A falsehood conceived is not and cannot be an error in the act of conceiving, but in the content judged and determined. Does conceiving itself imply reflections, since the act of conceiving without reflection is just a happening in the mind? An immediate judgement is necessary if we are to understand this happening, but a second stage of reflection about this judgement sets us on the road to reality, from existence. We cannot deny a happening in the mind no matter how unrealistic our immediate judgement is. To deny reality is not to deny existence. Though conceiving and conceiving something are simultaneous, conceiving itself can certainly be considered separately from its content. When see and conceive that there is a dog which in reality is a cat, it is about an error in conceiving reality as regards its content, and not as regards an absence of conceiving. Hence if such a separation is allowed, conceiving and the content of conceiving are two things that help us in the separation between existence and reality.

Further elucidating conceiving and existence

With this truth neutrality in existence, one does not have to deny the existence of anything without reality. A thing may not be real, but cannot be a non-existent, as soon as it is conceived and perceived. In this way, conceiving a chair is about the existence of the chair, but the veridical content of this conception, is about reality, in the reflection of its existence. Therefore for every existential question, not of 'what there is', but of whether something exists or does not exist, there should be a further question of reality, that is, whether something is real or not. This separation of existence from reality must allow the acknowledgement of phenomena as existents but not necessarily as the real. Seeing a phantom chair, if it turns out to be unreal, should not render the act itself in experiencing a phantom illusion, as non-existent.

The act of conceiving existence, is not an act that can be denied by the lack of criteria of reality applying reflections; for an act of conceiving or perceiving guarantees the existence of at least one content, that is, the act itself calls for no judgement. Only a judgement can imply a falsehood and therefore a possible denial. In an immediate conception as an act of conceiving itself, analogous to an immediate perception, there is no room for the denial, since it is the given. In the Cartesian sense, conceiving involving a reflection concerns one's own existence. This owes much to the act itself, in not fading away for the lack of incorrigibility in the judgement of its content. However erroneous our judgements may be, the existence of conceiving itself is not something to do with an erred judgement. I can refer to the idea of a squared circle, and the impossibility of such conception, if true, cannot deny me of thinking such semantic impossibility. That is not to say that an 'impossibility' can be conceived in the same way we conceive nothingness. Consistency demands that I accept that 'impossibility' is not an empty conception, and it is not a matter of whether impossibility can exist or not, but a matter of whether it has any mileage in reality.

The separation of existence from reality must also compel me to accept the possibility of conceiving all universals, the reality of which is to be considered by separate reasons. But as regards the generality of conceiving without having a particular content, in contrast to the act of conceiving itself, this general conceiving must be ruled out as impossible. Conceiving nothing in particular and indeterminately cannot be conceiving at all. Conceiving must be conceiving something other than an indeterminacy. We can say that conceiving of conceiving is a determinacy; that impossibility is a determinacy, a squared circle is a determinacy as is a unicorn. But conceiving things that are not determinate (indescribable), as a matter of fact, is impossible. There is a difference between conceiving the act of conceiving and conceiving generally. In the latter, conceiving generally is an act of indeterminacy that we do not know how to pursue. An act of conceiving a particular, is not indeterminacy. In an expression like 'I think', there is no indication as to what is being thought; hence there is no ontological deliverance except what may be implicit in the word 'I'. Thinking of nothing in particular, or just thinking generally, is impossible, unless it is thinking of thinking. For this expression, 'I think', to mean thinking, the minimal content of thinking itself must be a determinacy, implicit in the expression which makes it undeniable. In this sense, 'I think' can be replaced with 'the act of thinking itself'. Thinking of an impossibility itself is not something that can be struck out as 'never happened', even if its possibility may not exit; for we are conceiving the act of conceiving itself.

From existence to reality

Of reality within existence, we say that a unicorn exists in being conceived but not perceived; that a table exists in being conceived as well as perceived in space and time; or that a universal exists only in being conceived. We have extended existence with qualifications by further asking: 'existing in what sense?'. This is an extension of existence being considered as a concern for reality. The difference between seeing a plastic apple as a real apple, is not a question of existence, for the real question is not whether there is no apple in the absence of a plastic apple, or whether there is no plastic apple in the absence of a real one. It is a matter of misjudgement which only negates the reality of what is conceived in error, but not of what there is, which has caused, or been presupposed by, this misjudgement. It is in this conceptual test, we bring out more to a question of existence, and this outflow is the idea of reality. Is it the mistaking a plastic apple for a real apple or is it the non-existence of a real apple, which raises our doubts about reality? This is an important point. For the non-existence of something is not an error of nature itself, and the reality in this case is simply that there is no such 'thing' existed, not that there is nothing existed. Nature errs not, and men who err, make reality a question for them. So a plastic apple and an ordinary apple are either real or unreal depending on what we make of them in our judgement. This is not even about appearance versus reality, but about appearance or reality that do not conform to our conceptual expectation.

Hence, I will not think that a statement such as 'a chair does not exist when not perceived' is a shock to our common sense. The reason is not only that we can think of things being real or not, even if they are unperceived, but that it is more important for perceived and conceived existence not to be denied, than it is for it not to be real.

'Appearance' in a muddle

Appearance and reality are two alternatives that set the parameters for metaphysical discussion. But what is appearance once reality is defined? The answer is: nothing. If appearance is something that is not real, how is it to be perceived? How is it that reality only appears to us and yet we lay claim to experience reality beyond appearance? Does appearance exist? If appearance is not existence, what is it since it is not reality? If existence does subsume appearance, what else that exists is not appearance? Perhaps these are things that appear not to our senses but are conceived in our mind. If so, how can appearance be conceived without being sensed or appearing to us? By the measure of this metaphysic, they may exist only in thoughts, but they are not appearance since they appear not, and may not be real either. What is left to be conceived not in thoughts alone are sensible things that appear to us. Therefore, appearance must be all or at least part of existence that can be real or unreal. But we cannot deny the appearance of existence the criteria of reality, if appearances are not real. If whatever that is not real, cannot exist, as it is claimed by some, an appearance that is not real has no part in this consideration. Appearances must exist even if they are not real, otherwise how do we separate existence from reality? We can see how muddled this word 'appearance' is. Therefore, the term 'appearance' is only meaningful within the definition that all reality is within existence, instead of that all existents are within reality. If the latter is accepted, there is no place for appearances within reality even if they can sensibly appear to us as existents. For, if existence must be real and if there is a reality beyond existence, the concept of 'appearance', being not a concept of reality, must lie outside existence as well. In this case, what is something that does not exist and is not real? It must be nothing, the inconceived. So, what is appearance then? Consequently, if we hold the view that all that exists is within reality, we cannot make a distinction between reality and appearance.

Existence is more than reality

Existence is more than reality, and this idea may take some hardship to 'elucidate'. Perhaps examples will help. People may say that conceptual 'objects', such as infinity or 'the square root of minus one' or real numbers, exist, and yet they cannot say anything of their existence in the same way we can say of a chair we see or touch. The distinction here is of course one of spatial content. However, making two distinctions and yet retaining the use of the same word, 'existence', somehow indicates a serious confusion in reasoning. Hence it will be wrong to say that things that are real may not exist, since it is existence that underlines reality and not the reverse. Certainly, where there is a distinction, there are two senses of existence. This is the distinction I shall put forward as a distinction between reality and existence. In saying so, I am not suggesting that these two are totally distinct and independent of each other. What I am referring to is a distinction conferring more than existence to constitute reality. When we conceive an existent, and if what we can say of this existent at one time is not the same as what we can say of it at another time, are we not concerned as to why it is so, or what it really is? Whether an existent is everything I can say of it at different times, a veridical view of what it is must be in doubt. The concept of reality is to deal with this anomaly.

Abstract essence is relation

If I say that there is an honest man, in what sense am I committing to an ontological reality? That there is a man may be less problematic, but that there is an 'honesty' in the man is something hard to justify. To bestow it as a part of reality is even harder. I am not saying that this 'honesty' is in my consciousness. I may be saying that something other than the man is honest. It is certainly possible to conceive 'honesty' and say of something being ascribed by or not ascribed to it. But to conceive something having or being ascribed by honesty is not the same as conceiving the notion of honesty itself. To conceive something having honesty is not about the existence of honesty, but the existence of an association between the thing and something else, and 'honesty' is a reference to it. Is 'honesty' a thing that can exist, or may it be a property of something both mutually existing? If the man turns out not to be honest, did this 'honesty' as a property ever exist from the outset? Or if the man is honest, how is the existence of 'honesty' possible or how do we perceive it? Am I entitled to say that if I am more convinced of this man's honesty, I am more in tune with reality? Certainly, when someone is judged by everyone else not to be honest, and yet I believe him to be honest, must I be thought of as unrealistic? It is not a matter of whether honesty can exist as an entity, but a matter of whether reality asserts more than what there is in relation to something else. This is a vital point, which I shall further elaborate.

Again, to show what I mean by the separation of existence from reality, or of epistemology from metaphysics, I ask a question: 'Is there a sense in saying that if God exists, He is not real'?. For those who have not seen God, touched God, felt God or talked to God, God is not an entity of existence in the same sense as that of tables and chairs, if He exists this way. He can exist as a conception of a God-idea, within the meaning of existence in an epistemological 'reality' as opposed to a metaphysical reality. If a conceived essence or a thing cannot exist without a spatial content (perceived), God is not such a conceived entity. Whether God exists as well as being real is another matter for our judgement. However, before we begin to discuss reality, we must put this spatial and non-spatial distinction in perspective so that we can resolve the distinction between the existence of non-spatial entities like unicorns and spatial entities like tables and chairs. Sensible existents in reality are regarded as being in a separate category of existential reality. We say that this is a metaphysical reality. The other is an epistemological reality. The difference here is a relational content. Things of no relational content are epistemological reality only. To establish this separate category, I shall mark out reality from what there is, described as existence. Let existence justify its reality, but not the reverse.

3.2 Space and reality

Is space independent of being conceived?

In the search for what constitutes a sense of reality, I shall look for things in the content of existence, which is not dependent or wholly dependent on being perceived. I consider that there are three aspects in existents that may decide what is real. Things that are in space are different from things conceived without space. The first criterion for reality is of course space associated. This is the outer sense in the perception of what there is. Perhaps thinking is spaceless, and conceiving existence itself is spaceless, but the content of what is conceived may not be spaceless. How is it that something in space can be conceived in spaceless conception? Kant is known to have written that we can imagine space without objects, but not objects without space. Is there an idea in this Kantian wisdom that space can be conceived alone as well as being experienced with objects? Thus, when space itself is imagined (not perceived), and if the act of imagining is itself spaceless, is pure space in being imagined or conceived, spaceless? That we cannot imagine objects without space is undoubtedly true, for the simple reason that objects and space are inseparable; but to imagine space on its own is as problematic as conceiving space in a spaceless mind. Kant obviously thinks that geometrical figures with imaginary lines alone are pure, imaginary space and not imaginary objects; and that is his prejudice with which he favours the reality of imaginary lines in preference to the solidity of perceptual lines and their outer sense.

Conceived space and perceived space are difficult to distinguish

If space itself is considered as being conceived in a spaceless consciousness as everything else is, the content of this consciousness cannot be spaceless, since space cannot be spaceless no matter what. How can space be conceived without itself being the content in a spaceless conception? Either pure space may be outside our conception, therefore not conceived, or our conception itself is not spaceless, which would be very odd. But if pure space is not conceived, how do we know of its existence? The point about the 'spaceless' conception of pure space is highlighted by the difference between direct perceiving and conceiving ideas in consciousness. Of course, direct and immediate perceptual experience involves conceiving too, but the difference between these two types of experience is in perceiving and conceiving, one spatial and the other non-spatial. In dreams, we may 'see' objects as if we have seen them in 'real life', inseparable from space or extension. In as much as I would like to cast out a difference between the veridical perceptual space-objects and dream objects, I can find no satisfactory basis for contrasting these two positions. Still, it is not unusual for us in dreams to believe in the dream reality at that moment. The denial of the reality of dreams is only possible in the awakened state, by the comparison of these two states of consciousness. The difference between dream perceiving and veridical perceiving lies in another criterion for the assessment of reality, to be discussed later.

Reality in space

Space is of course a constituent of reality. All existents that are in space are real. Existents that are conceived not in space are epistemological existents. Whether there can be existence by conception alone is a matter for the belief of whether our own epistemological origin lies beyond empirical experience. Space is not only the space associated with sight, but the space associated with touch and hearing. To conceive a particular space is to understand and perceive data inseparable from it. There is no such thing as pure space on its own constructed out of imaginary lines, except perceptual nothingness. A space with lines as a particular space with extension and sensibility possibly created by the mind. I aim to expound this aspect more precisely in a later chapter (see pp. 103-144). For now, one aspect of reality is the recognition of an existence through space.

For something to be in space is for it to be perceived anywhere other than the point of visual perceiving (the originating point of perceiving is itself unperceived, but a condition for an identity of particular spaces: for further discussion of this point see, (*Nature of the Self*, Empiricus Books, London, 2000), Therefore, something that is in space is more than just being perceived and conceived, and more than being an existent. Being in space in this sense, is not only about having sizes and shapes, or being extended and voluminal, although these may be regarded as space associated. Extension, size and shape always accompany an object. Whether we dream or think of an object, or have a direct perception of it, we cannot make a distinction between them by considering only their extensions and shapes, even if it may be suggested that imaginary objects or dream objects are not spatial in the same sense that perceptual objects are.

Space in reality is a particularity referenced to a permanent point

What gives us the idea of objects in space is that objects are seen as being at a distance from the perceiving point. In this particular conception of 'in-space', all sensings, and particularly visual sensings are in space, just as touching and feeling are in space, or at a distance. Distance is space itself and it is not circular to use distance to introduce space, since distance (an aspect of space) is not determinable without a perceptual point that conditions its spatial value and identity. This in-space is not only about conceptions, but in particular about visual perceptions. To what extent does this 'in-space' concern visual perceptions?

I would say that it is total, because, without perceptual identity, determination or understanding, there is no perception in space. That space is perceived intuitively without any condition to determine its particularity is denied. We think of a visual perception of an existent as being more vivid and real, than its smell or touch. It is not that vision itself is totally unavoidable in conceiving space objects, but that a permanent perceiving point to determine a particular space in a window of vision is unavoidable. Its absence is inconceivable. It is this indispensable point for spatial references that enables all spatial determinations. If we close our eye to deny a visual perception, there is always a point from which all other spatial sensing and sensations are determined, to give an outer sense to them. This point is not a point in space, which, if it is, would have to be perceived and determined in turn by a reference to something else, and therefore dependent, instead of being depended on. This point is a metaphysical point of the self, and a measure of an outer sense, as I have hitherto argued elsewhere.

An existent conceived in space is more than just an existent conceived. An existent conceived in space may or may not be real. The imagination or dreaming of objects in space does not support the claim of a reality by this 'in-space' criterion alone. Thus, the second criterion of reality is introduced.

3.3 Reality and the totality of experience

Existence cannot be denied; only reality can be denied

We may have unusual experiences over which we may not be in agreement; this could lead to our rejecting them as part of reality. It is not the rejection of them that is troublesome. It is the lack of reason to reject them; for to our mind's conviction, an experience that has occurred will not be erased. Imagine that I see something clearly, and others ridicule my report and dismiss the claim of this reality. If I truly have this experience, what sense does it make to say that I have not? Again, without reality coming to the rescue, or without reality being distinguished from existence, any rejection of my existential experience will seem absurd. If what I see is what there is, both in existence and in reality, its denial will lead to the rejection of both reality and existence. But, if what I see is not real, I can deny its reality but not its existent; if not, how would I have seen it? This is a very unsatisfactory affair. When we reject a conceived reality, there is some sense in saying that we reject it not because we have erred in our immediate perception, but because we have erred in our reflections on its existence. Thus, we can reject reality without having to reject a perceived and conceived existence. To deny the 'existence of a cat is not to deny that a 'cat' does not exist, but to deny this determination of reality - an object being a cat. This confusion lays down the roots for many paradoxes in the denial of existence.

Reality in totality

Reality, thus, I say, not being identical with existence, is a conception of an existent within the context of a whole or a totality of experience. If I meet a man who says he is my brother, and if my experience confers no existence of such a relation, I will be reasonable to think that the situation is not real. If I see a woman who can disappear through a wall, and who I was told, lived two hundred years ago, I would not hesitate to question this reality. A brother turning up suddenly in total disconformity with everything else in my experience, stands out unconnected to the totality of my experience. Either I have to reject this reality or I must reassess my past experience to find room to accommodate such 'detached' existence. If the totality of experience confers no similarity in experiencing walking through a wall, this phenomenon has no relations with the rest, and should be questioned as to its place within the coherence of a total reality. Nor can I envisage that a woman who has lived for more than two hundred years is anything other than the dead or the perished. A man lives in the satisfaction of his reality because his totality of experience gives him a consistency or coherency so that he expects all facets of reality to fall within this consistent realm of experience. This is the reality of existence.

Distinguishing spatial and non-spatial existents

By the first criterion of reality, we put the non-spatial existents in the rank of unreality. This is not unproblematic. By this second criterion of reality, images in dreams and imagination not consistent with the totality of experience, are now consigned to unreality. Not everything that is conceived alone is spatial and consistent with the totality of experience. There may be existents conceived alone, that are not related to the totality of experience. Hence, to separate dream experience from veridical experience, we apply this second criterion since we cannot reject the reality of mental images by the criterion of being spatial alone. We wake up from a dream and find its content in total disharmony with our immediate and recalled experience. Our experience in its totality is continual, so that bits of happenings now can be conceived to be associated with, therefore, part of the past. Experience in its totality has its every bit firmly associated with or related to other bits, so that when something is introduced (perceiving an existent), such as a dream or a new experience, it becomes part of a whole reality fitting into a tightly knitted totality. Apart from being inconsistent with the rest, dream experience cannot slot itself into a continual experience in which we find ourselves when we wake up. I would be in wonderment if I was flying an aeroplane a minute ago in a dream, and now find myself lying on a bed. There is no continuity found in any recalled experience before the sleep and in flying an aeroplane during dreaming. Perhaps, we are bestowed with a sense of reality because in each individual, there is only one, and never more than one, totality of experience that carries each individual through his or her passage of life. This totality can be enriched, but never inconsistently disjunctive within itself.

Conceptual existence and perceptual existence

Earlier, I said things that are not real, may nonetheless exit. This is a conceptual existence. Although I may be happy to accept a conceptual object such as a unicorn as a conceived existent, but not real, am I prepared to say that a conceptual 'entity' such as a 'morality principle' or 'truth' exists, but is not real? If 'morality' or 'truth' is not real, it has no place in a totality of experience and its consistency. Unlike a conceptual object such as a unicorn, a 'morality principle' may not be conceived like any spatial object, but as a relation or value which is spaceless. Unicorns may not be part of a totality of experience for the lack of perceptual confirmation. The reality of a thing like 'unicorn' lies in whether it is part of a space-time experience, for it is conceived as a 'spatial' object and not as a relation. The lack of perceptual confirmation will be enough to deny it of this reality. Whereas a conceptual entity like a 'morality principle' is not conceived as a space-time object, hence its reality lies not in a perceptual confirmation, but judgements of relations within a totality of experience. And this reality will be denied if these relations are not established. But is conceptual existence a metaphysical reality or a conceptual reality?

A non-space-time conceptual entity, if conceived as a relation, cannot be in relation to another relation within a totality of experience, since there will be an infinite regress. Hence, either it is not real in the sense that it is not relational to other spatial things, or cannot be conceived as a relation. Furthermore, the reality of relations must be dependent since they are relations among things, and not things themselves conceived without relations. This reality will not be, if objects on which these relations depend, do not exist. A 'morality' not conceived as a relation to humanity will not be a reality. A badly conceived 'morality' has no reality if it does not explain a totality of relations among its objects - i.e. individuals themselves. This is a situation when we can claim that redness is not real, if there are no objects on which it depends for its conception. Therefore, relational, conceptual entities are not real if there are no existents to carry them.

There is the other alternative as to whether conceptual entities such as 'moral principle' can be conceived not as relations, but as a non-space-time 'objects' themselves. These non-space-time 'objects' are curious things that can only be conceived by philosophers. The idea of 'God', the Hegelian Absolute or moral principles may be these conceptual objects not conceived as relations. How and whether non-spatial things can be conceived not as relations are a matter for debate. If they can, they should be regarded as existents by conception, but not by perception. Their reality will be discussed in a later chapter.

3.4 Reality, relational consistency and value

Public reality and relational constancy (not repetition)

A self-consistent whole of experience on its own in reality can be criticized for the lack of a consentaneous agreement. It may be a solipsistic state of affairs no matter how firmly one believes in one's own reality built on such tightly fitted experience. We introduce the third criterion of reality that others must share one's totality of experience in its most consistent constitution.

In the convention of philosophical thinking, relations among things are seen as a means to detect the existence of dependence. For anything that is related to others is not independent. The construction of a reality from relations is not what I am looking for. Nor am I trying to bring forth simply a consistency or constancy subsumed under a so-called inductive repetition, in the same sense that the repetition of a planet circling a star would give a sense of constancy. Some may speak of reality as a permanent possibility of perception. A permanency may certainly give a sense of reliability, but reliability applies to both reality and appearance. Permanency has a sense in conceiving reality as being independent of ourselves, for something that is permanent owes nothing else for this existence. A permanent existent cannot depend on our perception which itself is not permanent.

By this term, relational constancy, I mean an underlying constancy which connects possible (perceptual) differences in relations, and not repetition itself. I think this relational constancy can be an objective basis for a consentaneous agreement on reality. Take colours for example. As one's perception of colour is a private experience, it is sensible to ask: how can we agree on the colours of things if our respective colour sensations are private, inaccessible or perhaps different? This is how an agreement is possible. If a 'real' colour red is seen by one as 'blue' and by another as 'green', and if such an anomaly is constant, that is to say, if one always sees what is 'really red' as 'blue' and another always sees it as 'green', then, whenever they point to the red, they can agree on a constancy in their respective perceptual data. This is an agreement on an underlying constancy and not on colour sensations, which are private. It is not an agreement that is dependent on identity, or a mutual knowledge of the same, but the reverse; and the identity in this sense is a mere consistent reference. This can happen, irrespective of whatever colour sensations they may experience privately, not verifiable by a shared sense-experience. This consistency of colours applies to sense-data (whatever they are) being constant throughout in a relation with sensible objects, to both perceivers. This is a relational constancy such that whenever I experience sensations, their relational constancy allows me to name things without anomaly and without a reference to sameness, and allows others to agree to the same by pointing to this relational constancy and consistency.

What we can agree among ourselves is not our respective colour sensations, but the constancy in the association not only within a range of sensible objects, but also between this range and others. This aspect of reality is the reality of relational constancy and consistency. This objectivity should not be trivialized; for I see that this relational constancy appears again and again in our understanding of nature underpinning the agreement among ourselves.

How can a relational constancy construct reality?

Seeing a star through the interpretation of radio signals or light waves is to see a constancy of relations. Take another example in the size of objects. It is said that a thing looks bigger when it is nearer and smaller when it is farther. Before men knew the secret of the cosmos, the size of the moon was thought for centuries to be larger than that of the sun; and we would not have convinced a single individual if we were to find ourselves living in that past. It is not that people in the past were stupid, but that they lacked the understanding of many cosmic facts, in a relational whole, at the time. For it would not be reasonable to think that people of a given past period did not know that things appeared smaller at a distance. Hence, lacking a constant factor to explain two stages of appearance of a same thing can and will distort reality, and different or contrary perceptual situations will be unified by a consistent, whole reality; constancy in relations can always explain such an anomaly. The size of a thing that looks smaller at a distance or bigger when it is nearer, is not a hopeless anomaly begging the question of what the veridical size is. This deciding factor lies in the distance that is consistently proportional to such anomaly. The distance of the object is in relation to the size of the thing (that is not to say that space is in this sense relational), and as long as this relation is constant, measurement is possible, and sizes can be veridical. That a thing is five feet away is only a relation to, and measured by, the length of a thing used as an approximate standard. Of course, there may be other types of constancy, such as seeing through glasses, water, angles or other perceptual media that may complicate a relation, without resulting in a nightmare of anomalies. The size of a thing is in a constant proportion to the measure of distance, using an approximate, standard length; this standard itself is also in a constant relation in size and length with everything else. When I see a thing smaller at a distance, I will not be alarmed to think that there is an anomaly in the size of this object; for my understanding is adjusted to this constant factor from an apparently distorted reality. Yet, I may not need to know what others' experience in what this 'big' or 'small' is; our mutual agreement is nothing but that of a constancy of a relation by a particular measurement. I shall come back to this when I examine the notion of space.

Relations are quantitative, rather than qualitative

The old philosophical idea of relation since Aristotle cannot survive this question without an answer, that is, what is a relation? Many may be satisfied with an answer that relation is, at best, a quantification. For example, if one pound of beef is 'equal' to four loaves of bread, and four loaves of bread are 'equal' to six nails, this relation (equal) can be extended to eternity, and will remain the measurement of quantity only, but never of quality or value. And value is the thing that is always lacking in a relation alone. In a way we may say that a relation is value itself, if we think that what is not 'in' an existent, is value. In fact, that is how I shall define value. What gives a content or a quality to a relation? What makes up the content in the relation between four nails and four loaves of bread? Perhaps, in most cases, the content of a relation is more or less understood and implied; without putting a content to a relation at the outset, a relation simply is quite empty. Why do four nails always equal to four loaves? In reality, four nails may not always 'equal' to four loaves of bread, without referring to human conditions. Whatever makes a relation constant is a minimal content in a relation. Therefore, whatever a relation is, and whatever its content has besides this, a relational constancy is a content in a relation. It underlies a connection among appearances, or the conceptions of appearance, so that a relation, no matter what it is, can explain one appearance in term of another, and another in terms of others, through a constant but veridical reference. Consequently, the appearances of things (as seen to be appearances of the same source) provoke a sense of 'sameness' if a fixed point of reference has an account for this. We can say that relational constancy is the value that underpins all relations, if relations are of any metaphysical significance. Perhaps this is the only objective 'value' that is not dependent on human conceptual power. Besides, there are many human values, epistemological or otherwise, that can underpin relations. This will be discussed in the chapter concerning universals (see p.240).

Let us see how this relational constancy works in our perceptual veridicality. The colour sensation from, of or in, an object gives a sense of sameness to two or more persons, if there is a relational constancy. This sensation is in space and fixed in a region (the object occupies). If there are different colour shades on the surface, it is due to sunlight or some perceptual conditions; eliminating these conditions will restore it to the 'original' shade. This is not to say that there is an 'original' shade, being a veridical sensibility in reality, but that there is a relational constancy that exists among all colours, interpreted in terms of other things through their relations. If a red object has a white shade on its surface, I understand that this white shade is there because of the light source. My yellow spectacles may make a red object look orange, but there remains a sense of sameness among all colours seen through these spectacles, that is a fixed condition that explains all anomalies.

Qualities in constant grouping

Various sensible qualities have a sense of reality because they exist within a definitive space, and it is in this space that this constancy among all anomalies is intricately confined. A definitive region is an area marking the boundary of an object to which this bundle of sensible anomalies is constantly related. Why is it that a certain bundle of sensible qualities always appertains to a particular region space? In any object, there is a representation of a particular set of sensible qualities in a space; it is this constant spatial grouping of sensible qualities that persists throughout. This is a point about the constancy in perceptual bundles of objects as regards grouping. A stone has hardness, colours, shape and roughness, but seldom a noise. A fire has colours and heat, but never hardness. This is the reality within the constancy of grouping (relation).

That a certain object is perceived as a particular set of sensible qualities and not otherwise, is a sense of reality even though these sensible qualities may not be, or cannot be outside our scheme of perceiving. This sense of reality by grouping, conceived over and above the spatial confinement, is consisted in the constancy in the natural grouping of sensible qualities. If the solidity of a stone is a sensible quality in Berkeley's sense (being an idea of sensibility), and if I can refer to this quality by correctly and constantly pointing to other stones, tables and chairs, there must be a constancy in the relation between this solidity and the sensibility in my touches confined to this group of sensibles that we call an object.

If there is a common aspect that I can identify from touching three objects, and if this aspect is always associated with each of these objects, I only identify a constancy among them. There will be an agreement and mutual 'identity' by both of us. If one does not accept that an agreement can follow from this identity of constancy, an argument from presupposition may be appropriate. When I refer to something constantly in my touches and others are able to refer to the same, it presupposes that such identity of a relational constancy is extended to others' experiences, otherwise no agreement can be reached. It is possible that the thing we both agree to, be it colour to you or solidity to me, are different things, even if the relational constancy among objects is the only thing identified.

Others may talk of sensible qualities or sensibilities in term of phenomena. Phenomena are appearances that have no substantive qualities independent of being sensed. A phenomenal world will make no sense if there are no relations conceived and understood by us. I doubt if we will be able to say even that it is full of these or those colours. Understanding of reality and having a sense of it are one and the same thing. We do not understand or identify things in relation first before we ask a question about reality. Why does water always boil when put over a fire, if water and fire are separate and unrelated groups of sensible qualities? To understand boiling, we must understand all the relations between fire, water, distance, and so on. Why does water always flow, or why is sugar always sweet? Here, we are not speaking of the things' nature, for there is nothing else known of them within or without, except our limited senseibility. We are not speaking of the repetition of events involving sensible qualities, for repetition adds nothing extra to the mere sensibility. Nor are we speaking of a permanent possibility of perception, for the permanency of a particular unrelated sensation, without referring to other things, gives rise to no sense of an extra-ego reality. We are here talking about a permanency of relations among sensibilities, presupposing an agreement among us, so that a sense of reality is rooted to this permanency that is not of our own making, even if it may be subjective and private in its conception. With these three aspects that I have discussed, we can construct a reality out of existence.

4 Substance and reality

4.1 Substance

An underlying reality

As I have asked before, why does water always flow, why is sugar always sweet? If there is an essence of water in flowing or an essence of sugar in being sweet, we can find nothing more in the moving water or in the sweetness that is not a mere sensibility, the origin of which is probably in perceiving itself. If there is a relational constancy in sweetness or in flowing, in the measure of things, what is this thing called relation, or a constancy of relation? What is this metaphysical reality responsible for a relation and a constancy in a relation? The conception of a relation, is of course, the making of the mind. We can conceive a relation that is false, only in the sense that such relation is not constant and consistent with others. That sugar is always sweet, is wholly a constancy, not a taste. The question of substance is a question of permanency. The traditional philosophies ask what underlies sensibility; our question of substance is what underlies a relational constancy, or perhaps, what a relational constancy itself is.

This is reality in what we can know and this is an epistemological reality, since all the constituents of this reality are not independent of perceiving and conceiving. But there may be more to what there is in reality. There is a sense in asking whether there is a reality beyond, if we do not know or if we misconceive all there is to know about an existent outside our sensibility. The question is how real things can be, rather than what is there. Besides this, there is of course the traditional ontological question of reality that concerns what supports independent beings unsensed or unconceived. If a thing can be independent of anything, it must also exist independently without being perceived; and, also, if perception is not an issue here, it must exist without relation to anything. Furthermore, a thing that has no relational dependence must not have parts; for if not, its parts are every bit as real of the whole and there must be some relational dependence among them. Thus, for a thing to exist independently of anything else, it must not have parts or be part of something else. Consequently, we are leading down a road, to search for something that conforms to these metaphysical demands: a simple thing that will be called substance.

Substance of rationalism

This is a reality, the confirmation of which can go beyond the senses. Senses apart, it is also beyond the linguistic discourse to 'discover' such a thing. Whether or not language and logic can be a safe reliance without the 'rawness' of senses to give us a firm ground for this discourse, the existence of substance is not something metaphysicians can ignore. Traditional rationalists argued for the reality of substance, starting not from the given sense appearances. Descartes uses his trust in God to establish a reality from appearance. Plato's reality in the Forms or universals transcends the senses into a third realm of reality. Leibniz likewise has his own reality in the Monads, the independent, simple metaphysical singularities. There are philosophers who apply both the sense experience and non-empirical knowledge in search for this reality. They see reality beyond the senses in things-in-themselves, or a substratum underlying sensible qualities and existence. As reasoning and logic are considered to be firmly rooted in the realm of extra-sensual conceptions, a rational reality will remain a reality by conception only, or suffer some confusion, if not inconsistency.

The acceptance of the reality of Platonic Forms as well as the reality of 'concrete', individual and sensible objects by Aristotle, is a case of such confusion. Hence, many think that Aristotle has two differently developed metaphysics, which are not within the scope of this book. Kant is another example. Hence in one sense, Kant can be regarded as a realist, an empiricist or in another sense an idealist, albeit only a transcendental idealist, whose reality is presupposed through an objectivity in the nature of our perceptual judgements, beyond sensibility. I think, Kant's problems are laid bare in his proposal of the synthetic-a-priori infusion in judgements. If a judgement of reality is inescapably a pure, *a priori* concept, it must have an *a priori* necessity; and, if so, a judgement is necessarily either *a priori* (not synthetic), or synthetic (not a priori) purely because of this necessity. The reference to 'synthetic' is superfluous in this connection. For one must admit that even mathematical truth must have some synthetic content, at the very least. As Kant has argued, our knowledge cannot be totally devoid of sense experience or it would be like something flying or floating without air, all human judgements and concepts must, in one way of another, have some synthetic content. However, Kant does think that there is a pure, *a priori*, knowledge. The argument on this issue is whether senses or sensibility are all there is to reality and nothing more.

Idealism and immaterialism

Of course, there are philosophers who take the exclusiveness of sense experience to the extreme; extreme, that is, according to your view. John Locke, Bishop Berkeley and David Hume typify these philosophers. Berkeley's reduction of reality to mere senses and sensibility, which are intra-human, leads to a label of his philosophy as 'idealism'. That all we can know of this world are our senses and sensibilities, may not imply that the world is made of our ideas or sensibilities. In fact, idealism cannot be confined to Berkeley's philosophy any more than realism can be attributed to the philosophies of Descartes and Plato. If the Cartesian or Platonic reality is substantiated by innate knowledge and reasoning, or by God's given assurance in its conception, this reality is ideal too, though not in the same sense as it is in Berkeley's metaphysics. Although Berkeley concludes from his arguments that the reality of the world independent of human perception is sustained by the idea of God, one cannot accept such a conclusion, without having to reject his premisses. The reactions to Berkeley's metaphysics for many years, may have missed the point, just as the person who came to the church and kicked the stone in front of the Bishop to show him a 'concrete' reality might also have missed the point.

To me, Bishop Berkeley's metaphysics is a philosophy of immaterialism, rather than idealism. Berkeley's arguments are meant to refute the notion that there are things that underline all the primary and secondary qualities, independent of our senses. However, to what conclusions we think the arguments will lead, is not easy to know. If we are comfortable in drawing the conclusion that all things that exist are nothing but ideas of sensibility, Berkeley is of course an idealist in this sense. Hume, true to his brilliant, rational self, does not draw conclusions like this, hence many think that he is a sceptic. Immaterialsm has had such a profound impact on philosophy since Berkeley that all contemporary Anglo-American and continental philosophies to this day can be seen as reacting to Berkeley's immaterialism, one way or another.

That the reality of this world is nothing but our sensibility (a product of our own subjective conception) is, understandably, disturbing to many. But the notion that a reality is made up of Platonic ideas, logical entities or God's given assurance, should be more disturbing. Sensibility is necessarily a human sensibility which can be shared and agreed upon; whereas Platonic and logical entities can be seen as beings imposed from 'above' by objectivity. We may reject the arguments for immaterialism that we do not like, in order to construct a reality by ignoring the reality made implicit by these arguments, or we may accept and use them to deal with a misconception of reality contravening our common-sense beliefs.

Sensibility and words

The persuasiveness of immaterialism that there is nothing other than sense and sensibility cannot easily be ignored. It is almost as if this persuasiveness does not come from the truth in immediate perception itself, but from the notion of 'how to know of anything'. The relation of language to the world is bi-directional. It is said that the world is a yardstick for the meaning (or truth criterion) of words, and, conversely, that words have notions by which the world is understood. If one looks at the sense of priority, both epistemological or metaphysical, one can easily see the difference in these relations (if there are such): whether the world is a prior condition for the meanings in words or words are a prior condition for the understanding of the world. This is important if we try to find the world through words. If words were an analogy of senses or sensibility (or even ideas), then, to find the world through words is like finding it through senses and sensibility. It cannot be true that words precede the world unless you worship the theory supporting the innateness of conceptual knowledge and words. If the world precedes words, inevitably there is a possibility that the origin of meanings of words comes from the world, but not the reverse. Thus we form the meaning of or give the meaning to words from the content of the world, through sensibility. If not, how is it possible that we can find the real world through words? Or, for that matter, how do we find our sensibility or even ideas from words?

Just as sensibility cannot identify reality, words too are not references to reality

Are not sensibility and ideas, words themselves? Perhaps words confer an implicit reality hidden behind logic, but such a claim is simply about a reality implicit behind understanding without the world, in which case such knowledge must be innate and outside sensibility, and therefore the world. If we have only words to discover the world, would it be difficult for us to identify words in turn with an unworded reality? On the other hand, given the prior existence of the world, we will have no problems in bestowing meaning to words or symbols for everything and every sensibility, without having to find a bit of world to fit the predetermined meaning of a word. Every meaning that is understood, will be implicit in presupposing the existence of a bit of the world or sensibility. This implicitness is not an innate implication, but an acknowledgement of the origin of words' meanings with a prior condition - the world. Our confusion seems to lie in the failure to recognize these two contrasting positions. One easy option is to label the world with words, which may raise problems of consistency and of mutual agreement among us, but never a problem of identity, that is, an identify of the world in terms of words but not words in terms of the world. Having accepted this, one cannot say that a statement is true, if and only if, there are facts corresponding to the statement. For that will be finding the world through words. In this way, I can call a table a chair, or a book a table, provided there is consistency in the relation between the word and the objects to allow an agreement among us.

The defining method to find reality, is not about labelling the world with words, but identifying the bits of the world with a consistency in applying them to words. This will create mutual understanding in words so applied. The labelling of the world with words would surely fail without the assumption of an innateness that can determine a criterion for labelling. It is easy to think that if we label something, we can later easily find this something by referring to the label. Reality does not have such simplistic labelling. It is because the world is not made of bits that are unconnected, and because relations cannot be labelled without having to refer to a large portion of the whole (or events) sufficiently to bring out the relation we seek to label. To find bits of the world with labels cannot guarantee a complete reference to what was originally understood, even if any labelling of the world is only about labelling a definite chunk of sense experience that is in principle unverifiable. Hence the persuasiveness of immaterialism has this aspect of truth in telling us that the world 'found' through words, senses or sensibility will always remain a world of words and sensibility. This is far from a conclusion that the reality of the world is made of words and ideas.

Is it possible to have substance beyond sensibility?

Yet, Berkeley's arguments go beyond this. If we follow Berkeley's arguments, there is the inevitability that senses and sensibility are all there is for us to know about the world, and there is nothing beyond the senses that can provide grounds for the construction of a thing called substance, independent of being perceived and relational to nothing except itself. Anything that is totally independent has to be known to exist. If something is known for its existence, it can only be dependent. The magic here is not about the mystery of independence, but a connotational parameter of the word 'exist'. Thus there is another aspect in the persuasiveness of immaterialism, in that if something existed must be known to exist, how do we know of an existent if all we have as a tool are words and sensibility?

Kant's slogan that we cannot know things-in-themselves beyond the limitation of our judgements has the same sentiments of immaterialism. But it misses the point concerning the difference between reporting (or finding) the world with words limited by our knowledge and submitting the world to our understanding. Words alone cannot lead us to an independent existence. Hence, Bertrand Russell may have grasped the aspect of this reality when he attempts to show how words or statements can point to the reality of particulars. He thinks that the only sure way words can 'name' particulars, is in the use of words like 'this' or 'that'. The point is not that words like 'this' and 'that' have a magical referential property that goes beyond human limitation. Rather, it is that the use of a word that has no referential meaning except to the speaker or the hearer in the presence of an utterance and has a function in pointing to a chunk of experience with sufficient relation in reality. This presence may or may not invoke a definite identity of a thing at all, depending on the speaker and the hearer's understanding. In this sense, an intended 'reference' is a variable for this reality. If there is a definite identity of an intended object or affair of the world, this reality is seen, understood, rather than verified, given that there is a connection between the words ('this' or 'that') and the world. This connection is immediate perceiving and mutual understanding through a relational constancy. In this sense 'this' and 'that' serve not as a reference, but invoke an understanding. Last, are our senses and sense experience, words? The issue is not vital here as they are both intra-human 'reality' in sensing and understanding.

Words cannot guarantee identity

If the world exists before words, there must a time when man experiences reality speechlessly, but surely not without being conscious of it. The difference between 'from reality to words' and 'from words to reality' emphasizes an epistemological gap between reality and words, in that a reality is never fixed (as opposed to being relationally constant). Words are rigid, limited by definition, and symbolic in their application. A world is not fixed because its conception is by a mind that can be both finite and infinite in the way it conceives. When I see a new thing to which I shall attach a word, there is no problem in finding the thing by referring to the word, if it all happens during a continual, immediate perceiving. The problem of course emerges when there is no immediate perception or when there is no temporal continuity in perceiving this bit of reality. If in those circumstances we have to rely on words to find reality, we need a full and precise description of what the original thing of perception was. Then the seemingly infinite description of all relations and details of this thing will be impossible for a logical, absolute identity. Whereas with an immediate perceptual experience, space and time, found lacking in a non-immediate perceptual situation, will help to make an identity possible. Would it be the corruption of our mind by formal logic that prompts us to think that a bit of reality can be designated by a symbol? If not, why is it that a bit of the world can be designated by a word and not that a word is designated by a bit of the world? If the latter is the case, we must find the bit of the world first before we can find the word it 'designates'. Let these men of brilliant intellect search for a true reality from words alone.

Substance and identity

The search for substance is a search for more than mere existence, or an independent reality. Reality is such an odd thing that exposing ourselves to it involves both its recognition (the speakable) and its vividness (the unspeakable). That a man can never grasp every bit of reality is undoubtedly true, for a man is not a machine made to capture every aspect, every tiny dot, or the inclusive whole, of reality, even though he may be in the centre of it. Hence, he will find the original concept recognized with a bit of reality, not always conforming to what he sees of reality the second time, or third time, as he originally did. It is not so much that reality may have changed through time, but that we may have different understanding and cognition of reality at different times, especially when closer examination is applied. Identity has always been taken as discerning a sameness between two entities, but seldom as a criterion for the determination of reality. I believe it is the latter that is more appropriate for the definition of identity.

Rejecting the doctrine of identity of the indiscernibles

There is a slogan that there is no entity without identity and also another that there is no substance without identity[3], which sum up the importance of the criterion of identity in substance. The first slogan goes beyond the idea that existence is merely in being conceived. The existence of a 'unicorn' is ruled out in this case. But, identity is a dubious concept if we consider it in the traditional sense. This traditional notion of identity is formulated or understood as this: if two things are indiscernible, they are identical; or A is A and B is B. Without a further introspective examination of my own rationale, postulating two entities and then asserting them to be identical and therefore one, even if there is an added indiscernibility, are self-contradicting. If there is an ontological commitment of two entities, which may be 'indiscernible', there are necessarily two things, no matter how absolute this indiscernibility is. But if such indiscernibility is absolute, there is necessarily one entity and we cannot postulate two entities from the outset. Indiscernibility implies more than one entity, therefore whatever is indiscernible cannot be one, in conclusion. That A is A has a dual ontological commitment, even though we say these two are one and the same. Logic and mathematics encourage us to postulate variables, which are conceptual presuppositions that have no place in reality; reality certainly cannot have ontological presupposition disguised as conceptual presupposition.

No substance without identity

In this method of identity, that is, A is A, any identity will certainly presuppose two entities which are identical. The slogan that there is no entity without identity is no more than a tautology. But, this slogan may not be a tautology, if it is only possible to postulate entities before identity. There will be an examination of identity later. But an entity without identity is a curious thing and it must be mentioned again. Identity may mean determinacy or minimal awareness of an existent. If it is possible, this entity prior to 'identity' (determinacy or awareness) must mean whatever is conceived as an indeterminate. But can we conceive something as an indeterminate? This is highly unlikely. A minimal awareness is not an identity in this sense. But if it is, it is only an identity of awareness itself. We do not know what an entity is before it exists prior to its identity; nor do we know how we can separate entity from identity. Should we decide to say that there is no existent without identity, we face the same problem. Can an existent be conceived or perceived, but not identified? Only if there is a difference between conceiving (or perceiving) and identity, can we say that something is conceived but not identified. Still there is a hesitancy to say that something is identified but not conceived, since identity implies conceiving or perceiving. If we can conceive without identity, then it is quite consistent to say that they can be different. The problem, I think, is found in what amounts to 'having identified something'. If we say that seeing an image or mirage is not identity, as identity has a say in reality itself, then an entity with identity must be something of reality and not just of existence. As we have argued before, an entity that is conceived is an existent not necessarily of reality, it does not make sense to say that there is no entity without identity implying an imprecise ambiguity as to whether this is an entity of existence or of reality. To find out what reality is, is to find what substance is, for the criteria for seeking reality and substance are the same. Hence it makes sense to say that there is no substance without identity (whatever the latter may be).

Realism constructed by words

The quest for the meaning of substance is the quest for reality, hence the consideration in our discussion on reality must take notice of what substance is. This discussion can take many forms including the questions of meaning involving linguistic items such as naming, referring and identifying, each of which is transitive, looking for something outside either as a means of confirmation or, again, identity. A linguistic method of investigating reality may be, to some, a way to realism, but in fact, and in my view, is nothing more than rationalism revisited. For whatever a word can refer to, name or identify, is necessarily something that depends on the one who utters, hears or understands. If reality is true as the words are, it can only be true as the meaning itself anchored to the one who utters, hears or understands. That is nothing more than saying that reality can be worked out within our rationale.

That reality is construed by us and by words, the meaning of which can be innate, is not new. But that reality construes our understanding of words, is another matter altogether; and how this is possible is older than Plato himself. In the latter, the reliance on identity to underpin reality, albeit with untold difficulties, is hindered by our misconception of this word 'identity'. The idea of postulation between two entities and confirming that they are the same, runs deep in many philosophical schemes, such as the causal theory of perception, or the so-called naive realism, because they postulate a reality on the one hand and intra-human qualities on the other hand, and proceed to find a indubitable link by whatever means. Identity is not about finding something indiscernible between two entities, conveniently presupposed, for logic will ensure that it will fail. Identity is about uniqueness of a thing together with knowing its uniqueness, its determination and nothing more.

From Russell to Quine and Strawson, the Russellian criterion of identity using 'this' and 'that' to invoke a speaker-hearer identity, tinged with a bit of Wittgensteinian idea that language has its meaning in being used, relies on what is called the immediate perceptual experience, with public agreement of course. The failure of a linguistic, descriptive reality gives way to the situation of an immediate, perceptual reality, without the actual need to mention it. For the words 'this' and 'that' are of no true meaning without an immediate experience in a speaker and a hearer; such is the persuasiveness of this reality that these words are almost redundant except in their function of pointing to something. This pointing to something is interpreted by Wittgenstein as the use rather than a referential pointing to something; Wittgenstein has missed the point because in saying that the meaning of words is their use, it still begs the questions of how, why and what.

What substance are we looking for?

Substance is sometimes taken as something that is permanent, unique or independent. Identity in a way, calls for a permanency that raises the possibility of 're-identification'. Independence, uniqueness and permanency are not three totally unrelated notions. They can be inclusive in some aspects and exclusive in others. Something which is permanent may not be independent or vice versa. If the success of identification can serve the cause of permanency and perhaps uniqueness, it may not underpin an independence. For to be identified is to be dependent; if something is unique, it is so identified as unique among other things and the knowledge of other things becomes a precondition for this uniqueness and, therefore, there is a dependence. It can be imagined that a dependency may not be a dependency on other things, but a dependence by other beings, so that others would not have existed if it is not for this thing (or substance). In other words, an independent thing may not be something that is known through other things, but rather, a thing the existence of which is presupposed by the conception of other beings through their dependency on it. This will be expounded on p.90. Still in this way, a thing presupposed by this possible dependency, may not be independent.

Identity alone cannot resolve this epistemological problem. Whatever is independent absolutely must also be independent of being known, and hence of being identified. Perhaps we can say that if we resolve this problem of independence, permanency and uniqueness will follow.

The sense of permanency is two-fold. In one, it is about enduring changes and remaining the same essentially, and in another, it is about persisting through time and space. A piece of wax through melting and solidifying and a person through ageing, can exemplify these two aspects. As all qualities are susceptible to changes, the first notion gives rise to an idea of something underlying all changes and remains the same. As re-identity implies that what was identified before can survived to be re-identified, it also implies an existence survived beyond being perceived, and therefore independent. Overall, the substance we are searching, is something that is independent (that implies being basic, simple and without parts), particular (unique) and permanent. Surely even if all things in the world are not appearances of sensibility, but real, concrete and independent beings, we are still entitled to ask as to whether they really have all these substantive characteristics. This again is a question of 'how do we know', therefore a question of dependence.

Problems with identity

The difficulty we have concerning reality itself is the same as that which concerns substance. Why should men want to pursue the enquiry into a substance that is simple, unique, permanent and independent, when all things in their experience give no hint of being like that? Perhaps understanding bears the burden of re-identification, in an indelible sense of things being able to exist in between one moment and another, unperceived. If I were to assess two temporal things for their discernibility, perceptual conditions cannot allow two sets of data at the same time for us to judge if the present bits of reality were the same as one another. Reality supplies only one set of immediate sensibility, with which others can agree. In this way, the identity of bits of reality is the same as its reference to incorrigibility. Without two comparables to determine an identity, even if logic allows us to postulate two entities from the outset, failure is readily obvious. Still it is a person who can identity and it is his fallibility and limitation that pose the problem in identity. Changing conditions, values, judgements and the break-up in the continuation of perception are all there to see. The identity of, and the enquiry into, reality or substance cannot be done with unreliable memory to determine the indiscernibility of two things at different times. Re-identity presupposes existence. Identity is really about determination alone and nothing else.

This old way of thinking of identity must be abandoned. There is another way to see identity, since there is a sense of identity in every judgement such as 'This is the same chair I saw two hours ago'. Without the notion of indiscernibility, identity is not a unique state of mind outside every perceptual judgement of reality. Nothing is conceived if nothing is understood in being seen and put into a realm of reality. Even the percept of a simple colour has a conceptual category of judgement, or a judgement of identity. Identity is nothing but determinacy. But a particular statement of determination should be an identity of a particular, and not of a generality. We say that to identify is to identify a particular. If that is the case, one must find the wisdom of how this is possible. This is a very ancient problem that simply will not go away. The idea of identity is now reduced to a judgement of understanding. If identity cannot guarantee particularity and if determination is in fact identity, what is a thing without identity, or determination? If identity is paramount to the existence of anything, it says nothing more than that determination is paramount to its existence, and that is nothing new. If something is not determined, it is nothing.

Determination itself cannot add anything more to an existence already confirmed, or to its reality in terms of dependence, simplicity and permanence.

Problems with simplicity

Let us look at the notion of simplicity in a 'substance'. Simplicity in extension is not possible because it is strictly contradictory to say that something which has no extension is still a body, or that something extended has no parts. Simplicity by definition is naturally unextended; thus Leibniz dares introduce his Monadology of unextended entities. Epistemological simplicity is not easy either. To conceive something simple is to conceive an existence not connected to anything else, and therefore to conceive an independence. This is difficult, since every existent must be perceived and conceived. The obsession with either a monistic or a pluralistic nature of things, has persuaded us to accept either one; for a thing cannot be one and many at the same time. How are we to find, let alone conceive a thing that is simple and yet extended, monistic but relational, or simple but pluralistic? As for the notion of persisting through changes, human perceptual faculty is a slave to change and can hardly condition a perception unchanged through time.

In all the parameters suggested for the existence of 'substance', the search for this elusive thing is nothing but human endeavour to construct an ideal objectivity cleansed of all human contamination. What is wrong with human contamination, after all if religion is right, humanity is part of a divinity? Humanity itself can be as objective as anything, if we do not look upon human perception and conception as a means to perpetuate this permanency. Perhaps the search for a substance is a crusade for common sense constructed out of a reality that we cannot dispute among ourselves; but it is exactly human fallibility that makes our common sense. A lover of reality is the one who accepts what there is given and still retains an inquiring mind to know more, but not the one who assumes a reality.

Substance and a human reality

Suppose it is possible to have a state of affairs in a world, so that there can be pure perceptual, intuitive data without humanistic judgements, if pure human sensibility is clearly separated from these world-data. In this state of affairs, primary things are seen as data unconnected since there are no human judgements. If colour is only human sensibility, a thing without any human sensibility can be colourless, odourless and shapeless, without hardness, coldness, hotness, and so on. It is not certain that what is left is extension. But judging a perceptual existent has an inevitable impression of objectivity, otherwise there will be no sense of a reality outside. Without sensibility, there will be nothing outside to serve as a target for these perceptual judgements. Whether we can identify anything outside is another matter. This is to say, that if colours, shapes and sizes are all subjective judgements and not what we judge, then what are we judging? The answer to this has two insights. One is a sense of objectivity in our perceptual judgements, but not of reality itself. The other, it can be argued, is a reality or substance to which perceptual judgements are directed. In this sense, whatever we are judging perceptually is a reality comprising the whole and consistent experience that also delivers to us a sense of objectivity in its relational constancy. On the other hand, more appropriately, there is an instigation and a motivation of human nature in these judgements of reality. This need stems from a vacuum of knowledge, which persons of action cannot deal with. For such persons' actions are both outwardly directed and world-related, even if their purposes lie nowhere else except in their own egos. With this and with a proposition that values are said of things but not inherent in things, I shall argue that perceptual judgements are evaluative and hence human values, which include not only sensibility, but relations in understanding. This is not inconsistent with the claim that all properties said of a thing, are ideas in us. The difference in these two claims is that while ideas are rootless and endlessly relational to other ideas, values are rooted to our nature, and directly to our need for knowledge to serve our actions in pursuing our own ends.

Here we return to the point of considering when and where non-evaluative reality ends and evaluative reality begins. But the non-evaluative is the 'unspeakable'. This is the ancient question of 'substance' dressed up as a question about humanity. If we hold that every cognitive judgement is evaluative, then the Berkeleian immaterialism still holds true. Any 'substance' of colour, shape and properties assumes an objectivity when it becomes the subject of our judgements, and is effectively a sum total of evaluations in sensibility. Such an assumption is not a logical consequent, but a necessitation by human nature. For the lack of logical necessity, the relational consistency can provide a sense of objectivity.

Human actions and their needs demand a sense of reality in all existents, hence the judgement of reality by relational constancy has parameters rooted to our nature instead of an extra-human nature. Sensibility in phenomena is not something 'floating', so to speak, in a subjective self. We constantly test this reality in our actions for its relational consistency and for its successes. A piece of bread that alleviates hunger is a reality firmly linking the bread to our real nature. Hence it is 'bread' rather than a bundle of sense-data. A car that takes me to another place is a reality that cannot be ignored. The hardness of a thing is used for many purposes by us, but hardness is a (valued) sensibility and not in the thing itself. If substance is what is responsible for, or underlying all sensibilities, this substance must be human nature itself, without which there can be no hotness, coldness, hardness or other sensibilities. Without human nature, there will be no bread. It is not the mind that is the substance giving rise to all these things; for the mind, an entity responsible for thoughts and considered to be the 'centre' of thinking, cannot explain, by pure thinking alone, what coldness or pain is without a reference to the whole being of the creature in which the mind dwells. Thinking alone will only provide relations, but never evaluative determinations for all things sensible. Human nature is the totality of our being including our mind (or brain, if you like), out of which sensibility in relational judgements emerges; human nature stands outside this sensibility as distinct. How can I know why an empty stomach is always associated with the feeling of hunger, or why we sense colours and shapes? A scientific explanation is not an illustration of events composed of these feeling and sensing, nor an explanation of their substantive existence with a purpose. That is to say, a sensation exists, albeit that may be seen either as an electrical impulse or a brain occurrence, but we cannot know why it should be so, which is a question of reality.

Still the question of what can be independent of our evaluative judgements, can be ignored. A subjective shifting to human nature and its needs, does not prevent the possibility of an existence of essence in things, considered as a reality outside. Whether or not it can succeed is another matter. It was David Hume who opened our eyes to the possibility that the so-called objective reality in causality, induction or indeed moral 'facts' had nothing but evaluative content that could not have come from nature itself, no matter how detailed our examination and analyses were. This is Hume's famous view on the unbridgeable chasm between facts and values. This breach exists only if we allow that there are facts which are not 'contaminated' by human values.

4. 2. Substance and relations

Substance within presupposed parameters

Within relational constancy, where there is a change, there is a relational explanation of such a change in terms of other things, so that if such relation is excluded, the change is seen as something that would not have taken place. Therefore, there is an underlying constancy in relations notwithstanding that there are changes. In this, all changes are explainable in terms of relations among all things. The veridical position in reality within relations is found in the perspective under a chosen or assumed reference (relation). This gives us a sense of the unchangeable beneath sensibility.

There have been philosophical arguments, in the Wittgensteinian fashion that a discourse among us presupposes a reality through the way we talk about things. Hence there must be a reality presupposed by the 'objectivity' in the meaning of language, otherwise, how can such a discourse about reality be possible? This objectivity can be seen in the same light of the modes of judgements, since it is about something that is rid of our subjective prejudices. Logically, such a transcendental argument is by no means necessarily true in that reality-in-itself must be the case if our judgements have this kind of objective (*a priori*) content. Transcendental argument proposes a possibility, albeit a reasonable possibility, through presupposition. There is no direct deduction to such conclusion from all considerations. Also to argue that repetition of events presupposes a reality or order, enabling us to succeed in the discourse about real things is to argue on shaky grounds. There are no reasonable grounds for this conclusion. The argument for relational consistency is not an argument for a presupposition. It presupposes nothing since it is only a constancy of relations that is judged and evaluated. Depriving our understanding of this relational constancy, nothing can be understood and determined.

Understanding apart, reality cannot satisfy all metaphysicians as to what substance is, and the history of philosophy is littered with many well thought-out possibilities. These possibilities more often are beyond the test of common sense, rendering an assumed reality a risky presupposition.

That there should not be changes in a substance or that a substance should not change, is not knowledge, since we do not know what a substance is. It is but an analytical expectation based on the ways we define substance. It certainly makes no sense to investigate whether or not substance really changes, as this will be self-proposing and self-justifying something we do not know. Can there be something unchangeable if we do not know what it is? This is at best a science. A philosophy of substance starts from what can be known. So, the postulation of a substance according to our prejudice is well avoided. Having said this, there is still a sense in thinking that if there is a reality outside sensibility, it must involve permanency and changes. This may seem another postulation of 'substance'; the latter is a question which stems from the quest for the origin of perceptual sensibility, which is not presupposed, whereas the former is a question posed from a definition not triggered by a perceptual reality. This extra-sensibility question concerning reality is prompted by human experience, without which the human connection will be overlooked. Credit should be given to a postulated reality of substance in human nature to which all evaluative understanding depends.

Relations and entities

Let me use a mathematical 'language' to illustrate a relational constancy pointing to the existence of a relational reality. Examine a number of formulae as follows:

$$X = 2b + c - 2d$$

$$X = 4\,e$$
$$e = 1/2b + c/4 - 1/2d$$
$$X/4 = 1/2b + c/4 - 1/2d$$
$$X = b + 1/2c - d + 2e$$

The relations among the variables, x, c, d and e are expressed in these equations, and the value of each will not fail to satisfy any of these equations if these values are in the same relations, even if we do not state their values. If we know the value of 'e' and therefore what '4 times e' is, we can use X to signify this quantity (value) without stating the value of 'e'. As long as their quantitative relations are constant, X will always end up with the same quantity of '4 times e' which is an indication of constancy rather than a quantitative value. It is not argued that these equations are deducible from within, but on the contrary, that the equations are synthetically acquired but found to be consistent within. In the reality of relations, a thing regarded as having two atoms of a certain kind in virtue of chemical phenomena, may be seen deemed to have passed two atoms to another thing, which has been assumed to have one atom of the same type before, having now three atoms of the same. We can contemplate this relational reality without having to name what this atom is, in the same way we can state an equation of relation without giving a value to the variables. The scientific reality of atoms is considered to be as real as tables and chairs even if we can never observe them. These atoms are postulations but substantiated by the underlying constancy of sensible things to explain their existence. Without a relation, an atom cannot exist or be conceived. If these relations, assumed or otherwise, enable the postulation of entities persistently throughout a great variety of things (variables), a certain belief in a substantive entity must emerge. And this is not an inductive repetition because the constancy of relations is far more complex than the mere repetition itself. There is a need of conformity to a relation for all things existed. Therefore, as I have argued before, the reality constructed from a relational constancy is a reality of the whole and not of a part of experience.

Changes and constancy

Then we have to consider if substance is really posited by relations and not just our psychological conception. Symbolic postulates such as mathematical variables or word symbols do not ontologically commit to anything. This way, we can propose relations by abstraction. But the mind cannot grapple with pure relations without concrete particulars; so symbols are the sure way to explain and help to conceive relations, and they themselves cannot commit to any existent, since relations must go hand in hand with sensible things. The water that is H_2O, is not the same water that washes the dirt off my clothes, whether or not I have learned chemistry. For we are not referring to the same relation. We see how semantics and connotations can play an important part in fooling us about reality; for the criterion in recognizing the same and unchanged 'substance' called water, depends on how much I know of this thing. A medieval man will certainly not identify the H_2O water as that which washes dirt. How easily can we identify the same substance 'unchanged', in the same way as we can easily be convinced that water can run downhill? Water can have a persistent nature in having the chemical property of 'H_2O', in allowing the washing of dirt as well as in giving out steam when boiled or oxygen when put through a chemical process (in contact with other 'substances'), but it does not say much about what it means to have this H_2O property being constant through changes. If 'H_2O' is a reference to the basic, unchangeable composites of water as a substance, it does not refer to or stand for, other non-chemical properties. We do not perceive a 'hydrogen atom' (let alone count two), or an 'oxygen atom', like we see tables and chairs. Scientific methods and indeed, all methods of conceiving reality, construct a constant and 'unchanging' entity by supplanting observations with what I called a relational constancy. Atoms, or any other elements, are entities referring to a constant relation among changes (chemical) in things. Therefore, it is the relation and not the entity that is constant. And it is never a substance that is unchanging, but a constancy underlying these changes. Let me explain further.

The properties of water may not be tested by human sensibility directly. These 'properties' can be seen as relations, such as gold never dissolves in most acids. Without an underlying constancy, relations can hardly be seen as entities or substances. This way, 'properties' have a sense of reality, if they are constant. Of course, water can 'have' a temperature, which may not necessarily mean 'hot' or 'cold' in human sensibility. The water that can melt butter has a different temperature than the water that cannot, without having a temperature that is either hot or cold. In this sense, this temperature is only a measure of relation between two waters in contact with butter. To explain why one water has a different temperature (having a definite relation with butter), and remains substantively the same water as the other, we have to introduce another relation. If the other water is heated over a fixed amount of combusting fuel for five minutes, it will have a temperature to melt butter, then, the difference in their respective temperatures (not in terms of 'hot' or 'cold') is stated in the relation between the amount of fuel, the combustion or the duration. The same quantities of time and fuel in combustion, will be a constant factor to determine the property water stated in a constant relation. This substantiality is about constancy, the constancy in a relation. The relation is of no value until values are introduced or added. Without them, it is a pure relational reference. Relations always remain relations without value, which is an input of human perspectives. It is hard not to see that it is us who observe relations in the nurture of our intellect, and it would be inhuman of us not to see everything without our imbedded values. Relations without constancy have no reality and will suffer the same fate. 'Seeing' the temperature of melting iron as 'hot' is inevitable, and yet if we detach this hotness from this temperature, we cannot see an underlying reality of hotness itself. We see a constancy of 'hotness' that can only come from our nature, since 'hotness' is not in the melting metal.

In the same way, the wisdom that water is made of hydrogen and oxygen atoms has no more reality in our sensibility than that the permanency of this 'substance' has a reality in our sensibility. If 'atoms', or other entities thought of as the constitution of all things, are not seen or confirmed by direct senses, what colour, shape and size can we attribute to them? The periodic table of basic substances with their chemical or atomic structures is a table of relations among them. It gives a sense of reality about how things are composed because the constancy of relations can explain well the postulation of this hypothesis. Take the atomic weight for instance, the unit of 'weight' is not so much an intrinsic reality as it is a measure against a basic substance called hydrogen, which in turn owes it 'existence' to another relational reality with some consistent phenomena. In the same way, the weight of things is seen to be an underlying reality not because we know how it feels to lift a ton of metal, but because this 'weight' has a relational reality in the measure of all things by various devices without inputting the human sensibility like 'heavy' or 'light'. Weight in this sense, like temperature, is compared to a mathematical postulation of a variable without value, but nonetheless a constant measure of relations among things. This is relational reality in substance, postulated for better understanding like a mathematical variable.

It should be noted that when it comes to a descriptive reality, mere quantitative relations, constant as they are, may be quickly abandoned for speculative reality based on unsound reasoning to introduce personal values and prejudices. For instance, some people think that there are in existence, as many things as there are many mathematical constants such as $\sqrt{I}$ or $\sqrt{-1}$. Many scientific exponents of reality, especially in physics, will have no hesitation in substituting a relational reality with an 'object'. Thus, the ordinary notion of substance is an entity referring to a relational constancy. Water gives out steam as well as gases. The reality of these gases relies on relational testings, just as displacing air or reacting with something to form something else tests the property of water. Men certainly thought at one stage that water and ice were two different substances. If a gas can be formed by chemical reaction with water, it was believed that water was made of this gas. The claim of gas substance as 'hydrogen' is secured by testing in constant relations with other things. The claim of a composite to a thing (substance), water or hydrogen is not a thing seen with extension, but a reference to all these relations, which give us a sense of reality as to the content of constancy. Hence, we see that this existential claim of substance and that of property are interchangeable, since they both refer only to relational constancy. If the postulation of a substance is determined only by the presence of these relations, then such a postulate can be an 'existent' not in terms of sensibility but in terms of pure relational constancy. This we have rejected earlier, for we cannot conceive relations alone without sensible things within them. In conceiving mathematical relations, we postulate symbols as variables to help to conceive these relations, but they are by no means entities of existence. Therefore relational consistency gives us the sense of reality in all things, but is not a reality in itself. If things are real, it is so because they are in relation with the whole, in constancy.

Naming a relation is not naming an existent. I can never see how linguistic terms, even if they are used as subjects, should confer particular existents. The composites of water can be named differently without altering the nature of its composites in terms of their relations. Any entity so postulated by reference to relations, gains no extra content, no extra extension. Postulating an entity called atom should not confer to it any sensible quality or extra extension. An atom may be extended or shaped, but we have not seen it and cannot know it. If hydrogen is a substance, it is composed of only one kind of indivisible stuff (as earlier scientific theories believed), just like other substances postulated as relations in terms of weight, chemical reactions, or other conceivable compositions.

There are those who think that things are sometimes sensed by many senses and because of this, reality has a more-than-one-sense dimension. Sense impressions from different senses are inseparable since they are closely associated to produce one existent, in the same way we say of secondary qualities are inseparable from the so-called primary qualities like extension and motion. Quite obviously, things sensed by more than one senses have more enduring reality than those sensed by one. It is exactly this multiple sensibility that can invoke or raise an expectation of reality, since multiple sensing provides a more immediate perceptual relation than a relation, which is merely contemplated. A multiple sensing is not a multiple reality; it is only a 'multitude' of expectations of a reality depending on more than one mode of sensing.

In his work, Berkeley wrote:

> Now, if it be certain that those original qualities are inseparably united with the other sensible qualities, and not, even in thought, capable of being abstracted from them, it plainly follows that they exist only in the mind.[4]

In this, Berkeley insists on the inseparability of multiple sensibilities in order to refute his critics. Here, I shall add to this argument, a question of why primary qualities are inseparable from secondary qualities or why we sometimes infer the sensibility of other senses, from one simple visual sensing. It is not that we cannot imagine that a table has no solidity; it is because a reality conceived in constant relation is best found in many modes of sensing.

Common sense and an irritating doubt seem to come up again and again with the impression that there must be something that is behind sensibility or value persisting through space and time. Bearing this in mind, the search for a 'substance' outside a human reality and sensibility is a search for another reality outside. In the following chapters, when I come to examine other aspects of the metaphysics of space, time and oneness, I shall have this problem in mind.

We have rejected the notion of substance based on available knowledge and the improbability of independence, but the existence of substance remains a possibility. It is possible to conceive the notion of substance by individuation instead of conceiving it as a natural essence. We say that essence is nothing but relations with an underlying consistency perpetuating a reality in all things sensible. But essence itself is not conceivable without sensibles, therefore they are not existents, or independent existents within our definitions of existence and reality. To conceive it as something outside our sensibility, I need to examine other aspects such as space, time, universals and perception.

Apart from the consideration of individuation of reality and its outer sense, there is a peculiar aspect of reality considered to be substantial; that is the aspect of sensible qualities being 'welded together' in regions of space. This coming together of qualities must have a sense of relation, and since spatial relation is a totally mind-consuming subject, I shall investigate it in a separate part of this book (see pp. 103-144). The persistent desire to find a substance is curious. But the answer as to what things are made of, is important to us to further our interests over nature. Yet, if one of us 'knows' the atoms and the wave-lengths in a piece of bread and an another knows its life-saving 'property', who has the better grasp of reality? Reality is to serve our actions and to provide a content for our projection and expectation. In this, the reality of the whole in constant relations can serve men best.

PART II

SPACE AND TIME

5 Space

5.1 Space and oneness

Is it possible to conceive of space without time?

When a question is asked 'what is space?' (or time for that matter), I would be cautious in answering and wonder whether this is the right question to ask. For, if we ask what something is, we are asking about this thing, about its 'nature', in terms of what we know or can know. But space is emptiness basically, and there is nothing we can say about it except through other things. It is the same problem as regards 'substance'. However, there are things at the forefront of our knowledge, where we can no more explain the thing than to stretch our language to the limit with much dissatisfaction. In asking what space is, are we supposed to treat it the same way we treat physical objects, or mental concepts? Take an example of the colour red. We can no better describe what redness is than we can point to a series of red objects. We can only talk about space through other things.

The difficult notion of space involves some crossover between itself and time since they are closely related. To begin with, I ask myself a question: can there be space without time, or can there be time without space? Space is important because the reality and the existence of things outside us involve space. Without having to consider the existence of space, can I even imagine or conceive of space without time? To answer this, I have a problem because the act of imagining or conceiving of something alone involves time. If I can conceive of space without time, it may not be because space can be independent of time, but because conceiving of something cannot be independent of time. So, a positive answer may not be conclusive, even if it is reasonably argued. What types of space can I conceive of without time? Is it the void itself, a region, distance, a volume or a pure extension without content? One thing I think is certain. I cannot imagine a space associated with motion without time, for the simple reason that there is no motion without time. So, if I can imagine or conceive of space without time, it must be a static space or space involving no motion, provided that I can ignore the involvement of time in the very act of conceiving of it or imagining it. This can be done by considering that conceiving (or imagining) and the content of what is being conceiving are distinct, so that a static affair of nothing is independent of the mind's temporal influence. If there is a state of affairs in that both perceiving or conceiving of 'timeless' space and perceiving static things are possible, then why cannot space be independently conceived of without time. Of course, there is the possibility that nothing in this universe is at rest, in which case, such a state of affairs is impractical, since perception can ignore or may not perceive motions it does not notice. Yet, I cannot say that such a state of affairs is beyond imagination.

Can space be conceived without objects?

There is the other question of whether pure space can be conceived without objects, even though objects cannot be conceived of without space. This is the famous Kantian position in rejecting space as being composed of relations. Kant thinks that we can imagine (or conceive) pure space without an object occupying it, by imagining a space with lines and curves. In this way, the conception of a space does not depend on the extension of an object and that extensions, considered to be spaces, are not dependent on the sensibility that 'constitutes' or goes with these extensions of objects. This is in contrast to what Bishop Berkeley has maintained. Also this Kantian argument can take away the possibility of objects in being individuals by virtue of their spatial regions.

The mind makes boundaries of space

It is my thinking that space has a duality role in being a void and composed of parts. Thus the conclusion of this Kantian argument may be acceptable, but for the wrong reason. So in order to dispel Kant's reasons and to lay down a premiss for the separation of space from objects, I shall put forward my view. In a sense, space is nothing but a void that has no boundaries, no lines, no curves, no self-definition and above all, no reference to any part there may be. It is the mind that creates boundaries, lines, curves and defines a region. Just as an object has all these demarcating lines that determine its spatial confine marked out by its sensible qualities, space without objects cannot be said to have all these defining parameters, since it is a void. The mind that distinguishes two shades of colours, can conceive their separation. And whatever separates two distinguishable colours is conceived by the mind to be a line. It is not the case that lines and curves are properties of space, but 'properties' in sensibility. How the mind distinguishes one colour from another is not irrelevant here. But it is through the distinction of sensible qualities that the mind conceives many geometrical marks that may not be given to us *a priori*.

Boundary, limit, oneness or unity

The other thing that the mind derives from this act of marking out sensible qualities is the concept of oneness. It is not surprising that many have found difficulty with the philosophical problem of how a thing can be one and many (parts) at the same time. The mind 'defines' a region of space by the help of sensible qualities, or indeed by its own imaginary boundaries; and it also defines oneness this way. Oneness is nothing but the confinement of whatever is determinable or a content within a defined parameter. If we extend this act of 'defining' to a non-spatial content (a thought), setting a parameter to it is possible without a reference to space. In this way not only is unity itself a defining parameter, but a series of numbers can be defined too with a limiting parameter, as can thoughts or their content. A mind sets limits so that it can focus its attention; thus in perception when limits are set by the mind, attention is possible. The mind, in its acts, cannot wander aimlessly at any one time seeing many and one, all at once. It can see either all as one or one as all. This we shall discuss again when I examine the notion of time. I can perceive 'all' things in front of me as one scenery, but every particular attention to reality is only possible first, with a defined parameter. Needless to say, a chair can be parts and one as the attention of the mind changes, and with it the defining of a whole and its parts. I hope that this proposal has implications in the philosophy of mathematics.

Two aspects of space: the void and the parts

Space is a void but also has parts; these parts are mind made. Space as the void has no demarcation itself and cannot have parts. That is why these two conceptions of space are necessarily distinct. The void in being limitless and boundless, is not the making of the mind in this respect, but the regions of the void conceived as its parts are mind made. If space has occupied regions, these regions can be vacated. This should not alter the nature of the void itself, and should make no difference to the conceptual parts of space, occupied or not. The mind sees the difference between the occupied and the vacant, and thus conceives space to be made of parts, especially when these regions are identified through its 'defining' parameters. The question following this is: is occupied space not space at all? When an object occupies a space, and if this space, which was a void, is now no more a void, then what do we call the extension which an object occupies? Is this extension part of the object or of a void it fills? Are they distinct? When an object is removed, there is the void again; does it mean that space can exist (before being occupied), cease to exist (when occupied) and come to exist again (when the object is removed)? If space is the void which is nothing, it cannot exist and come into being again. How is it that we cannot imagine or conceive a situation where there is no space?

Whether a space filled is still a space or not

If a 'whole' space cannot be conceived to perish, no parts of it can be conceived to perish. Hence, when a region of space is occupied by an object, we cannot conceive this 'occupied region' as having lost its void, as much as we cannot conceive objects without space. This is our difficulty. Consequently, it is erroneous to conceive of space as a void to be filled as well as to conceive of its filled parts as not being a void. Perhaps there is a verbal confusion in saying that an occupied space is still a space. When one says, 'I cannot put another thing in there [space]' because it is occupied and because there is no more room, one clearly does not recognize that an occupied space is still a space. Thus it is perhaps that occupied space is not the same as no space, and this is the crux of this verbal confusion. It is precisely because there is space that something can occupy it. Perhaps space is more than just the void, but a void that has the possibility of being filled. If space has parts through being identified and filled, then these filled parts must be space still, since they are its parts. So if we hold that space has parts, it will be inconsistent of us to hold that there is no space if its parts are filled. For a whole cannot lose its parts and remains the same whole. But, if we hold that space has no parts, what do we call the extension of an object? For if space has no parts, we must conclude that an occupied space is not space anymore, in which case an object can occupy no space. This cannot be the case. A space occupied must still be a space.

That object can occupy no space is not satisfactory, but that occupied space is an occupied void, seems reasonable. The idea that space has parts is mind-made does not allow the idea that a part of space once occupied is no more. Space as the whole void with no demarcation and boundary and thus having no parts, can be occupied and will be no more a void, provided that this occupation must also be boundless and limitless. When this happens, there is still a boundlessly and limitlessly occupied space. An occupied space is a space that allows no more occupancy. So, the distinction between occupied space and no space is credible, but the idea that there can be no space or that objects can exist without space, is inconceivable. A particular void when filled is a filled void, and not necessarily a space no more.

There is the logical problem in an apparent contradiction that a void (unfilled) when filled is still a void, albeit being a filled void. But still, a void is a void, how can nothingness disappear or become filled nothingness? Could this be a verbal confusion in 'space is the void' and in 'a void when filled is not a void'? What do I mean when I say 'a void is not a void'? When a void is filled, it must continue to be a void, if whatever filling it can subsist through a continuity, otherwise whatever filling it will perish too with the void it fills in persisting not through its own existence. If so, depending on what fills it, a void will remain always, whether it is filled or not. In this sense, the distinction between a filled void and a void-no-more can be firmly linked to whatever occupies it. For without the continuation of this void, whatever filling it, will have no space. Therefore a filled void is not a void that is no more. If a part of the void can cease to exist, having not been occupied, there is no possibility for the existence of sensible qualities within the void, since all sensible qualities cannot exist without space.

How can a void persist to exist when filled?

As I said earlier, a space or a void (as opposed to the limitless void) must be not only a nothingness, but a containment of nothingness within a mind-made parameter; in this way, a negation of nothingness (in having now something) should not deny the parameter of containment itself. A void filled is nothing but its limiting parameter. Space as a limitless nothingness is not comprehensible without the mind's preparation for its parts, and its conception can feed us with contradictions. Space as limitless void, for reasons given later, is an objectivity, but space as a containment of nothingness with boundaries, is a subjective vessel in which sensible qualities are conveyed in our totality of experience. Beyond all markings of particular regions of nothingness, there is still the void, which is limitless with no demarcation, no boundary, and which cannot cease, and of which regional spaces are parts. This limitless void the mind finds difficult to understand fully, since the mind can only apprehend and comprehend within limitations.

There is a passing interest concerning this conclusion. It accidentally refers to the Hegelian primary 'being' that is supposed to be an indeterminate and yet has being. This Hegelian absurdity will be discussed later (see pp. 410). Perhaps, oneness and setting parameter for a unity can be the minimal determinacy in this Hegelian being. It may be difficult to put a boundary on a thing that is indeterminate, but it is not so in putting an imaginary, but imprecise boundary in space. In this sense, together with what I have argued before, the first minimal existential content is a determination of limitation, oneness and space. Having proposed this, it does not follow that I think all the Hegelian 'deductions' from this being will become acceptable, let alone comprehensible.

5.2 The void and space

Relations of parts of space

The void is indeterminable without markings. Now that if my argument is convincing, space has to be 'marked' out into parts or regions by the mind. Only a determined region or a place with boundary can be comprehended by man, even if these boundaries are in our imagination. This is different from the Kantian idea that we can imagine space without objects. (Kant thinks that space is that which conditions our perception of things in how they appear to us.) Though I cannot decide what region there is without an object and its markings by my mind, I can imagine standing in front of the big void and being decisive about it, even if the void is a perceptual nothingness, without a region of itself. But how do I identify this limitless space? This cries out for a relation between all its parts. Consequently, since the void is usually taken as synonymous with space, the premiss accepted by many well-known philosophers, that void has no parts, must be re-examined closely, especially as regards its determination.

Difficulty in space having parts

For example, F. H. Bradley[5] says 'For any space must consist of extended parts, and these parts are clearly space'. The traditional problem centred on parts of space itself lies in the difficulty in establishing what type of relation exists between these spatial parts. For being parts of something must entail a relation of some sort. If my argument earlier is good, then that space has parts must be logically lacking a constructive relation. In fact, self-contradicting questions will emerge from many deductive inferences from the proposition that space, as a void, has parts. This difficult is usually compelling enough for many to reject that space is relational or hold that it is absolute. For if space must have parts, the relation between its parts is difficult to explain, either in terms of space itself or in terms of an absolute space. Without the separation of the void from space in the way I did, I cannot see a way forward. Hence, this is my answer to the earlier comment that space as the limitless void is objective, and space as parts, is subjective.

Separating the void from space of parts, the objective from the subjective

A part of space is mind made with or without the help of objects. The act of the mind is peculiar in demarcating regions, in that there is no need for definitive lines and curves to mark out a region (contrary to Kant's claim). I can look at the big void without an absolutely clear boundary and yet I can more or less say, that area, that part or that region. Whether I use imaginary lines or not, there is always another void outside a mind-marked region or a line-marked space. The subjective 'creation' by our mind of the parts in space, cannot change these parts within the reality of the void that is limitless and has no parts without the mind. We must accept that these are two realities, the subjective and the objective. The subject is what I will call space instead of the void which is the objective. In this way, how space is seen as absolute or as relative with parts, can be accommodated.

How the void is conceived

The void is emptiness and nothingness. Nothing cannot be counted, cannot be many, cannot be quantified, cannot be infinite or finite, and cannot be one. The void has no quantity to be infinite or one (finite). To be one is to be conceived and defined by a mind. To acknowledge infinity is to acknowledge the subjective nature of demarcating and the impossibility in a real boundary, since there is always a void outside a marked region. A mind cannot limit nothingness or the void, so that the implication of something having been conceived in being limited may not be necessary. In this situation, the mind can only confine a region of the void for its perceptual attention. Without this limitation, the attention of the mind is impossible.

The vastness of the universe provokes our thoughts to speculate whether it has a boundary. But if 'space' (as a concept), which we can talk about, is conceived as limited, the mind must be able to find a scheme to explain how this is possible. If this is conceived as limitless, we are conceiving this 'space' as one void, since the mind cannot know how to conceive infinity and limitlessness. We can talk of the void as one, because its enormity defies our parameter-setting and gives us a false sense of limitation, until we carefully consider it again. If the universal void is infinite, it is not because we know or perceive it to be so, but because the void is inevitably limitless, boundless or unquantifiable. Since we have no idea of the nature of this universal 'void', whatever we judge it to be will invariably give us a sense of its nature according to the word we use to describe it. Therefore the deductive truth about the universal 'void' is only verbal. Space seems to have parts because the parts conceived by the mind as regions are parts of the perception, and not parts of the void. The void has nothing; nothing cannot have parts and it has no sensibility or something involving sensibility. If the void is something for something else to fill, it may conceivably be considered as an existential support of whatever that fills it. Apart from this, there is nothing more that can be said of the void, a nothingness. Existence is therefore first and foremost to fill nothingness.

If the void is nothingness, how can we know of nothingness since nothingness has no sensibility or no possibility of being sensed? If a child is born into the darkest void and sustained by a miracle, he would not have known this void, for there would have been no sense-data whatsoever to feed the learning. The point is not that the child cannot learn anything, but that the child could not have learned about a void in front of him or her. We conceive the existence of things by conceiving or perceiving a content, even if our identity of it may be mistaken. If we can conceive an existence, we can certainly conceive the opposite of non-existence, which is not nothingness, but a conceived absence of what has been conceived as an existent, and the negation of such existence. So the claim here is not that the void can be known on its own, for there is nothing in it to be known, but that the void is known through existence in its negation rather than through a direct perception of it.

Space and extension

The void, like a vast span of 'landscape' of nothingness, has its reality within and without objects in the measure of its dependence. Without objects, it is the objective void and within objects, it is the space of parts. Let us look at the subjective space of parts first. A void has a potentiality to fill with things and this is its reality within objects, so that it reveals itself as a part in the boundary and extension of an object itself. An extension of an object can be seen as permanently associated with the object, or being the property of an object, depending on your views. Hence when an object is removed from an original space, its extension is 'carried' to another region; and yet we cannot say that the original region has lost its space. Therefore we can consider that an extension is quite different from a region of space, unless, of course an object can 'steal' a space for its extension when it changes its occupied regions. This is our dilemma. If extension is different from a space (a void), care should be exercised as to whether it is the object that occupies a space that is also its extension, or whether it is the extension that occupies the particular space. Or is it the object or its extension that really occupies a space? If it is an object that occupies a space, and if the space is not its extension, what is the object's extension about which philosophers have been speaking for centuries? Does an object have an extension over and above the space it occupies? The idea that an object moves in space shredding the old and gaining a new space-part in a continuum, is not satisfactory. For it implies that this disposable space, exchanged for another, is dispensable from an object. But an object cannot exist without an extension. If an object can 'come out' of a space and if its extension and the occupied space are one and the same, what is the void it leaves behind when removed?

Extension and a void are two aspects of a part of space

For me, at least, an extension is something that fills and the void is something to be filled. This is the two sides of the coin that constitutes both extension and the void that I will call space-part. In this sense, the mind's determination of a parameter can be seen as an imaginary extension that marks or fills a particular void. Thus a particular space-part is not a void, but a determined void. This distinguishes itself from the universal void that is limitless. It is easier to accept that an extension occupies a void than to accept that it is not space. For, if it is not space, what is it? The answer lies in the duality that I have mentioned: the one that fills is an extension with a parameter; the one that is filled is a space. They are coexisting aspects of a space-part, so that an extension is space in one sense and its 'filling' in another. The relation between extension and the void is a curious mutual instigation, so that one cannot be excluded from the other, and yet inclusively they are not identical. A void without extension or a boundary, is not a space-part, but a void is not an extension itself. We can see the importance of the void through extension that fills it, and yet without the void we cannot understand what an extension is; for there is nothing more to be said about extension except this fateful association with the void. It would not be comfortable for me to call a void not a space anymore than it is comfortable for me to call extension a space. Perhaps a void is not space in the universal sense, but a space-part. Hence it is why we make a distinction between the universal void and space as a space-part.

Dual aspects of space, space and the construct of reality from the void

If a space is that which is not filled (a void) as well as what is filled (an extension), it still leaves us with the question: 'what is the thing that fills?'. If the extension in, or of an object is not a space but that which fills a space, may it be said that this is what underlies or supports sensibility? Is there no extension without sensibility or no sensibility without extension? The former may seem more acceptable than the latter, since there may be, arguably, some sensibilities that are not considered spatial. But are we convinced that extension itself can subsist without sensibility? In Kant's argument, space can be imagined without an object occupying it, and this is not a proof that extension itself is separable from objects. As I have argued, this conception of space 'without' objects is not strictly an imagination of a boundless space, but a bounded space of the mind. Thus an imagined space in Kant's argument, cannot escape from being a bounded space with lines that are imaginary sensibility. But if extension is not space but that which occupies it, there must be a sense in saying 'that-which-occupies-a-void' is besides the void which should exist without that-which-occupies, or sensibility.

The problem is this. Without sensibility how do we know a space is occupied and how can we identify the occupied region? Or if we take away all sensibility, what is left of the extension? To these questions, there is a possible reply relying on the relational consistency discussed earlier. An object in, or of, an occupied space is not isolated so that it will not affect other sensibilities in a constant relation with it. A heavy thing on soil leaves a mark; a thing travelling towards an occupied space will recoil, shatter or bounce away; acid poured into a volume of space will cause chemical reactions that may suggest its prior occupation. The claim of relation is not about whether something occupying a space can exist without sensibility, but that such an occupant can be conceived through a relation with other sensibilities. Therefore, direct, regional sensibility in a space is not the only indication of having a space filled or not. We distinguish space from the void by the marking of the mind and in the absence of sensibility it is the boundless, therefore the void. The void is the unfilled and unbounded and its imagination cannot be confused with the imaginable space with lines or objects. Consequently, a void is separable from sensibility but a space is not. That a local sensibility is not the only indication of an occupied space (as opposite to void), shows that the void's filling does not depend on sensibility in that region. In being capable of being filled and conceived to be so without the local sensibility, the void must belie reality. Nothing more can be said of extension in reality, except that it is not considered as the void, but one aspect of a space that fills it. Thus the void is 'something' capable of being filled; and the void is no more when it is marked out and 'occupied' by sensibility and becomes a space-part. Every space is potentially a void to be filled. Hence 'space' in the conventional sense can be conceived to be both separable from sensible and not separable from sensible, depending on whether we conceive it as the void or as a space (part). This is not a realism independent of sensibility, but a realism of the void, that is capable of being filled and that underlines the construction of reality from sensibilities.

The potentiality of the void is to be filled and filling it is an existence, a spatial existence

In the construct of reality from the void - the very prerequisite of conceiving sensibles - there can be no room for things that do not occupy space. This immediately raises the problem of whether certain mental content that occupies no space deserves to be the outcast of reality. In the beginning, I have made a special separation between existence and reality and in being consistent with this, we say that this outcast of reality can exist but may not be real since existence is defined only in being perceived and conceived. This is not to say that there are things that are real but may not exist, but that there are things that exist but are not real. In this way, the conception of existence is potential for a reality underlined by relational consistency, and also the void. So too, much of my mental content that is non-spatial and not relationally consistent, may have an existence but not necessarily a reality. Some people may not be comfortable with this conclusion. However, we must not forget that we can consider the existence of my thoughts in constant relations with other spatial existents (bodies and actions) and conceive of their reality in this sense. These thoughts are not merely in constant relations with our body; they exist in an intimate understanding and knowledge, for we can in principle be aware of all these intimate details. How I understand that my thoughts are closely related to my movements owes no debts to neuroscience to explain the causal scheme between the brain and muscles. Without a diversion into the world of values, I hope the value aspect of mental content can also be understood, which, when discussed in the section dealing with universals (see pp. 215-240), will illustrate how reality and values are intertwined.

5.3 Space as parts and its relation

Quantity and distance are mere relations

Apart from the void and extension, there are other notions associated with space. I am talking about distance, size and position. These can only be conceived if space is regarded as parts. If space is a big void without border or demarcation, there will be no measurement of size. If there is no identifiable region or point, there will be no position and if no position, no distance. All these are relations only between two or more parts. But distance, common a term as it may be, is only a quantification without a value to indicate how long, how short or how far away. Pure quantification of space is the construct of geometry, which most people consider as a satisfactory description of the physical world, in the so-called physical space. We can say this thing is five feet from that, or that thing is five miles from a hill. We immediately know what a foot or a mile is, even if there is no indication of its value in the words, symbols or drawings illustrating it. A foot is a measurement relational to an object, standardized to give a 'universal' constancy of this relation by comparing it with all else; a mile is nothing but a further relational quantification of the 'foot'. A foot is the distance from the tip to the end of a thing used as standard, assuming it does not shrink. Again, we may reinterpret this 'foot' relationally with other objects assuming the same. This can go on forever and still we say nothing more about the value of a distance or length. This is purely a quantification of relations assuming a constancy without value. There is little point in stating what this relation is. When I say that this object is of the same length as that of another, I say nothing except a relation, unless what is meant by 'length' is more than a relation and clearly spelled out.

Our immediate recognition of the value of a 'length' blinds us from questioning whether there are two distinct things in these words, 'quantity' (relation) and 'value'. Thus philosophers who hold that space is relational are desperate to state what this relation is, since it cannot be a relation of space as a relation of a relation will be circular. A better analogy can be drawn from the notion of temperature, which inevitably has an immediate association with hotness and coldness. But temperature itself is only a relational constancy in changes between things in the presence of 'heat'. Suppose I have no experience of this standard distance measured as a 'foot' and I do not know what a 'foot' is in my experience, I cannot fail to construct a 'physical space with its parts' using this unit of measure. There is a lack of spatial value in me saying that a mile is an enormous length or an inch is a short distance, if none of these has a spatial value. This is what inspires Plato to ponder on what is called a relation term. What is big, small or indeed what is good, eventually seduces Plato to 'discover' his world of Forms (broadly speaking, universals). If I do not know what a 'light year' is, I may be foolish to suggest that I can walk through this 'light-year' distance in a lifetime (a relation, nonetheless).

Spatial value - being far or close

Since all measurements among parts of space are nothing but relations in constancy without values, and even a distance of one foot can be measured in many ways using different standards, standardization cannot guarantee an absolute length or distance. If things are comparable in lengths, they are not the same, exactly. All measurements can point to a similarity but not sameness. But there is still no spatial value, even if the things measured are absolutely the same, or if the 'physical' world can be mapped out by a supercomputer so that all possible spatial relations among all possible things are illustrated. By spatial value I mean a value that enables us to say whether the length or distance is long, short or enormous. If I say that a door is seven miles high, I will find no consolation in redefining a 'mile' as having the same length of a ruler. A world constructed merely of units of measurement will continue to be a world of constant relations between its objects. There is no value; nothing will be long, short or enormous.

When I see an object in front of me, I need no measurement to tell to me a value of distance in terms of 'far' or 'close', just as a cat needs no geometry to catch a mouse by judging how far away a mouse is, before it pounces. If I have not a sense (value) of distance, all methods of measurements will not help me at all. If a man sees things only as a relation to all other things, he sees no distance (with value). A child not conversant with measurements will not fail to grasp things in front of him; or a supercomputer that 'knows' all relations of objects, cannot determine these relations with a value of 'how far', 'how near' or 'immediacy', unless this 'value' can be programmed into it. If a programmer were to 'instruct' it to define 'near' as 'ten inches', it has no sense to comprehend this 'near' in a situation when there is no appropriate application.

Space considered by the mind as parts, has this value, a humanistic value, already entrenched in it through sensibility. A man sees things in relations, not only with other things, but with himself and his nature that provides these human values. These values are extra-physical. It is these values that give a sense of 'being far', 'being close' or 'being out there'. A thing is heavy without comparison to anything else because it is referring to human strength that is known. A distant is far or close without reference to any spatial point except to the self that knows human endeavours in covering distances. 'Being heavy' and 'being far' are both value judgements concerning strength and distance. These are what I shall call spatial values. A spatial relation is not only a relation of space, but a relation in human values. This term 'human value' is not about 'ethical values' or the like. It is a term signifying something that does not come from objects themselves.

Relative terms have no significance unless there is a rigid reference. This is more an insight than a problem of relations. Without a fixed reference, everything that is far away can also be close, just as a mouse is small (compared to an elephant) and big (compared to an insect) all the same. This 'fixed' point is supplied by man's nature that puts limits and parameters on his capabilities. He sees things with a human aspect in a relation to his needs, pains and pleasure; in relation to his possible actions, his past and dispositional desires, rather than seeing things with the intuitive or perceptual aspects only. This is our departure from the mere physical.

We are not talking about the relation of an object being five feet from myself, being a spatial relation to myself. This is only a relation not different from that in which an object is five feet from another thing. We are talking about a distance (five feet) being not only a quantity in relations of constancy, but a quantity with a measure of value. Otherwise, relational quantity will remain always quantity and nothing more. The 'five feet' from myself is not strictly spatial without a sense of direction and distance. Two objects of five feet or five miles apart, cannot be distinguished without a sense of distance from a perceptual viewpoint. An object of five feet away has the same outer sense as that of an object of five miles away, without a value of distance understood. A young boy may think that the moon is as far away as a distant mountain. He is wrong not because he perceives the wrong relations in space between him and the mountain, and between him and the moon. He can only come to a right judgement if he considers it in a total relation that explains what 'far' or 'near' is. Perhaps he has not yet seen a rocket landing or understood the space in which the earth is in relation to himself.

The values of 'far' and 'near' are not values of 'in space' or 'of space', but the outer sense with a measure of our own efforts and movements, that, of course, includes an evaluation of time. If there is a language of space made up of pure relations without value, it will make no sense if we say that an ant can run a long or short distance of five feet. If we say that it is a long distance for an ant, it is because we imagine ourselves to have the size of an ant but still retain the same human capability. If we say that this distance is short, we surely must be talking in terms of human capability solely. Five feet is five feet that has no sense in being long or short, even from an ant's point of view. What can 'decide' what is 'long' or 'short'? This value sense is not gained by measuring spatial relations between things, but by using our experience gained. Thus, there can be 'mistakes' in conceiving something being 'far' and 'near', since they are subjective. But that five rulers can always fill up a space (distance) which can also be filled by sixty match boxes or ten thousand sheets of paper, is a relational constancy without values.

Space value - the outer sense

I cannot conceive that things seen are not in space. This is not to say that objects in space only function in filling a void. An object in space is an object that has a sense of being in-distance, and this in-distance is not about a distance from other things. For, if so, it can only lead to an infinite regress by referring to another relation that in turn depends on other relations. Even if there is only one single object in this universe, I still will see it with a sense of in-distance, that is no measure of other objects, except of myself. This is not an introduction of a sense of absolute distance, but an absolute relation with one thing - the perceiver, and intuitor, indispensable in perceiving. (There are detailed arguments for this case.[6]) A thing is in-distance if it is in a distance from a fixed point accompanying its perceiving always. This is an unavoidable and indispensable point that must be postulated in all perceptual values in space. This point is a metaphysical being of the self presupposed by the understanding of all spatial values. A sense of distance is a sense of something being away from the point of perception, with which come the values of being 'far' or 'near'. We measure this outer sense in terms of our capability and possible acts, perhaps also with time, without which we cannot hope to catch a ball thrown at us. In catching a ball thrown at him, a man does not go through a geometrical and temporal calculation. He has this intuitive sense of something being 'far', 'near', 'fast' and 'slow'.

Spatial value - positions

With a spatial sense of value, a man will not run when he sees a stone thrown at him from one mile away. A man does not see a thing in terms of how many rulers he can place between the object and himself; he sees this thing in terms of a spatial value dispositional to his reactions to things outside him. A positional sense of objects is not different from this, though geometry can tell us how the position of a thing is calculated in terms of other things at different 'positions'. But a position has to be identified, or there is no position at all. A thing that is five feet away at a particular angle to another thing has no position, unless the other thing is identified as to its position relative to the perceiver. A distance from a thing needs a direction and there is no understanding of a direction unless a perceptual point can supply a fixed reference. East, West, South, North, up, down, left, right, over or under are not things that can be understood by drawing on a sheet of paper without our being involved in their references. A position in space must have a permanent point of fixed reference that is not in turn identifiable through the positions of other objects. A perceptual point is a point that is the self's metaphysical being. That the North Pole is at one tip of the earth tells us no position unless there is one known (valued) position that can determine all positional references of other things.

A known position on which another positional relation can be established is important because if all positional references, no matter how numerous they are, are relational, variable and not determined, all resultant positions will remain variables, even if they can be stated clearly in terms of all things. Therefore, I must know where I am in relation to the earth before I know how to get to the North Pole, even if I know that the Pole is relationally a position on the earth, and covered with ice. In this sense, a spatial position also has a human aspect, in not only recognizing the positions of things for human interaction with the outside, but also in providing a fixed, permanent point for a direction and their positional relation with ourselves. All directional terms such as 'left of', 'right of', 'in front of', 'behind', or 'underneath' cannot be position indicators without ourselves as their perceptual points. Something underneath something can be on top of something depending on the frame of reference. The point of perception provides always such a rigid frame of reference.

The left and right relation

In the dispute between whether space is absolute or relative, there exists a well-known argument by Kant against relativity. He thinks that the relativism of space cannot justify having the sense of the 'left hand' and the 'right hand'. He thinks that the spatial relation between the left hand and right hand is such that if their distinction is relative, it is only because there is reference to a clockwise or anti-clockwise direction, and yet clockwise and anti-clockwise directions are not distinguishable without an arbitrary point of reference. He says that if there is one hand in the universe, it still has to be either a right hand or left hand. He thinks that right-handedness and left-handedness are absolute in this sense. Simply saying that a solitary hand in the universe contributes no significant meaning in its being a right hand or left hand cannot dismiss this argument.

The point Kant misses out is that the distinction between a 'left hand' and a 'right hand' presupposes a third reference to another dimension. He is right about 'rotation', 'clockwise' or 'anti-clockwise' being arbitrary. But the 'left' and the 'right' have a meaning additional to their relation, and this is a meaning in virtual of the third dimension of space. The 'right' side of a 'right hand' has a special positional relation to its 'top' and 'bottom', as has that of the 'left hand', in a three-dimensional space. Now, what the 'front' or 'back' is, is indetermined, depending on the observation point. Insofar as the front and back of a hand are indistinguishable, the left and the right hands are also indistinguishable, without a third-dimensional reference. But in the reality of three-dimensional space, the front and back of a hand is distinguishable, not as a logical necessity, but a matter of fact. Hence the 'front' and 'back' are distinguished in relation to the 'top' and 'bottom'. The perceptual point supplies this reference. If there is only one hand in the universe it cannot be a hand of either left or right if the 'front' and 'back' are indistinguishable.

In a three-dimensional space, there is a distinction between the front and the back of a hand, but not so in a two-dimensional space. Therefore, the left and the right can be established by a three-way reference, that is, top-bottom, back-front and left-right. The relation between the right-left and the top-bottom may be arbitrary without the back-front relation, or the relation between the top-bottom and the back-front may be arbitrary without the left-right reference. But when these three sets of relations are in place together, the left of a hand must be in a special relation to the top and bottom without changing its relation with the back and front, or conversely with the back and front without changing its relation with the top and bottom. If there is still a sense of arbitrariness about the left, the right, the top, the bottom, the front or the back themselves, our idea of the self being a permanent referential point will see that they are spatially valued in the way we discussed before.

Hence, that the positional sense of the 'left' and 'right' can be arbitrarily determined depending on one's reference point, is clearly wrong. If I revolve my left hand 180°, the back of my hand is still the back, but I do not call this surface facing me the palm. If I turn my hand 180° so that the bottom is now the top, and in a world where there is no distinction between the top and bottom, I still cannot call the bottom of this upturned hand the top of this hand. If the self gives a permanent and fixed positional value to a special feature of the hand in a veridical judgement, we can dismiss Kant's argument as one based on an imaginary geometrical, two-dimensional world of lines and curves. In a world of only lines and curves, a hand, of course, cannot be identified as left or right, without an empirical content that supplants spatial values. One cannot be more accommodating than suggesting further that if an imaginary line-drawn hand of three dimensions is painted with colours so that one surface is distinguishable from another, then we can say that a right hand is one having its coloured surfaces in a particular position reference to its thumbs. Spatial values of 'left' or 'right', 'clockwise' or 'anti-clockwise', 'up' or 'down', 'East' or 'West' and the rest, are perceptual human values.

Spatial value - size, big or small

Earlier, we were concerned with the spatial values of 'far' and 'near'; 'long' and 'short' without a reference to, or a comparison with other things, but the self. Still they subsist as relations with nothing else but the self. There remains a sense that a distance in a relation to other things can be seen to be longer or shorter; farther or nearer, bringing us to the attention that other relations also exist without the self. But this is besides our point, because it is not a claim that there cannot be relations among things in being longer, shorter, farther or nearer, but a claim that these relational terms can continue to be so, even if there are no relations with other things. That is to say, the sense of being 'long' may have come from being 'longer'. Yet, from where does the sense of being 'longer' originate? Hence a value from the self provides a basic permanent relation, dependent on the point of perception but not on anything else. These spatial relations cannot be said to have disappeared if the association with other things is taken away. It is the thought that if these terms are only relations between things, there cannot be a tangible, permanent reality in these relations that constitutes a relational space, as opposed to an absolute space. A relation is no more real than the things that give it its existence. Being 'longer' and being 'long' are two different relations, the former subsist in a comparison and the latter in a value laden in perception.

In considering the value of the size of a space, and in addition to its determination by setting parameters, we see that there are volumes, which are larger than some and smaller than others, in a relation among themselves. By comparing two regions, we may see an excess of space left by the 'bigger' regions. This 'excessiveness' of space does not determine what is large or small, but what is larger or smaller. In the same way, the concept of 'large' or 'small' will not disappear, even when there is no comparison. A region of space on its own can be conceived of as 'large' or 'small', simply as a value-laden perception. We have a value of what is large or small, that is more basic than the spatial relation between two things other than between it and ourselves. This is the input of a humanistic content, just as distance has a basic value in being far, long, near or short without the measure of things other than ourselves.

What belies extension is not value or sensibility

It is arguable whether 'extension' itself has a humanistic measure too. That sensibility, conducive to shapes and sizes, is at least mind dependent (if not totally), is not debated here. There is shape, size or perhaps solidity in an extension. Shape depends on the angle of perception and size has its largeness and smallness firmly entrenched in a relation in distance. Solidity is felt by senses; if we can argue that size and distance are not parts of sensibility, we have to consider where they come from. As I have argued before, size as merely a relation of being bigger or smaller cannot constitute the sense of size. In the same way, distance is mere longer or shorter, never the long or the short. What is a size, if all different volumes of space are merely different? It makes sense if size is a relation subsumed under a value of distance and position, which call for a fixed reference. Without a fixed reference, there is no value, therefore no sense in distance and position and consequently no size. A human evaluative source is such a fixed reference.

This leaves the question of whether extension itself has relations with other things (apart from the self), or is dependent on them. Bishop Berkeley, in his arguments against the independence of primary qualities, also suggests that there is an indispensability of sensibility in extension. That is to say, if we take away the sensible qualities of an object, there will be no more extension. If there is something left when sensible qualities are taken away, a reality that transcends sensible qualities is certainly possible. However, even if there is nothing left behind after the disposed sensible qualities, there is still the possibility that perhaps sensible qualities are themselves extended. This is certainly possible because extension can be a precondition for all possible objects and we do not see any object that has no extension of space or into space. A hologram is certainly extended, but lack solidity. Thus there is a sense in making a split between extension and solidity, even though solidity may not survive extension. Solidity is sensibility, no doubt.

A hologram can be regarded as a space filled. What fills the space of a hologram is colour and light, which are not at all different from that which a mind can use to mark out a region by imaginary lines and curves. Thus, if solidity is a sensibility, we can say that there is still more to this sensibility of solidity.

One distinction between the physical and the mental usually made by philosophers, is the criterion that mental events are not spatial while physical events are. This argument is usually put forth by those who are sympathetic towards the possibility of the existence of a non-physical realm of reality. Here I can see a glaring inconsistency. For if sense-data are mental, they must be non-spatial in this way of thinking; it is to no avail to suggest that physical objects represented by sense-data can be distinguished from mental 'objects' by this spatial criterion. Therefore, for the 'idealists' generally, if everything is mental, there should be a way to distinguish perceptual objects from imaginary objects. Hence, Descartes asks: how do we know that our dreams (of objects) are real? It is therefore difficult to maintain that sensibility is spatial and yet the mental is spaceless. For sensibility is in a way also mental. If we cannot grant such a distinction by a spatial content, one may say that 'space' is something that is beyond sensibility and perceptibility, and something that is known by inferences. This again is contrary to our common sense.

As I said earlier, 'space' is nothingness and therefore has no boundary, no sensibility; yet it has the sense in capable of being filled. Being filled and filling a void are two sides of the same reality. One aspect of reality beyond sensibility must therefore be nothingness itself, even if it has only one sense in being capable of being filled. Whether we speak of extension alone or of extended sensible qualities, the inevitability of space, being an underlying void that permits extension, must come up. Since the void is void of all things, it is void of all sensibilities. And in this sense only, extension is not wholly sensible, or dependent on sensibles. Hence the reality outside us is emptiness.

The void is a reality underlying sensibility

It is not certain whether an occupied space can prohibit penetration or whether impenetrability implies occupation of a void. But extension itself is not necessarily always impenetrable. A rainbow has an extension but we do not regard it as a separate physical object distinguishable from its vapours and cloud. Impenetrablility has a sense in something that occupies and therefore exists in a space. This sense of reality is a reality construed from experience, in that penetrating an occupied space by displacing its sensible qualities, perpetuates such a reality in filling and displacing of space.

Penetrability is sensibility relational only to the self if it is by touch; it is relational to other things if there is a displacement of sensibles. Whether extension itself is totally dependent on sensibility is hard to say, except that at least the capability of being filled is somehow independent of sensibility. But they may be reciprocally indispensable from each other without exception, in the sense that if there is no sensibility, we see no extensions. The reality of space in the absence of sensibility must revert back to the void, which has no sensibility. The underlying reality beyond sensibility must be the void itself. Again this justifies our separation of space as a part filled or marked out from the void that is boundless and senseless. In the conflict of this interdependence, between sensibility and extension, one will disappear into the void.

An object (of sensible qualities) replaces and occupies a space, and in turn is replaced by another, in a chain of occupation and displacement in a space continuum. When sensible qualities are vacated from a particular space, it continues to dwell in another, without having disappeared and re-emerged again. An extension has this sense of spatial continuum and existential continuity in this reality. It is therefore this 'chain' that connects an extension and sensible qualities and perpetuates the continuous existence of sensible qualities extended in space. For this to happen, there must be a presupposed existence of the void itself, in capable of being filled. Even though we may say that the concept of capable-of-being-fill entails something that fills, we cannot say that in the absence of a determination of this something, this conceptual presupposition does not exist. Hence a spatial content of an extension in being filled, is not mental, in the sense that being filled does not require sensibility for its existence, or that the void does not require sensibility for its 'existence'.

The non-exclusiveness of the mental and the spatial

This distinction allows us to conclude that even if everything that is mental is not spatial, everything that is spatial may not be mental; if sensible qualities are spatial then they may not be mental. We must decide whether dreams and imaginations are spatial or not. If they are not, and are mental, it will not contradict the idea that all things spatial are not necessarily mental. A comparison between a state of being awake and one of dreaming or hallucinating, can provide a basis to reject that dreams and imaginations are spatial. We have come to a point where we do not need either to reject that all things mental are non-spatial, or to reject that they are spatial. By rejecting the former, the distinction between mental and physical will disappear, leaving a materialistic world. By rejecting the latter, we cannot explain the extension of an object in terms of space, if sensible qualities are all there is to it. That at least some sensible qualities, especially secondary qualities, are non-spatial, is not inconceivable. For instance, the hotness itself may be conceived as pure sensibility. But hotness itself without an association, even if it is an association with the self, cannot support itself in an existence. Once an association is established, a reference to my body or an object, i.e. a steam iron, is inevitable.

Ordinarily, we say of thoughts and conceptual entities as non-spatial, but images and impressions of perceptual data are not clear-cut cases. For if I make images by imagining or visualizing objects indirectly from perceptual memory, these images have 'mental' extensions indistinguishable from the extensions of objects in a direct and immediate perception. The distinction between a 'mental' extension and a 'real' perceptual extension is made (and must be made) by the test of relational constancy. We cannot touch or smell an extension in an imagined image; nor will such an image fit into a coherent relation within a world of our immediate perceptual experience. An imaginary meal cannot satisfy our hunger for instance. By and large, I cannot see too much of a problem in distinguishing 'mental' space (space associated with imagined images) from space of immediate perceptual experience to raise a question of whether mental things can be non-spatial.

If some sensible qualities are invariably spatial, they are not mental at least in so far as the void allowing extension to occupy it, is concerned. Thus, a sense-datum of colour may be absolutely mental, but has a content in extension that may not be mental. This content and the datum itself are inseparable in the sense that one's disappearance will annihilate the other into a void absolutely. This is this sense of being spatial and non-mental that adheres to the sense of objectivity and a reality of spatial sensible qualities.

Two kinds of nothingness and perceptual duality

The void has two senses. One is that of a conceptual nothingness and the other is that of a perceptual nothingness. A conceptual nothingness is the inconceivable and there is nothing can be said of it. It is a total eclipse of consciousness. A perceptual nothingness is the perceiving of a total nothingness. Imagine there is nothing in the universe except myself for a moment before I perish, I can see nothing but a void, if I am not blind. How we can 'see' nothing in front of us and still have an act of perceiving? Some may say that to conceive of (as opposed to perceive) nothingness is to conceive of something about this conceiving itself. This is a sense of conceiving the conceiving of nothingness. In this way, the Cartesian impossibility of self-denial of thinking is parallel to this, in that denying the conception of conceiving nothingness is impossible. Can I deny the conception of nothingness? If so, my denial is a conception itself, just as thinking of not thinking is a thought itself. Therefore, I cannot say: I conceive of nothing, which would be self-contradicting, since I must conceive of the conceiving itself, which is not nothingness.

The situation is different with perceptual nothingness since we are not talking about the conception of a perception. I can deny a percept in perceiving without denying perceiving itself.

A state of perception unlike a state of conception, has a duality in that the percept and perceiving have separate ontological status; whereas the concept and conceiving are existentially the same. For one cannot think without a thought. The Cartesian 'I think' and 'I am' are mutually inclusive because they are both, existentially speaking, conceptual things. The peculiarity in perceptual situations offers a duality in which at least one, albeit minimal, is non-conceptual, so that there is no mutual inclusiveness, without ruling out the possible relations between them. This non-conceptual thing is space as a void to be filled. In this way, we can certainly perceive nothingness without ourselves disappearing into nothingness itself. The absence of nothingness in our thinking, including thinking of thinking itself, will surely mean an absolute non-consciousness into which our being must fall. Such a sense of duality in perceiving not only serves us with a sense of reality but also renders possible perceiving 'nothingness', in contrast to conceiving 'nothingness'. Thus it is perfectly possible for us to see a vast void in front of us without this perceiving having to depend on the existence of a perceptual content.

But I am not here introducing a metaphysical dualism, but an epistemological dualism perhaps. This duality in perceiving is experienced by everyone, in one way or another. Even a lifelong physicalist or materialist will not dream of cooking a conceptual (imaginary) 'egg' for dinner, if he makes no distinction between the mental and the physical. Space as a perceptual, boundless void provides us with the other entity in this perceptual duality, and still remains a nothingness. The dependency of perceiving or conceiving on the existence of a perceiver or conceiver, may not necessarily bring about a duality, if all that are perceived or conceived, are necessarily in perceiving or conceiving itself. For this dependency to bring about a duality, sensibility or concepts at least, must have a content of objectivity to mark them out from the perceiver or conceiver itself. But the case as with space is different. As nothingness cannot be part of perception, perceiving nothingness must be perceiving something other than the 'perceiving' itself. This cannot be said of conceiving, for conceiving nothingness can never be separated from conceiving itself, or it will be a total unconsciousness. Perceiving nothingness is not having sensibles as a content in the act of perceiving. For in nothingness there is no sensibility.

Therefore, in perceiving nothingness, there is a real sense of subject-object reality that cannot be found in 'perceiving' sensibility. In this way, that the void can be perceived without being a part of perceiving, is not at all analytical as it is experiential. That the perceived entails a perceiver is analytical in their mutual containment.

Absolute or relative?

Whether space has parts or not, is a reason for the debate in whether space is absolute or relative. We see that conceiving a boundless void as having parts is not possible, as many have argued. For parts entail a relation that is hard to find. This is so, without a fixed reference point. In this metaphysic, space parts are mind made and spatial values are provided; if space is relative, it is the content of the self that makes this relativity possible, providing a constant association of perceptual values with spatial content. Having constantly a fixed point of evaluative reference, space can be conceived as relational with the self. This desperate philosophical question, 'if space is relational, what relation is this?', is answered in this relation to the self.

If space is relative, all its properties, such as position, direction or size, are dependent on something else for their identity and value. If space is absolute, no such dependency is called for. Since we have separated the void from space parts, it is inevitable that in this metaphysic, space is seen as both absolute and relative, albeit relative with a fixed reference. Certainly, space can be also conceived as absolute, if the void is the totally indetermined nothingness. Since the void has no value, no sensibility and is boundless, it must be absolutely independent of everything else. I do not think there is anything inconsistent in conceiving space as both absolute and relative, since we have distinguished the void from space parts. It all depends on how we look at space, and on what aspects we focus ourselves. If there is no mind to dissect the void into parts and regions, for the lack of sensibility a big void is certainly independent of the mind too. If there is any doubt as to how we can conceive a void without perceptual content, this has been explained before. We can either perceive nothingness without losing the act of perceiving, or conceive a void by the negation of existence of existents known after. The void exists and is absolute in this sense.

The outer sense and the void

Unlike the deprivation of sensations, perceiving a void comes with an active search for a perceptual content outside us, outside the act of perceiving. There is an outer sense represented in space. A deprivation of sensations does not provide an outer sense in a perceptual consciousness, as perceiving a void does. A mechanical device (say, a camera), given the human perceptual capability in every imaginable way, cannot distinguish between a void of perception and the perception of a void. For in both cases, there is only one situation where there are no sense-data received. But it is different in a situation where there are no receptible sense-data, for these will imply an expectation in perceptual consciousness. Perceiving a void is certainly a perceptual consciousness in action. Perception is a peculiar thing so that we cannot say if there is nothing to perceive, there is no perceiving. It is in this sense, perceiving is not dependent on content to give us a sense of reality in the sensible qualities. This is an outer sense in the absence of sensibility. An outer sense is a sense of 'distance' from the point of perception, made possible by a void for things to fill or to move. Whether an outer sense is in our act of perceiving or in an act of reflection, it is difficult to say, but we can comfortably make a distinct outer sense itself in perceiving the void. An outer sense also implies the existence of something other than the void. This is perceptual consciousness in action. The fact that perceiving can take place without sensible content, will convince me that an outer sense, that comes with perceiving a void, is most likely mental (non-physical), since there is nothing spatial and sensible. The existence of an outer sense can be further enforced by many of life's instances, such as 'seeing' three-dimensional space in pictures (with depth) from data of two-dimensional space on a television screen. The mind can create a sense of seeing enormous distances between things within a small screen.

To understand a thing moving through a void, the mind creates parts that cannot be allowed to subsist in reality independently. For if it is reality that a thing can occupy a part, abandon it and occupy another in due course, a paradoxical situation will surface. By considering the parts to be infinitely dissectible into even smaller parts, as Zeno (Greek Philosopher) and others have shown us, it can be paradoxical. I shall not get into the details of these paradoxes. Thus the parts of a void are not an independent reality allowing the perception of movements through the void possible. This will be considered when we discuss time (see pp. 145-200). Therefore, in considering the void and space parts, these two aspects of reality will have to be distinguished. The one that is the void itself without parts is an underlying reality; and the other considered to be parts enables us to see a world of objects in a coherent whole and in all its movements, individuations (demarcated) and space values measured through our nature.

In a perceptual void where there is nothing, the mind has no need to make parts or regions; this metaphysical reality is clearer and more profound, entailing the existence other than the void - a self, so solipsistic that it can resonant in a world of objects to remind us of the loneliness in each self and in its metaphysical origin. This way, one may say that this philosophy is an empirical idealism in the reality of nothingness. We take comfort in the fact that every perception we have, has its association with a body, a minimal inducement for us to see the body in space in order to underline its reality.

5.4 Particular and public space

Space is particular

If the void has no parts, no quantities and no boundary, there appears no reason for us to think that there is a possible existence of different spaces (not space parts but different voids of no parts and boundary). For if there is another void again, how is it to be distinguished from the other? If the void is so conceived, then it must be one void and a particular void.

As to whether regions of space marked out by the mind are particulars, we have to see if they can be duplicated so to give a multiplicity of the same region. Since space parts are filled or marked out, they are no longer the void without content. It makes no sense in saying a part of space is in the same position, or of the same volume and size, if there is only the void. Once a region is marked out or filled, it cannot be anywhere elsewhere but in a definitive place determined by a fixed point positioning this marked region in a unique relation. The position of any particular region is unique in virtual of its reference to a fixed point which is also unique. Without a uniquely fixed point of reference, positional identity is far from being established, let alone unique. In this sense, space considered as parts are particulars.

Can two objects occupy the same space?

The consideration that two or more objects cannot occupy a space, appears to be conclusive without too much dispute. If a space can be occupied by more than two objects, it is necessary that the extension of a body and the space it occupies are different, so that two extensions or more, from two objects or more, can occupy one space. Otherwise, if an extension and its space are one and the same, two objects occupying the same space must have the same extension shared between them. This is absurd. Practically, as well as by imagination, a situation of two things occupying the same space cannot be created. I have heard of the suggestion that 'particles' of an object can occupy the 'holes' between the 'particles' of another object so that the same dimension of a space can accommodate two without excess space required or left behind. That such an absurd argument has been allowed to run, says more about philosophers than philosophy itself. Needless to say, such an argument is more about identity than about the occupation of space by two objects.

An extension is that which fills and demarcates; a space is that which is filled or marked out. They cannot be separated, nor can they be one and the same. If two objects can occupy one space, there is a logical problem in defining what amounts to one and what amounts to many, since there is only one boundary. By our theory of oneness, such a possibility is not a matter of empirical fact, but a conceptual fantasy. In this, we can say that every object within a boundary of space can be two or more, if we can identify a particular group of 'particles' to constitute this oneness, leaving the rest to constitute the other. This is a way to mark out sub-boundary within a boundary. Hence one extension cannot be for more than one object, simply because an extension is what marks out one particular object in a particular region of space. That no two objects can occupy one space serves the claim that a region of space is always a particular. The impenetrability by another object to occupy it may help to understand what an extension is, but will not provide the means of laying this ghost to rest; the ghost that there can be two objects in one space.

This particularity of spaces occupied by objects actually cements and brings about a determination in the particularity of every individual in space. Every object has its unique space that constitutes its being a percept of particularity. Every object is a particular in space.

Private space and public space

Finally, there is the question of whether sensible qualities, assuming they are all mental, reside, as it were, in a private space or a public space, since sensible qualities are private and not shared. Though sensible qualities are essentially private and since there are features and aspects in them which may determine whether they may be shared, even if the criteria of their identity are difficult to establish. An exception can be said of the void, that has no sensibility and therefore no features for us to compare with. If we are convinced that the word 'void' is public, then I cannot say how it is so. The verification of seeing the void is very peculiar, since there is nothing, and there is only nothingness we can offer to others to make public my emptiness.

Such a luxury cannot be awarded to sensible qualities in a public understanding. In this sense, Bertrand Russell may be right in saying that public space is the one in which geometry and mathematics reign. But geometry and mathematics are not spatially informative as we think they are; for they are nothing but stating constant relations between things in terms of length, position, size and shape without values or without the imposition of human understanding. What do we mean by the length of the hypotenuse of this triangle is 'five times' that of the circumference of that circle? By this alone we may understand this relation, but not the triangle or circle that are in real space. We have triangular things in real space, but never triangles. The position of this triangular thing five feet away from a circular object cannot be found, if we cannot pinpoint the position of the circular object. And the position of the circular object depends on something else or being seen. Geometry is about relations for the sake of relations and nothing more. The point about this is that even if the variables are substituted by the so-called determinates (such as X (a variable) is now substituted by, say, 'two inches'), the resultant 'value' of an equation is only an expression in terms of this 'two inches', which again is a relation to a 'ruler' and so on in a circularity that answers nothing concrete. The Russellian public space is nothing more than a big web of relations from which we cannot extricate an understanding to serve our perceptual space. A blind man with no touch hardly knows space as we know it, even if he excels in geometry.

To me, sensible qualities, spatial demarcations and positional references are undoubtedly mind made and mind dependent. Does it follow that if they are mind made, they must reside in a void that naturally is also mind made? Can the mind make the void itself? Nothing can be made from nothing. Therefore a void cannot be made of anything or from anything. Nothing is nothing; a void is nothing and a void cannot be made by the mind. There is no sense in making nothing out of nothing, except in marking out a space from a void. This is the space that is subjective and private, beyond relational measure. The demarcation of a region is helped by the natural disposition of objects in having colours and shades distinguishable from neighbouring regions or by imaginary lines learned from experience. This space, many regard as public, is not geometrical or mathematical relations. This space is a space of objects. What concerns Russell is the constancy in spatial relation brought out by geometry. A small thing at the horizon can be judged to be big by reference to the distance, not by the appearance conceived by the mind. But geometry, if not fitting to perceptual reality is not the representation of reality. A public space, first of all, must be a space in perceptual reality.

In reality, these shades and shapes are of no significance when there is no sight. But underlying these sensible qualities, there is the void in which they all fill. In total darkness, there is perhaps no demarcating lines except by the sensation of touch which may or may not give us an idea of a line. Lines and imprecise marking are best served only by sight. If demarcating a region is helped by touch, it is in the mind. Still it is sensible to say that it is also spatial, in the sense of filling an emptiness, but not in the sense that concepts and images are non spatial. In this way, it is not an inevitable conclusion that the space where these undoubtedly private sensible markings dwell, is private, unless we can find no distinction between the imaginary-conceptual space, and the space of our immediate perceptual experience.

The void, being nothing, belongs to nothing, and to no beings; and in this sense it is public, not because it belongs to the 'public' or is accessible to all beings, but simply because it belongs to no one. However, an individual mind that marks out a space from the void seems to share the same public, positional sense. This is an agreement that seems to suggest an objectivity of space mapped out by the individual mind. How this is possible, if we consider all activities of the mind and its sensibility of which we have a privileged access? The easy way out, to which I do not subscribe, is to reject that the mind's activities and sensibility are not private at all. This will create enormous problems in explaining the cognitive underpinning of the mental. Thus it is only the relational constancy between things in space that will allow us to agree upon positions and other spatial items in space. In such an agreement there may perhaps be an assumption of a sameness or of a similarity in our mutual perceptual nature, operating through a constant relation between things in space.

5.5. Summing-up

Space as the void is perceivable and conceivable independently of time, since the void has no distance, length, region or any items that may be considered as time related. These conceiving and perceiving the void are distinct from the void of consciousness. Hence in perception, the absence of a percept may not be followed by an absence of a minimal perceptual content, which is the perceptual void sustained by consciousness.

The void must underline all representations and sensible qualities in reality, since all sensible qualities are in space where the void is filled. In this sense, a space in its representation of reality is mind dependent. The void itself, having no sensible qualities such as length, region and distance, must be independent of the mind. It would not, therefore, be outrageous to claim that there is at least nothingness or the void outside us, even if everything else is mind dependent. In other words, human reality depends on the existence of the void without which our sensibility will not be extended and has no outer sense. The time-dependent aspect of space lies in motion, which is what we shall analyse next.

6 Time

6.1 Aspects of time and movement

Time is unobserved

Time cannot be defined, but explained through things. Time is in every perception and every thought, so that any attempt to define it will presuppose it in turn. In this first section on time, I shall bring out all the problems in order to resolve them one by one. Many have said, as there is in space, there are objective time and subjective time. If time is something outside us, what would it be? It cannot be a tangible thing or sensibility, for we do not see time itself, except what appears to be a feature in movement and change. Nor can we say that time is a cause, a quantity, a quality or a substance. It is not a cause because time itself is not an event; it is related to events perhaps, but certainly not an event itself. Time is not a quantity because every interval we shall call time has no tangible measure except in terms of space and movements. It seems that time cannot be determined, except through other qualities, without which it is nothing outside us. Hence, it is not a quality since there is no sensibility for us to see it. It is not a substance because again, there is no quality associated with a substance, such as extension, independence or individuation.

Is time a thing of nature that 'governs' events of things? If that is so, imagine a situation where we are alone looking into a universe in which nothing moves; will time be considered to have stopped? If not, then, time will continue to exist with or without movement. Is this possible? Or imagine that a man is looking into a vast void in which the absence of all things will surely deny a perception of time. But it is hardly likely.

Perceiving movements

Time raises its head whenever we see movements in space or perceive a change; we cannot express the notion of time to ourselves unless we 'describe' it in terms of a movement or change. In fact when we talk of time, we often talk of movements in its measurement, its understanding and nothing more. Of course, we can refer to the memory of movements, but it says nothing about time being outside ourselves. Can time exist without space? If I propose a negative answer, it is not because there is not a necessary link between time and space, but because without space we can hardly perceive anything at all. Certainly perceiving and time itself may have a close association, from which we may mistakenly infer that there is no time without space since there is no possible perception.

Is there time without movement and change? By movement, it is meant a motion through space or a change in a thing's positional references. Perhaps a change may not involve a motion, as a change of colour in leaves will show, and yet time can hardly be excluded from this consideration. Let us see how it is to look at a thing in motion and yet not 'in motion'. If a camera, which flashes at one-thousandth of a second, is used to capture a moving object, the object will appear stationary or 'frozen' in motion. The 'captured' object is stationary because all movement can only be photographically captured in still 'motions' in any case. It is curious that, if our perceptual faculty is like a camera, how can we capture a thing in motion? It is only through our reasoning that we add a time element to the reality captured by the camera, by saying, for instance, that the blurred edges signify motion. But if the motion of the object is slow enough or the camera is fast enough, we may not even see the blurred edges.

If men's perceptual physiology is like the mechanism of a camera, we only see a moving object in many stationary frames, and nothing more. No continuous motion of an object is seen, unless inferred. But in ordinary perception, we do see continuous motions. Inferring a motion is only possible, if we can compare the picture of the camera with my true perception of this movement. If a true perception is not possible, no inferring of this continuous motion is possible. To capture a motion, we must have a large number of frames of the object in a series of spatial positions, so that we can say that these frames are a representation of an object in motion through a series of positions in a definite duration. Then, would it not be sensible to say that how the camera captures each frame of reality, is as important as the number of frames taken?

If the camera takes a frame every five seconds and if the motion is at five hundred miles per hours through a short distance, the camera cannot possibly capture this motion, no matter how many frames it takes at this rate. It can only capture a moving object at different positions every five seconds. Even if this is possible, can I infer motion from these different positions? It is only because I have a concept of time that I may plausibly infer there has been motion involved. If I have no such concept, I may think they are static positions of different objects. Perhaps I have no need to think that an object has moved, or perhaps it is moved by divine intervention. Therefore, if we perceive like a camera, we see no motion and at best we only see a series of positions of a static object.

Internal movements

The illusion of movements in cinematography is not always an unconditioned exercise. To create an illusion of motion, frames of pictures are played back at a speed - not at any speed, but at a speed of the 'real' event they captured. A cinema playing back at a frame a second will give us a sense of stillness in the pictures, albeit in a sequence. If perception is just about sensing and processing, no matter how complex this processing is, we see only things in still frames leaving God to explain its continuous motion to us. The point about the speed with which a playback of frames is employed is important here, because it tells us that to see a motion at speed a separate movement at a particular speed in seeing is vital; just an illusion of motion is only possible when the frames are played back at a particular speed.

To demonstrate this further, we shall notice that every computer and its central processor has an internal clock to arrange what is before and after in its output. Its counting of hours and days is not so vital informing of the time, as it is in organising temporal sequences. I am not suggesting that a clock is time itself in whatever form, but that a measure of time or a timeframe is necessary in processing data. Perhaps, if perception is akin to processing data, there may have to be a similar need.

With this insight, can I imagine what it is like to perceive motions without a 'perceiving' motion-camera rolling, and without a preordained timeframe or timescale? Timescale here is analogous to the variable speeds employed by the camera. If I were to imagine that objects jumps from one place to another without a sense of spatial or temporal continuum, would it be a reality? Time provides a temporal continuum for sense-data from within, irrespective of whether there is time governing the temporal continuum of things perceived from outside. Without an internal time - not just time itself, but a timeframe or timescale, we cannot see a continuous motion and we cannot see data in a temporal continuum?

Even if someone can show us that this is possible, we will still have the problem in lacking the notion of 'before and after' in the perceptual data that construct a motion perceived. A thing suddenly appears in different places, but in a sequence implies a notion of 'before and after'. Still, there is a problem of how long my 'timeless' eyes can open without closing or blinking. If they are open in a series of split seconds or for long intervals, again, it will be necessary to link up these broken-up data.

To see motion, we need both motion and timescale from within. If my eyes are like a still camera, unmoved, unclosed and unblinking, how will I see objects in motion without a motion within and without a timescale within? If things occupy different places without a continuum, it will be impossible for me to see a particular thing. Imagine a camera that opens up and does not close, its still film will be scattered with images (perhaps of one object only) all over it, imprinted from an object at different positions in motion. Looking at this picture, we cannot see which image is before and which is after, and, therefore we see no movement. Again, the longer the camera is kept open exposing to images, the more images there will be; we must have a finite duration for exposing to images, without which this camera perception is one big blur or darkness, filled up by images until no space on the film is left. Imagine my eyelids can open and shut in a definite interval, I can only capture a static state of affair of immovable objects, unless I can make inferences of motion. Even if I can do so, each opening duration is only a measurement of time and not a continuum. How a series of different positions can prompt us to think of time without a preconception of it, is a mystery.

Continuous motion

If motion is about jumping from one position to another, albeit in a sequence, how is it that I do not see things 'jumping' from one place to another when I perceive a continuous motion? For if motion in space is possible, it would have been like hopping, even if the distance between each 'hop' is infinitely small, otherwise there is no other way to conceive continuous movements in space. But time itself is supposed to be perceived in continous motions as opposed to being deduced from changes of positions. What is this time that is perceived and not inferred? Is there a time inferred from without and a time perceived from within? Just as a camera rolls in motion while capturing a moving object, perceiving motion needs another motion. If I do not see this 'hopping' but a continuous motion, there must be a different 'time' within, that allows me to see a continuos motion. But if this internal time is different from the objective time, how is that I can imagine in an objective time, seeing things 'hopping' through an imaginary space? Still, whether we have an internal time or not, seeing a disjoined movement is not possible without having a notion of 'before and after'. What is this time that allows me to see continuous motion, not hopping from position to position?

There are motions too fast for us to see and motions too slow to detect. If we stare at the minute-hand of a clock, we do not see a movement though we can deduce a movement from two changed positions. This situation is very close to the situation of deducing time through a thing 'hopping' from place to place, without seeing a continuous motion. Can we say that there is no time, if no motion is perceived? Yet we do say that time can only be seen through motions, even when the temporal notions of 'before' and 'after' are considered. I suspect that there are several aspects in time itself. One that enables us to see motion not as 'hopping' from place to place without intervals, and another to consider the concept of 'before and after'. Perhaps there are more.

6. 2 Timescale, perception in motion and rhythms

Timescale or timeframe

Returning to the case about the clock-hand, I find it fascinating that something clearly in motion cannot be perceived to be so. When something is travelling too fast, we cannot see it except in a flash. If it is faster, we may not even see it at all. It seems to me that to see something in motion, we must have in our perceptual faculty something that regulates this perceptual process, akin to the function of a rolling film inside a camera, so that it governs a continuum in perceiving movements through space. This is the speed of perceiving. This is what I shall call a private timescale or timeframe, which enables perception to be slow enough to see certain slow motions and fast enough to see certain fast motions, setting a limit to our perceptual capability. Perhaps such a limitation may have something to do with our physiological make-up.

To see motion, we have limitations. For if our ability to see motion is not limited, the strain placed on us in seeing light travelling like a train would be a burden beyond imagination. Yet it is not exaggerating to compare the speed of light with that of a train if we can imagine what the speed of a bullet would appear to an ant. If the speed of perceiving is fast enough, we will not see motion as a sequence of disjoined positional 'hopping'. If we run a cinematographic projector fast enough, all motions will be continuous. If our speed of perceiving is adequately timed within a definitive scale, we shall see a smooth and continuous movement through space; any 'hopping' may be seen still but only as a movement at a erratic speed within this internal timescale in perceivable intervals. If our speed of perceiving is slow enough, we shall see slow-moving objects in motion. We cannot see the clock-hand move because it is too slow for our internal perceptual speed. Perhaps we can actually see the hour-hand move if our perceptual nature is different.

Perception also involves an internal motion

Here, an empirical example may help to introduce this notion of private timescale or timeframe. When we observe other animals, birds for instance, we wonder how birds can fly among other birds at such speed without crashing into one another. We are curious because we see the speed of the birds in our own timescale or timeframe, suited only to determine human experience; at the speed of the birds we cannot hope to cope with similar judgements and reactions. The sooner we allow that birds may have a different timescale to perceive motion to go about their business, the better we will understand. The films in a cinema are made up of numerous frames that are put into an illusion of motion in sequence, enabling us to see a continuous motion through space without 'jumping' frames. To do this, the speed of the projector is vital, otherwise, a slow-moving thing may become stationary or a fast-moving thing may 'jump' from position to position. We can take the speed at which a film is rolled to capture or to project images, as analogous to the speed of perceiving in our private timescale. In this view, perception definitely involves an internal motion, and is certainly not a static affair like a still camera with its lens open.

At this juncture, I can almost hear a roaring objection from the Wittgensteinians. They may argue that if we all have our own perceptual motion in a private timescale to see a public motion, how can we agree, for instance, to catch a ball thrown at us at a speed formulated in someone's timescale different from our own? I have dealt with this problem in another book.[7] The gist of it lies in the possibility of a relational constancy in temporal relations which I have elaborated before. When we agree, we agree not on our respective private experiences, but a relational constancy of our motion and its timeframe or timescale. Imagine playing a video recording at different speeds, the co-relations among all motion in the play are constant at all different speeds.

It is improbable to perceive motions in a static perception

In perceiving a percept changing positions in motion, it is conceivable that the process of perceiving cries out for an internal motion in response to, or to follow the changes of the percept, just as a camera must change the film for a second take, and to keep up with the changes of its object in projecting a continual motion. However, if the percept is itself all sensible qualities that are mental, the sense of motion must be generated only from the mind. Any suggestion of a perceptual dualism analogous to a cinema and its objects, must be postponed for the time being. The question of how we can generate an experience of a motion from within, let alone perceive motion from without, is not easy to answer. We can say that sensibility is about sensations, sense-data (mental), impressions or images, but who can say that all these have to be in motion? Again, if they are not necessary motion related, how do we perceive motion? Is motion itself, like the void in space, the candidate for reality underlining sensibility? Assuming this possibility, we shall continue along the line of enquiry of how we can see motion if it is external to us.

Imagine, in perceiving, there is a static, stimulated impression upon our physiological organ (the retina, for example), an image resulted from this static impression is clear if there is no movement. If changing impressions are impressed upon the same organic surface, our perception will be imagined like this: the impressing sensations are sent to our brain (or mind) to make judgements or sense of these static stimuli each lasting a very short time between the changes. If this is the case, the same receptive area (organ) must endure millions of changes of these impressions, in an almost infinitely short duration, not to mention millions of other impressions that the brain (the mind) must distinguish in terms of 'before' or 'later'. For if a continuum is to be perceived, there must be a contrast of what has been and what is after. If motion is to be perceived in spatially differentiated durations in a vast, or almost infinite number, data or impressions must be spatially represented in a temporal order. Most of the discarded impressions have to be retained (in memory), recalled to be assessed in a relation of this temporal order, in order to perceive motion.

Such a discrimination of sense impressions is an improbable scenario, and if recent impressions are not marked out by the mind from old impressions, how can we see changes and motions? That is the case when the 'blackboard' for impressions is never wiped clean before the next lot of writings arrives. If we see the present frame of motion without the past or the one before, impressions are static, or if we are to see all the before and after impressions at the same time, it will be difficult too. To see motion in a duration with all the data or impressions before and after, all being present, the past will be as vivid as the present; all past impressions are forever present with us in this static perception. If motion is seen in one instance as a static frame, even if it is helped by a memory recalled, we see no motion, just as we do not see the movement of a clock-hand. And this view of static perception, scientific as it may be, is a very unsatisfactory affair.

The necessity of internal motion in perception

Thus to see motion, in an alternative view, is to imagine a continuous change in the receptive surface, like a cine-camera rolling its films, to accommodate moving 'impressions' in the motion of things. Paradigmatically, a mirror that can reflect every frame of a moving thing must itself move to accommodate this motion. If static perceiving of motion is impossible, we have to consider perceiving in motion itself. Perception by part is a motion - an internal motion, as it were. It is with a motion that we see other motions, which also entails the possibility of two timescales or timeframes.

If I am to catch a better glimpse of a fast car passing by, I will move my head in the same travelling direction of the car; the speed of turning my head, albeit for a few seconds, can actually 'slow' down the perceptual timescale in seeing the car passing by. For the same reason, if I move too fast I can hardly see anything that is stationary, except blurred images in a flash. A motion to see accompanied by another motion seen, not necessarily of the same timescale, can determine what motion we can see. I am not saying that we need to move our heads all the time to see motions, but that a static position to perceive a motion is not probable. The motion that enables me to see other motions without turning my head is an internal motion within.

Private time and its timescale in perceiving

Where there is a motion, there is time. Therefore, if the motion of percepts involves time itself, the motion to perceive must also involve time. This is an internal and private time not necessarily subjective in being under the influence of our arbitrariness and prejudice. It can be objective in the same sense that human nature (perceptual faculty) itself is objective. We cannot hope to erase or alter their nature, except to misinterpret it. We cannot alter or erase an internal time and still hope to perceive and think. With this 'internal' time of perceiving, comes a timescale. By 'timescale', I mean a set of temporal relations among perceived motions determined by particular, permanent speeds, relationally consistent throughout. An example can be demonstrated by the use of a video recorder to simulate reality, a video recorder that can play back recorded motions at different speeds, giving a varied sense of seeing the same event, being 'slow', 'normal' or 'fast' in a disguised reality. Since they are all representations of the one and the same event in reality, we can imagine that each of us actually sees that event at different speeds.

This would not result in a disagreement among us in the reality of this motion, because the relations among all the durations in all these speeds recorded are constant. That is to say that though I may be running at a faster speed than another person (if we are both allowed to see each other's speeds objectively), the time taking me and that taking another person to run the same distance will be the same quantitatively. If we have different perceptual speeds, I will catch a ball thrown by him to me at a higher speed (timeframe), or he can catch a ball thrown by me who may see the same 'speed' in a different timeframe. But I do not need to know the thrower's perceiving speed because my 'slowness' is compensated by the slowness of everything else in motion in a constant relation within my own private timescale. These different speeds in our private worlds are the timescales of a private time.

The duality in perceiving motions

It is not inappropriate to say that a private timescale is a temporal structure within our human nature to see motion, variable according to our physical make-up as well as our 'mental' make-up. What supplants this timescale with a relational constancy among different perceptual times, relies on the existence of an external motion implicated in the motion perceived. This duality in perceiving is not a duality of two motions seen, from within and without, but an implicit duality in the necessary existence of two motions in the act of perceiving all motions, of which perceiving itself is one. The reality of motion in a relational consistency guarantees a agreement on our subjective timings of perceived motions. A perceived motion is one that is, within this relational consistency, presupposing the existence of itself as well as the motion in the act of perceiving, since every perception of motion needs two motions. Seeing motion involves also a motion in perceiving. A singular, perceived motion will not exist if only one of these motions exists, therefore, we can say that any one of these implicit motions is not independent of each other. They are realities, one relational constancy and the other, human reality, underlying all perceived motions. Thoughts have a temporal order, and therefore can change, and its temporal aspect can be perceived through these changes. In this sense and in line with what we have argued, thoughts and thinking of thoughts are two interdependent but distinct things, just as the external and internal motions are distinct, but interdependent. Thinking is an internal motion just as thoughts are changes to be conceived in the motion of thinking. This is our temporal nature that has an implicit identity of the self in a duality that runs through time, motion, thinking and perhaps a whole reality.

The impossibility of having the same external timescale to see what we see

Of course it is possible that we all have the same timescale in our respective private time-world, so that with or without a temporal relation constancy, a publicly perceived time world is possible, even though I have shown that a public agreement does not necessarily depend on having the same private timescale, by appealing to a constant relation among motions. All the movements of a ball in a video replay at different speeds, are always measured with the same distance a clock-hand (inside or outside the video event) travelled, and the clock compensates for this speed anomaly by moving in the different timescale of each speed with a constant relation among them. But if we think that the possibility of a public timescale for all, is a better alternative, we must ask ourselves a question: if we all have the same timescale in perceiving motions in the world, do external motions not have the same timescale to ours? How do we know?

Whether we all have the same timescale in us is not very important, but whether this same-for-all timescale is the same as that in external motions, is an important point. If the same-for-all timescale is the same as that of external motions, we must be able to see all external motions no matter how slow or fast they are. We shall be able to see the 'motion' of light, the motion of a flying bullet, as well as the motion of a hour-hand (clock) or the continual change in the colour of leaves. This is not possible, as I have argued, therefore, our private timescale must be paramount if motion is perceived the way it is, discriminately, according to our limitation. This is a limitation imposed upon us in perceiving motions.

I consider it possible that each of us has a different timescale analogous to the different time-worlds with various motion speeds in video replays. Timescale, in a sense, is a private time-world of relational constancy, so that our actions are all but determined by this limitation set within this scale. If so, some people are faster in their reactions than others, albeit not by as much as we can find in the reactions of birds or bees; how much of this is down to our respective alertness and skill, is not certain. Setting this possibility aside, I must consider how different timescales can condition and set limitation to seeing motions and yet retain a constant relation in measuring spatial movements within the same time-world.

Construction of a time-world based on temporal relations

If I cannot see the movement of the hour-hand of a clock, it does not mean that the hour-hand does not move. If I walk for a duration equal to the duration travelled by a train at a certain constant speed, and if I find these two durations equal to that covered by the hour-hand, I can construct a time-world totally out of temporal relations without putting a subjective value of time to any of these durations, and without seeing the hour-hand move, since a change of position of the hour-hand can infer a movement not seen. Therefore, a change and indeed an unseen motion can be interpreted in temporal relations to all other motions. For the same reason, when we do not perceive a very fast motion, it would not stop us from using a change of position as an interpretation or a measurement of this unobservable motion. In this way, the time-world of temporal relations is one that can be very real indeed, and yet still private.

Rhythms in perception

A motion that allows the perception of external motions, is not like these motions perceived. This motion of perceiving is not itself perceived and its existence is a necessary postulate for all possible perceptions of motions. If this motion is not perceived and is positionally 'static' (i.e. the retina), it does not preclude the possibility of its being a 'motion' to facilitate the perception of motions. To consider this perceiving motion as changes instead of moving in space, I cannot conceive of it to be anything else but rhythms.

In the modern-day, popular theory of space-time (as opposed to space and time), velocity is supposed to be the only thing to postulate and interpret time. There was this premiss that light travels in a constant speed under all conditions, therefore, all units of time can be translated into the speed of light as a constant. Without having to consider all the scientific facts, it is plainly true that the manifestation of time, that is, whatever enables us to conceive of time itself, is not just through the perception of velocity and objects moving through space. There are many aspects, and above all changes, that must manifest to us the notion of time. Rotations, changes in shapes, sizes, or sense-data, and rhythm are some examples. Certainly the time that it takes a leaf to change from green to brown has nothing to do with the speed of light or a car. Measurements in change may involve speed as a relational pointer, but not the manifestation of time. If rhythms, the time phenomena, enable the temporal perception of changes, there should not be an implication here that rhythms in a time-world is distinct from another time-world through the perception of motions.

Life's rhythms, its temporal constituent

Is it a speculation on my part that perceiving itself needs an internal 'motion' that, being not a motion across space, is a rhythm to perceive motion? From an empirical point of view, the only perceivers of time are living things, and living things are entities that have movements in themselves. A man does not calculate the force and velocity before he plays football or even kicks a ball. In a man's actions, a certain timescale must have become familiar to him before he is confident to act instantaneously.

Time is instinct to us; it is not scientifically taught to us. If an individual's timescale is changing all the time and when the individual sees and expects motions at different speeds, he or she does not have a veridical frame of time to apply the familiarity of motions, within a multi-timescaled world to cope with his or her reactions. We not only need motion within ourselves, but a rigid and constantly relational timescale. Movements and their temporal judgements demand a temporal relation and the sense of time; without time, there will be no movement, and without movements, men do not live. We are temporal creatures just like birds and worms. Time, in this sense, is the rhythms of life. The internal motion of perception is the perceiving rhythms. If I may imagine a physiological model, it is the rhythmic changes on the surface of a receptive organ, pulsating and forever changing, carrying one set of images, disappearing and regenerating a new surface to receive new data or impressions, to carry out the task of this internal motion of perception.

6.3 Subjective and objective time

Time and its value

Subjective time is in how we feel about a duration, being long or short sometimes, without having its relation with other movements or changes. I may feel that a day is very short, but a day has twenty-four hours. In this sense, a private time is the feeling about duration of time in a private value in being long and short. An hour full of busy affairs will seem very short,whereas an hour of idleness will seem longer. Such a feeling about the duration of time is not in the perception of time itself. For feelings apart, a duration is first and foremost marked out from a relation (i.e. the clock-hand has moved from A to B), no matter how long or short it may seem to us; a subjective time is about how we formulate and determine this duration, giving it a value. The 'long' and 'short' of a duration are values we impose upon a duration of time and they are not objective. Whether time is more than being merely 'long' or 'short' remains to be discussed. Time, if it is like space, can only be said to be mental (in the sense that all sensible qualities of objects are mental) by virtue of being inseparable from movements. Again, whether time is a quality at all remains to be seen.

Time and space, their dependence or independence

Earlier on, I argued that space is an objective reality in the void and yet subjective in its parts in being created by the mind. If time is an objective reality, its relation with space must be clarified. Many think that time is inseparable from space. This may be true enough, and there are many reasons for this. If time is a perceptual necessity and if space is inseparable from sensibility, time cannot be independent of space. But, if space and time are both the same objective reality without this perceptual dependency, their coming together in one inseparable whole, is not so obvious. Can time and space be related in an extra-perceptual reality? A velocity has both space and time so that one can be quantified in terms of the other only in a relation, but is velocity independent of being perceived? That is to say, if P is not an observable thing, but a relation, can we say the same of velocity? A velocity has a notion of being high (fast) or low (slow) that is beyond being a mere relation. A light second may be 186,300 miles, but can a light second be conceived without a relation to things perceived? Apparently not. For I know that a light second is a very, very fast velocity, or a very, very short duration, or a very, very long distance. These are values beyond space-time relations. Or for that matter, if one mile is one one-hundred-and-eighty-six-and-three-hundredth of a light-second, how can we conceive of one mile without the conception of a second or foot or yard? These relational terms, seemingly having values by playing on our immediate understanding and experience, are relations without values. Constant relations are in a reality, but are not reality itself; for reality must be within the existence of sensibles and their conceptions. This has been argued before. Constant relations can supplant our sensibility with a sense of reality, but never replace it.

There can be no pure relations without the sensibles and there can be no relation between space and time without the sensibles. Therefore, time and space are interdependent not in themselves, but through the sensibles. That we do not usually conceive of time as a distance or space in a duration, is in no doubt. When I say that a mile is a distance measured by a travelling object in time, I am referring to a relation, but not a mile in space. Nor am I saying that a mile is a duration of time itself. Conversely, when I say that a second is a duration measured by a distance travelled by an object, I do not mean that it itself is a distance or a velocity to travel a distance. For I can consider a duration without this relative measurement. I can see the century-old habit in mathematics replacing time with its spatial relation, or space with its temporal relation, that allows a conceptual, categorical mistake in thinking that space is identifiable with a temporal relation, or time is identifiable with a spatial relation.

Time and space are not logical equivalents of each other

For example, the distance travelled by mercury in a thermometer, can be constantly stated by the number of matches burnt underneath a test-tube of water, in a relation of temperature or quantified energy. But if we were to say plainly that the increase of mercury volume is identical with the number of matches, the absurdity of this is clear. A judgement of quantity equivalent (constancy) is not a judgement of identity. The former is a judgement of relation and the latter an existential judgement. I suspect that the problem lies in the idea that the relation of space is space itself, and of time, time itself. The velocity of light is a relation of time and space, and yet the distance itself and the duration taken to cover it, are not about this relation. Therefore, for time and space being two separate entities in a relation, not capable of being separated, there is a verbal confusion, if not a muddle.

If we were to take the distance of 186,300 miles as a space (distance) itself, it cannot be its relation also to a duration of light's motion. Hence, to say that a distance of 186,300 miles is identical or interchangeable with a light-second in time, is a mistake of identity. Still, we can surely say that what this distance is can be a tool to measure a duration of time with reference to light's motion. But there is a difference between saying something is relationally equivalent to another thing, and saying something is identical with another thing. In reality, the distance of 186,300 miles is not a distance we cannot perceive in principle among objects. Consequently, the distance of 186,300 miles is not a duration of time, but can be measured by reference to a duration of time through a relational constancy. If we talk of space and time being interchangeable, we are talking of relations alone and not of their respective beings. What can be deduced from a space-time relation is anyone's guess, just as $\sqrt{-1}$ can be 'deduced' from and to all kinds of mathematical relations. To illustrate finally this muddle, if I say that 186,300 miles is a light second, how long will it take light to travel a light second? This surely is nonsense.

Time can exist independently from space and objects (the subjective time)

Space and time are closely related, only through the sensibles. That is to say, if they are inseparable from each other, it is because of their mutual dependency on the existence of percepts. It is groundless to say that they can be interdependent outside this criterion. If so, in the void of space and in the absence of any sensible object, there is the absence of motion and change, therefore, there is no time perceived with motion in a sense. But conceiving of or perceiving itself is a temporal process as much as thinking is. If time can exist without sensibles, it will exist without space, since a sensible object always carries a content of space with itself and it is space (not alone) that gives rise to motions and changes. As it is so proposed, time has the objective sense in being associated with space and objects, and a subjective sense in being associated with thoughts and other mental acts (perceiving is one). This subjective time is not about a subjective judgement of time independently of sensible objects, but is the rhythms in life itself that govern perceiving and thinking. Thus subjective time, if it is metaphysically distinct from an external time, has a sound metaphysical origin or basis in the composition of our being.

The possibility in the objectivity of time in motions

I imagine Berkeley would have rejected the objectivity of time being external to ourselves. For in the absence of all sensible qualities, there will be no motion and therefore no perceptual time. Since it is hard to disagree that all sensible qualities exist, one way or another, in the mind, it is difficult to see how things seen together with them can be anything but mental and subjective. Putting aside the possibility that time exists in the act of perceiving itself, space as a region and as a distance or position, has no need for a temporal relation with anything else, if there is no change in them. For we can perceive a region, position and distance without measurement. The idea that time has a say in a position of an object, is not a sustainable claim of a space reality, unless there is such a thing as space-time (as opposed to time and space) coexistent. It has always been taken for granted that space and time are parallel problems; if you solve one, you will solve the other. I think this is far from the truth.

Kant puts space as something that gives us an outer sense whereas time will give us an inner sense. The acceptance of both as two sides of the same perceptually intuitive condition has been the cause of much misconception, even if sufficient arguments have been put forward. The interchangeable identity of space and time, as I have argued before, lies in measuring the constancy of relations, which is an easy option to see a relation as a thing itself. We may refer to distance in terms of time and velocity, but they are still relations. Distance, position and region can be determined relationally by reference to other distances, positions and regions without having to appeal to motions in time. Our direct experience of a 'distance' involving the length of a ruler allows us to imagine a distance in multiples of this ruler, without having to measure it by velocity.

However, objective time itself does not possess the luxury in being self-subsisting, in the way space (the void) is undoubtedly self-subsisting. Objective time (time not associated with thoughts and sensibility), if it can be so distinguished, is wholly determined by motion and change, and nothing else. Save the act of perceiving itself, objective time has no place in static sensibles or static perception; nor can it be presupposed by them. So, if time is something that is not in static sensibles and if motion itself depends on a time-regulated perception, the key to its mystery must be found in the perception of motions or in the motions themselves. The (Berkeley-inspired) idea that time is mental because all sensibles are mental must be questioned as to whether motion itself is mental. I have argued that perceiving motion is not possible without an internal motion. If this implicit duality in time of two motions in perceiving is necessary, then the proposition that all motion in sensibles are mental may not necessarily be true. This does not mean that time is not subjective. At least one side of this duality is subjective. But an objective time will not be known without this implicit subjective time that enables the perception of motion.

Memory and spatialized time

As space itself has a relation to an object in being occupied by it, being inseparable and yet distinct from its extension, being positional to it and around it, and being within or without 'its' sensible qualities. But the relation of time to an object is not so observed without considering its motions and changes. The time-object relation we can investigate thus lies only within motion or change, and nowhere else. A motion that is a change of position from a previous one, cannot be a spatial change unless the new position is recognized, to presuppose that there was an old position available as a comparison. It may be difficult for us to imagine a situation where a new position cannot be determined, at the 'moment' of perceiving. Much of this peculiarity about motion was seen by Henri Bergson, when he wrote:

> The consciousness which will accompany this sensation cannot remain identical with itself for two consecutive moments, because the second moment always contains, over and above the first, the memory that the first has bequeathed to it. A consciousness which could experience two identical moments would be a consciousness without memory.[8]

Here, Bergson thinks that memory is the key to capturing this change of positions in the conception of motion. Although it is true we can conceive that motion can be broken down into stages of changes in spatial positions, still it is not at all certain if these broken-down moments of perception have to be held by memory in order to give a sense of continuum and sequence. If perceiving is a moment of reality, how is this perceiving moment divided and how are the divided durations determined? Should it be true that the moment of immediate perception is subdivided so that all these sub-moments of the perception of motion must be supported by memory? But, in perceiving a motion, we are not conscious of applying our memory to see a motion. We think of seeing a motion as immediate, but if memory is applied, should there be a judgement of identity and determination of every 'sub-moment' linking the chain together? This is highly improbable.

No spatialized motion without the sense of 'before and after'

If we leave out the intervention of memory, motion as a series of changes of spatial positions cannot be captured or conceived as a motion. For a motion which cannot itself distinguish a new position from an old may not be a motion, since there is no temporal organization of spatial positions, and no sense of 'before and after' existed in it. This temporal order is already implicit in such a series. If, in reality, bodies 'really' do move in space, we cannot imagine what this motion will be like without conceiving different positions in terms of the old and the new. Notwithstanding the inadequacy of memory itself, the conception of the 'old' and 'new' does not lie in the objects themselves. It is because our perception is a slave to this temporal concept, that it is hard to imagine motion without this temporal sense. This imposition of temporal order on spatial positions is of course mental. This is why I cannot imagine what an external motions is like, without my mind's temporal sense. If there are external motions, I can only infer their existence by the duality necessary in perceiving motions, which I have proposed before, and my temporal sense therefore may not be in the external 'motion' itself.

Spatializing time is to perceive static 'motion'

I can see the dilemma like this: on the one hand time is expounded by the motion in space with definitive distances to mark out durations, and on the other hand, spatializing time this way creates enormous problems. The ancient paradoxes of Zeno and many others have shown unsatisfactory consequences in spatializing time, or worse still, in dissecting space. (Since they are so well known, I shall not bring out their arguments.)

Earlier, I proposed that to see a motion presupposes the existence of another motion in perceiving it. We assert that whenever a motion is observed there are inevitably two motions inferred - one, the perceived; the other, the perceiving. To capture a duration by marking two spatial points cannot be a simple affair, for there are problems lying between two durations. This is to say that in dissecting a space for the duration of a motion, there is always a time when a motion has not left the first duration and yet not completed the next. This calls for an infinite subdivision of a duration. A motion through dissected spaces, is motion seen as a series of static impressions at every temporal moment. This is not an impression of something in motion, but a series of static impressions. If this is the case, then a spatialized motion is composed of frozen 'motions' at many broken moments, without an explanation of how a motion can cross from one point to the next. To do so, we must again dissect the space between these two points in order to show a series of sub-motions, and so on to infinity. A series of static, stationary positions can never become an impression of a motion. This is the failure in using static impressions to construct a motion; implicitly numerous as they may be in considering motion as crossing a number of points in space. Therefore, dissecting space to explain motion and the concept of time, is misconceived in a way that can only confer a motionless state of reality, even if we can impose an imagined continuum in the static series of impressions.

To mark two points within a length through which a motion takes place is difficult, if a motion is a series of static impressions; for such marking will not be determined by external motions, but by the arbitrary mind. If an object is motionless, there is no marking of points for a duration of this motion, since there is no space crossed. The illusion of cartoon movements whereby a static object is placed at different points of space and filmed by a still camera frame by frame, can be created by projecting the images and rolling (moving) the frames in a sequence at speed. Therefore, the absence of an external motion does not necessarily mean there is the non-perception of motion. The possible reality inferred from this example is that perceived (external) motions are the product of the internal motion of perception and that external objects 'hop' from place to place without the continuum of motion. This may be true, but we have no hope of knowing it if we are restricted to our perceptual nature. If perceiving itself is static or motionless like a still camera, there can be no motion perceived (this I have argued before) whether or not there are external motions, as a still camera cannot capture motions. Spatializing motion and time begs a static state of affairs at every moment represented by a spatial point, and since static perceptions and stationary percepts cannot produce the perception of motions in continuum, hence spatializing time to explain motion (and time) is impossible, or the reality of external motions is 'space-hopping'. But this does not mean that time cannot be measured and contained within motion itself, if we do not conceive motion in this way. If 'space-hopping' is the reality of external motions, the proposal that every external motion perceived implies an internal motion, must be quite credible since motions in continuum are what we ordinarily observe.

Points of space and points of time are different in their nature

I am therefore cautious about determining the duration of time using definite distances, however small they are. Ordinarily, when we mark out two definite points, we mark a distance, not a motion. A film-rolling camera can see stationary objects, and in the same way we can certainly see stationary things in space even if there is a perceptual motion within, since stationary things can be repeated in unchanged impressions of themselves. At a point of space, a motion has arrived and is there and will pass from it, all at once. This is the sense of 'motion in continuum', not 'hopping in space'. Static series of impressions cannot give us this sense of continuum. This sense of continuum can only be provided by the motion within perception. Without allowing a motion within our perception itself, we cannot explain how a thing at a point of motion can be coming, being and passing away all at a particular moment. But, coming, being and ceasing to be, are things conceivable without motions. Hence external motion is unlikely to exist without the temporal conditions in the perceiving mind. These are temporal points and not spatial points. The distinction must be made.

The problem in freezing a moment in time as a point in space, is that a temporal point is different in nature to a spatial point, even if they have a constant relation. There is always another point preceding that at which the motion has ceased, and how can we capture the precise moment when a motion is being and not passing away? This is difficult because we are looking at it as a temporal point. Whereas a point of space, and with sensible qualities, has an extension that is undiminishable, which leads to the thinking that a temporal point must also have an extension in itself so that a moment before a moment, is like a bit of extension next to another extension in space. If we consider that there is an internal motion in seeing a motion, we may consider that this internal motion has durations determinable independently of any spatial representation. To mark two points in space is simple, but to mark out durations is difficult. To mark two points in a motion through space is to mark a motion without a static reference for our imagination. This marking is only possible by inferences from relations; we cannot mark two points passed by light travelling across space, but we can calculate it by reference to its relations.

Distinguishing motion through space from non-spatial changes

Still, if time is conceived only in motion through space, I must persevere with my thoughts on what motion itself is. What can I find in motion that is more than a change in spatial position? Changes on the surfaces, in the shapes and sizes of things involve the notion of time, and so too does a movement through space. The common, accustomed way of measuring time is using linear movement. Yet, time seen through pulsating and changing is not a time measured through spatial positions. The difference between these two types of movements, as I can see it, lies in the sense of direction. Motions through space, whether circular, elliptical or linear, are directional. What makes motions always directional? And this is not a question of what a direction is. For every directional movement, there is a previous position chosen, and a possible prediction or expectation of future positions. This is not about the identity of a direction of whether it is going west, east, left or right, but a possible projection of a position from another. This projection requires a temporal notion of 'before and after' as much as a non-temporal sense of direction in space. Imagine motions through space that have no directions and we will imagine only changes, pulses not crossing a space. Hence motion in space may not be the only phenomenon from which the notion of time can be extracted. Direction in space has a temporal sense because it involves a sense of motion in 'before and after'.

Consecutiveness and simultaneity

I see in changes nothing more than the notion of 'before and after', separating each perceived change from another. Perhaps, the idea of 'before and after' is not the only temporal concept contained in changes, for they also imply something that was and is no more, a state of being and non-being, replacing and replaced, and a sense of consecutiveness to the exclusion of simultaneity. As for a motion through space, the predictability of a direction has more than a sense of 'before and after'. Its sense of direction is not just 'what-is-after-this', but 'where-is-after-this'. It is this combination of both temporal and pure spatial considerations, that none of these two senses can be a determination of the other. That time has its measure only in duration may have blinded us from seeing that this aspect of time is primarily about consecutiveness without simultaneity. Spatialized time in motion through space is about the consecutiveness of all positions it passes through to the exclusion of simultaneity, since simultaneity within one motion is inconceivable.

The consideration of time in the motion of an object through space is about one motion of one particular object and not two. There cannot be more than one motion within a definite duration involving one object. There cannot be one motion within one definite duration involving two or more objects. If a motion within a duration involves a singularity, then the idea of a simultaneity within one motion does not arise. When one motion is divided into sub-motions within a number of sub-durations, there is still no simultaneity as all sub-motions are necessarily consecutive. The idea of simultaneity involves more than one events and is independently understood from consecutiveness. It is consecutiveness alone that raises the notion of time in a singular motion through space. To create a consecutiveness in a motion, one has to dissect a duration into sub-durations. But it is motion itself that implies this consecutiveness, and not the division of a space. Dividing a motion means an introduction of many objects at different durations across a temporally dissected space in consecution. If I cannot see many or a infinite number of objects across the space at different points consecutively, I will fail to see that one object crossing a series of points in space. But if I do not see this consecutive crossing, how do I establish time in a motion, if consecutiveness is the essence of time? This is not a fruitful way to understand time.

If the sense of simultaneity is a sense of time, it is about the simultaneity of two things, not two objects or static affairs, but two events or durations. Two simultaneous durations must begin at the exact moment and cease at the exact moment. This sense of exactness in a moment is also a sense of time. The sense of simultaneity may be only a feeling of temporal exactness since the mind cannot see an absolute simultaneity. Some even believe that simultaneity does not exit. As consecutiveness and simultaneity do not presuppose motions through space, but are presupposed by them instead, they are understood independently of motions through space. This is also the reason for the failure in the claim that seeing motion as a series of instances joined together, involves static perceptual impressions, which require no consecutiveness. Seeing a motion is seeing one object passing through space, and not seeing many temporal images of it through a series of points in space. The duration of a motion measured through space begins with a point from rest, and finishes at a point of cessation; this is only a marking of two points in space to define a duration travelled in space; everything else in an imaginary dissection of space into sub-points for crossing is nothing but the creation of the mind in a representation of time in space. I see no reality in this unless the division of space duration can bring out the concepts of 'before and after', of consecutiveness and of durations, all of which can be conceived independently of motion itself.

6.4 Motion and duration

Motion and change are more than sensibility

Motion, as long as it is conceived to be a temporal item, is more than what there is to be perceived, since there is a precondition for perceiving a motion in assuming the existence of another motion or rhythm to enable the seeing of an external motion. By 'perceived motion' I do not mean only the sensibility accompanying all that is moving, but also the movement or motion itself. I am not at all perturbed by the slogan 'no motion without sensibility'; for I think that the idea of motion is self-evident within ourselves without relying on sensible qualities as it is so in the perception of the void. Consciousness is a motion in itself. If sensibility can move and change without having to attribute its motion and change to our own perceptual conditions, motion and change are not pure sensibility. Changes in sensibility in a perceptual reality cannot have causality within the mind, unlike sensibility itself. If I have to close my eyes or squeeze my nose to perceive a change, I can 'blame' this change on myself in a causal link. By this, I do not mean that there is a supposedly existing object that can cause a conception of a change in me, but that factual considerations do not warrant a constant connection between the change and the mind. While we can say that sensible qualities are all but our sensations within, what distinguishes a static sensation from a sensation involving motion and change, even if they depend on this sensibility? Yet, this does not mean that motions are necessarily external in the way they are conceived.

Time is in the act of perceiving

As regards the sense of time itself, I can see no indicator of anything conceived as a temporal sense in the moving and changing of sensible qualities, except in the ideas of 'moving' and 'change'. If time itself is necessarily part of external motion itself, as opposed to being an internal awareness in perceiving a motion, it can be argued that if there is no motion seen, there will be no time. This can not be true. If I can imagine myself alone in a static world, time will not exist without motion, but this can hardly be the case.

Time undoubtedly continues to exist at least in our awareness; the misconception that time will cease in a static world lies in the lack of measuring criteria, which come from movements. In a static world, we have no seconds, no minutes, no hours and no years, but this is not to say that there is no time or duration of time, even if we cannot measure it. This argument is not an argument for an absolute nature of time. That time exists in a static world, does not necessarily entail that time itself is absolute and independent of anything else. This is the argument that one cannot imagine there is a perception of anything (time for instance) without oneself always remaining the perceiver in such a situation, imaginary or otherwise. Of course, what is perceived in time is necessarily the content of perceiving awareness and not only what is perceived. If that is the case, if time still exists when everything else is static, it may entail that time is in the act of perception. This is different from saying that time is in our sensation and sensibility.

If time is in the motion itself, and not in perceiving it, it is possible that capturing a motion by perception will inevitably capture time itself. If perceiving has no temporal control, it would not have mattered at all, for time itself will come with the perceived motion captured by any imaginable perceptual method. How is it that a motion cannot be captured by a camera if the shutter is open permanently or closed with a timely operation? How is it that a duration cannot be captured by it, but only measured by the operation of the camera itself? If the assimilation between photograph-taking and perception is not a comfortable one, a man, in practice, sees a duration only when he defines a moment for himself in the act of perceiving. This defining act is like shutting the aperture of a camera to determine a duration of a motion, or to create a change from opening and shutting.

Is motion absolute or relative?

Motion without a timescale to perceive it, is a motion not perceived. If a train and I were travelling at the same speed and direction in empty space next to each other, I would see the train and myself as motionless. Some relativists will say that there is no motion of the train with reference to me and no motion of me with reference to the train. If so, it will question the original premiss that we are both travelling at the same speed in the same direction, without which we are of course both stationary. Suppose there is a third person seeing these motions who is unknown to me, would reality he or she sees of these motions also be unknown to me? If there is an absolute reality, we can see none of it. What we can see is only a relative reality. The absolutists will argue that there is a mutual compensation in the motions to explain that these motions do not happen. That is to say, the sense-data supposed to be impressing upon our senses by a moving train will remain on the retina as static data, because the retina moves at the same speed and in the same direction. How is it that perceiving a motion depends on the condition of the retina, if the reality of a moving train is contained in all the physical, moving data? Hence we argue that moving itself cannot be in the data, and it is a perceiving act that determines a motion. In this case, the train's motion is not seen because there is no motion determined by me.

Suppose the situation is such that I am moving or the train is moving next to another stationary train, and seen by a third unknown observer. This situation creates moving data from the second train, whether or not I am moving or the first train is moving, and if so, how can we tell which object is actually moving? When I see a car passing, how can I know whether it is I who am moving or the car that is moving? If the observer's reality is made known to me, there is an adjustment to accommodate both perceived realities, without having to accept two relative realities. Why is there a necessity for the intervention of the mind to adjust our perception to accommodate a reality seen by a third party? If the train and I were travelling at different speeds, observed by someone travelling and known only by the train, I will never know the 'true' speed of myself or of the train by reference to the observer. Perhaps you may say that the 'true' motion is the one only observed by the third man, but does he know that the train and I are not moving at the same speed?

The relative reality in this is not so much that we do not know what is absolutely moving, but that if all things are moving, what temporal values are there in these motions? And the absolute reality is not so much that there is an absolute motion by which all else is measured, but that if there are absolute motions, are there absolute temporal values too? If so, what absolute standard can confer these absolute temporal values? In other words, whether motions are relative to some absolutely stationary thing or not, we have no way of finding out. We are concerned with the relativity or absoluteness of spatio-temporal determinations, such as 'where a thing is', 'how far it is' or 'what the speeds of the trains or myself are', or 'what the duration taken to cover a distance is'. In this sense, until someone can find an absolute reference to determine the existence of absolute motions, motions can only be understood relatively. However, temporal values are considered as having a relational constancy with which we can adjust perceptual anomalies, by pointing to the relation between the old and the new references. Without this constancy, such adjustment may not be possible. I cannot see that the way in which an absolute reference outside us can be conceived, since whatever is used as an absolute reference for a motion can always be seen as relative to the motion itself. In this sense, anything can be selected as a fixed point provided that the relations among all motions referenced to it are constant. An seemingly absolute system of motion can be in principle determined by this constancy. If the sun is taken as a fixed point, all motions on this planet and every other planet are absolute in this sense. If a distant galaxy is taken as a reference instead, there will still be an absolute motion, if the relation between the sun and the galaxy is reconciled in a constancy. Humanity cannot bother with the inconceivable absolute reference; it serves humanity well to use the earth as a reference point and this is as absolute as one can get in every-day life.

Thus a motion perceived must not be a motion of anything absolutely, but a motion hinged on a particular, selected space timeframe. A motion is not determinable within moving things, but by the act of perceiving. Consequently all relative motion of the train, myself and the observer is motion depending on a determination. Since 'I' is a permanent perceptual existent in all perceiving, a reference to this 'I' can be considered as absolute in this sense, spatially or temporally.

If there is any true motion, 'I', the perceiving act itself, must be the only reference assuming a fixed and permanent point in space and a frame of time, irrespective of whatever other viewpoints are hidden and unknown. If motion is so elusive, what can be said of time that is supposed to be within motion itself? There is very little to be said. Seeing a moving train at the same speed as my own shall suggest a static affair between myself and the train. There may seem an absence of time since there is no motion perceived. The time measured by a relativity centred on the self, is by no means consistent with relational constancy of time measuring all things moving. For if no time existed during a mutual immobility of the train and myself, I would never grow old or manage a sequence of thoughts. Thus time exists not in the moving things perceived. In a mutual, relative immobility, we may not see motions, but we cannot lose the conception of time. And this is not a belief in an absolute time, but in a belief that time must exist in perceiving and in myself. We see moving things but do not see time itself in moving things, and time is in the act of perceiving.

Marking out duration by the mind

The consideration of time in motion lies in the determination of duration within a motion, because all 'times' are measured through a thing called duration not observable in a continuum of motion. But duration has a beginning of and a cessation of motion that may be observed. Duration is inevitably mind made, the markings of the mind, like a region of space marked out from the void, except that the temporal 'boundary' is now a beginning and an end. Nature's motion in having a beginning and a cessation, just like the boundary of the extension of a body, helps the mind to mark out duration as natural as it can be.

Duration

What is duration? Or perhaps I should ask: what is a second, a minute or an hour? Is there anything that is not motion-related which can give us a duration of time itself without having to refer to a motion or an event? The second, minute and hour are measurements of a movement of, or a change in, a clock or many clocks, many growths, many sunrises and sunsets, many seasons or many circling celestial bodies. On closer inspection, we find that these are no more than a constancy in the representation of space-time relations, such as the distance of a few inches travelled by a clock-hand being equivalent to a few miles travelled by a car, or being equivalent to a distance travelled by the sun in the sky. If 'S' is a speed, 'D' is the distance, what is the relation between D and S? We may not call it a duration or anything if we do not understand speed and distance, therefore understand motion. Motion has already implicated the notions of time and duration, and cannot be understood by a quantitative relation alone without the understanding of the constituents of this relation, namely, time and duration.

With these relational representations, we can safely make the clock measurement redundant by substituting it with the car's five-mile distance measured and in turn by the distance the sun travelled in the sky. These measurements are nothing but empty variables. Without the content of temporal experience in time's passing, they cannot be evaluated as durations. We can compile a vast amount of representations of spatial equivalents to give us a sense of reality in the comfort of this constancy. We cannot call this the constancy of relational the representation of 'time'. This will be unsatisfactory, for a relation is always a relation and nothing more. And the concept of time in the real sense of the word does not exist in relations. However, we may ask the question: what is this thing that we say is the distance travelled by a clock-hand, equivalent to the distance travelled by the car? We are surely not talking about distances since the distance travelled by the clock-hand and that by the car, are certainly not equivalent.

This equivalence between two different distances of motion, being equal in a constant relation, must cry out for a recognition in reality. And if we call it a duration in terms of its spatial quantities, there still lacks a content. Is duration time itself?

From a private point of view, duration can be felt without the measure of speed and space; duration has a sense of being endured by a perceiver throughout the motion until its cessation. The absence of anything perceivable, contributing towards an understanding of duration, together with the sense of endurance in perceiving, point to the possibility that 'duration' exists in the mind in perceiving and not in the distances measured; for an equivalence in distance (albeit different distances) amounts only to a relation.

The sense of duration is more clearly marked in the consciousness in having a sense of 'short' or 'long'. A duration without this inner sense is something that has no identity except a relational constancy. If we have experienced the passing of a duration equivalent to a distance travelled by a clock-hand, we know very well what this duration means to us in our experience, and yet we cannot but label it with our subjective reference without which it is just a constancy of 'nothing' in a relation. A computer can sense and measure the start and ending of a motion more accurately than human perception, and no doubt it can mark out numerous duration-equivalents, but can it know a duration like we do? Duration is quantified by relations and stated as relational equivalents. But somehow, at least one of these equivalents has to be an endured experience for all to mean anything to us.

Irreversibility of time and motion

If time is subjective duration does not tell us that time is irreversible. Such an obviously subjective nature of time always sows seeds of doubts in my mind as to how the lack of objectivity in time should create an reversibility of changes in a physical world consisting of random movements in an indeterminable affair. To say this is to ponder why growth, life and death are somehow irreversible if the motion of a stone can be conceived as reversible by replacing it in its original position. This may not be a conception of reversibility. For it is only in the conception of motions or events that changes in time can be said to be irreversible. We can certainly imagine a repetition of a movement through space from point A to point B, with the possibility of retracing its 'original' course. Yet the only thing that prohibits us from saying that these repetitions are not identical, is the sense of time, so that one earlier movement is necessarily a different movement (hence being irreversible) because it happens at a different time. It is time that separates events, no matter how indiscernible they are. Therefore it is this time element that makes all motions irreversible. Time is irreversible and that makes events in it irreversible. Stripped of this irreversibility a motion is inconceivable. Consequently, that duration is in itself unique and the conception of a duration in terms only of space is totally misconceived. If I say that a minute is a distance of one-quarter of an inch travelled by a clock-hand, or a number of miles travelled by light, it would appear that a minute, or a duration, is a generality or universal representation of space-motion constants. This is far from the truth since motion itself is irreversible.

The making of duration

Still if we look at duration itself, it must undoubtedly consist of two temporal points: beginning and end, otherwise there can be no identity of a duration. A beginning and an end are not always determinable by spatial points. A motion in nature is necessarily continuous and a continuity cannot be dissected in segments between its beginning and its end. If time is not a continuity, but consists of duration and sub-duration, motion must be capable of being divided. To consider motion as divided, is to consider only the related space as divided, but not time itself. Since motion is both time and space in a relation, time understood in terms of divided space should assume a division too. To divide time is to consider time as space in being reversible and stoppable, and capable of occupying the same point again. This is inconceivable.

If time consists of durations, how do we identify them and what relations do they have with other durations without space? If the beginning and cessation of a motion are perceived in space, the beginning and cessation of a duration are not so perceived. Time's beginning and cessation are only the relations to these perceived points of space, and never identical with them. The beginning and cessation of a duration are the marking of the limits of thoughts, attention or perception by the mind. In this sense, the conception of unity and oneness that we have discussed before bears a significance on the sense of time. When I see the pendulum swing to its higher position, I do not always take this cessation of motion as the end of duration. When a clock-hand moves to a marking, I do not always consider that this is a natural marking of a duration I am referring to. Therefore a natural event or a movement does not necessarily supply the markings we follow to determine a duration. Duration is nothing but the important and useful creation of the mind. Temporal points are not spatial points.

If we recall Kant's famous words: 'we cannot imagine objects without space but we can imagine space without objects', we can imagine that what a duration is to time is exactly what an object (extension) is to space. Hence, I say that we cannot imagine duration without time but we can imagine time without duration.

If time is a part of any external reality it does not have physical (spatial) points to mark out a duration of temporal 'points'. If the mental is non-spatial, temporal points are mental. Temporal 'points' cannot be physical points in space, even though they may be represented in this way. In this sense, therefore, time has no objective duration and a duration is, just as a region of space is, subjective. The cessation of motion of an object does not mark the cessation of time in that motion, but the cessation of a motion which is perceived to have ceased. It is the cessation of thoughts, attention or perception. The possibility of motion itself being external is not denied by this. For it is the determination of its temporal aspects that is relative and mental. Without duration, time is perpetual and continual. If time has no duration and is not one duration, time is not something that has a beginning or an end. The conception of a beginning or an end is not time itself. Similarly, just as the void is boundless and cannot consist of regions, places and positions without the mind, a boundless time of perpetuity cannot be grasped by the mind. Space comes into our understanding through our marking of regions and similarly time comes into our grasp through marking of durations by the mind.

Subjective and objective time

So when one says that time is duration itself, one would not contradict this philosophy, for time is conceived through duration, which may not be identical with time itself. Hence there is a subjective time and an objective time. A time in our perception is a time that is continually defying its own dissection into parts. This is the time that enables the perception of motion itself, and underlines all changes and motions. Time is not perceived in the things in motion, but perceived through a condition instilled in life that provides life's rhythms, movements and timescales to perceive motion itself. It is so that the claim that time is unreal, is true insofar as it cannot be perceived through things in motion without a humanistic input; and the claim that time is real, is true because seeing motion has an implication in a duality of two motions, the subjective and the objective. Staring into a void of no movements, one does not extinguish the sense of time because of this perceiving consciousness that carries the rhythms of life and thoughts, and all its temporal aspects.

The mind, in conceiving all sundries and particulars, cannot occupy itself with unlimitness. Its attention cannot be a general mechanical device to capture various things all at the same time without a clear marking of limitations within which it focuses. Thus the concept of oneness is also a temporal necessity in its acts of perceiving, thinking, defining or analysing. Thus the boundlessness of time is not conceivable because the mind has no capacity to conceive anything other than what is limited in time (duration) and in space (regions). In space, the mind marks out the regions, and no doubt, in time, it marks out every duration necessary for particular understanding and for the measure against all relations. The working of the mind in conflict with external reality is not a problem in metaphysics if we can understand the difference between metaphysical and epistemological realities. This does not determine whether metaphysical and epistemological realities are the same or not the same. This is still open to philosophical debate.

6.5 Past, present and future

The present is not an objective duration

The imposition of duration by the mind on time cannot be more demonstrative at the 'moment' of direct perceptual experience. St Augustine brought this to our attention many centuries ago when he asked what it is that separates past from present: Is it a moment ago? Two moments ago? And, if so, what about those sub-moments within a definitive moment? It is not time that imposes on, or presents itself to us through duration, for it is so, the elimination of durations would have eliminated the conception of time altogether, or duration itself would have been objective in itself, in which case time will be identical with durations each having a beginning and an end without disputable definitiveness. In that case there will be a absolute duration that is called the present, and the durations before and after will be the past and the future. Also, time (a duration) will cease before the next begins so that the continuation of time is questioned, and a spatialized motion that determines a duration passing through two sub-durations will create havoc in the mind.

Separate the linguistic use of the present from a definition

This Augustine-inspired analysis of the present is not suitable for a linguistic discussion of this word 'present'. For if I use it in the sense of 'the present state of the economy' or 'the present Queen of England', I shall reduce this word to a mere measure of duration that may involve, arguably, an implicit past. So the present is all a matter of defining, as the present Queen and the present economy may show implicit events and objects that existed in the past. That the present may sometimes include the past is not so much inconsistent, as it is lacking clear concepts available for the understanding of time. Thus in this temporal meaning, depending on an undisputed use, and unless a clear definition of duration is made, we have no satisfactory answer of what the present is.

The present, no matter how one can mark its limits and label as such, is always inescapably linked to the 'now'. 'Now', again, can be a duration implicit of the past if we think of its linguistic use (perhaps not too far into the past as the 'present' is). For me, how we use words has never been a problem in philosophy in the wake of the popularity of Wittgenstein's influence, as long as an understanding or a definition is possible. Again, this is the 'now' of the immediate 'now', which is what I will call the immediate perceptual presence. Hence I must define the present as the time (leaving out the limit of its duration) in an immediate perceptual presence, despite many linguistic uses it may allow.

The difficulty of marking duration goes with marking the present too

When I am thinking of and seeing things in front of me, I am in the present. The presence of my consciousness reveals itself in the Cartesian sense, in a state of my awareness. However, at this stage of immediate awareness, the need to mark out the past from the present will not go away. As I sit here looking at things, there are moments that pass away and a moment when I can no longer see what I have seen a moment ago. At the moment of contemplating, I am also aware of what I was contemplating a moment ago. Consequently, there is no possible way for me to define exactly what a moment of the present is, separated from the past. If there is one time, there can be no veridical duration that can pin down the so-called 'present'. In this sense the unreality of time is a distinct possibility. This further enhances my belief that duration is mind-imposed and time itself has no duration and is boundless (eternal). If this is the case, how do we have a sense of past, present and future?

Changes cannot determine the present

Some mention 'event' or 'events' as if events themselves in their constitution have no time elements within, except in the measure of time. Events are movements of things and thus must be time-constituted. Why they are so is a mystery, since occurrences of events must have duration. Some are allowed to think that occurrences do not involve changes. But, it is only when there is change, there is an event. There can be no event without a change. In this sense, motion is considered as an event of a change of spatial positions. If an event has duration, it must have sub-events with sub-durations; so why should an event be a complete event instead of being a part of another event or its other sub-events? Is time itself only the constitution of past, present and future, even if the present as a duration is an impossible conception?

McTaggart[9] thinks that there are changes of events (as opposed to in events) from the future to the present and then to the past, and these changes are the bases from which we measure time as the present and past, just as we measure time from other changes within an event too. That is to say that if we consider time itself as one big event, the changes within this big event can subdivide itself into past, present and future, if we can determine what this 'change' means when we say that there is a change of the event from the past to the present. Indeed, to explain this change is difficult, not least as it is already implicit in past and present and as an event itself. He also thinks that there is no conception of 'before and after' without the conception of past, present and future because 'before and after' does not involve change.

To start with, if the present cannot be marked out as a duration, there can be no event called the present, and if there is no such event, how can there be a change of a non-existent event (as opposed to 'in a non-existent event')? McTaggart relies on changes to determine duration, but every duration is heavily implicit of changes. It seems that the conception of duration must precede that of a change or be implicit of it. But, the past and the present are distinct as well as continual, that is the problem. To have a change there must be two distinct happenings through time, but one cannot posit an event of the present receding into a continuation of the past by having two distinct happenings. For to use one happening as the present and the other as the past to define a change in turn, is a very circular affair, since a distinction made of two happenings either implies 'past', 'present', 'before' and 'after', or is totally irrelevant to them. In both cases, such distinction cannot determine the present and the past.

Still, McTaggart's change is not the happenings, but a change for the sake of change itself. It is a 'change' that determines the past from the present or a change of the past from the present. This is not what we normally conceive as a change. As we see it from St Augustine's writing, a moment of the present can equally be conceived as that of the past. If there are more than two changes, what should determine for us which one should mark out the present, instead of the sub-events of the past. Yet one seriously ponders: what is this McTaggart change that can determine a present from a past? Is there a change that is labelled 'the present' to mark itself out from the past?

If 'before and after' do not involve change, according to

McTaggart, 'It will be universally admitted that time involves only changes, then it will follow that time exists not in the constitution of "before and after"'[10] Can we really conceive of a change without 'before and after'? This is indeed very curious because the mere constitution of 'before and after' raises the question of time itself, with or without change. I shall discuss this later.

Past and present presuppose time but do not determine what time is

In an immediate perceptual consciousness, the present is full of changes. In changes I see events, and I see events within events so that in a solipsistic, static world without motions, the duration of the present is even harder to define. In such a world there is nothing passing into the past except my thoughts and my attentions. McTaggart thinks that we cannot avoid talking of time in terms of past, present and future, in all their inclusiveness. Take motion for instance, an object passes through space in the sequence of positions A, B and C in a temporal order where C will be the future when the object reaches B and A becomes the past. As we found out earlier, to consider motion as having definite staging points in time is to spatialize time so that time and motion are considered as capable of being frozen at different points. This will raise many problems including how we can actually perceive motion at all. To consider time as past, present and future is to consider time in the same way, and St Augustine has shown us the impossibility in making a real distinction between these durations. Since the conception of past, present and future is nothing but a verbal convenience, time must be conceived of in other ways. Therefore McTaggart's claim can be dismissed by taking away the basis on which the claim was made, that is, by affirming that there is no real demarcation between past, present and future. It does not however take away the verbal convenience used to measure duration by motion and by spatializing time. Thus there is always the present, if two people can agree upon the duration in which the present dwells.

Reality is not that which can be arbitrarily defined or redefined one way or other. When I sit down and see things in front of me, what is said to be the now, the past, involves changes (as distinguished from a change for itself) distinguished from one another. We cannot use a beginning or an end of a change to determine the present. If reality is composed of more than what we can see, the event that is passing away from now must have bits already passed and bits not yet passed; therefore, the reality within the moment of passing into the past also constitutes the present, that is unobserved, let alone pinpointed. How can we conceive time in terms of the present? A change I do not see now is in the past, presupposing a conception of time rather than telling us what time is.

Present and past; 'before' and 'after' are not mere separate durations

It is with the habit of measuring duration through motion that we conceive time as a progression moving from past to present. This cannot but be presupposed by time itself. For the irreversibility of time ensures that the past will never be the present or the future again. Time is in a sense, an irreversible progression and one directional. A motion with direction and with an irreversible progression must consist of time. If the past, the present are an irreversible progression, it would be true to say that they are inseparably conceived within this progression and direction, so that the conception of the present is implicit of the past and perhaps the future too. In the same way, 'before' and 'after' are also mutually implicit of each other. We cannot say something is before or after without having to ask the question of 'before what' or 'after what'. This mutually implicit nature of these time progressions, prevents an independent existence of each and every duration we call 'present', 'past', 'before' or 'after'. In this sense, a duration before, after, present and past is not just a duration determined by separation and change, but implicit understanding. There is no past without the present, no 'before' without 'after'. This is only true in terms of this dependence. Whether the reverse is true depends on whether the present can be stated without reference to the past or future.

Since changes can only determine a separation of durations, and since separation itself cannot fully explain the present and the past, therefore, changes alone are not the main constitution of these temporal terms. The same can be said of the before and the after. All these may well be verbal confusion in which philosophers inevitably from time to time find themselves. Certainly, motion too cannot be perceived without the implication of 'before and later' or even 'past and present' in a temporal progression. Without this crucial temporal progression that explains the uni-directional nature of time over and above the mere separation of durations, past and present are nothing but the notions of 'before and after'. That is certainly the case. If there is a definition of the present without the past, it will be a definition without the implication of anything else. But an independent past without the present is hardly likely.

What is the future?

What is the future? The future is not, therefore it exists not. If time involves the future, it involves something that does not exist. The future is not an actualized reality from an empiricist's point of view. A 'future' event is so-called when it is the conjecture of the present, and therefore implicit of the present. Therefore, without the actuality of the present, there can be no reference to the concept of the future, let alone events of the future. The future is the expectation of the present and nothing more. When there is no expectation of the future at present, there is no conception of the future; and that brings up the question as to why we have expectations at the present implicit of the concept of the future. The expectations in the present within the concept of time can also take time for us to conceive of and ponder upon. This contemplation is not the future.

All temporal notions point to the present

When I see a speeding car passing by I have no time for contemplation, but I perceive this passing, through an 'intuition' (I use this word to avoid the necessity of time taken to contemplate the 'after'). The mind, if it can think at the same speed of the passing car, or faster, will no doubt conceive expectations during the sight of this passing. The 'future' of the car after this moment or before this future, can only be understood by retrospective contemplation. If an event occurred miles away after another observed event, and if there is no causal connection between them, I shall not call the faraway event a future event, which, by implication, is connected to the 'present'. There are many events happening after this present moment, and I shall only call them 'events occurring at different times'. Therefore, 'future events' are categorized into those that are connected to the present by expectation or causality, and those that are not, are merely temporally before the present.

If these events are after the present, and have no exceptions from the present, they hardly deserve the label 'future events'. If 'future events' are the expectation of the present, then there is more to be said about 'future events'. When people say that events are becoming, being and perishing in time, an implication of the present is clear, because becoming is forming into a being, an expectation from a being of the present. An event faraway and long before the present cannot be said to be becoming without an inference from the present. If I see a fountain with its water continuously spluttering out of somewhere, the reality of the yet-unseen source is real to me because of my certainty about its happening that is not temporal in any sense; it is the happening being prior to the present event, that is temporal. As we can see, all temporal notions of the past, the future, the before and the after, point to the present, depend on the present, and are born out of the present.

What distinguishes 'before and after' from 'the present and the past'

Events do not come into being; they just happened. They can be conceived to be coming-into-being only through our expectation. Still becoming can only be conceived in retrospection. There is no metaphysical significance in the temporal notions of being, becoming and perishing. They are simply the present, the expectation (future) and the past. They too are mutually implicit of one another and derivable from the being, that is the present. To stretch the point even further, we can say that 'future' events can be subdivided into events that are either before or after. But what is a future event that is after another future event? Is it not that a future-after event of another future event will be its past event? This application of past and present to events that are merely before and after, is inappropriate. This is what distinguishes 'before and after' from 'present and past', since the notions of 'present' and 'past' cannot always apply to events that are merely before and after. If so, 'before and after' is somewhat independent in part from the notions of past and present.

Using 'before and after' to determine past, present and future

What the 'future' is, is not fixed by time itself, but conceived through expectation as being after the present, at the present. For those who are not interested in the mere temporal distinction between future and present and wish to see an absolute certainty of events becoming the present from the future, I propose the establishment of past, present and future, from the notion of 'before and after', in a coherent relation among events in the inevitability of becoming and in the identity of the past with the present. We see events in many relations including causal relation (whatever they may be). Related events are the reality of a whole in relation. Future events are a necessity of the present because we conceive within these relations no possibility for their non-existence that can question the credibility of the present.

What then is the present? The present does not rely upon being what is before the future or what is after the past. The present is a state of awareness or consciousness of thought and perception. The 'present' is only a label, if it has an implication of the past. But without such implication, perceptual awareness itself is a state of reality that transcends the temporal notions of present, past and future. This is not to say that there is no temporal sense in the present, for time is a sense and a condition to enable the perception of motions, thinking of thoughts, and to regulate the limitation of both. Of course, in the same way, the mind can impose arbitrary durations within the present, by which a duration of the present is subjectively marked out. That durations of the present are arbitrary explains St Augustine's inability to pinpoint a particular, fixed duration that is the present. When a mind defines and marks out a duration in the present perceptual consciousness, it defines a 'now'-moment, then, what is before this is the past, and after it the future. In this way, defining the present is not presupposed by the past or the future. It is the defining of the past and the future that relies on this notion of 'before and after' using the perceptual awareness or consciousness as an absolute measure.

Therefore, within a moment that I say is the present, the present is understood in terms of both an immediate perceptual awareness, and a subjective duration with arbitrary limits.

Again, a present moment itself can be constituted without the notion of 'before and after'. This is so especially when I define a present moment being a moment after another, as the past. This is labelling a 'now' of the perceptual awareness in terms of the past. In a solipsistic world of no motions, a moment past is the moment after the present without events seen. Thus the importance of the notion of 'before and after' in our temporal nature cannot be ignored. In a state of perceptual awareness, a moment of the present depends on how we wish to mark out a duration. A past moment is possible in a static world if we have this notion of 'before and after'. In the awareness without change and motion, the temporal reality will seem eternal without duration marked. At this point, one may feel that it is not the genesis and cessation of an event that determine a duration, but rather, it is the mind. Time itself does not have its own duration that allows its own beginning and cessation in the absence of motion and change. Time really is composed of 'before and after'.

How do we mark out the present?

When I have sat down and observed everything I can see for three hours, there are events that are no more at any particular moment, having been perceived before. The receding experience in a perceptual awareness has an association with 'vividness', but this vivid, immediate experience cannot be so vivid, determined and comprehended in isolation from my memory. This is the implicitness of the past in the present, and its dependence on the present. And such must be the implicit reality of the past, in being part of the present. In an epistemological sense, what I can see vividly at the present moment must include all things implicit, so that the construction of reality and the identity of an immediate perceptual experience are possible. In this way, when I see a man vividly singing in a concert, his past profession as a singer, his childhood, or any similarly relevant details, may help me to know him, but may not help me to form my intuition of this singing as part of the present reality. But the lyric I have heard a moment ago must constitute the part of a song being sung at the present moment. In order to construct a present reality of my perceptual experience of this singing with all the happenings around him, past understanding (the words sung a moment ago) must be epistemologically included, even if those words were already sung. Seeing reality as a whole or a related whole, determines how we call a moment the present. We may call the present, in a historical reality, a duration of more than many years. And yet, when it comes to a sub-atomic reality, a scientist may call a short moment the present, when he is paying attention to some related activities of sub-atomic 'particles'.

'Before and after' is the constitution of the past and the present of events. This constitution is not only a separation of events in a temporal order with nothing. The thing that makes the present and the past, more than an order of 'before and after', lies in their mutual implicitness, anchored to an immediate perceptual awareness that is self-defining without duration. Any defined duration that is in this awareness is the present. The past is whatever was before it. The past is of the present, and the future is of the present, not because of the temporal connection, but because the notions of the past and the future born out of the present are existentially dependent on the construct of the present reality. Hence the 'past' can be metaphysically in the present, but epistemologically it is the past by being implicit in the present, definable by the mind within a perceptual consciousness that is without duration.

Time and reality

Time is not a verbal reality. It should firmly cement itself in reality and facts. But when facts are 'flying in the air' in scientific conjecture, time travel is possible if men can construe their reality through mathematical relations without considering their assumptions. In this case, possibilities may play games with the reality of the past and present. I have earlier concurred that time-space as a entity, not a relation, is absurd. The fact that time can be represented by motion through space or that space can be represented by speed and time, does not necessarily allow the creation of a space-time entity. Apart from its relational representation, time itself is quite a separate thing from space. It is only because perceiving demands the constitution of time, and because any percept including a motion in space, cannot rid itself of any aspect of time itself.

I am quite convinced of the existence of our subjective time which I think is more than a conceptual thing or rather it is a nature in man that enables him to see motions, to think and to handle perceptions in limitation. In the end, his knowledge as well as actions cry out for a timely collaboration with other external motions. It must be highly possible that there is external time in perceived motions and internal time in perceiving motions. Scientific conceptions of physical objects are such that each and every part of this physical world is the constitution of either motions or wave motions of unseen particles of some sort. If that is the case, external motion is not only a seen phenomenon, but a reality behind the reason we see anything at all. That being so, in time, our perception of the world has a distinct permanency in a temporal irreversibility. Is this irreversibility imposed by time of world events, or is it a condition in perceiving things that cannot be otherwise? What is before or after, and what is temporally irreversible lie at the heart of understanding time itself, since motions are of their constitution. But if external motion exists, we cannot know what it is like since we see them in our subjective timescale. It is quite possible that external motions are 'space-hopping'.

Time is outside events

Why are events, instead of stationary objects, commonly used in conceiving time? We see that there is a time between events as well as within an event. If time is something that constructs an event, then what constructs the temporal gulf between two events? It is not, therefore, a good idea to think that time is always represented within events, or we can only conceive time through events alone. Between events, there is nothing temporal that can be mentioned as regards external motions or changes. Between events, a temporal 'gulf' exists in our perception and nowhere else. Time is within but not between the events. In this sense, time itself with all its temporal characteristics must primarily be in the mind, in perceiving and in thinking.

The eventless past, present or future

Depending on the temporal direction we choose (from the past to the present, or from the present to the past), the future has no end (the distant future) and is not perceived or known. It begins (the actualization of expectation) with the end of the present. The past has no beginning (the distant past) perceived or known but ends with the beginning of the present. Duration that has no beginning or end is not duration. The past that has no beginning and the future that has no end, are not durations. They are therefore conceived outside events. I can say that a particular event with a beginning and an end is a past event, but not that the past in the general sense is an event. What is generally the past, is merely what is before the present. Thus the generality of the past or the future is conceived outside particular events that are in the past or the 'future'.

That the past, the present and the future can be conceived generally as three temporal sectors, without themselves being duration or events, must be a metaphysical reality based on the notion of 'before and after'. Since the notion of 'before and after' can lie outside an event itself, the measure of what the past, present or future are, may not be found within an event. An event cannot determine itself to be the past or the future, it is determined outside itself. Something that can be put into a temporal order must itself be temporal; hence we only consider motions and events (never objects) as the things that are capable of being before and after. An event is itself temporal at its conception, enabled by the dual motions within and without. Therefore, the conception of time is outside the event itself, that is, in perceiving or conceiving an event. But in order to have a sense of what the past, present or future are, without events, one must find a first temporal premiss to infer all others, otherwise the temporal relations among past, present and future will be circular. This premiss, as I have said before, is the reality of the immediate perceptual awareness that may be labelled as the present.

Time is in perceiving; it is not a nature of things, but nature of the living

In this way, the 'now' is independently defined without a reference to the past and the future either of which has any ending or beginning. Any event that lies after the 'now' is an event of the past, and before, the future. An event is in the past or future but not in the event called the past or the future event. Metaphysically, events are in time and seen in time, even if there are changes and motions within. To see aspects of time within an event is not about seeing the event itself, but changes and motions that constitute another sub-event. Or we can say an event is nothing more than motions and changes in time. It is simply these things. Again the past, the present and the future are not events themselves though we can say of an event being in the past or present and being conceived to be so. As many have said before, time is within conceiving, rather than without. Living things are temporal beings who can see the world not only in terms of their temporal values, but also within their temporal make-up and their time-frame to which are fixed their way of conception, organization and expectation in their reactions to the world. Time, if it is not taken as a concept, is a part of the construct of their nature.

6.6 'Before' and 'after'

'Before and after' presupposes past and present

The motion or change in an object in an event, and the conception of events in terms of past, present and future as well as conceiving of this temporal sequence, are products of this notion of 'before and after'. They do not explain 'before and after', but rather, are explained by it, since every conception, every change and every motion of the past or the future, rely on this notion. I hope I have satisfactorily argued the case for this already. And this notion, that is really the essence of time, deserves our final investigation.

When we see a motion, we do not see every moment and spatial position the object passes through, because if a thing is in motion, it cannot be static at any moment and at any point no matter how minuscule this moment or point extension may be. Believing that this is the case is only the work of the mind in its understanding and analysis. We see a motion as having a 'moment' after another, only if there is duration long enough for us to perceive, and for a motion to complete. In this sense, the concept of 'before and after' will arise to enable us to mark a duration. A parallel can also be drawn from perceiving changes in objects; where past, present and future also reveal this notion. Duration is conceived in time, but time is not conceived in a duration. Thus to conceive a duration, the notion of 'before and after' is presupposed. And McTaggart's argument that it is 'past', 'present' and 'future' that explain this 'before and after' is finally rejected.

The difference between Kant's time and this theory of time

Kant thinks that 'before and after' comes from perceiving a motion as changes of positions in a before-and-after sequence. Kant thinks, in his so-called metaphysical exposition, that time is a precondition for seeing things existing in one and the same time, and at different time. Thus he writes:

> Only on the presupposition of time can we represent to ourselves a number of things as existing at one and the same time (simultaneously) or at different times (successively)...Time has only one dimension; different times are not simultaneous but successive ...These principles cannot be derived from experience.[11]

This insight does not say much about how time can help our temporal intuition because simultaneity and succession are temporal terms anyway. Here, he recognizes the significance in treating time itself and its parts (duration he calls times) separately. For different reasons, I arrive at a similar insight as Kant's, in that time has two 'aspects' as regards limitations and parts. Further on, Kant writes:

> The infinitude of time signifies nothing more than that every determinate magnitude of time is possible only through limitations of one single time that underlies it. The original representation, time, must therefore be given as unlimited. But when an object is so given that its parts, and every quantity of it, can be determinably represented only through limitation.

Of course, Kant's times of the limited and the unlimited are necessarily the same one time. Without a metaphysical separation of these two (as opposed to being separated through the epistemological aspect or what he called the transcendental aspects), one cannot really explain the impossibility of seeing motion taken in parts of time (or what others will call the spatialization of time). Without this spatialization of time, there is really nothing can be said of time in motion itself.

Motion is not about change in position in a 'before and after' sequence

Hence in the next section ('*The Transcendental Exposition of the Concept of Time*') of Kant's book, he writes:

> Here I may add that the concept of alteration [I think he means movement or change], and with it the concept of motion, as alteration of place, is possible only through and in the representation of time; and that is this representation where...no concept ...could render comprehensive the possibility of an alteration [...]
>
> Only in time can two contradictorily opposed predicates meet in one and the same object, namely, one after the other.

Here he thinks that our perception of motion is only about seeing two or more spatial positions with one after another. If he does not allow a metaphysical separation of time the eternal from time the duration, he cannot see motion as being different from positional change in terms of 'before and after', since, as we have argued before, a motion is necessarily moving at all possible spatial positions without being stationary at any one point.

For this will imply the perception of the movements in a motion in a stop-start situation having to divide each and every moment into infinity. This entails the notoriety in spatializing time. But if time is an intuition, even if it is a *priori*, how can we perceive time from a motion without duration to give a sense of progression and uni-direction, since seeing such progression is time itself? If the intuition of time is not an immediate process, in supposing that there is the sense of 'one after the other' in the change of position, either there must be an implication of more than one object such that one is before and the other is after; or the existence of objects at different positions lies in our memory. If the former is committed, how we do we see different objects at different positions and how can we join these objects in a unity of motion together as one? This is a mystery and the sense of its being a *priori* will not save us. If the latter is committed, whatever is in our memory, will already have presupposed the sense of 'before and after'. If the mind can see a infinite number of objects through a limited motion, an infinity does not constitute oneness in a motion. Factually, we do not see unconnected sub-motions within a motion in the order of 'before and after', to claim that they are one. It is unlikely that we discover this notion of 'before and after' from the change of positions in a motion.

However, if time of the unlimited and times of the limited are metaphysically distinct; 'before and after' will be the essence of time itself. In that case, one does not have to explain this 'before and after' within a motion of an object because we simply do not see motion in terms of a series of objects occupying a series of positions in a progression, and because a singular reality of time cannot accommodate both realities of time in being unlimited as well as limited, let alone of motion and duration. 'Before and after' with the implication of countable 'onenesses' can only be considered in durations.

Thus to think of 'before and after' is to have more than one thing to sustain that one thing is before or after another thing. 'Before and after' must be outside motion itself even though motion can project the duality of time as I have explained before. Since an event has a beginning and an end and therefore the concept of oneness, we can look at this 'before and after' in much clearer light without the problems of motion. Again, it is not universally the case that the cessation of an event can be so unproblematic as the 'cessation' of a movement in motion. To consider 'before and after' in the change of position or points in motion of objects, is to consider 'before' and 'after' not in terms of events. This is impossible since 'before' and 'after' are about events.

In the consideration of something that is after another or before another, there are at least two things being considered. This entails the postulation of parts of time itself and hence of duration. These things cannot be objects, but time-things, such as events, duration or motion. It is only time that can be in time succession. Conceiving something temporally (in terms of time) is not the same as conceiving it in time, or in its succession (before and after). Again, this distinction is justified by our claim of the duality of time. Seeing a movement is the former and seeing things in a 'before and after' succession is the latter. There is no duration without a movement, the beginning and cessation of a movement. Cessations of movement are mind-determined rather than a reality deduced outside a perception. If events are distinct within a duration, the notions of 'before' and 'after' apply to them. But events are durations too and cannot be within themselves unless they are sub-events. A 'moving clock hand' is not seen to be moving, and flashes of lightning are seen as instantaneous, so the movements of both are a matter of deduction by the intellect through changes, instead of being seen in a progressive change, point by point. But deduced events are not excluded from being considered as being before or after.

The difference between the successions of 'before and after' and of 'the past and the present'

Henri Bergson (1859-1941) thinks that it is memory that creates this succession of before and after. Again the succession of the memorized past and the present cannot give rise to the notion of 'before and after' since memory itself presupposes the past. This, as I have argued, cannot be the case. And, according to St Augustine, the so-called 'present' includes things that are seen no more. Things are no more but in our memory. If so, how incredible is it for us to retain a present event of the singing of a song, without having to include those words passing into our memory? If things in our memory are things past, how is it that the present should include them? Thus defining the past is not satisfactory by the criterion of memory. The past is only what is before the present. This will inevitably form our memory. And the reverse cannot be true. Let us compare the succession of the past and the present with that of the before and after.

Events of the past can be before and after within the past. Events of the present can be so too. Hence events can be before and after without being the present and the past, even though the present may imply the past and thus also imply a notion of 'before and after'. Therefore the notion of 'before and after' is independent of the present and the past whereas the latter depends on them. The notions of the present and the past exist within the notion of 'before and after' and the latter is more than merely the present and the past. Consequently, if memory can provide the notions of the present and the past, it is implicit already in the notion of 'before and after'. The missing premiss that memory is responsible for the notion of before and after, is not a conclusion, but a premiss to be agreed upon.

Temporal succession in the temporal identity of events and its existential root

The application of the present and the past as a succession needs more than the notion of 'before and after', in that there is a so-called temporal 'direction' from the present, whereas 'before and after' is merely a direction of time without the sense of the present. Past is a specific temporal direction from the present whereas the succession of 'before and after' is a general direction. That the past and the present are not constituted without the 'before and after' is obviously true, but the past and present are not just a temporal succession. In the succession of the past and the present (a particular succession), there is a possible temporal identity of events. By this identity, I mean a temporal value by which the reference to the present is understood. Two years before today is a temporal identity whereas two years before 'he started drinking' has no temporal identity until a reference to the present is known. There is no temporal identity of events in a 'before and after' succession. This particularity in a temporal direction is not a mystery but something that is anchored firmly to the present considered to be an existential necessity (involving the perceiving self that determines the present). The past and the present are separated and distinguished from other temporal successions by this existential criterion. The succession of the past by the present is sustained by memory. This is a temporal succession for beings who can remember. It is a succession that has temporal values and identity.

All these cannot be said of the succession of 'before and after'. The succession of 'before and after' in a generality, without a particular temporal identity, is in the making of temporal beings such as human beings; for we cannot conceive of the notion of past and present without this temporal sense. We can see events in succession in our perceptual consciousness without having to think that a split second of an after-event calls for the aid of memory. 'Before and after' implies the existence of two events. If there are two durations in continuum they cannot be simultaneous but only in succession, and if there is one, a prior event must be adopted by memory for its existence. It is time that conditions us to look for an event outside every event, or makes it impossible for us to conceive of something that is no more (in the past) to exist again. Therefore it is time that ensures that what existed before cannot re-emerge from an existential oblivion. In understanding how we come to have the notion of past and present, we can see our temporal nature and make-up and as a temporal being, manifested in the notion of 'before and after'.

Temporal successions within the present

Existence is about the present and the present is a perceptual consciousness. This is undoubtedly true. An event has an end and a cessation; once something ceases, it is no more. The past in a sense is no more. This is the irreversibility in past-present succession. Perhaps you may say that the succession of 'before and after' does not necessarily encompass this irreversibility. The past is the cessation of what was previously a percept, but if A is after B, we cannot say that B is now no more, or A cannot be after B, unless B is also in the present. Without placing A and B in the context of the past and present, there may be no controversy whether A is after B or B is after A, as long as they are in succession. This temporal sense in A and B as succession either way, must be independent of the context of past and present. But it is difficult to imagine a 'before and after' without the context of past and the present, therefore, the argument that 'before and after' can be also uni-directional and irreversible is not opposed vigorously.

Simultaneity

However, if the temporal succession of 'before and after' is applied to the context of the 'past' not being always a past event of the present, but as a before event within the present, then the mind has to mark out these two events by limitation. When I see two trains in motion, I can say that one train is before the other without having to wait until one train disappears out of my sight into the past. This raises the question as to what simultaneity is within the present where a temporal succession without the past may exist. Sometimes we say that a train that will reach a particular point earlier than another, is a train before the other, even at the point of measuring this temporal priority there is no cessation of motion that concludes the events. In this case, it does not mean that the succession of 'before and after' is not found outside a duration but within it, since the present (being a perceptual consciousness) is not a duration. It is an event that is within the present and seen in succession of 'before and after'. If we mark out the present in a duration, the past will surely follow and a past event will be that which is before this marked-out period called the present.

If I can call a perceptible instance the present, whatever happened before it is the past or a before event. If two or more events occurred in this instance, we may say they are simultaneous. But ordinarily we do not confine the present to an instance, after all, an instance may be a long duration to some and short to others and we have no objective criterion to set a duration of the present. The present is not a duration, but the perceptual presence, though duration can be marked out from it. If we use a second or a fraction of a second to define a duration of the present, there may be events simultaneously occurring within this duration so marked out. But they are not simultaneous when finer fractions of the duration are applied. This problem is a parallel to that of spatializing time to capture motion as points through space.

Still, in our ordinary use of this word 'simultaneous', we regard some events as simultaneous when they occur within a relatively long duration. We may say that two football matches are being played simultaneously or two trains arrive simultaneously, when the occurrences are not instantaneous. Simultaneity or its application depends on a defining limit of a duration and if this is so, it cannot be an objective reality. Since motion has objects, and since objects have extensions occupying space, whatever movements there may be, the movement of each object must originate from different lengths of space. If so, unless the speed of the movement can compensate exactly the difference between the initial locations, then simultaneity in a motion is impossible. If we consider the speeds of two objects to be accidentally compensating, given that no objects are of the same size and extension occupying the same space at finishing, there is still a matter of two different speeds marked out by the front and the rear of an extended object, just as the front of a train may arrive before its rear.

Again, if two sub-events are simultaneous, they are indistinguishable; if so, how can they be seen as two?

A conceivable moment and simultaneity

This is only a minor irritation. To have simultaneous movements, we can consider a simultaneity at the start of the movement and its finish. We can say that two movements start simultaneously but do not finish simultaneously, or that they finish simultaneously but have not started simultaneously. Thus, simultaneity is not about a sameness in speed and time taken, it is about a moment being 'at the same time'. Again, a moment is itself a duration, no matter how short it is. To consider two moments as simultaneous, we again have to consider each moment's beginning and finish, since each moment consists of a beginning and end, and so on to infinity. When we say that the trains arrive simultaneously, are we talking about the moments of arrival being simultaneous or the arrivals being simultaneous? Or are we talking about one moment in which both trains arrive? Does each train have a moment of its own arrival so as to be compared to that of the other to see whether they are 'in the exact time'? If so, do we not need an outside time to measure moments? Only if time is outside us can we conceive simultaneity in this way. This 'simultaneity' is a moment conceived.

A moment is definitely not a spatial thing that can be divided. A conceivably short moment is duration marked out by the mind, inconceivable to be composed of sub-moments. This is so because human perceptual and conceptual capability sets its limits. We can infer minor moments by using instruments, but the limit in which a humanly conceived moment is set, is incomparable. Things are perceived simultaneously but measured to be simultaneous. Since it is with time that we perceive things in motion, consequently it is with time that things are perceived to be simultaneous. We perceive events to be simultaneous if they are within a conceivably short moment that has no conceivable sub-moments.

Without the subjective criteria that define the shortest moment within conceivability, there can be no conception of simultaneity in all things moving. Therefore, simultaneity is very much a perceiving thing. If we were to consider from the perceiver's viewpoint, simultaneous events suggest that there are two percepts in motion in simultaneity; light that arrives at the same moment (assuming there is only one eye) from the percepts is not the moment of a true event, and it cannot be a simultaneous stimulus from two things that are placed at different positions. If the events are really simultaneous, it would not be simultaneous at the point of perception, and if they are simultaneous at the point of perception, it would not have been simultaneous at the points of origin.

Perceiving things simultaneously is not at all simple. Even sense-data that are spatial, must have parts and all parts must be simultaneous for the whole to be simultaneous. If there is a simultaneity in events, we cannot see it. Simultaneity must therefore lie in seeing events as appearing to be simultaneous, rather than seeing events that are simultaneous. A mind sees simultaneously because it cannot distinguish the perceptions of events in terms of a succession of 'before and after'. Perceived events in reality are not necessarily simultaneous even they are so seen.

The present can contain 'before events' that are not in the past

We now return to the consideration of before-and-after events existing in the present. The temporal sense of 'before and after' does not always turn an event to a past event, as we can see that a temporal succession can be all at once perceived in the present (without a duration itself). It is only when the present is marked out as a period, will the past then emerge. If an event is a before-event but not in the past, it does not owe its priority to our memory to sustain its existence. Though we may say that all past events are 'before events' of the present, not all before events are past events. If before events can exist without being in the past, then certainly before events can be independent of memory itself. Henri Bergson and those who think that memory plays a part in instituting the temporal notion of 'before and after', would have regarded before events as being synonymous with past events, letting the sense of the past and present constitute the sense of 'before and after'. This I believe to be erroneous. The sense of 'before and after' is certainly independent of the past, and therefore memory.

Oneness in events and succession

When I see two events as before and after, I do not need to recall any event that is memory. What I see is a succession in two events both in my perceptual consciousness contemporarily but not simultaneously. A succession, if I consider it carefully, cannot be at all different from a succession of mini-events within a duration, since a succession is not about objects moving across points in space. An event has a limitation of quantity of time in encapsulating a motion or change to determine a succession. Yet, not all motions or changes have a beginning and an end to determine their successions. What separates two events? Is it time itself? One would almost say that time is in between events that have beginnings and ends. The notion of 'before and after' can quickly remind us that it may not be the case. Consider a case when a before event is immediately followed by an after event without an interval, or at least a perceivable interval in between. If there is no interval between them, there is no time between them. And if so, an interval between two events may destroy the constitution of a succession of 'before and after', if the marking of a succession is by time.

There is now a question of whether two events are or are not really one, if time cannot separate them. If they are one, then there is no sense of 'before and after'. The battle of Leipzig may be before the battle of Waterloo, but is it a separate event within the larger event called the Napoleonic War? If every cessation of movement will constitute the ending of one event, why should not the cessation in every bridge taken, every soldier killed, every musket fired, or every sword struck be an event marking out the end of this battle? Certainly we may do so, but, just as certainly, we need not do so. When and where do we mark out an event from a bigger event, if the help of time is at our disposal? So it is not time that separates two events considered as being before and after. Again it must be men who mark out one event from the rest. The world is a flux of motion even if we do not always see them all.

It would appear that what is needed in conceiving of a succession of events, is the making of a distinction between the two, by using the cessation of an event. The idea of 'before and after' comes after this distinction. Once the marking is done, being before or after a cessation point is immediately apparent. Imagine two separate events: say, a football match starting at 3 p.m. and finishing at 4.45 p.m., and another event, say, singing from 3.30 p.m. to 4.00 p.m.. As these two events are not simultaneous at the start or at the finish, there is no sense in saying that one of these events is before the other. The second event can be said to be later by reference to the starting point, but earlier by reference to the cessation time. The sense of succession in these two unrelated events is by no means as strong as that of events such as tuning a guitar before playing a piece of music from it. The difference here is that the tuning and playing of the same guitar form a naturally continuous event, but football and singing are not considered to be so. The notion of 'before and after' is more than the notion of succession if by succession we mean two events are consecutive, perhaps in the same vicinity. Events of different vicinities can be in the order of 'before and after, and we may be hesitant to call them a succession of events. Again, in considering this sense of 'before and after', it is not the whole duration that is important, but the points of the beginning and end that count, just as it is in simultaneity. The notion of 'before and after' is more to motion, movement and events, since this notion survives the events which are clearly not in succession.

Our temporal nature and our temporal being

Looking at temporal succession, how does seeing the beginning or cessation points of events in 'before and after' set itself apart from seeing motions and changes? We do not see motions occupying intermediate points of space, but we do see beginnings and ends of movements forming duration, and we can infer changes from perceivable differences in the positions of beginnings and ends. These differences are not only spatial, but temporal. And this inference does not proceed from this notion of 'before and after' since we do not see these events. Still, the possibility of inferring a movement does not mean that all movements are inferred. Again, can a movement be inferred with the notion of 'before and after'? Movement too can be perceived no doubt, but only within a perceivable duration, only if there is a perceivable duration in which a movement can be seen.

Since temporal contents are not always deduced from changes, but are in the act of immediate perceiving, it would be unlikely that this notion of 'before and after' is a concept under which perceptual data are pondered and subsumed. Since we can never separate this notion from the very act of perceiving, this thing must be an intuition, just as Kant would have said. But intuition is a mysterious term in that it lies between raw sense-data and conceptual judgements. Not many philosophies actually explain what an intuition is. It is a dust bin for those things we regard neither as raw data nor intellectual judgements. It is for things that we cannot analyse into constituents of concepts, and that we reject as raw data given with an understanding but without an origin. This sense of 'intuition' I shall reject. This thing, 'before and after', is one aspect of our nature; the temporal nature of our temporal being that regulates movements. Without this temporal nature, how can we move at all, let alone act?

Time is not so much seeing an order of things, a temporal order as some may say. Time is seeing and differentiating perceptually the flux, the changes and motions in reality. Berkeley's immaterialism is the philosophy of the static, so that sensations are only impressions within, and it has no answers as to why they are in motion since motion itself cannot be explained alone by our sensibility. When I see an object, it is not only a bundle of primary and secondary qualities or sensations, but a bundle that can change and move. This theory is not suggesting that time and movements are external things perceived by us, but that time has a dual reality, one is minimally external, presupposed by the other possibility of time in perceiving motion, and the other is both subjective and objective. It is subjective in the sense that time itself is internal and in the act of perceiving. It has its objectivity in our nature, as a temporal being and with this nature we are able to perceive motions, and ultimately actions. It is subjective because temporal duration is the marking of the mind. It is objective because time itself does not have duration and parts.

Perhaps time is real in the sense that our subjective, temporal make-up needs such a reality for us to be aware of our own temporal sense, our timescale and temporal organization in thoughts and perceptions. If we ask a question: does motion need time? We shall say time is motion itself.

PART III

IDENTITY, PARTICULARS AND UNIVERSALS

7 Identity and determination

7.1 Identity

Are all things composed of universals ?

Earlier in this book, I argued at length that reality is within existence, so that something can exist without being real, but cannot be real without being an existent. The application and the elucidation of the definitions of 'real' and 'existence' are in this chapter. We reject the notion that existence is within reality, in that something can be real without being an existent, but cannot be an existent without being real. This I shall maintain. This way there will be no beings that are real and not part of empirical existence.

Universals, the things or properties that are never unique and particular, have their place in reality if we believe that they do exist or that they are real. It would not be controversial to say that there is a common belief among us that most things seen to exist are particular things. In fact, the world is full of particular things and it will be a shock to imagine or to be reminded that every particular thing, when analysed into its basic details, is composed of nothing in particular at all. From colours to shapes, in the names and proper names that we employ to label these particulars, we find that they are all but things shared among many other things. This creates obstacles for us in considering anything as a particular if it is totally composed of things shared by many others. Is this world, a world of particulars or universals?

This metaphysical position is important not only because it gives us a reality of abstraction in things, but because the ontological credit given to this abstract reality must entail the possible reality of other even more abstract things than the universals in objects (such as moral principles or mathematical entities). The existence of these intangible universals in reality is very contentious indeed; for if they do exist, many dubious and conceptual entities, such as goodness, truth, virtues, courage or authority may also exist or exist in a reality independent of us. What kind of reality is this world? This is a centuries-old battle fought over with words.

Identity by postulating two entities

Not only do I think that there is a connection, an important connection, between identity and universals, I also think that universals can be explained outside the rationalistic tradition. Identity is a difficulty subject. Identity, as many may see it, seems to concern whether two things are identical or if they are indistinguishable in every respect. Identity can be seen in many metaphysical ways: determination of a substance is one way of identity; identity of things by names or vice versa is another; the sense of independence and uniqueness is also identity in itself. When the Platonists ask, 'This thing is a bed, that thing is a bed and many things are also beds, why should this bed be uniquely a particular bed?', they are applying the same method of identification. For a bed needs to be identified with another bed to sustain the meaning of this word, 'bed', by which it is so called. It is well known that Plato (perhaps as a spokesman for Socrates) was the author of this epistemological problem of universals.

When it comes to identity, one cannot forget what Leibniz has to say about identity. Leibniz in his well-known principle of the identity of the indiscernibles, thinks that if two things have indistinguishable properties, they are necessarily identical. Bertrand Russell thinks that this entails also that it is impossible for two things to be exactly alike in this sense.[12] But, if there is such an entailment, there is a need for another premiss: no two things can have the same properties. This proposes a caution in postulating two things and claiming that they have the same properties. The point here is not whether two things can be the same if they have all common properties, but that the method in identity is not satisfactory by postulating two entities prior to deciding on their identities by referring to their properties.

This erroneous way of thinking about identity can be traced back to mathematical methods which postulate variables without values and assignment of numerical quantities. That variables are 'entities' without properties, is a curious thing in philosophy, since there can be no entity without properties. Variables may be acceptable in mathematics, but are not at all sensible in ontology. Whatever exists must have something that can be conceived for it to exist. The trouble is that it is assumed postulating variables ontologically does not commit us to anything conceivable, and can still commit us to an ontological assertion of entities. Variables that have no specific content or properties demand qualities and values for their inception. Perhaps the property of a variable is in being a variable; but in being variable, it cannot offer an identity, let alone be identified with itself. When we say A, B and C are variables, and if A, B and C have the same quantity, say, 10, then A, B and C are identical. Why must there be an ontological commitment to three entities in the first place? In the spirit of the philosophical principle, 'no entities without identity', any assertion of an entity must cry out for an identity. When there are two things, there must be something that separates them into two and for them not to be one. The postulation of two entities implies a distinction to make a separation so that two things instead of one can be conceived. If there is a distinction, there is a difference (in properties), and if there is a difference, two entities cannot be the same. Thus merely supposing two entities at the outset, embraces the analytical truth that two entities are necessarily distinct. Whatever is distinct from something, cannot be identical with this something which may have common properties with itself. This postulation of two entities in identity has a contradiction that will be carried through to its conclusion.

This Leibnizian way of committing to two entities to find an identity of indiscernible properties is very contentious for me. For I posit that any two entities are by definition and by nature discernible. Therefore, it will be inconceivable to think of and postulate two entities as having indiscernible qualities. This method, I can see, lies also at the heart of Plato's conception of forms or universals (not necessarily the same). A Platonist may say a bed is a bed by virtue of something else. If a bed is a bed by virtue of another bed, they are in this respect the same, and if so, why are there two beds? If the second bed is a bed by virtue of another bed, we can no longer justify the three beds to be so without bringing in a fourth and fifth. An infinite regress is in the offing. This problem is not new and Plato realized this in the so-called 'third-man argument' (Parmenides). Of course, they may reject that bedness itself is in the physical object, and has its own realm of reality in existence. Still, bedness is bedness by virtue of what? My point here is not concerning the truth in Platonic Forms, but the method of identity that partially leads to a conclusion in the existence of Forms (or universals). The similarity between Leibniz's postulation of entities in the method of identity, and Plato's formal identity relying upon another, is quite clear.

Individuation by the identity of position

The individuation of particulars alone is not sufficient to establish successfully their identity, even though we can say that successful identity can imply the individuation of a particular. To start, I shall borrow the premiss that no two things can occupy the same space at the same time. This has been argued before and I do not think that it is very contentious except for the scientific relativists of space and time. I too have argued before that space-time (as opposed to space and time) is not an acceptable reality. For a distance of 60 miles is not identical with

1 hour in a car travelling at 60 miles per hour, even though there is a definite association between them. Nor do I think one needs to commit to the existence of an absolute space to hold that two things cannot occupy two spaces at any one time.

As I have argued before, the relation among parts of space is a constitution of relations upon relations and nothing more, without an input of a fixed and permanent point of reference. The location of a region among other regions in position and direction is only conceivable with reference to a fixed perceptual point (the perceptual self). Thus spaces are relative in regions without being somehow indeterminable since there is a fixed reference. In this way, every space position perceived is in principle identifiable. To be a particular, a thing must be identifiable in its space first. And this identity of space position is not the only consideration over and above that a particular space can only be occupied by only one object.

Individuation of space - two objects cannot occupy the same space

The determination of whether or not the extension of an object is the same as, or distinct from, the space it occupies is not indispensable to a spatial identity either way. Whichever belief we hold, it is not possible to separate the extension from the space an object occupies. Thus the space marked out by a definitive boundary and a definitive position of a body is a particular space and, could not be anywhere else. In this way, an inseparable space marked out by a body, belongs necessarily to the body and cannot be that of another, or occupied by another and still retain the same unique extension it has, in a particular position. We are not trying to imagine a Kantian space (without an object) in order to introduce bodies in it, since it is an extension-cum-body that concerns us - an extension inseparable from a body. Whether a body can shrink or expand its volume, at a certain state of affair, it has a definitive extension, which is impenetrable. A body has an extension and two bodies have two particular extensions, both impenetrable, therefore two particular extensions cannot merge into one because of this impenetrability. Consequently a space or an extension of a body can only be that of a particular body, and a body in space is particular since it has an extension in a identified position belonging to no other except itself.

When we impose a positional reference to this space, it creates a particularity through this identity (of position). Even so, one may argue that if the size and extension of the body are interminable, the body must be of general size and generally extended. If so, it must be said that the body has no particular extension or that it has an indetermined size and shape depending on where and how we look at it. But, if a body has an indeterminate size, how can it exist as a body and in a space that is marked out (determined)?

Particularity of space is the particularity of objects in space

It must be remembered that it is the mind that marks out regions of space, and as such the anomaly of why a mind cannot conceive two objects in the same space, must be explained. This centres on what we have discussed earlier: whether sensibles are inseparable from the extension or the body itself. The problem is that the sensibles are regarded as mental, whether they are sense-data in the Berkelian sense of 'ideas', or as Hume's 'impressions', or Locke's qualities, or as the 'given', but we do not manufacture them in our mind. The marking of a space according to the boundaries of bodies and the contrasting shades and colours, is mental in the same sense as colours are mental (sensations); but colour sensations and the marking of space according to bodies' boundaries, are not manufactured, but applied.

Although the inseparable extension of an object or the space it occupies, is known by sensibility, and if we accept that the sensibles in objects are necessarily inseparable from their extensions, or the spaces they occupy, then they must be inseparable as a matter of fact. Consequently, if every space or region is a particular, and since no other objects can occupy this same space, an object that has extension and occupies a space must be a particular in virtue of this space, even if all properties associated with this space are universals. We may have many beds in front of us and we may not be able to distinguish one bedness from another, but there is no doubt that each of these beds occupies a particular space that can be uniquely identified. Hence we can say, 'this bed is different from that bed'. An object carries with it its extension always, and the consideration of vacating a space at different time is not really relevant, for when we talk about this extension/space, we are talking about an extension that will always occupy one or another space in time, no doubt. An object is particular, whether it is seen with sensibility or regarded as the construct of sensibles, if it occupies a space that can only be a particular space. If a unicorn is a possible percept, it too must be a particular if it occupies a particular space. The question is not whether a unicorn is a particular, but whether a unicorn can be a percept in space. If a unicorn is a mental entity that will never be perceived in space, then the question of whether it is a particular does not arise.

Generality as an identity method cannot provide a particularity

Although identity in the sense of 'A is A' may not lead to the identity of particulars, there is still an expectation that identity can progress towards a confirmation of particularity. If establishing a particularity depends on the success of identification, identity again is problematic. As I have rejected the way of identity by postulating two entities prior to the examination of their sameness, I can see that this postulation can only bring about a generality in every property compared between 'two entities', since it is shared by two entities. I am not sure whether it is a linguistic muddle that such unhelpful postulation of two entities can immediately cause a problem to the determination of particularity in any property referred, since a property which may confirm a particularity by a distinction, will also destroy the identity of the two entities in being one.

I can say that a bed may not be a particular bed by virtue of its bedness, since it is a particular only by virtue of being an object, first and foremost. This way of identity leads to an identity without particularity. How can two things with the same universals be particulars even if they are said to be identical? I see that without the confirmation of particularity independently of identity, the failure of one always undermines the success of the other. For an identity by descriptions is an identity of generality and generality can never substantiate particularity. Perhaps the exposition of this failure should highlight the real function of language, in all its description power that has long been exaggerated in the function of identity or definitive descriptions.

Identity by descriptions

Aristotle sees a way of enquiry into identity, particulars or metaphysical reality, in the subject-predicate form. That is to say that a subject is seen to be predicated of many things and not of itself. Particularity and independence in this way remind us of the quest for the existence of substance. According to Aristotle, a cow is predicated of all colours, shades, sizes and shapes, and still remains a subject with cowness that is more substantive than it is descriptive. This proposes to us a belief that the substance of a particular is constructed out of an objective or innate understanding. This again is a postulation of two entities, the subject and predicates (or a substance and its attributes) proceeding to link these two in an identity question. This time it is not about whether a predicate and a subject are identical, but what relations there are for them. The problem is whether a subject is really independent of its predicates, or whether there is a subject at all without the predicates. For if a subject cannot be independent, there is no sense in any relations at all. If they really belong to each other, why are they two distinct things? If they do not belong to each other, in what sense are they one? What can a thing be without a conceivable predicate?

The problem I see here is the gulf between description and reality. A description will always be a description and can never be the reality it describes or purports to describe. In this scheme of thinking, a subject or a substance is a postulation of reality and predicates are only its descriptions. Reality can only be confirmed if descriptions are 'identical' with reality. Postulating a bit of reality with a description will always be a description in all its verbal reality. In this sense, the pursuit of identity and the pursuit of substance may be seen as one and the same. To leap this quantum gulf is very serious indeed.

Nevertheless, a reality needs to be understood and confirmed, thus, it cannot do without descriptions. And yet this epistemological dependency cannot but create an illusion of reality through a mutual identity, and a possessive relation between reality and its descriptions. But what more can we do, even if we see the problem?

Identity and reality

The hope that a subject is an identity to its predicates, is of course the hope that this identity can confirm the reality that goes with it. Plato saw the impossibility, hence, he rejected the reality of concrete things in favour of that of predicates of generality, which he formalized and called 'forms'. By formalizing, I mean that instead of referring to something by description, say something being 'red', one can turn this predicate into a 'predicate-ness', that is linguistically a subject or conceived as a mental object in itself, in order to avoid a circular question concerning its dependency.

This is the philosophical legacy in postulating qualities (predicates) as well as what is underlying these qualities (the subject), so that the unity of them makes up what particular things there are. Such is the legacy of identity, that the earlier version of Aristotelian philosophy used a subject-predicate form or the Cartesian philosophy that admits the reality of an unchanging substance, is also there for our benefit. This also lays a foundation for the problems in the dualism of mind-body philosophy, since the description of the physical may propose the mind's existence. It is not until Berkeley, that such a dualistic postulation of two entities for an identity exercise was questioned. Berkeley rejected the existence of matter that is identical with or supporting our sensibility (the descriptions, if you like). But Berkeley and Plato's are totally different philosophies that should be disentangled from the similarity both held in rejecting an extra-descriptive reality; one in matter and the other in concrete objects. The distinction between Plato's form and Berkeley's sensibility are epistemologically different because sensibility is confined to empirical experience permitting no sensibility of unicorns and conceptual things such as 'good', 'justice' or 'equality'. This distinction is important in my view so that two kinds of idealism should be marked apart because of their respective epistemological origins. Plato's idealism, of course, can be the modern-day realism, but not Berkeley's.

The attraction of describing our way to identity and reality will not disappear. Nor can there be a definite description succeeding in the attempt to solve the problem of identity. Or, for that matter, that logical variables can be substitutes for such descriptions is not tenable. The root of the problem lies in the inevitability that no matter how persistent and diligent we are in describing an 'object' into reality, the words, descriptions, sensibles, concepts or whatever else we may use, are derivative not only from our understanding first, but from our understanding of other things and applicable to other things; this presupposes a prior understanding which of course renders all descriptions of reality universal. Perhaps one who is Berkelian at heart may try in vain to construct a particular object by descriptions alone. But one must not forget that Berkeley is talking about the sensibility, which is merely descriptive. If we consider descriptions and predicates as logical variables, these variables can never be substituted with definitive values unless there is such a thing as a definitive value of reality. To construct a reality with variables is to avoid a commitment to the definite identity of things, it may succeed to tell a relation, but it will have no epistemological value to men.

The popular view that there is such a thing as intersubjectivity suggests that the identity of things can confer itself upon our understanding by the mutual agreement between a speaker and a hearer. In my view there are two ways of looking at speaker-hearer identity of things. First, an intersubjective agreement between two persons conferring a definite identity of things is arguably possible, because if reality is only a private affair how can agreements be possible? The other way is the confirmation of an identity by others who share our respective, immediate perceptual experience. I hope the more plausible is the latter. The idea that an agreement may presuppose a reality and identity relies not so much on the truth and meaning of the speaker and hearer's common beliefs, but on the presumption that reality and identity somehow must be presupposed if agreements among people are in fact possible. There cannot be a collective test on, or justification for, their respective private experience to determine the validity of this identity claim.

Intersubjectivism is (mythical) subjectivism all the same. As to the question of why there should be any agreement, if reality is nothing but private and subjective, it should be observed that any presupposed reality is no more certain than a presupposed similarity existed between the speaker and the hearer. Nothing in our search for reality or an identity through sensibility and descriptions, can be said as lacking an understanding, and yet we are discontent with all descriptions that may well be shared among us. This brings out a question as to the strength of speaker-hearer identity, in terms of the number of speakers or hearers who so happen to agree or understand an identity proposed. Even if it is not, can both speaker and hearer make the same mistake? Or can more speakers and hearers reduce the chances of misidentification? What is the significance of an interpersonal agreement confirming and identifying reality or things, if one person should fail? This applies too to mutually agreed perceptual experiences between two people.

Identity in my view is not about whether something is the same as another, or several entities are identical through a space and time continuum, for reasons given before. To me, the way of identity is to lay bare what we can say of it. This may or may not be complete in identifying it, but at least we have not committed to the existence of two entities to begin with. A successful identity of a thing depends on the object being identified as a particular, and this is conferred by the space it occupies particularly; therefore a successful identity is space-associated since all particulars exist with space and in space. This can only be done in an immediate perceptual presence and nowhere else. Everything else we can say of a thing in space consists of descriptions, sensibility, concepts or universals that are not of particularity, since they presuppose prior understanding of other things.

7.2. Universals and identity

Generality needs particularity for its exposition

If a thing is the sum total of all that can be said of it and all that can be said of it is nothing but generality, a thing is nothing but a complex generality, save for the space it occupies. Generality, no matter how complex, cannot be particular and therefore cannot identify an individual. Of course, it can be disputed as to whether all that can be said of a thing is necessarily of generality; for instance, is colour sensation general or particular? Without going too far into this at this juncture, I shall remind myself that the space, which is inseparable from this bundle of generality, is not something that is said of this generality; instead, it is the generality that is said of this space. For space is the void or nothingness that adds nothing to generality, but generality has content that can add to the emptines of space. Let us take colours or other sensible qualities of an object for example. They are a bundle of generality because a 'red' in one object can also be the 'red' in other things. How then can a space, being inseparable from redness, be something apart from the generality of redness? But, I do not see there is any inconsistency here. An answer to this should breach the divide between the epistemological and metaphysical realities. It lies in a claim that generality is not separable from the instances of its manifestation.

Imagine seeing a patch of redness in front of me; calling it red is not an admission that this redness (of this particular patch) is a general redness. Far from it. Even though I call it red and call something else red too, this patch of redness is distinct from all other red things because of the space it is associated with. If I see two patches of redness, I can distinguish them not by reference to a colour, but by their spaces connected to this redness. Redness may be a generality, but a patch of redness is not. Redness itself may be conceptual, presupposing and sharing with something else, but a patch of redness is a combination of a direct perceptual content and its conceptual identity (determination). We cannot imagine redness without it being of a definitive spatial shape and in a position. Hence there is the distinction between the instances of direct perceptual, spatial content (which confers particularity) and instances of conceptual determination (which confers generality). A generality is conceptual and whatever is conceptual requires instances of particularity to be conceived. We will consider generality as relations later so as to reaffirm this claim. Perhaps mathematical concepts are not conceivable without the assumption of the existence of the instances in its variables, just as numbers cannot be conceived without objects or limitations.

Spatial content and the sum total of its properties

Again, the idea that a thing is the sum total of its properties can sometimes be taken as an acknowledgement of an existent falling or being subsumed under the properties that are said of it; this kind of identity requires positing an entity to subsume these properties under itself. It is not clear whether there is an ontological priority in the things subsumed under another or in the thing under which others are subsumed. If not, space that is emptiness can be said to be something over and above the sum total of all properties, or that under which properties are subsumed.

Of course, if there is an ontological priority, there are two distinct entities, and an identity cannot be established; for if one thing can exist before another, this thing must not be identical with the other. Therefore, a thing that subsumes all its properties under itself, has an identity problem in explaining why they are one or why one belongs to the other. In an attempt to say that a thing has properties, instead of positing that a thing is the sum total of the properties, one has to commit to an ontological existence of a thing over and above the properties. The question is whether the properties belong to a thing, or whether there is nothing else except the sum total of these properties. The former is problematic as explained, but for the latter to be sensible, we must see what these properties are. If properties are nothing but the 'thing' itself, are they more than mental? This is the question we have looked at in discussing reality. If properties are mental, they certainly are not different from concepts. If a 'thing' is not identified with its properties, we can we go down this route without positing a prior entity apart from its properties?

Space occupied by a thing, coexists with its properties, and there is no need for a consideration for its priority over these properties. A space is emptiness and may perhaps be the source of all the minimal identity of all things.

Of all the things that are mental and that can be said of an object, they may be of two types. One is that which cannot be dissociated from its space, its content and position. The other is that which has no spatial content and position. Perceptual concepts are of the first type that is always spatial and positional. The rest are conceptions and images assuming that generality can be conceived without instances. This distinction is a convenient assumption. Thus, a patch of redness as a perceptual content is of the first type and redness itself is the second type. A perceptual image recalled from memory is the second type. In this way, perceptual content together with its particular space and position can be considered as having both of these aspects. The empirical reality in this sense is either metaphysical, which reveals itself to us without words in our immediate perceptual awareness, or epistemological which reveals in our understanding.

Determination and identity

Postulating two entities to determine an identity is self-defeating. Postulating two things in an immediate perceptual experience, in order to determine an identity can be absurd, since two things in space are necessarily distinct. But there is a sense that to identify something is not to identify it to be the same as another, or a thing in our mind (memory). To identify is to understand what a thing is, without going through a process of comparing. It does not mean that we do not borrow conceptual properties shared among other things, in order to understand about a thing. This is a way of substituting 'identity' with the understanding of a particular. Properties have a reality in the constancy in association, and this constancy of association will allow us to answer the question: 'is this stone the same stone I saw yesterday?'. How do we call this 'identity' if I have already dismantled the meaning of identity by substituting it with understanding?

The identity posed by the question is an identity with the postulation of two entities, this we have chosen to abandon. Two entities in space cannot be the same, and this we have abandoned too. There is still the possibility that two posited entities are in space and in the mind. When the mind cannot conceive a distinction, the question of distinction and sameness will not arise. If an object in memory is distinct from the stone I see now, this is only a temporal distinction. The fact that I can mention them as two entities, implies a temporal distinction which renders them not logically the same, and there is no sense in supposing that they can be the same. If I claim that this stone is the same one I saw yesterday, I must have many assumptions such as its continual existence without interference. In this case, the expression 'the same stone I saw yesterday' is not an identity statement, but a description that I remember from yesterday, about the stone at present. Therefore, if it is an 'identity' by comparison, it is effectively an acknowledgement sought about something being seen now, in having a property of being 'a stone I saw yesterday'. For a stone of yesterday is not a perceptual existent for comparison. We are now changing a purported identity into a descriptive property involving the past. I shall call this a predication of identity. This is a proposal of predicates or of generality, and not an identity of a particular. Identification is practised by attributing predicates to a perceptual space that will guarantee a particularity. If one can say that the concept of a thing is the concept of an identifiable, I shall say that the concept of a thing is the concept of the identified (in space). For 'identifiable' is determinate; anything that is indeterminate is non-existing.

To the idea that there is no substance without identity, I would add that, at this metaphysical level, existence and identity are simultaneous; space and sensibility are simultaneous and inseparable. The importance of what I call perceptual content (involving space and time) cannot be marginalized, so that this important combination of spatial and conceptual content all at once, lies in the heart of my way of thinking not only of universals, but also of reality as a whole. These contents are our determination of a thing in existence. Determination should therefore replace identity. There is no substance without determination, and there is no determination with spatial identity and particularity.

Singularity and universals

Particularity involves the term 'singularity,' which is really part of its concept, rather than its substitute. A class is more a singularity than a particularity. The conception that a singularity by virtue of its meaning is indivisible, is not conceived by importing an imagery of a region of space. For a space by virtue of its nature is forever divisible. A singularity without space is only conceived as 'oneness' and oneness itself has no natural property except in its conception to be so in the mind. Oneness is a limitation defined by the mind. Hence if one seeks a singularity, one may also consider the identity of a class or a class of classes and so on. In this sense, a singularity is no longer an individual marked out in space, but a group marked out from the rest. This again will show the peculiar way a mind can define a singularity by limitation. Without an imposed singularity, a class of two classes is nothing but two classes; merely subsuming them into one will not make them a class. Classes have similarity and differentiation as criteria and by their mere imposition we cannot make a class of things as a singularity. Perhaps mathematicians may allow classification as a number game, all the same, even if deductions are possible involving classes of classes. The idea of universals is the idea of class and classes, in how we see similarity and distinction among all things. Or we may say, it is the idea of how all things are seen in class and classes, within their similarity and distinction. Or we can say, all things are understood or identified by describing their similarities and distinctions with other things.

Universals and reality

The problem of universals, as I see it, lies at the heart of the philosophy of reality (metaphysics). The argument of whether 'reality' is mere appearance or more than appearance, should pave the way to determine whether one should believe in the existence of universals or not; or what kind of existence or reality there is to subsist universals. For some will have you believe that universals are real, but do not exist. There is a fatal logic in both beliefs that universals exist and do not exist. For those who believe that all that exists in reality is only sensibility, as well as that there can be a logical and substantive world, independent of sensibility, it would be hard to reject or dismiss the existence of universals altogether; for they say that we cannot talk of things without presupposing their existence, just as we have to presuppose the existence of things in order to find their place in our sensibility.

To talk of universals, we must first focus on differences and similarities. For generality is no more than a similarity shared by many things. And every difference not only implies an understanding of the similar, but also an understanding of the difference. An understanding is of course possible through the understanding of generality, if it is not of generality itself. But to say there are similarities and differences, we must assume the existence of two or more things. Therefore, the determination of one thing in fact relies on the understanding of two or more; every aspect of this particular thing will become a generality since it involves more than itself. If all sensible things are particulars in space, no sensible things are general. And yet every sensible thing is arguably reducible to items of generality. How is this so paradoxical? One would be an empirical idealist to reject the reality of universals in the belief that reality should not go beyond things that can be sensed and perceived, and that the distinction between universals and sensible things is not metaphysical but epistemological. Plato is not a phenomenologist or an empirical idealist whose reality is merely appearances. But he does not reject the existence of sensible things, which he holds, though not being real, partake in the reality of universals or Forms. It may be odd to some that such two 'similar' idealisms (both reject the reality of concrete objects in their own ways) can be so significantly different in their approach as to embrace the existence of universals on the one hand and to reject them in a contrasting way, on the other. Again, I remind readers of my slogan, 'reality within existence' instead of 'existence within reality'. Thus the Platonic reality of universals is a reality rejected since it is outside existence. By rejecting the reality of universals as outside our realm of sensible existence, we are in a position to say that there can be things that exist but are not real. Whatever reality universals have, it must therefore be within the existence governed by our sensibility.

Abstraction and being simple

The rejection of universals cannot be argued from within our sensibility; this is seen in the problem in attempting to abstract concepts from particular things. For if a generality is not seen as a part of a particular thing without its ceasing to be a particular, and if whatever can be abstracted does not come from the particular thing itself, what can be abstracted that are said of this particular thing? If there is anything that can be abstracted from an object, it must be first identified with the object; and if so, what is this abstraction of something not identified with the object? This is the problem in the abstracted thing, being, on the one hand, identified with that from which it is abstracted, and on the other hand, not identified with that which is abstracted. In both cases, abstraction is futile since it does not help the identity of the thing. When I say that A is abstracted from B, I assume that A originally belongs to B and this abstraction is a way to show that 'A-ness' in B can be abstracted from it. If redness comes not from the object, it makes no sense to say that the ontological origin of redness comes from an object and can be abstracted.

If whatever abstracted is a concept, and if universals are concepts, then there is no need for any abstraction if concepts do not belong to objects. For an objective reality demands that whatever abstracted is part of that reality. What is necessary for the identification of a thing is more than having concepts for it to fall in. Hence space and its particularity are this additional thing by which a thing is identified over and above the concepts it falls in. In this respect, I cannot say that because things in space partake in concepts, they are concrete objects, since things in space are already concrete objects with or without partaking in concepts. Instead, I would consider that it is concepts that are attributed to objects in space. In this sense too, a particular cannot be simple since being simple, it will not have a number of properties or have parts within itself. Every object in space has parts. A tree has branches and leaves and yet a particularity is conferred to it in being one, unifying all parts through relations and space. When one talks of being simple, one is possibly talking about a substance, the simplicity of which allows it to be independent of other things. In this sense, concrete objects are not substances.

Universals considered to be mental, but objective

Plato thinks that his Forms exist in a separate realm of reality, outside the subjective realm (the mind perhaps) and the physical realm. There is also the possibility that universals can be thought of as objective and still being mental. Some think that things mental may only be subjective, in the sense that being subjective lacks the sense of regularity, law, reasons or necessity in the things considered, conferring a sense of arbitrariness. To be mental as well as objective is to have all these things. This philosophy (particularly advocated by Kant) may regard universals, as being objectively mental. Russell regards Kant's transcendental philosophy as an attempt towards an epistemological truth rather than a metaphysical truth. He thus wrote of Kant's philosophy: 'The transcendental (or epistemological) argument...is more definite than the metaphysical argument'.[13] He obviously regards any truth coming from a transcendental argument is epistemological, rather than metaphysical. Thus the metaphysical reality of universals is not a foregone conclusion even if we accept the epistemological reality or its transcendental arguments. From a rationalist point of view, these ideas hold the key to whether there is a difference between the understanding of reality and reality itself, or whatever a transcendental reality is all there is for us.

For if how we see the world is not imposed upon us from outside, but from within, what else is there from within, apart from reality? If reality is imposed from within, why not everything else, including perhaps our freewill too? In our experience, given closer investigation and reflection, things are conceived differently at different times. Objectivity, or mental objectivity, cannot explain errors, misconception and disagreement, unless you blame it on our frailty. But if you do, what is the sense of this objectivity? If such objectivity has any truth, that which is imposed upon us to see things as they are, cannot be otherwise. Things mental are naturally disputable. A mental objectivity, such as some a *priori* knowledge, depends on the idea of an independent way of thinking and seeing the world, so that our understanding of it cannot be questioned even if it is mental. One can almost hear readers shouting out that it is the understanding imposed by objectivity that is unalterable. In other words, it is our mode and way of thinking that are objective rather than the content of our thinking and conceiving that is objective. This objectivity lies in the 'rules' of thoughts (or perhaps intuitions). Still, if this is the case, how can we say that something is independent of our thinking or intuition and yet constitutes the thinking itself (the mental aspect)? This is a great mystery.

Generality and meaning

There is the view that universals are conceptualized generality, by nature mental, subsumed under the particulars of things; and that universals are verbal so that their representation is general, but their referential meaning is not. Although I have sympathy for the former view, such a scheme cannot lead to an identity of particularity in things already presupposed as particulars, since subsuming a particular is to admit its existence first. If we subsume things under general concepts, the things will always be general concepts, albeit in bundles of them. This view cries out for an identity of something else, without the sole reliance on general concepts. In the latter, the introduction of a general representation by words is even more problematic. We must first explain the role of language if words are the third thing that separates the world from the conceptualizing 'mind'.

It is possible, perhaps even true, that words can never confirm or definitively describe a particularity, and all that there is to be referred by words is nothing but generality. If words are all about generality, how can we arrive at a reality of particulars through words? And how can we arrive at a third reality of generality distinct from the generality of words? This of course demands an explanation for the world-word relation. The philosophical enthusiasm in words' magic, their expressional content and their importance, seems to help many accept a hope propelling the significance of language to a new height, in being the key to the confirmation of reality.

Let us examine this argument: since words reflect generality, they must reflect the generality of the world, otherwise how can we explain the general conditions under which these words are to have an objective meaning understood by many? This argument is effectively saying that the public meaning of words presupposes a factual condition by which the meaning is understood publicly, and that if the meaning is referring to generality, there must be a factual generality that serves as a condition for such a public understanding. This is, of course, Wittgensteinian in origin. To say that every public meaning must presuppose a factual condition for its understanding, is to say that there must be a factual condition for every word, such as unicorn, squared circle, class of classes, and so on. A detailed refutation of this philosophy is not within the scope of this book. But, basically, the objection to this lies in the denial of the entailment, from the existence of public meaning or understanding, to the necessity of factual conditions for public meaning or understanding. Such a denial must of course be supplanted with an alternative explanation of a possibility of how public meaning or understanding is possible without such presupposition.

Traditionally, the problem of universals is seen as a problem of whether they are merely attributes, properties or predicates and never the substance, particular objects, or even conceptual objects. Plato's 'objectification' of attributes or predicates is too religious in its connotation for many to take it serious. However, serious debates will be found wanting to determine whether these attributes can have an existence independent of the mental. Furthermore, the origin of a general term and its problem in identity should be explained. We shall now explore this.

7.3. Universals and human values

Defining a particular

Earlier, I have made a distinction marking out the perceptual attributes from the conceptual attributes, by reference to the particularity of space, which is inseparable from the former. All we can say of these 'spatial universals' is that space is inseparable from them without assuming a priority of space or its universals, or each identity, by discerning each other. 'Basic particulars' are these bundles of spatial, perceptual attributes, inseparable into two, and not mutually identical. These are not particular things with their separate and independent perceptual attributes. A particular thing is a particular space with a bundle of attributed perceptual qualities. I use this word 'attributed' not to mean that they are attributes of something, but attributes to a nothing, that is, a space. 'Nothing' here is not the inconceivable, but the capacity to be filled (with attributes).

Apart from these perceptual attributes, there are no conceptual attributes that are said to be seen within objects or found in objects. A bed has no bedness seen in it. There are no sense-data that can mark out a courageous man, stoneness, tableness and chairness. Anyone who tries to construct a bed from sense-data will be foolish. Courage, stoneness, tableness and chairness are conceptual 'attributes' not found in our sensibility nor in any basic metaphysical exposition of our senses. Only sensible data of a spatial particularity, such as a patch of blue or red (as opposed to blueness or redness), a position, a size or a shape, are purely perceptual 'attributes'. That is not to say that there is no conceptual element involved in a perceptual attribute marked out by a space. It is the nature of our perception that data are necessarily conceptualized (conceptualized because we need to recognize them and understand them) but inseparable from its spatial content which marks them out from other bundles of conceptual attributes.

Determination of generality

Since all conceptual 'attributes' are not necessarily seen within and contained in an object, they must be imposed by the mind. Here comes the question of arbitrariness in such imposition. In this way, the attribution of concepts to data in space has two aspects in both being rigid and changeable. It is rigid (not in the sense of being logically necessary), when public understanding and agreement are called for; it is changeable when these attributes vary through the course of time, influenced by knowledge acquired. A bed is a bed by convention that is not wholly arbitrary, since conventionally men sleep horizontally, and have a general range of heights, the love of softness and warmth. These are determinable human features that decide a generality of a thing. A generality is not determinable outside us, but within us. Of course a bed can be used to sit on or burned as fuel. The generality attributed to objects of perceptual attributes, is not a matter of arbitrariness manufactured by the mind, it is partly imposed by our nature through our intellect, which explains both the rigidness and variety. Our nature supplies this rigidness and our interpretation of this nature supplies this variety.

Relations

There can be no universals if there are no similarity and distinction among things and thus they can be thought to be relations of things in this respect. It is through similarity and distinction, a thing is understood, or identified (in the sense of understanding in terms of something else). This 'in terms of' is a relation, and can only be a relation. To understand something is to understand in terms of something else. There is a circularity in that if something is understood in terms of another, how far do we have to go to justify the understanding of this 'another', without relying on this 'something' in turn. Thus, a relation is ultimately anchored to something within us and is not understood in terms of something else.

Universals and relations conceived outside the physical and the mental

Some have argued that universals are independent of both the world-things (like Plato's) and of the mental governance (like Kant's). Bertrand Russell wrote:

> It seems plain that it is not thought which produces the proposition (relation) 'I am in the room'. It may be true that an earwig is in my room, even if neither I nor the earwig nor anyone else is aware of this truth; for this truth concerns only the earwig and the room, and does not depend upon anything else. Thus relations...must be placed in a world which is neither mental nor physical.[14]

Russell here puts the problem in the setting of a world that can be known without a perceiver. If the earwig and the room have a relation that is not known (as opposed to 'being seen') to anyone including the earwig, there is no possible conception of the proposition - 'an earwig is in the room', and the truth as such does not exist since the proposition has not existed. The existence of any proposition implies the existence of its owner, and therefore a perceiver of facts, who can confirm or disaffirm this expression. I regard this to be self-evident. This is the classic case of the no-ownership principle that cannot be defended unless a world independent of perceptual minds is assumed, and even such an assumption cannot explain the extra-sensual (physical) conception of relations, such as a simple bed or the room-earwig relation. As I have argued in the earlier part of this book, relations are only possible when an existential being (i.e. a self) is postulated as a permanent reference point to measure them all. Still, relations are forever relations without a sense of value in their determination. A earwig and its room are evaluated entities and identity, hence a relation is conceivable. Where the earwig is within the room, is determinable if a perceiver of this fact (a reference) is presupposed. To say that an earwig is in a room generally (somewhere) but not in a particular place, is also a determined relation since we all know that a room has a space inside it, and this general assumption is based on another relation. To speak of an earwig in a room without a particular perceptual point for its identifiable relation with the room, is to speak of the non-identity of the room, of the earwig or of its position, for any earwig in existence must be at a particular place. If this relation is understood only through the physical world and if this relation depends on the understanding of physical things, how can this relation be even conceived without the understanding of identity? An earwig cannot be conceived to be in a room, if we do not understand at least that a room has a space within and an earwig is an extended being. A relation is a generality of particular things, but never a generality of another generality. The latter is a conceptual relation rather than a world relation. Russell has put the relation of a earwig and a room, in a relation of another generality, in the world of the conceived and the unperceived. This ultimately depends on other world-relations. Even Plato, the originator of this problem, was aware of this circularity, hence he has his 'third-man argument' in *Parmenides*. If we take it a little further, we can say that a most general statement still requires relational understanding, even if we reject all its physical, mental content or origin.

The point here posited is to reject the idea that relations and universals are not mental, or worse still, that they are neither mental nor physical. The possibility of a third realm of reality (not mental and not physical) is not necessary and cannot be grounded on a no-ownership principle, which is itself unsustainable. Berkeley has attempted the same and he ends up with a third reality in the consciousness of God.

Russell also thinks that a spatial relation (the example he gives is a positional relation between London and Edinburgh) can exist absolutely without anyone knowing what the North and the South are. A person cannot detach himself from his imagination to conceive a spatial position. Without a permanent reference point there cannot be a determined position of the sun, or the 'top' of the earth; there cannot be a determined direction of the earth's spinning motion, and consequently its North and South. In positing directions and positions, we take it for granted that our imaginary survey of space carries always ourselves as a referential point from which all notions of position, such as left, right, top, bottom, East, West, North or South, are marked. What we should not forget is that the London-Edinburgh relation (or indeed other relations too) is not just about Edinburgh being at a different place from London, but rather, that the conception of North or South speaks more about two different places. This additional something is the human connection associating with things in a way that cannot be explained in terms of mere relations. There is a difference between saying London is South of Edinburgh and saying they are at different places.

The typical dilemma in the philosophy of universals is this. On the one hand, it rejects that relations exist in the mind, maintaining that relations are there whether there is a perceiver or not. On the other hand, when the question is posed as to the origin of these relations, it will say that there is nothing physical that can determine a relation itself. (There is nothing in London or Edinburgh that suggests a North-South relation.) So it is not a coincidence that relations as well as universals have to come out of the physical and the mental realms of reality. Russell wrote:

> ... that the relation 'north of' does not seem to exist in the same sense in which Edinburgh and London exist. If we ask 'where and when does this relation exist?' the answer must be 'Nowhere and nowhen'. There is no place or time where we can find the relation 'north of'. It does not exist in Edinburgh any more than in London.[15]

This difficulty is so profound that it needs the invention of a third realm of reality to get out of it.

Basically, it all reduces to something like this: either it is something that does not exist in the mind, but is 'apprehended' by it, or it is something, such as whiteness itself that is not in the mind, but the thought of it is in the mind. It seems that we are stretching the meaning of 'existence' to its limit. To say that something is 'apprehended' by the mind and yet exists not in it, is to say that we can comprehend in our mind something that does not exist in it. That is totally unsatisfactory. If there is a different type of existence, we must find out the sense in which it may appear to our understanding. If one type of existence is of the lower order, being temporal, or limited in time; this I can imagine. If I am forced to consider a timeless and absolute existence, I cannot imagine the existence of such; for I am a temporal being who can imagine no situations where I am not the supposed perceiver in a time that goes beyond my consciousness. And even if there is such a possibility, I would not know it. Still as this is the writing of Russell, his reputation must add extra-verbal truth in whatever he writes giving comfort to lesser mortals than himself.

Universals are relations, or references to relations

Let us consider the distinction between an object of thought and thinking itself. It can be examined in conjunction with their mutual implication. There is no thought without a content. Therefore a thought does not exist independently of its content and the object of thought cannot be separated from having a thought. Even if a universal in a thought is distinct from thinking itself, it will be a particular thought to take away its universality, if the object of thought is considered independently of everything else. I think of bedness in its generality so that one or more objects of bedness are considered in this relation; this makes bedness itself a universal. If bedness itself is given as a thought's object or content without relating to anything else, it must be a particular thought; so, how can it be a universal or general thought? Furthermore, what do we say of the thought of a thought of a universal? If every thought has an object distinct from itself, will the thought of a thought of a universal, have an object of a thought of a universal?

If a universal can be thought of by another person too, it is not only a private object of thought itself, but a public object of thoughts for us all. This brings to mind Wittgenstein's idea of public language by which a reality is assumed because of the public, linguistic reference. If so, these thought-objects may be publicly understood not in terms of other things (relations), but 'apprehended' publicly without them. And if so, what is the need for language in being instrumental to public understanding? It is my view that what we can agree among ourselves is not our private thought or private object, but a constancy or consistency in relations among things (as opposed to relations themselves). There are no objects of thoughts, but content of thoughts so that this content is not something that is ontologically distinct from thinking itself, for thinking without content is not thinking at all. If we take my line of reasoning, there is no need for us to postulate a thought of a thought, or an object of thought, or the risk of an infinite regress.

Universals are relations conceived of things and not in things (whatever that may be). They are the determination and understanding of things by relations, hence they are relations. Their generality comes about because a relation is an understanding in terms of other things; if these things are nowhere to be found then relations remain forever relations without evaluation through experience. In other words, universals are like mathematical variables that confer relations without values. We can only determine and understand things through relations, that is why we claim that one aspect of reality is in the totality of all things in conceived relations. Evaluation of relations comes about in two ways. When we speak of particular things in space and time in relation, we evaluate these relations, endowing them with true particularity of our present, immediate and vivid perceptual content, which is the 'unspeakable' and raw. Speaking of these data is in fact putting them in relations with other things through understanding and determination. In this sense all words are universals too.

Universals and natural attributes

Even though the attribute of 'bedness' may not be unshakeably associated with a thing, there are attributes that may seem to confer an 'essence', without being the accidental and conceptual nature of the thing. When we focus on something close to its basic making or essence, the question of its being, whether accidental or essential, will surface. When we speak of gold or oxygen for instance, we do not refer only to its conceptual generality (for what it may amount to), but also its perceptual attributes and its constancy in a relation to other things. For instance, when I say that this is a piece of gold, I am referring to, among others, a relation exemplified by what may happen if it is dropped into acid, or a relation referring to its assumed atomic composition, such as the atomic-weight ratio to hydrogen. This universal relation concerning the essence of a thing is not only about our conceived relation but is in essence the constancy of certain relations among things. Whereas other conceived relations may not have a constancy in this way.

If diamond and graphite are supposed to be composed of the same element, i.e. carbon, one would expect their respective nature and essence are the same. The sameness is about 'carbon' basically, and not diamond and graphite themselves. But, in fact, many of diamond properties are not the same as that of graphite. Even if a conceptual excuse is brought about to explain this anomaly, their constant relations remain. The nature of things in being what they are, is not due to their 'elementary make-up', basic and fixed, but due to a permanency underlying their relations among things. What is elementary to a thing is not only what can be observed, but also what can be conceptualized through testing, associating or comparing. That is to say, if the arrangement of the atoms of carbon can explain the difference in properties between these two things of the same make-up, it is a permanency or consistency in these relations that explains, rather than anything considered as elementary, physical and observable.

The permanency of associations is a matter for nature unseen, discovered by the understanding of relations, and not by the conception of being (a conception independent of empirical verification). For instance, the relation between the redness of a bottle and that of a book is a relation of resemblance, but if every bottle we see is red and every book we see is also red, then there will be a constancy of relation between these bottles and books, making possible the claim that this paper and that glass are of the same make-up. It is through this reality of constancy that things are associated with phenomena, so that a scientific reality can suggest a possibility of the existence of things in having more than their sensible qualities, without sensing what they are.

So far universals are not sensibles, or inherent in sensibles or in what we may call, the physical. We have rejected that they are outside both the physical and the mental. Universals, we say, are relations and also constant relations. These relations are judged and determined in the mind. The reason for the Platonists in rejecting the claim that they are mental is not so much based on metaphysical grounds, as it is based on the epistemological significance of their origin. By admitting that they are mental in origin, the Platonists cannot reconcile between the arbitrariness of the mind and the absolute nature in the standards of these things acquired by the mind. Hence this ambiguous ontological claim of the non-physical (sensible) and the 'non-mental' is rejected by us.

Relations and values

Still for all the questionable conclusions, the epistemological origin of universals must be explained if they are not in things or in our subjective thought of things. This origin is actually well implicated in all the perceptual data that require judgement of relation and identity, since we are not 'seeing' and 'thinking' machines looking not for justification of these judgements. For it is in judgements that universals will appear, whether they are judgements of something or not of something outside ourselves. Universals are not outside us even if they are not inherent in things outside. If so, universals must be in some ways mental in origin. If they are considered as connected to all existential questions and yet not the existents themselves, they are, therefore, relations among existents, measured through the self. If there is nothing outside pointing to their origin, we must look deeper beyond our rationality, because rationality only explains and understands an ontological source, but is never itself an ontological source. If we look at our perceptual data and our judgements of them, we see how these universal relations are determined independently of sense-data - the 'unspeakable' data. For, no sooner do I speak of a sense datum, than it immediately becomes something verbal (judgemental). By this, I mean sense-data without determination and judgement are epistemological nothingness, which we can only point to, never describe, since describing them is to make judgement of relations, or to determine by relations. Universals are relations. But a relation cannot subsist on its own without things other than itself. The self comes in at this stage, not in an act of perceiving or judging, but as a standard and evaluation of relations.

In our constant search to fulfil our nature, we plan our acts, anticipate nature and understand one another's actions, so that the world is not just a world of sensible qualities, but a world bearing on us and our needs (not necessarily desires of the flesh), that subsist within our nature. Intellect is not self-subsisting to be nurtured for its own sake. Intellect is to serve man's nature in all its vanity, eagerness to know, among many things of his needs. These needed judgements are judgements of relations, since all judgements (from that of a simple colour datum to mathematical formulae) are about relations. Demanded by every judgement and determination to serve our actions, are our values.

It is through these values, relations are no longer variables and quantities, but qualities. Everything named has in itself a reference to something else so that it is so determined and understood. But as to this 'in-terms-of-what' is to be used to determine a thing, we say that it is determined in terms of human values in human nature, which is the origin of all universals.

Consequently, values - human values, are conceived as things that are not contained or inherent in sensible objects. This definition of universals fits in both relation and its value. Hence universals are also relations with values. A chair has values in terms of its functions or in terms of whatever way that may serve me in a moment of need. And my need is well etched in the meaning I conceive in determining this thing called a chair. Let me go through some explanations to see how relations or universals are derivative from the human-world relation; how their origins are explained and how their 'abstraction' (not from objects) from understanding is possible.

Particularity in metaphysical reality (sensing) and generality in epistemological reality (understanding, identity and determination)

First we shall look at a sensible attribute such as a patch of white. A patch of colour is not an identity or a particular, unless we are referring also to the particular space. But then colour (not a patch of white) is a general term that cannot be associated with a space, since we only see a patch of white, blue, or red, and never a patch of colour. The particularity and the existence of a patch of 'white' cannot be doubted, but we can doubt what we mean or determine as 'white'. 'White' itself is a general term needing something else for its ontological determination, but the 'white' in a patch is a sensation that exists with or without our verbal determination. Since it is so, how do we come to name or determine it or understand it? To say something of a sensation or to understand it, is to bring it under a general term (a relation) and not to give it an independent identity. If so, there must be a distinction between the sense-data (spatial) and their 'names', 'understanding' and 'identity' (their relations). In other words, there is a distinction between the unspeakable sensations and the speakable sense-data (ones that are brought under relations and generality). Some consider that to be impossible, because if we cannot identity them or bring them under relations, there is nothing there; or because if the public understanding of them (in term of the names we use) is possible, it will have presupposed their metaphysical reality; or because if the thing that can be identified by more than one persons, it cannot be an exclusive existent in our own mind.

To overcome this, I have to mention again the constancy of relations. Assuming in the example of 'a patch of white', that the term 'patch' is understood without raising another issue, and if I see a patch of 'something' about which I deliberately do not tell others (i.e., what it is), others may ask me what is it that I have seen. I point to the same feature in several objects. Others seeing these objects will understand what this 'something' is, without knowing what sensation I have had. If the features of these objects have a constancy in similarity, and are always there for our verification, this constant 'similarity' is in fact what we agree upon which is not the actual sensation itself. In this way, a generality about which we all agree is a constancy of subjective relations, and the particular sensibility itself is beyond words. We come to understand our sensible things according to their constancy of relations (through words and concepts) and never understand them as things in themselves. Understanding and verbal identity are never about our perceptual particulars, which are beyond public or verbal identity.

The question as to how I know that this 'white' is constantly 'similar' to all other 'whites' I have experienced of several objects, is a matter of true identity or determination. This I have said is not about contemplating two entities to see if they have all the same properties. Identity is about how we determine what a thing is, within the scheme of understanding in terms of relations and values. For in my private world I cannot make a determination, if the whiteness at this moment may be different from the whiteness of another moment, postulated as two entities. And being two, they are necessarily distinct. However, how we can determine and understand a thing in relations, presupposes a prior understanding of other things in these relations, in their identity and determination. In so doing, I do not need to accommodate the argument that an agreement of our private perceptual content presupposes a universal reality independently of my own perceptual particularity.

Similarity and identity

The explanation of an identity with or without postulating two entities in a search for an indiscernibility, depends on the term 'similar' and whether this term presupposes a prior concept of what it has picked out. Again, the postulation of two entities to find a sameness or similarity between them, will presuppose the knowledge as to why two features in two entities are discernible or indiscernible. Certainly this way of marking a distinction or sameness needs a conceptual standard to pick out distinctions and sameness. Now if we imagine that men are computers and machines, one must supply the machines a criterion to mark out differences or pick out sameness. Even if we say a machine can memorize what marks out distinctions and similarities in differentiation or identification, there must be a time when such a criterion is first introduced to the machine. This is as far as machines are concerned. In human understanding, we are seeking an origin of their conceptual criterion that determines a difference or sameness. What we are discussing here is at the very edge of human knowledge and what is true in whatever outcome must be an intuition rather than reason, for if it is reason, we need to justify it in turn.

When I look at three white objects, I can see the colour resemblance without having to resort to memory, or to set an image of whiteness as a standard, to determine a similarity. When I close my eyes I can imagine a patch of whiteness; the mystery is how I can imagine a patch of whiteness without having to admit that memory can serve me in this task. I cannot argue from the point that memory recalls all white objects seen in the past instead of whiteness itself in the present identity; for recalling all white objects seen in the past will certainly need an immediate white standard to pick out all white objects of the past. Even if my present perceptual experience tells me that my differentiation or identity of colours is instantaneous, I cannot rule out the possibility that I had not made such a differentiation or identity instantaneously in the past.

Although universals are not sensed because of their generality (for only particulars are sensed), we can still say that there are no universals without particulars.

This dependency on particulars not only questions the independence of universals, but also proposes an inference that particulars precede or at least coexist with universals, and are never posterior to them. If this is the case, there must be a logical possibility, if not a certainty, that a resemblance can be intelligently conceived from the sensibles in front of us without having to call upon a preconceived standard for this a resemblance. Otherwise, universals must precede particulars, which is rejected. If there can be no universals without particulars, it makes sense to think that universals originate from particulars, or from the conception of particulars, and nowhere else. This reinforces the possibility that the so-called abstraction of resemblance from sense-data by the intellect, is more apparent without the necessity of a standard. Furthermore, we must not forget that using a standard to determine resemblance not only requires postulation of two entities, but also a standard of a standard that may lead to infinity. Perhaps we must also not forget that we are intelligent animals and not machine. If there is anything that helps us to see generality, it must be in the mental act of marking distinction and picking out sameness intuitively, and not in the form of a preconceived idea of distinction or sameness. If a standard is preconceived, how can we learn new things about the world or make mistakes in the course of learning? These two problems are exactly the products of the Platonic Forms that Plato created. He thinks that knowledge is already born with us and remembering it is what is needed. He also thinks that if we only believe in what is true, then there is no false belief. For there are as many universals as there is conceptual knowledge, virtually covering all linguistic expressions and words. If we believe that universals are complete entities in a realm of being that can be apprehended by the mind, we must not stop at one or two, we must believe in the existence of all of them, all capable of being apprehended at the same time. If so, it would not conform with the belief that our knowledge of universals clearly is acquired through experience, in the determination of relations among things.

Relation of relations

Some people think that there are universals and there are relations of universals, if the conception of a universal can be modified in the light of experience. In other words, it is only the relations of universals that are modified, but never the universals themselves. For example, the earth was flat centuries ago and is now round; some will argue that it is the relation between flatness, roundness and the world, that is modified, and never flatness and roundness themselves which are unchangeable. Since a universal is a relation that presupposes an understanding, and every understanding involves multiple concepts with more than one relation, therefore every universal may contain a relation of some sort, apart from itself. Even nothingness contains a relation between fullness and existence. A bed is relational to sleeping, lying down, resting, luxury, intercourse and so on. It is not a philosophical accident that words fail to pick out particularity without an immediate perceptual content, for generality is always a multiple dependence on many things.

This dependence in turn raises the question of how we know of the relations among universals, if universals are not known through sense experience or even the intellect. Such is the necessary condition for the Platonic universals to be absolutely complete, independent and self-explaining (being rational), that we seem to forget: 'what is there to advise us to make a connection between a universal and another, or between it and an object'? If universals signify such a necessary reality, there can be no arbitrariness in the association between one universal with another or an object. But what is there to help us, except universals again? Universals are relations but never relations of relations suggesting that they are content for yet another level of relations. You either have to reject the idea that universals are relations or there can never be relations of relations. If universals are not relations, all the problems raised in this chapter will be difficult to resolve. It is all very well to say that universals are the reality of identity; that is only perfect when there is no mistake, no loss of memory and no frailty of the mind in old age, that may render us in a state of confusion. This state of confusion, mistake and uncertainty, are not permitted if we seriously consider the existence of an independent reality of universals, being not relations of something else. For if a bed is a bed, it must be absolutely a bed; who is there to reprimand me if I call it a table and dine on it? If we do not believe that men can distinguish and assimilate from sense-data without a preconceived standard, we will plunge into the world of universals, where every standard is provided for every judgement, considered to be rational; demanding that we are rational too in following this predetermined standard. This conclusion is plainly absurd. The only premiss we need is that humankind, given the necessary intellect, can distinguish or assimilate without any standard of difference or sameness, and we can quit the world of universals.

Sensations and values

I share the same sentiment with J. S. Mill in his *A System of Logic* where he writes:

But when we speak of the sensation itself, language, which adapts itself for the most part only to the common uses of life, has provided us with no single-worded or immediate designation; we must employ a circumlocution, and say, The sensation of white, or The sensation of whiteness; we must denominate the sensation either from the object, or from the attribute, by which it is excited. Yet the sensation, though it never does, might very well be conceived to exist, without anything whatever to excite it. We can conceive it as arising spontaneously in the mind. But if it so arose, we should have no name to denote it which would not be a misnomer.[16]

We say that the distinctive sense in the existence of sensibility does not require us to use words and general concepts to label it. What there is in ourselves to recognize it lies in the need to subsume it under the whole picture of world objects, so that our interaction with world objects as demanded by our nature, has a potentiality and possibility, if it is understood in terms of everything else and in terms of our values.

One may like to enquire: if reality is all about sensible qualities in particular spaces, and if all we do in communicating is to report reality, do the words we use to describe reality go beyond these bland, cruel and unspeakable basic sense-data constructing the particular and sensible world? If not, this will be a world of nothing but extensions in space and time. But our world is a colourful world of all conceived and conceivable possibilities, of all forms of humankind transcended excellence; a world equally of horror and in all forms of unpleasantry. It is not so much that we see a tasteless world of extensions and add to it our human sensibility, but that we see the world instantly as a human world. We see every tiny aspect of the world in our own being and nature. We cannot explain why we add this bit of human functionality to that part of the world instead of another; we can only predicate a world seen with human aspects by considering that our nature imposes upon us to see the world with human aspects.

Human nature - the sources of world values

This is a human reality: a reality that concern humanity and its nature, so that this reality is full of dispositions, potentials, expectations, relations, desires, beauty, ugliness, and understanding. These are not connections through world things themselves, but through each and every individual in that individual's perceiving and conceiving opportunities, to exploit all there are in world objects for his nature. It is right for Plato to point out that things said of sensible things are not in the things themselves. Of course, they are not in the things but in a subjective world in which human nature imposes its conditions. The reality of sensibles in a totality of relations is now combined with the reality of human nature, so that everything we see (judge), every sensible datum, has at least an aspect that originates from human nature, from where the determination with values is derived.

One who does not sleep or lie down cannot have the concept of a bed, nor does an object in its natural state, contain an aspect intrinsically human or functional as such. Sands and stones can be functional, but there is no function in sands and stones. We see things as food, not because 'foodness' is naturally a dispositional essence in these things. 'Food' as a general concept cannot identify things in a metaphysical reality, without humanity. In this sense an epistemological reality is a metaphysical reality with human aspects. Once we can see the two realms of reality: the metaphysical and the human evaluative, we can also see clearly why an identity always fails to match both realities at the same time. If someone says to me, 'How can you say that this is not a bed when I have slept in it for the last two years?', I shall reply, 'We both understand this 'bedness' because we both share the same human convention to sleep horizontally, on soft surface and in warmth. Hence if I use it for a different purpose, am I entitled to call it something else? If a bat could speak, it would not probably agree with you or me that this object's identity is a bed since bats sleep hanging upside-down vertically.'

If there is a third realm of reality to accommodate this extra-objective universality, it cannot be unexplainable as to how it is acquired or known. For it would be an incoherent way to explain reality since an extra-object ontology (therefore an extra-sensual ontology) is not within our conception even if you apply logic and reasoning. There is an extra-object or non-sensible existent, conceivable and apprehensible; this existence is apprehended through the understanding of values (same as the understanding of universals), and not through sensations (at least not until they are determined or identified). It is known not in sensible objects. This existent is our own nature that propagates all our values, and in turn our intentions and actions. I find this objective source firmly rooting us to all our desires, vanity, beliefs, convention, survival and needs. These things outside world-objects are human values. They may sometimes be seen as being attributed to world-things not because they have a natural identity with them, but because men have to see world-things in terms of their needs and wants, and see them as functional for these needs. They are relations between human nature and world-things. Since human nature in its implication is in our awareness (of wants and actions) in principle, then the value of these relations can be known; unlike pure relations themselves to which only a constancy can be assigned. Hence many philosophers, such as Bradley, argued for the impossibility of relations; they have forgotten the human connection in them.

Universals are also verbal

Trying to use words to describe successfully or identify a world-thing is immensely difficult. This foolhardy attempt will not beg our understanding; for is it not that we talk and write about the world with words? In this book, I have on several occasions made a distinction between the unspeakable and the speakable 'reality'. The difficulty in language, to identify or refer to particularity will be considered, but to do so in great depth is beyond the scope of this book. If universals are verbal, this will explain why the identity and its referential function are difficult, if not in vain. It should be noted, that universals are verbal is true if language is not used to refer to objects directly. In this sense, all words and expressions are universal in their nature - universal in that if words are not universal they cannot be understood. But understanding is one thing, identifying or referring is another. Universals may be all verbal, but the task of language is not to identify and refer to world objects, but to refer to experience (assuming there is a separation of experience from the determination of experience), in a way so that a particularity can be pinpointed by immediate direct experience. The details of this will be argued in another book.[23]

Some say that universals are concepts under which objects are brought. This is possible if these concepts have an origin not relying again on the same objects for their content, in circularity and in arbitrariness. This depends on universal concepts being totally independent and absolute. Take for instance the word, 'in' as a relation or universal, everything is at least in one thing or another if we look at the big picture of time and the universe as a whole. When a realist imagines a world without a perceiver, and says that this 'in', can be made absolute by something being placed inside something. This is an absolute 'in' without us knowing what these two 'somethings' are. Do we really understand this 'in' this way? That something is or is not inside something is basically a human term. That something is always 'in' something is not absolute as it depends on a reference to the existence of something to be conceived as extended (by the perceiver). Whether something can be 'in' something else depends on a minimal existential determination of this something. Still, can we really conceive of something that is not a particularly something, but a general something? Not only is this general 'something' inconceivable (unexplainable) rationally, but unimaginable empirically. In an unperceived and conceived world, there is no such a thing as 'something is in something'. Something is within something because there is a oneness assumed, therefore a limitation assumed. A world without a perceiver cannot have such an assumption. Any attempt to disassociate universals from particulars is bound to fail. This type of universal has to be explained in spite of, but not instead of, sensible particulars to which it may not belong.

Direct perceptual identity as opposed to verbal identity or conceptual identity

Therefore, a fork has, in a human reality, an identity (determination), with values, and has, in a metaphysical reality, an existence invoked only by an immediate, direct perceptual experience in space. All the considerations that words or concepts can be used to refer to the world, are superfluous. Thus we attribute to every unspeakable 'colour' (sensation), every unspeakable hardness (sensation) in space, with the knowledge from the repertoire of the past in their determination. The two levels of metaphysical realities cannot be mixed. A sensation will always be a 'this' or 'that' sensation; a redness will always be a relational determination that is not the sensation itself. This may seem paradoxical, but then the separation of metaphysics from epistemology is paradoxical, if we think they are one and the same. Therefore, the words 'a red book', do not refer to a world object and identify it. This object is 'identified' by our unspeakable direct perceptual experience and the words are referring to this instance of experience, rather than the world object itself. As to whether sense experience and the object are one and the same, I have already made out an argument.

Treating an identity as an 'unspeakable' and direct instance of perceptual experience, avoids the metaphysics of universality (which is impossible), which will in turn be firmly understood in the realm of epistemological reality. This way of looking at the world releases me from the obligation to postulate two entities for identity through indiscernibility. Even though I think that we can distinguish and assimilate without a prior standard, identity is not established this way. We have an in-space-object, the particularity of which is not in doubt, and all else attributed to it according to our values and understanding of relations, may be agreeable through a constancy and a shared common humanity that imposes our ways of seeing things. Since all universals are relations and values, they are the abstraction of relations and the interpretation of immediate and functional wants and needs.

Classes, values and essence

To what extent is relation based on, or imposed by, human values? In this, I have to deal with things that are purely general as well as things particular. The distinction is whether something is in space or not. Everything that is an object is an extension in space and time first and foremost before it is functional. In this way, every value-object has two aspects in its identity - one in terms of space and time, and the other, evaluative. That the world is full of value-objects, is not in doubt; how are they not incapable of being considered in the light of their natural 'identities' without humanistic or functional aspects? A fork is foremost an object in space, before it is something functional. To resolve this, I shall return to the earlier discussion on the 'natural' essence of things.

Consider a chicken or a tree for example. The critics may say that certainly there are things which, by virtue of their being identified as such in a certain class or species, are undoubtedly things judged to be in their true nature specified by their class or species. Being a bird, an animal, a living thing, or something that can fly with feathered wings, must surely be essential in being a chicken. Being a growing green thing with leaves and buds, must surely be essential to being a tree, without someone thinking of it in terms of his own needs and wants. In asserting something as having an essential nature, one puts this thing in a category, a class by which its 'true nature' is judged. It can be argued that it is all very well to talk of a fork in having functional values, but when it comes to consider it in what may be regarded as a 'class of nature', one cannot easily subsume natural classification under human values. Examples of these may be these: gold, carbon, water, elephants or oxygen, and so on. Let us examine these objections.

First of all, let us look at classification, differentiation and exclusion. I want to see if the awareness of a resemblance or sameness is quite independent of an awareness of a difference, or vice versa. When I see a resemblance, it seems that if there are no differences in other aspects, it will be sameness, not resemblance, even if the awareness of a resemblance in whole does not need an exclusion of the non-resembling elements in parts, which sameness needs. If there is only one aspect of resemblance, sameness may still apply. If I see a sameness, I do not need to know if there is no difference, even if any difference will invalidate a claim of sameness. Seeing a sameness is independent of seeing a difference. But in a reversed situation, if I see a difference, it is not certain if I do not need to know any resemblance or sameness in order to see a difference. If two things are different, they are not the same. There is no other way to conceive a difference without having to say this is not a sameness. I would not know they are different if I do not know they are not the same. But, since I can see a sameness without knowing a difference, sameness must precede difference. When

I see a resemblance, I cannot say it is all sameness or difference, for if either prevails, there is no resemblance. If all that there is is sameness, there is no resemblance, and if all that there is is difference, nor is there resemblance. Therefore, a resemblance must have both sameness and difference. Since a resemblance is inclusive of both, we shall now only look at the dependence of sameness and of difference. Since sameness precedes difference, and since there is a dependence, all the notions of difference and resemblance must originate from the notion of sameness.

In the physical world, it must be admitted that everything is in a sense different from everything else, and there are no two things exactly the same. We say so because we do not find two world things being the same, not because we can see that the world objects are different among themselves. Thus we can say that the world objects are essentially difference-neutral. In a sense, our understanding of sameness and difference can be replaced by that of 'sameness and not sameness' so that we only need to know what a sameness is without the need to know what a difference is (difference is only a negation of sameness).

How do we then explain sameness and resemblance? If sameness implies an identity, then what is the purpose of resemblance in the judgement of two things being identical? So if two things are in the same class, do they have identical sameness or just resemblance? They cannot be identical since they are two separate things. If they are not identical they are not the same in every aspect. So, if two things are in the same class, they are only in a class of resemblance, that may include both sameness and difference (not sameness) in parts. When I say this and that are gold, I am not saying they are the same for it would mean that they are identical and yet I am saying that they are 'the same in essence' in virtue of being in the class of 'gold'. Again, if we return to the argument on the 'sameness of this essence', we will say that the essences of both things can only be a resemblance instead of sameness. I cannot say that they resemble each other in this 'gold essence', for what sameness is there? But the sameness in two gold pieces is nothing but the sameness of their physical aspects. There is no 'goldness' seen in these things, except in their physical appearances. To be gold, things must be identical in all the 'gold aspects' (physical) that make up this 'essence'. As to what we can call a classification or 'unnatural classification' of things, a class resemblance may suffice without an absolute sameness. But there is only resemblance in experience; sameness is a concept created by the mind just as a straight line is created, because the mind can never apprehend things that are exactly the same. Sameness in reality does not exist; whenever the mind cannot distinguish it says it the 'same'. This is resemblance based on a mind-conceived 'sameness'.

To classify things of the world, we do not need to know their differences: we classify them according to resemblance, 'sameness' perceived to be so. Furthermore, in classifying, we need to exclude not only those which have no resemblance or 'sameness', but also those that are neutral in respect of resemblance within a class. Before I can say this is a class of resembling things, I have to single out a particular resemblance in this class to the exclusion of others. So to classify a particular class we need to understand the criterion of exclusion as well as resemblance.

In a natural state, world objects do not supply us with an objectivity of 'difference'; and this exclusion from resemblance is a judgement of the mind. There is no sameness in world objects for us to assess resemblance, and sameness is a judgement of the mind. This conception of 'sameness', and therefore resemblance is possible without an absolute standard even if such conception of sameness may be erroneous. Having a concept of something and having an absolute concept of something, are not necessarily mutually exclusive. Hence we who have never found the absolute truth, do not stop thinking that certain beliefs we hold remain true. All the terms of 'difference' and 'sameness' are mind made, so that a 'difference' is conceived through the concept of resemblance; this is attributable to our imperfect perceptual and conception ability. If the world does not provide an absolute sameness and resemblance in things observed (even if it does, we cannot apprehend them), classification of things by an objective criteria identity into classes is not possible. Therefore classification is a mind-made affair, conditioned by human evaluative standards, and according to our limited nature. The so-called nature classes or essence of things are mere resemblance in classes. This is evaluative and not objective. In another sence, relational constancy may be substituted for 'sameness' and the classification by this constancy is not absolute either.

Universal and reality

Some may think that identity is the identity in a class or classes giving things their identity. This type of identity cannot confer particularity. Whatever is in a class is necessarily an 'existent' of the general type. But to identify an entity is not about classifying it into classes. Even if we consider classes as relations, relations or universals cannot confer a definite identity. When I say something is X, I do not classify it, but determine and understand it, perhaps by relations that may involve classes. An identified thing is first and foremost a particular before it belongs to a class; a class has nothing to do with this individuation. In fact it may prevent it. How this class essence or resemblance comes about is a main point of contention. When we say a thing is X without perceptual comparables available to establish a resemblance, we recall a resemblance from memory not only to establish a determination, but to conceive X in the context of the whole sensible world. Hence, when it is said that universals are relations, this is by no means a accidental conception of universals. Still, relations are rooted in human nature which serves as a third reference making the determination of these relations possible. We see things not only as dull sensibility, but see them in terms of the whole scheme of our experience, with an outside sense of reality, in relations with other sensibles, in the values of our nature. In Aristotle's view, all of us by nature wish to know, but to know things is not, in my view, an intellectual vanity, but a necessity guiding our actions through the world objects. Identity of things in relations is knowing reality to serve this purpose. Consequently things in relations, are ultimately in relation to men, without which men cannot dispose to act within their nature. To perceive and conceive things without relations is not natural for men.

A class in nature is conceivable, as I have argued before, through the permanency and constancy of relations, that agrees on resemblance in things; the way science explains the world is not at all different from this. For example, a match has the potential to light up, which is not our mind's indulgence. The potentiality here is an exemplar for a claim of relations through instances. That is to say, if I have lit this match only once, I would not dream of thinking that this match is a member of a class of things that can light up. This way, we can discount the possibility that a natural class of things is a Platonic idea within us, recognizing it or its absolute essence as a universal. It is repetition and induction that suggest a constancy in a relation, and in turn a universal and understanding. This lighting-up 'essence' is not known immediately upon striking a match.

The lack of ontological status for universals, and even shuffling them under a third realm of reality, may create ambiguity in Platonism. Platonism can be seen as a realism, but the realism of the common sense is a realism of concrete particulars in space and time. Platonism is a realism constructed out of rational absolutism, the epistemological sources of which are always taken for granted. The authority of this rational realism is necessarily divine, and yet the reality of divinity is not considered as realism in the ordinary sense. The intellect itself cannot be its source since human intellect is differently tuned from one individual to the next, so that disagreements will inevitably create division without a solution. It is certainly not empiricism, if considered from an epistemological point of view. Platonic realism is an idealism of the rationalistic type as opposed to that of an empirical type. Hence one cannot be a realist of the Platonic type without being an idealist too, unless one has no consideration for the epistemological origin of one's reality constructed out of rational absolutism. How one takes up a belief with respect to this realism has a bearing on one's ethical, political, and, ultimately, humanistic outlook. For if we submit ourselves to the reality constructed out of rational absolutism, we must conform to all its implications in all the absolute standards and laws. However, this philosophy is one that questions whether this rational absolutism can have any sound foundation upon which our final ethical and political beliefs can rest. The answer is surely no.

PART IV

EXISTENCE OF THE MIND OR THE MENTAL

8 The Existence of the Mental

8.1. The mental and the physical

Should there be such a distinction?

The duality question of the mental and the physical has been with humankind since the beginning. It is only the recent advance of science that puts paid to the idea that duality of the mind and the bodily is a reasonable belief. It is not as if science has found an answer to repudiate the existence of the mental over and above the reality of the physical; far from it, it is the science of the mind, restricting itself to the investigation of physical phenomena, that dismisses out of hand any phenomenon associated with what is normally called the mental. Science pursues its truths by examining and explaining physical phenomena, postulating laws and rules which it claims it has discovered; the causal investigations of the physical naturally exclude any admission of a causality between the physical and the mental, since mental phenomena are not directly observable. It would be uncharitable to say that science refuses to investigate mental phenomena by brushing them aside; but if it does, it would undermine the difficulty by putting mental phenomena on the same footing as physical phenomena observed. It is not unwise to say that if there is a science of mental phenomena, it is inevitable that new laws will be set up in contradistinction to those of the physical. And that will probably be 'blasphemy' to science.

The so-called physical phenomena associated with this term, mental, are typified by brain states, synapses of the nerves, genetic influences and constitutions, and so on. Although science has yet to explain satisfactorily the sense in which mental items are identical with physical events, scientific physicalism (the belief that physical and mental phenomena are identical or one and the same) is considered satisfactory in the hope that one day all mental phenomena will be explained in an 'identity' with physical events. Even where a scientist drops his jaw, trying to answer questions that cannot be satisfactorily met without assuming the existence of the mental, materialistic philosophers will not be ruffled in the least. Perhaps science gives philosophers confidence not found in words. I shall therefore meet the challenge of this mind-physical identity theory first before going onto examine the criteria for the existence of the mental.

We need to know what the mental is in order to claim an identity

This is the theory, inspired by modern science, that what we call mental events such as sensation, emotion, thinking, and so on, are identical with physical events in a sense, such as bodily behaviours, brain states or electrical discharges (or synapses). It says not only that mental events are explainable in terms of bodily or physical events, but also that they are ontologically the same. Something is ontologically the same as 'another' if the non-existence of one may mean the non-existence of the other. If 'I' and my body are said to be distinct verbally (an epistemological distinction), and if the existence of 'I' cannot survive when my body is destroyed, or vice versa, it is said that these two are ontologically the same with two aspects. In the same way, an analogy can be made out of brain activities and mental occurrences. By saying that they are ontologically the same through their existential dependence, one can get away with the obligation to explain away the epistemological difference between the mental and the physical as to why and how we normally distinguish these two types of events.

In using the words 'identical with' to assert one identity for two things is derived from Leibniz, among others, and is something that I have challenged earlier. Even if two postulated entities are epistemological entities, their identity can only be epistemological, not ontological. If such a postulation is allowed to succeed, the criteria for this identity must rest on how the contents of both types of events are determined as being the same. The content of a physical event may in principle be determinable, but what about the content of the 'mental' events? If not, this identity rests only on their existential dependency and nothing else, since there is nothing in the mental aspects that can be determined in order to make a judgement of sameness. The problem is: everything else apart from this existential dependency is either different from the other or indeterminable for a claim of identity. We cannot assume that the content of the 'mental' event is the same as that of the physical, or our argument would become circular. Brushing aside minor objections, such as that a mental content of seeing 'red' may include other mental contents not included in the physical content of 'seeing red', a requirement for the physical and the mental to be identical, begs the questions as to what a mental event is, in order that we can proceed to identify this sameness.

Mental and physical identity through existential dependency

If I want to be unkind to this theory, I shall argue that by postulating two events (the physical and the mental), a distinction must have been assumed. This is an epistemological distinction and cannot be an epistemological sameness, for that will be a sheer contradiction. But, can there be a postulation of two ontological entities (as opposed to epistemological entities) in the first place? If so, does it also admit two distinct ontological entities before making an identity of them? If I allow that it can, do I have to spell out the content of this mental entity, as I have argued earlier? An example of two epistemological entities is that of yesterday's and today's sun. So if I allow the postulation of two epistemologically 'identical' entities, can I proceed to affirm their ontological identity as well, and if so, what logical criterion do I need in making this jump? I imagine that the identity theorists will say, the existential dependency of these two entities (that is to say, the destruction of one will result in the annihilation of the other) will suffice. This is effectively more plausible than the identity via the principle of indiscernibility in all aspects of the two things. Still two epistemological entities cannot be identical. The question of whether yesterday's sun is the same as today's, is not a question of identity of two separate entities. Temporal constitution ensures that yesterday's sun is not today's sun in its sheer connotative content. These two do not exist at the same contemporary consciousness, just as we cannot see 'two identical tables' at the same time as two entities. Because of this temporal and connotative content, the reality of the two 'suns' in being one, does not come from this epistemological content alone. It comes from a content of relation linking what was yesterday and what is today. It is an identity by which the present entity, i.e. today's sun, cannot be understood without the parameters presupposed in our understanding of the past sun. It is also because we understood what a sun was that we understand what the sun is now. The assertion of a relation of the two as one is not an assertion of two metaphysical entities as one, since spatio-temporal reality ensures always that there can be no absolute sameness between two entities epistemologically postulated in the outset. The assertion of an identity of yesterday's sun and today's sun as one, is the assertion of constant relations among groups of perceptual data. There is only one sun, because what we have seen in the past and what we see today are constantly related in such a way, so that 'one sun' can be the only explanation for such a relational reality. What relations can we find between physical events or brain activities, and mental occurrences apart from this existential dependence? Does my understanding of my mental occurrences depend on understanding my brain activities?

However, two entities that are existentially dependent on each other may not necessarily mean that they are identical. For example, a cause and an effect are existentially dependent on each other and they are not identical. Still, it may be said that whereas a cause and its effect are consecutive in time, two mental and physical events are simultaneous in time. Also there are essence and existence that are simultaneous, but they are held by many as being not identical. Two things that are inseparable will not bring about an identity. Spaces and objects in them are inseparable and they are not identical. Two events that are inseparable ontologically may not be identical.

Physical states of thinking and believing

This brings to mind the question of whether the thought of, 'a physical event is identical with a mental event' is itself a physical event. If it is a physical event, then 'a physical event is identical with a mental event' is nothing but synapses of brain cells. What is the truth or falsehood in its context? Or truth itself is a definitive physical pattern of electrical charges in the brain. But the act of thinking itself cannot be true or false; it is the content of the thinking that can be true or false. So if thinking is a definitive pattern of synapses in braincells, what is the content of this thought in a physical state? It will be absurd to think that the pattern is the state of thinking and the synapses are its content. Still the content of truth or falsehood must be another state, the state of believing in the content. So if the state of believing in the content of a thought is another pattern of electrical charges, the thought or its content cannot be true or false unless another state is involved. Now we have two states of this thought in order for it to be true or false (one thinking it and another believing it). Since they are all physical events, there is no saying what their relations are; if they are not causally related, one state may occur independently of the other, and if so, we may have a believing state without the thought state. If they are causally related, we cannot show their necessary connection since thinking may not always be followed by believing. We do not know what we are believing, in any case, even if we are in a state of believing.

I do not want to get into a regress by further asking what a brain state is in the verification of facts in our belief system. We let the truth of physicalism stop at the first level of belief without a check. If a true thought involves two physical states, what do we make of these associated 'states' of belief? If it is only a physical pattern of electrical discharge, what criteria are there for a thought to be objectively true, without something that is truth-relevant being introduced? What is this truth-relevant thing? If there is, can this something be just a physical event? Physical events are, but can never be true or false. At best, physicalism is, but can never be true or false. The mere fact that physicalism can involve an argument of truth, must question what the physicality of truth is.

There are other examples quite similar to the above that one may contemplate. How the belief in a mathematical equation can be identical with a physical event in the brain is questionable. The belief of, say, '2 and 2 are 4', is a belief of necessity, but if it is a physical event, it is inductive without necessity. Even if a physical state can be a belief, a belief system as physical events can only work through the repetition in occurrences. Can there ever be intuitive beliefs like '2 and 2 are 4'? We may say that all logical certainties are contingent at most, through a matter of chance in the synapses firing contingently. In short, it is a problem lacking verifiability, which is the main crux in the scientific investigation of mental items; if not, how are we to prove a mathematical formula or affirm a belief, if the ontological constitution of thoughts is merely a contingency in the physical world?

Conceiving time cannot be a physical brain state

Suppose I am a scientist who wants to find out a brain pattern (or electrical charges) for a thought of, say, the duration of one tick of a clock's second hand. The movement of the hand in one click is my perceptual 'data', identified as a brain-activity pattern. How can I account for the time as a mental event, instead of a physical movement? For in order to claim that in the conception of this duration, the brain has captured the 'real' time movement of the clock, or that both durations are identical, I must assume that the timing within the brain pattern, i.e. the duration between the first and final synapses, is exactly the same as that taken by the clock. But the perceived time of the clock movement, will have to include the duration taken by light to travel to the brain to induce the brain synapses. And the brain's physical time must be different from the clock's time between the first and last synapses. Therefore, the durations of the clock movement and of its conceived time, must be different and not identical, if they are both physical.

We can conceive that the determination of sensations as the identity of sense-data can be immediate without a second level of cognition, but the conception of time or indeed space is totally different altogether; since space has no sense-data and time is no more without them. If 'sensing' time itself has a physical marking in a brain state, there must be another brain pattern to signify this and to conceive this duration, otherwise, 'sensing' time will have no identity in a brain state corresponding to a definite time event. If so, in 'sensing' time, there will be two mental events, one sensing spatial data and the other marking a physical time itself; these two states cannot be identical as it is in the perception of the clock's temporal movement, unless they are simultaneous. But if they are simultaneous, they cannot be two states. Also, if 'sensing' time is not more than perceiving sensible data in space, how can I explain the conception of time in a big void, which we certainly do? If there is no second level of cognition of time, how can we perceive time in isolation from spatial movements? For according to this all-physical reality, a 'second' in time is only a movement of a clock in space; where is the sense of time in it? In an all-physical reality there is always a physical state for every cognitive determination. Once there is an input of concepts in the determination of temporal and perceptual data, there are two brain states, not simultaneous and not identical. To conceive time, my brain has to understand the duration of a 'second', even if it has to recall past experience. Thus more brain states are involved. Consequently, if for every mental event of 'perceiving time' there is another physical brain state occurred, they cannot be identical; or if they are identical, there cannot be a conception of time.

If conceiving time is a physical event, the duration within cannot be identical with the duration it is supposed to capture. There must be another physical event responsible for the (cognitive) recognition of the difference and for the capture of a temporal sense which is not found in perceptual data themselves in spite of their movements in space. If the sense of time is not found in physical events, it should not be found in 'conceiving time' itself since it is a physical event. Also physical states cannot explain immediate intuition since every determination of an extra-event content rests on another physical event for its explication.

This is not a denial that there is no physical identity of a conceiving time, but that if there is, conceiving time is improbable. If brain events are the only physical reality, they cannot extract from themselves the element of temporal conception from the mere physicality, since time itself is in the perceptual intuition which, if it is again physical, will produce no sense of time over and above movements. Perhaps movement itself cannot be perceived as such. Even if we may conceive of events captured by a physical brain state in a temporal order of 'before and after', it is inconceivable that there is no preconceived or assumed existence of a temporal point of 'now' by which 'what is before' and 'what is after' are determined. If so, how is this temporal point of 'now' conceived as a physicality?

Conceiving space is not a physical brain state

If mental events and physical brain events are identical, how do we see space? It is impossible to have a physical event in seeing an empty space, since empty space has no physical events. In the absence of outside stimuli, brain states are not in a causal relation with whatever that is seen. They must be purely physiological and caused by other brain states within. Seeing space this way must be a physiological seeing. But as regards spaces that are occupied, we can look at it in another way. If the representation of space is unlike that of sense-data, which may be subject to interpretation, distortion or the lack of verification, a space or extension should be an identical copy of that of world objects inseparable from it. Since the size of the perceiving organ is limited, the representation of space in a physical reality must be scaled down so that the reception of it is possible within the size of the perceptual organ. In that case, seeing sizes of things has a certain judgement of scale built in. In order to see the physical reality as it is or is assumed to be, there must be a reinterpretation of the scale of size or distance to reconcile between a real physical space and a conceived space.

In order to judge sizes and distance, do we need a physical representation of scale? That is to say, one foot in size or distance in reality should always be interpreted as a definitive physical length in the physical state in the brain that captures it. Assuming that the particular capture of a size or distance involved here is identical with a brain state, we cannot say that we can actually 'see' this brain state, so that we can see also the spatial scale or proportion registered by it. If one state is identical with another ontologically, each cannot know the other or the scales they represent because each cannot measure the other to make this judgement. If so, how can physical space represent itself in a physical brain state, and how does it measure the consistency of relation in size and distance? Perhaps again, like that of time, the 'capture' of space involves more than one physical states.

It is difficult to imagine how a brain state can represent the identity of a mental, perceptual image that is already an immediate interpretation. If we allow two levels of sensing and interpretation, a brain state cannot be a true representation of the real world since it always has interpretations of it. If brain state is the cause of a separate mental state, and also its identity, physical laws will not allow a cause to be the cause of itself. If one state is the cause of another, they are necessarily two. If a bit of reality does cause a brain state, this is a brain state of reality unscrutinized, and we still need another level of interpretation. The point is that if brain states and the mental are identical, there is a lack of the interpretation of reality, because the strict physiological reduction of a psychological content, to a physical reality of space is not possible. How much reality is explained by interpretation, even if such interpretation is about relations among other things?

Physicalism does not need an identity theory

In arguing against this theory of physical-mental identity, one definitely has a disadvantage, for this theory does not, or is reluctant, to spell out the descriptive content of events it considers to be physically identified with the 'mental'. Therefore many intuitively implausible exemplars against this theory are lost in the verbosity hidden behind the interpretation of the physical, in the hope that its correspondence may be found one day. In fact, the materialists should not be alarmed if their identity theory should fail, for even if the so-called mental items are not identical with physical states, one still can argue that these mental items are ontologically physical. If both are necessarily distinct and physical, one has to go back to the traditional way to seek a source of their nature, and to explain a causal connection between them. The modern-day linguistic philosophy that sets out philosophical problems in terms of expression, meaning and truth conditions in the hope to find the metaphysical truth, should realize that the truths and conclusions involved in expression, meaning and truth condition will never go beyond their epistemological origin. If they are satisfied that philosophy is all about epistemological reality, there is absolutely no need to go beyond what we ordinarily consider as the mental.

Two states of perceptual experience cannot be identical through causality

Perhaps, there must be a difference between perceptual happenings and non-perceptual happenings both considered as mental. In the case of the perceptual and mental happenings, there is the sense in their being caused by external data in the process, as different from the non-perceptual happenings of the mental. Now, in the ordinary sense of causality, a physical state that has an observable causal link with world-objects, is considered in this connection as an effect caused by world-objects and not by mental events. Mental events, if distinct from the physical, must be said to be caused by the physical states. In this way, they are consecutive events. However, in the case of non-perceptual mental states, a causal direction, that is, from world-objects to the mental, does not exist since there are no physical stimuli in a perceptual situation. So, for non-perceptual states, if there is no separate causality accounted for, they must be concurrent or simultaneous without one being the cause of the other. Non-perceptual or non-stimulated brain states are impossible for the lack of a final, external, physical cause. This must be so if all physical events are supposed to be separate and yet 'glued' together by causality. But brain states without causes must be odd to physicalism, even if they are identical with the mental. What can cause a brain state without a stimulus? Still if they are identical we do not call them two different states or events. The crux of the matter in considering mental states as ontologically physical is the problem of how to explain these physical events in a total and necessary causal reality. Perceptually mental events part, non-perceptual mental events cannot be so explained and must be denied by physicalism for their ontological reality.

But perceptually mental events in a realist's plan, are considered as part of a chain of causes and effects from world-objects to the brain, they cannot be identical with the percepts or stimulus, since one is a cause and the other an effect. If brain states are caused by world-objects, the mental states, if distinct from both must stand in some causal relation to them. So what is this 'mental state'? If it is the same as the brain state, how can we causally explain the epistemological state that is in every aspect different from its physicality? Therefore if the causal theory of perception is true, it is incompatible with a physical-mental identity theory, since it admits different ontological events through causality, each of which cannot be identical, or if identical cannot be causal.

Speaking of causality in perception, one cannot help but subject it to serious criticism as there is no identical representation of world-objects, in images or in impressions of what we are supposed to have actually captured. World-objects impress upon the nerves and receptive organ without exception in every possible detail, otherwise, the so-called physical law of causality will collapse if something is missing out in this link. In this physical process we shall expect to have captured all impressions of things in principle, and of every minor detail that is in this causal link, if seeing in a mental state is corresponding to that of the physical state caused by this cause link. If this is so, and if a physical state is identical with the mental state in perception, then we will perceive world-objects in every minor detail in a final perceptual state so caused. But we know that this is not the case because what we can perceive is restricted to what our attention points out to us, and what we are aware of. Minor details that do not come to our attention may only surface if we are mindful of our attention to them. So a physical causality from world objects to mental states breaks down in perceptual situations.

This objection is only true if there is no ontological distinction between the physical and mental perceptions, for the physical causal laws to apply to both. By presupposing that they are identical, one must explain the causality between physical and mental. Until such explanation is given, a causal connection from the physical to the mental should not be assumed. Nor can we say that if there is no causality between physical and mental, all things must not be physical; for this will be presupposing the conclusion we wish to give. That there is no causality between physical and mental is also presupposed by the proposition that things mental and things physical are identical.

Sensing temperature in a physical sense

Consider heat or hotness. If I model myself on the materialist position, the hotness or coldness sensed by the body depends very much on the temperature of the body itself. This is to say that an individual who is cold will feel something warmer, whereas the same thing can be colder to another individual whose body is hot. Far from suggesting that this is subjective, I shall go out on a limb and say that this difference of temperature needs two media of temperature for measurement. I will imagine that the perceived temperature is registered as impulses or synapses in the brain state, and there will also be another state that shows the body's temperature in order to register a physical difference in temperature between these two states. Consequently there is no corresponding world-object that is the cause of this physical registration of difference in temperature, which is really the brain's own measure, even if it physical. In this case, though we can explain a perceptual source of the first temperature felt, we cannot give an account for the existence of the 'comparison' of temperatures, originated from world-objects. If it is bodily in its origin, it has no outside cause. How is it that directly perceiving a temperature will result in two distinct sets of bodily data, unless one has an unexplainable source?

Even if we consider both the state of capturing stimuli and the state of measuring and judging, as one physical state identical with a perceptual state, we need to explain the causal origin of measuring and judging which cannot be in the data so captured. If measuring and judging are of a different causal origin, they cannot be part of the same state capturing stimuli. And if they are physical too, their causal origin must be at best bodily or physiological. If so, does this physiological cause ultimately lie outside the body? If not, the physical law of nature must be shying away from the governance of the body. If it is outside, how can we explain the association between the immediate measuring and judging and the capturing of stimuli itself, since they always come together? An indicative probability will not do. It has to be a necessary connection such as a causal connection and we are back to our starting point. In fact, our mental experience of sensing hotness or coldness does not even involve two states of feeling hot or cold; this experience is immediate.

There is no cause for non-perceptual mental items

Even if we were to brush aside the difficulty in the causality of interpretation of data, those non-perceptual mental states, such as thoughts or beliefs, offer us no physical causes for their existence. If we say that mental states such as these can cause a physical state (an act for example), we have more problems. For if a physical state is caused by a mental state, they are not only non-identical, but outside the physical, scientific reality too. The mere assertion that mental states are physical cannot guarantee that they would inevitably be caused. If there is a cause but not a physical cause, the physical laws of causality must be rewritten. If one shall say that thoughts or beliefs are caused by stimuli acted upon some parts of the body, we should be aware of them in the same way that we are aware of perceptual stimuli. If 'should-be-aware-of-them' is not appropriate, why and how should outside stimuli cause our beliefs and thoughts? If they do, a physical determinism in beliefs and thoughts must be possible. And if so, why should there be false beliefs and erroneous thoughts? For if one stimulus is as good as another for a belief, why is it false? If the quality of a stimulus is a truth condition for beliefs or veridical meanings, what is this quality in the physical sense? And how do we perceive the truth quality of a stimulus, let alone identify it? If believing is a different brain state rather to its mere mental content, then we may be in a state of believing about nothing, if the content state does not exist. If that is possible, we can also say that there is one stimulus for the brain state of believing and another for creating its content; but then, how can there be an association between this believing state and the state of content?

Being physical and identical cannot be mutually implied

The mind-body identity theory cannot consistently admit that there is a mental state, even if it is ontologically identical with the brain state. By such admission, it sows the seeds of incoherence. This has been explained before. The identify theory, by affirming the identity of the mental with a physical state, must assert only that a mental state is physical and nothing more. There cannot be a conclusion that, if they are identical, the mental must be physical; for there is also an inference from this that the physical is nothing but mental, if they are identical. Conversely, if things are physical, it may not follow that they are identical. This, I am afraid, takes away the conclusion the theory sets out to achieve.

Physicalism must explain intentionality and non-spatial qualities of the mental

There is a widely known argument, that all mental items or contents are non-spatial (as championed by Descartes) or intentional (as proposed by Brentano). Descartes thinks that thoughts or the contents of the mental are non-extended, unlike the body, which is extended in space. But the intentionality of the mental in behaviour or expression is more complex, because the lack of empirical sources begs the question as to what intentionality is, without presupposing the existence the mental. These basically highlight the difference between the physical and the mental. The mind-body identity theory must therefore explain away the non-spatial content of the mental, as well as its intentionality and intensionality.

Another way of looking at this physical-mental identity is to look at mental states, not as causal-physiological bodily occurrences, but as behaviours. In this way, it is claimed that all mental items or states can be substituted by, or interpreted through behaviours. From the scientific point of view, bodily behaviours are not uncontroversial as physiological occurrences, since the latter have a regularity underpinned by physical science in medicine or the like. We cannot deny that mental events cannot have physical descriptions. For if mental events are descriptively independent of the physical explanations, one can no more ignore the ontological reality of the mental, than ignore that of the physical. Naturally, in turn, if all things are physical, they must in principal be capable of being described in terms of the mental, otherwise, how are we to illustrate an understanding of the physical reality in the first place?

Whatever ontological reality we may have of the mental, mental descriptions will stay with us all the same.

8.2 The problems in the understanding of the mental

The traditional philosophies on the mental, such as Descartes' or Leibniz's, courageously commit themselves to a specific view on the ontological status of the mind. This century has seen a retreat away from this position. Modern-day philosophies of the mind tend to restrict themselves to the epistemological aspects and the descriptive meaning of mental items. Without courageous speculations, epistemological theories of the mental will always be incomplete. Many descriptive philosophies of the mind cry out for an ontological explication of those mental terms they use. To explain the mental is not to explain it in terms of substituted words without having to give an ontological explanation. I have seen words like 'intentionality,' 'intensionality,' 'behaviours,' 'logical behaviourism,' 'psychological,' 'physiological,' 'qualia' or 'behaviour outputs' and so on. But, the term, mental is a term used in opposition to the term 'physical'. To distinguish this term from the physical, a distinction must be drawn before we can proceed to examine the ontological aspects.

Are mental items in the same category as the physical?

I start with Gilbert Ryle (1900-76) who has much to do with behaviourism or logical behaviourism. In short it is a theory that all mental items are in principle capable of being stated in terms of, or substituted by behaviours, and that it will be a category mistake in treating mental items and behaviours as two separate ontological categories, just as we treat a school as a separate thing from all its pupils, teachers and buildings. One wonders whether it was really a category mistake, because this distinction depends on our ontological understanding of the mental and the behaviours. We make an ontological distinction if we can make claims of their status, but we do not use a presumptuous distinction in order to make a claim. One can see Wittgenstein's influence on Ryle for there is the Wittgensteinian assumption that the acceptable use of these terms (mental terms) legitimizes the discussion of this reality in terms of that usage, instead of being legitimized by it.

The mental items we are talking about are certainly not the same things in the same relation as between a school and its contents. We are not saying that mental things are the content of the physical, but that mental things are of a different category from the physical, ontologically. Wittgenstein's influence on Ryle could not be more incomprehensible. Still, the fault in this theory lies not in a category mistake, but in not explaining what behaviours are, and how they are distinguished from movements or movements in biological things. The use of language cannot explain reality but is explained by reality. I cannot call things conscious things unless I can establish what 'being conscious' is. But 'biological' is not a word that is undoubtedly mental, nor can 'behaviours' arguably presuppose the mental. This presupposition is clear throughout Ryle's theory. Ryle thinks that the explanation of animal behaviours can subsist on its own without postulating what he calls a para-mechanical cause. It is clear to me that if one rejects a para-mechanical cause or a psycho-physical cause, one must seek to explain the difference between behaviours and movements, the failure of which begs this question in every step towards the acceptability of logical behaviourism.

Is a para-mechanical cause or the lack of it, such an irrational thought, so that Ryle would assume that no one would hold such a belief seriously, if one engages in philosophy?

Distinguishing the mental from the physical

We cannot rely on the Cartesian sense of thinking to distinguish the physical from the mental, by saying that things that think are mental; things that do not think are not. For things that do not think may be things that are objects of thinking or content of thinking.

It is not certain whether a perceived object in space is also a thought itself, or its content. According to this idea, doubting a thought is thinking itself, and perhaps the thing that thinks itself, but never the content or object of a thought. A thought must have content and doubting is a content as well as a thought; that is why a negation of thinking is impossible. But there is no such thing as thinking without thinking of something. To Descartes, it is only the thinking things that are indubitable; the unthinking, physical reality indubitably exists because of his faith that God will not lie to him. How can unthinking things exist indubitably so that they can make a metaphysical contrast to the other indubitable existent, the mind, without God?

The difficulty in knowing the existence of others' thinking

Thinking is uniquely an understanding from private experience. To conceive of a thing that thinks is not the same as conceiving of the experience of thinking outside the personal experience; this is not possible either. There are certain things as regards thinking of which I cannot conceive. I do not know how to conceive of a thinking being, without conceiving also a physical aspect of this being; or how to conceive two consciousnesses within a self (a public and private, or two minds); or how to conceive thinking outside a private consciousness; therefore, things are unlikely conceived as thinking things outside a private consciousness for the lack of these criteria. And everything conceived is not as a thinking thing must be distinct from the thinking thing itself in being conceived instead of conceiving. Everything else outside this private experience cannot provide these criteria. But this distinction lies only in the fact that we cannot know what it is like to be thinking outside our consciousness, without having to exclude the possibility that there can be thinking like ours in things, the existence of which we can only conceive by the criteria used for conceiving the existence of things. We cannot tell whether a stone can think any more than we can tell a person can think for the same reason, except that a person moves differently from a stone. Unless we have a criterion to determine what thinking is for all and sundry of the universe, not only ourselves, we cannot make such a distinction by our subjective knowledge in our own case. This is certainly a philosophical prejudice that if I cannot know by my own criterion, there may be nothing in it. The idea that thinking is the sign of the mental cannot be extended beyond the private sphere.

Nor can we say that the fundamental criterion for the existence of the mental is the presence of thoughts. Even if a thought implies the mental, it is not necessarily implied by it, for the ordinary experience of a thought is intrinsically intensional that cries out for an answer as to why it is so, instead of an answer to explain the mental. A thought cannot be described as physical like a table or chair, and its intensionality is well implied. In consciousness, there must be some content of consciousness, and consciousness is peculiar in that it can be distinguished from its content. This is undoubtedly the notion of 'self- awareness' that confers such a separation. A thought, and its awareness (or what Descartes will call the thinking itself) are not in the same relation as the relation between perceiving and the percept, because of the intensionality it entails. In the first relation, they can be all physical (if we reject all intensionality), or all mental (if we reject all material extensionality), but they cannot be physical in one and be mental in the other respectively, since thinking and its content are the same ontologically, and interdependent. In the second relation, a dualistic position is possible; the object of perception can be taken as being physical and even if it is assumed to be mere 'sensibility'; it can still be distinguishable from perception itself as something not manufactured by the mind. We can perceive without a particular object of perception, but we cannot think without a particular content. This is the difference. So the presence of a thought proves nothing, not least the distinction between the physical and the mental; as the physical, defined of the unthinking, in turn is not implicit by thought itself or vice versa. If this is taken seriously, nothing apart from our own consciousness can be seen as thinking, and that includes other persons and animals. Minimally, it begs the question as to what thinking things are outside our consciousness, in order that we can identify them as thinking things of their own account.

Uniqueness of private experience

Yet some may say that in spite of the indubitable private access to one's own mental content, it is difficult to determine what this 'privacy' is, if there is no alternate way to this inaccessibility. Certainly, being 'private' entails no existence of an owner of the mental content, and privacy itself is about inaccessibility and nothing more; in this sense, saying that some content is private is not circular, since 'inaccessibility' does not need the term, 'privacy' to explain it. To explain the inaccessibility of one's content of consciousness, one can say that one cannot imagine this content being conceived of or being aware of, in more than one way at the same time. This value of uniqueness is firmly rooted to a particular setting of awareness. It is the appeal to the sense of uniqueness in one's awareness that constitutes the notion of inaccessibility. Being unique, a thing has no need for alternatives to bring about this uniqueness; it needs only an examination of the particularity of the content of awareness to establish such uniqueness. For example, the uniqueness of spaces or regions in reference to a particular perceptual point can supply a criterion for the inaccessibility of mental content.

The difficulties of dualism

Nor do I think that the demolition of this indubitable, private accessibility of the mental, will result in the refutation of Cartesian dualism. If, being indubitably private, the access of the mental is not possible, as it is assumed by many since Wittgenstein, the Cartesian dualism can be stated on a different ground. If what is true is what can be agreed and understood publicly, then, thinking and consciousness must have a public understanding for dualism to live on. For if behaviours can be publicly understood and verifiable through descriptive words, so can mental phenomena. If not, why ridicule one and uphold the other? It is our own prejudice, as it has always been, that convinces us that certain words should be interpreted in this way and not that way. Ryle's prejudice is seen in his insistence on describing behaviours the way he thinks fit (the contrived, physical way), while ignoring that commonly we do use mental terms to describe things of the world to mean something more than physical, or something para-psychological to us. Hence it is perfectly trouble-free for both materialists and idealists to maintain the distinction between the physical and the mental, with or without the Cartesian arguments. This depends only on how we interpret what we call the mental. It is precisely because the private and the incorrigible access to mental awareness cannot be said to have a public criterion of verification, that the mental is always a thing that is 'felt' by each of us and cannot be expressed in words. Hence the criterion for both is difficult to find.

Nor do I think that extension can mark out the physical from the mental. It is not certain whether it is true or false that extension itself is indubitably a physical aspect on its own, or not a physical aspect of things. It cannot be so determined because whether an extension is intrinsically a physical aspect cannot be determined. The examples to illustrate this are those of sense-data. Whether sense-data are mental or physical; the cause or the caused; in the objects or in our consciousness; mere sensibility or objectively sensed; permanent or temporary, is debatable. If so, that extension can mark out the physical from the mental is debatable. Some may even suggest that things such as perceiving and thinking are not mental because they cannot be felt or perceived at all, by anyone.[17] Such an opinion, of course, is based on the Wittgenstein notion that if thinking and perceiving have no outward and public criterion, they cannot be private. I think it would be unfruitful to get into this, since I am convinced that Wittgenstein has misconceived. (There are many arguments against Wittgenstein in various parts of my writings elsewhere.) I bring up this example to show how contentious this topic is. Philosophy perhaps will not progress until Wittgenstein falls out of vogue.

Making a distinction between the mental and physical

It seems to me that to espouse a success in making a distinction between the mental and the physical, we cannot start with terms that already have the connotation of the mental and proceed to isolate the mental out of these terms; for to do so is to presuppose the mental from the outset. For instance, we cannot use the term, intentional, to explain the mental. How we understand something being intentional (describing events or actions) lies in the fact that we pick terms already laden with intentionality. There is no physical 'abnormality' from the events that give us a sense of intentionality. To say that every mental act intends (something) is to say nothing about what being mental is, because, that every mental act intends, is not the same as saying that there is an intention in every act, since an act is merely a physical, intentionless movement, in a manner of speaking. How are we to see or verify an intention in a movement when all there is to be seen is what constitutes a physical movement?

To introduce an object with which an intention is associated, is difficult even if there is no problem in describing what this object is. Why should there be an object for every intention? This is difficult to answer. We cannot borrow the physical causal law to explain such connection either, because of this so-claimed intensionality as distinct from extensionality. Consider this: 'a proposition is extensional if its truth depends solely on the truth or falsity of its constituents or possible constituents, when these are combined by means of logical connectives definable in truth-functional terms; it is intensional if that is not the case'.[18] In other words, this is saying that by defining what an expression of the physical is (as in an expression), the opposite of this is mental. Again such a definition relies on whether there is, in reality, an expression or understanding quite opposite to the description of the physical, without having to say what this so-called opposite is. Unless our intellect is so incredible as to make a description of the physical so complete that it can include all possible cases, we are unlikely to know what the counter-examples of such definitions are. I see this thinking as a corruption of the mind by logic. It is clear that to establish a distinction between the mental and the physical, one cannot avoid spelling out what is 'in the physical' that makes something mental, since most mental things are connected to the physical in one way or another, such as consciousness is connected to the brain. By showing what the physical is and saying that the opposite is the mental, we have assumed that there is really something in addition to what is physical; and that is not satisfactory.

Intentional objects

Returning to the terms of intentionality and mental acts, one says that an intentional object is 'internally' linked to the act, or is an existent relating only to it; and this has an epistemological plausibility, but is not ontologically convincing. For that anything can be said to be pointing to an intended object, is only conceivable if we understand it to be so in its intended meaning; that is to say that any entailment of an intentional object is no more than an analytic entailment that depends on how we understand the original terms. For example, if a judgement intends a proposition as an object of this intentionality, it says no more than how we understand the term 'judgement' (which entails a proposition). Overall, this way of proposing the existence of the mental is no more than asking the question: why are there so many expressions and terms that cannot be understood without the importation of the mental, having unconfirmable, anti-physical aspects? This is of course a very viable question to which I shall return.

A linguistic formulation of the intentionality of the mental, of course, would have missed out this question. It is because linguistic logic demands that if there is A, there is the non-A (the exclusion to A); and there is no indication as to what this non-A (which certainly has more connotations than merely being non-A) really is. For example, to answer the question, 'are there things that are non-apple?', we may busily define what an apple is hoping that a logical contradistinction can supply us with an answer without actually dealing with what a 'non-apple' is. But a chair is a non-apple and so is war and many, many things each of which has a distinct ontological identity or determination. For the understanding of the mental is not just the understanding of the non-physical, that is, anything that is a contradistinction to everything that is physical. Knowing what the non-physical is, is not knowing what the mental is. Leaving this linguistic diatribe aside, that consciousness is always directed to an object, albeit only an intentional object, is nothing more than saying that consciousness has a content, be it a thought, a sensation or anything else.

This is a testament to Descartes' error in saying that there can be a substantive thing whose property is thinking. For thinking is not thinking without a content and there cannot be a thing that thinks without a content, or there cannot be a thing that thinks generally not of anything in particular. A thing cannot have a property of thinking without also a content of thoughts. Hence the mental is not in the thinking, but in the content of thoughts. Thus the peculiar thing about consciousness is that it must have content and if this content is unique, it is inaccessible, and therefore private; and also this content itself can be thinking of thinking itself. The possibility of thinking of thinking is a peculiar introspective aspect of consciousness that tends to give us the curious notion of the self in being capable of thinking of nothing in particular. This is misconceived. It is the content that raises the head of intentionality; pure consciousness without content does not help to determine an intentionality. It is because perceiving or sensibility does not always serve as a parallel to thinking of thinking, as a content in consciousness, that I think that not all intentional acts involve intentional objects. Is our sensibility or, for different reasons, a sense-datum mental? It seems without doubt that our sensibility is within us, as Berkeley would have taken it for granted. This will be discussed again.

8.3. The ontological understanding of the mental and consciousness

Some movements have extra-physical aspects

Many people call all things, to which they can attribute actions, conscious beings. It seems that, to them, conscious beings are those that are capable of acting and willing, or those who can act are conscious beings. Perhaps no one can get out of this circularity unless one can first define what consciousness is. But being aware of an action is not the same as being aware of its intention. Acting is not the same as intending to act. Having an act is more than just being aware of it. In order to introduce the notion of the mental and consciousness, I shall look into these terms from two angles. One is from the 'inner', private understanding of consciousness that can satisfy the epistemological criterion; the other is to look at the terms in relation to the physical, so to satisfy the metaphysical criterion.

When I look at the physical world of hard facts and concrete things, I do not presuppose anything mental in them, not least that perceiving itself is mental. But this physical world is full of movements and changes of thing and in things; even science gives us 'laws of nature' for the understanding of these movements and changes. It is only the acceptance that everything physical is explainable by these laws of nature, that blinds me from the obvious fact that these laws of science cannot adequately explain every movement, or why a dog can jump up in defiance of gravity. I can see that their laws may plausibly explain why a river runs downhill or a rocket rises to the sky. Yet there are numerous types of movements that cannot be explained directly by these physical laws. For if a stone's falling down needs a causal law, why not the dancing of the swans? Swans and dogs are physical in the sense that they have weights, sizes and extensions, just like stones and chairs. In a way, throwing a dog that weighs 20 lb. is the same as throwing a bag of sand weighing 20 lb. This aspect of the physical law is no problem to me. What concerns me is what causes a dog to jump or how far a monkey will (as opposed to 'can') leap from a branch of a tree. There are no physical laws to determine this. Still I cannot argue that dogs and swans are not physical, or perhaps that this law of physics may not be discovered one day, with hope.

Movements without observable causes

We can distinguish two types of physical things by appealing to how we can or cannot subsume their respective movements and changes under the rigid laws of nature, and how we can or cannot find observable causes in them. By these criteria, we can separate physical things into the living and the non-living. I do not call them organic and inorganic because the mere structural, physical difference cannot explain the lack of causes and governance of the physical laws. A dead thing is organic and yet non-living. A stone is not organic but non-living. How can I tell a living thing from the non-living without this criterion? Again, I shall say that anything that is alive can move or change without an observable cause. In order that this demarcation is not carved out of my own prejudice, but is as natural as water flowing downhill, it can be observed that while living things can die, non-living things cannot die, become alive, or be alive again. This truth is as perpetual as our mortality.

It will be tempting just to attribute the mental or consciousness to the class of living things by saying that all things alive are conscious beings. That will be too hasty. For being conscious or having mental items involves the epistemological aspects that need to be expounded. So, even in the world of concrete materialism, there is a kind of dualism, an ontological dualism in the living and the non-living. This cannot be hastily dismissed. Still, it must be said that there may be many who would not hesitate to reject such a distinction, since an unobservable cause is not at all a cause that may not be observed later, or in principle observable.

There remains a possibility that a physical cause that constitutes a biological movement in living things, can in principle be found in stimuli upon the bodies of these living things, as biology may imply. Indeed, it may seem that some movements may plausibly be explained by outside stimuli. For example, a knife can stimulate pain and reactions. I use this word 'can' because pain may not necessarily follow from a cut, just as a match will not always light a fire. However, one thing certain is that in causal laws, what is changed by a cause may be reversed by eliminating this cause, as science can illustrate to us. A car can be repaired by following the law of causality. If living things are governed by these physical laws in all aspects, we will certainly see dead things revived back into life or life can naturally commence by applying a particular cause. This is of course my ultimate premiss, which, I hope, will yield few credible objections.

Behaviours are not mere movements

Earlier I discussed Gilbert Ryle's behaviourism concerning the claim that whatever is considered mental in behaviours, is no more than what we can see in the physical aspects of these 'behaviours'. But Ryle cannot restrict his descriptions of behaviours to the mere physical aspects of movements, and inevitably the use of many 'mental terms' which he rejects, is inevitable. So, according to him, feeling pain is nothing but behaving in such and such a way so that 'such and such' is not a mental description but a physical. If we are really honest to ourselves, our descriptions of pure physical movements are nothing that can be called behavioural in the ordinary use of this term. 'I move my hand up in the air' is a physical description, but 'I wave my hand in a panicking way' is a behavioural description transcending the physical. How we see behaviours instead of physical movements, is not clear to Ryle. If he can, it will beg the question as to why we see behaviours instead of physical movements. One cannot sometimes wonder whether it is Ryle who has committed a category mistake himself, by mixing up behaviours with movements. Speaking of behaviours, it must be admitted that a stone or a chair does not have behaviours, but movements, that are caused. Behaviours are movements attributed to living things, albeit not all living things. If it is not certain whether behaviours and movements are the same category of things, the demarcation between the living and the non-living will now determine this.

Physicalism or psycho-materialism has as its main claim that the physical and the mental events are ontologically identical. But how can the 'psychological' be satisfactorily explained by physicalism, without using terms (psychological) that offer no credible distinction in meaning from that of the physical? However, if the physical is indisputably dualistic in terms of the living and the non-living, physicalism cannot be true or it has to explain an unseen cause. Genetic is not an explanation any more than the program of a computer is an explanation of how it moves to execute a command. The most physicalism can say of this identity is that a mental event is identical with a physical, but living event. A brain is not only physical, but also living, just as a live body is. There are no events in a dead brain or a dead body that can correspond to or be identical with any mental events; perhaps we can say that a dead body or a dead brain has no mental contents or attributes. What then is the significance between the living and the non-living, if they are all attributably physical, and if science does not deny that there are living things? Science does not make the distinction the way I have done. Science cannot admit that the causality that determines the movements of non-living things, is not adequate to explain that of the living things as well.

Epistemological dualism

Therefore, a bodily state or a brain state alive is not the same as the physical state of a stone or a chair. Ordinarily, we can recognize this distinction without realizing the inadequacy of the overexaggerated scientific laws of nature to explain the world. By getting rid of this physical determinism based on the physical laws of nature, physicalism can hardly be so objectionable as before, because it is only the explanation for one half of nature, the non-living nature. To say that a living, albeit physical, state is identical with a mental state, is not the same as saying a physical state has a corresponding identity with another mental state. To admit a distinction between the living and the non-living is to admit a metaphysical dualism in all physical things from the outset, and this dualism lies in the heart of the distinction between movements and behaviours. It may be true that behaviours need no mental items for their being, but it would be a totally different matter altogether to say that non-causal physical movements need no mental items for their being.

If behaviourism or even logical behaviourism is true, then it must explain why it chooses this term 'behaviour' instead of 'movement' for the motion of living things. If we can ascribe properties adequately to distinguish behaviours from movements, we may call this criterion an aspect of the mental. There are other biological movements such as heartbeats that may not be classified as behaviours, but nonetheless they are movements not of a purely physical nature. Thus, in being alive, an object has more attributes than its mere physical attributes. A living thing is more than just an object. So far this concept of the mental has not concerned itself with those items like thinking, feeling or imagining. It is but a capacity to be a living thing. This way, we can say living things are objects with the capacity to explain life's movements. The lack of awareness in some of them cannot stop convincing us that all involuntary movements such as heart-beats are also life's movements. It can therefore be said that such an account of life's movements belongs to nature too.

As behaviours are movements ascribed only to living things, so all behaviours are movements of the living, but not all movements of the living are behaviours. The distinction here does not always hinge on finding a metaphysical distinction in these movements to isolate behaviours from them, but rather on having epistemological connotations; these connotations come from nowhere but ourselves. Not only seeing movements of the living, we see them in having more than that which constitutes their physical 'essence'. By this, painful behaviours are understood not just as movements of living things but, as private experience associated with actions. In this sense, an intentional duality exists in many things we see. Descriptions such as 'behaving as if one is in pain', or 'behaving as if one is happy', or 'a stone of immense value', are dualistic conceptions of things that says more than what there is in their physicality. This is the epistemological dualism, a dualism from within a private consciousness evaluating biological movements. Who can say this epistemological dualism has no metaphysical reality in live beings other than ourselves?

Epistemological duality and identity

In the same way that every living movement has an unexplained dimension, a brain state or a bodily state is exactly such organic movements with a dimension responsible for these happenings, which cannot be explained purely in physical terms. Nor can I say that what is responsible for an organic movement is the organic movement itself; for if so, it will make no sense of the initial question as to why a movement of a physical object without an observable physical cause must be explained. If we ignore this question, on what grounds can we distinguish the living from the non-living, or behaviours from physical movements? I am not here claiming that the non-physical dimension is the cause of life's movements, or that there is a non-physical 'cause', so that I can determine the mental as a cause distinct from its effect. It is simply that a brain or bodily movement is not purely physical.

As previously stated, if a brain or bodily state and a mental state are causally linked, they cannot be identical. The aspect of the living adds more to this claim in that there is a difference between the causation of the brain or bodily state by physical objects, and the unobserved causation of its organic changes and movements. For if they are the same, it would mean that the physical causes of all movements are observable. Still this improbability must tempt science to investigate. Thousands of years of human observations may still be wrong. If we accept that living things have no physical cause within the physical laws, brain or bodily states cannot be caused by the physical. If we say that they are caused by mental states, then they and these mental states surely cannot be identical for reasons given before. It is, however, strictly a sense of necessity to mark a distinction between organic movements and physical movements. It is also a necessity to ask for an explanation for the origin of biological movements, in order to complete an understanding, in the same way we ask for a causal understanding of all movements to complete an existential enquiry. And, in so doing, this necessity will render whatever is distinguished between cause and effect, to be totally unidentical. This epistemological dualism has no singular identity. Consequently, a brain state is not merely physical and a brain state is not identical with a mental state, because of the necessity needed to explain this living state and because only if they are all physical can they be identical.

The non-physical and the mental

Dualism is in almost everything we see physical. It is not that we need to impose mental descriptions to all physical things before we find ourselves being chained to this inevitable duality. This duality in everyday reality exists not only in the way we see everything as relational, evaluative and functional, but also with an implication of the mental that things alive are more than just being physical. The connection to universals seen as in values and relation is not unapparent; values and universals are non-physical items that provide a metaphysical argument for this epistemological duality. If physicality is about colours, shapes, sizes, hardness, substance (such as wood or metal), electric charges, light wavelengths, temperature, and so on, then what in these physical descriptions constitutes a book, a tool or a bed? Physical aspects are things that constitute a physical object in its nature, but a bed is more than just a physical object in space and time. What we call bedness is something outside what is physical, and inside our judgement of a non-physicality. Take food for instance, food is more than the physicality of a thing. Without pointing to the apparent association with our own personal tastes, needs or feelings, we can find these extra-physical aspects nowhere except in our introspective awareness, and ultimately our nature. Hence I say there is nature and there is human nature.

Metaphysical consideration of this dualism

Dualism may not need the postulation of the mind as a thing, in contrast to a physical object, in order to subsist. For it is the distinction of what is not merely the physical that marks itself out from the physical, creating a duality. The question is how we can account for this extra-physical item. We cannot account for it in terms of the physical again, even if it coexists, since it is its being not identical with the physical that marks it apart. This duality is prominent in physical movements that we call behaviours. There is no doubt that the reason we can mark behaviours out from physical movements, lies in what we perceive in them as the dispositional qualities of these movements, since the open-ended question of causality invites us to fill it with a dispositional quality to substitute it for a cause. Yet, these dispositions are not explainable in terms of movements in space and time, to account for the non-living physical things. By calling movements as 'behaving as if…', we cannot satisfactorily explain the metaphysics of movements in terms of these dispositional qualities. But a stone falling down cannot be said to be behaving as if it is so. The potentiality in movements of physical things, such as voltage or a potentially electrifying 'live wire', is predictable according to physical laws. It is not the same with the dispositional implications in biological movements, in which we see the dispositions in terms of intentions, wants and purposes, that give rise to expectations, but are unpredictable and variable.

Now these dispositions are not seen, smelled or heard by the senses. It cannot be too absurd to suggest that these dispositional aspects are all understood and measured against awareness, in the same way that physical sensibility is awareness. To account for the existence of these dispositional aspects we see in physical objects, we can only look inwards with our judgements, since there is nothing outside that can explain them. In a broader sense, the duality explains why some physical things are not just physical, but associated with something that is responsible for their potentiality in intentions, wants and purposes. Their metaphysical origin lies in an awareness that is no longer epistemological. The world is not a cold world, but a human world in which all objects are in principle associated with human purposes. In another sense, this is a duality not only between the physical and the mental, but between the physical and humanity which is extra-physical in its conception. Nor can we imagine that we can shake off every humanistic view of the world to see it as merely physical. This other dimension of the physical reality is not a mere appearance, for appearances cannot and will not explain all these dispositional aspects of intentions, wants and purposes. The dispositional terms can surely be understood in my own, private and individual case.

Exposition of the mental outside the self

If we see creatures with behaviours (as opposed to movements), or moving with an intention, a want, a purpose, an expression of feeling, suffering or an ecstasy, we have no reason to think that these extra-physical aspects are necessarily connected to these creatures, be they men or animals. However, we can judge that their movements are not just movements, but behaviours because they are alive. We do not know these behavioural aspects for the lack of accessibility, but we can understand them, even if it is an understanding through ourselves. Still without knowing them, we can say of these creatures that they, in being alive, have movements that are dualistic in both being physical in their representation, and non-physical in their cause. This non-physical item, though not sensed, owes its existence to the non-caused movement. Hence if it is not a cause, it is a non-physical item (mental) which epistemologically is a reason, to explain a source for the movement without a physical cause.

This is the exposition of the mental, in living creatures outside ourselves. In self-awareness, those dispositional qualities are certainly known as well as understood. To understand behaviours, we call for no explanation of their physical causation. To explain behaviours metaphysically, we explain the extra-physical aspects that constitute behaviours and not movements. But, epistemologically, we can also explain the extra-physical through judgements within our own awareness, whatever it is. (This is not a presupposition of the existence of consciousness.) After this, comes the problem of public understanding of this dualistic nature in most things we see with our judgements. For if the understanding of these intentional items is only from within myself, how can I guarantee that other creatures' understanding of the same is the same as mine?

Public understanding of behavioural qualities

The exposition of how we and others can understand private experience and indeed linguistic utterances, has been detailed in other books I have written.[23] Without being too elaborate, I shall explain this briefly. To understand the mental or dispositional items of others' behaviours, one can draw on one's own actions or behaviours in association not with others' actions or behaviours (for that will be a circular argument), but with the similar surrounding, condition and situation we face ourselves. One's understanding of one's own reactions to situations and circumstances is the basis for understanding others' reactions or behaviours. This is so if we assume that our respective natures are similar, if not the same. If a person is in pain without an outward expression either in utterance or behaviour, it would seem that we will not know or understand it, unless we draw on our own experience of the circumstances and physical conditions and our reactions to them. Since most mental items are associated with outward expression and utterance, we will have observable criteria to understand and make judgements. Outward expressions or behaviours can be similar in the sense that if I cry, I can assimilate my crying with others' behaviours in their outward physical manifestation in the reaction to similar situations. If outward behaviours can be recognized in others through my own, it is through the association with my own mental items and outward behaviours that this understanding is bridged. This cannot be done via a direct knowledge because it is simply not available.

Here comes an assimilation: if a physical condition can lead to my having an awareness of a mental item in my behaviour, and if others behave in the similar or same way under the same physical condition, there must be in existence some mental items similar to mine, in the others. These mental items are ontologically responsible for others' movements without a physical cause, and will epistemologically account for my understanding (therefore my judgements of their behavioural content) of them without direct knowledge. This is so if we do not emphasize only the description of all behaviours, but the physical situations and conditions. That is to say, if I have a knife stuck into my stomach and I feel pain, I would expect someone to have experienced the same under the circumstance, assuming that we all have the same nature. The description of pain is superfluous, but not so the description of the physical circumstances. Therefore, if we are the same product of nature, I cannot assume that a knife sticking into my stomach will provide joy to someone, even if I do not feel pain myself. How good this presupposition is, is open to debate. We see the reactions to physical conditions from others all our life and our reactions to the same cannot be more similar. It is this acceptance of the sameness or similarity in our respective reactions to conditions that constitute the understanding of others' mental items in utterances and in behaviours. This conclusion extends beyond human experiences and their interpersonal agreement, into all things alive. From the 'lowest' life to the 'highest', and because all lives share the same nature of being alive, there must be a minimal understanding among them by reference to physical conditions and the reactions to them. Here, I may have inadvertently supplied some ammunition for the animal-rights activists. This exposition of the mental is only a position as regards other 'minds' and the following section will examine our own consciousness as the mental.

9. The mind and dualism

9.1. Our own minds

Cartesian dualism and its problem in interacting

The understanding of our own mental items is of course quite different from that of the mental items outside our own consciousness, because the metaphysical explanation of these 'private' items does not rely solely on the explanation of the living. Everything physical has a epistemological source which explains its metaphysical make-up. A chair is an epistemological explanation of its metaphysical reality, whatever it may be. The physical world may have physical and causal laws laid down to explain motions, from beginning to end, but mental items, as they are extra-physical, share no such luxury. Descartes identifies the mind as a non-physical, thinking thing by pointing to the peculiar feature of thoughts in having no extension that is indispensable in all things physical. This is a dualism of the non-extended and the extended: the mind and the body. This is all very well until the sceptics ask for its origin and the causality between this thing called the mind and the physical if the mind is an ontological thing in the physical world. How can men find the mystery between the causal interaction between mind and body, if they cannot even explain how life begins? This is where a causal connection, if there is one, should be found. Our philosophy is not to postulate the mind as an entity in the physical world.

I think the problem lies in how we perceive things (with the mind). If all things physical contain nothing but our sensibility, how can we distinguish between the intension of sensibility that is mental, and the extension of the physical objects, let alone determine a cause between them? To regard perceptual data as mental, one may have the problem all the same; for it is not at all certain if perceptual data are mental in the same sense as feelings and pains. The difference between perceptual data and pains is that while pains may come about independently of a physical object, veridical perceptual data (not dream data and the like) are absolutely interdependent with the object, or may even be said to be identical with it. In examining our private mental items to the exclusion of objects, I shall exclude the sense-data of perception; but can I do that really? I shall to return to this later.

Brain state and its physical cause

Earlier on I said that a brain (or bodily) state does not depend on a physical cause for its existence, since it is a living thing. But if it exists in a causality, there must be another state apart from itself, since a cause must be distinct from its effect. A brain (or bodily) state is distinct from whatever that may be claimed to be its causal origin. But if there is no causal explanation for the existence of a brain (or bodily) state, the separation of a mental state from a brain state is not credible. Thus if we have a good reason to leave out the physical aspects in the explanation of a brain (or bodily) state, we must explain it as well as a mental state. I think most people may object to the suggestion that a physical and a mental state are one identity, but may not at all object to the suggestion that a brain state is extra-physical in its cause. Having divorced a brain state from a physical cause, how can we understand mental states in term of the physical?

Why do I feel pain when a knife is stuck inside my body, if I do not consider this physical object, the knife, as the cause of my feeling pain? The stabbing of a knife into me is a general condition under which I feel pain, and yet it may not necessarily be so. If I am anaesthetized or paying too much attention to another life-threatening event, I may not even feel pain. Since such contingency exists, that is to say, a physical bodily condition may or may not conduce to a feeling of pain, the feeling itself and its physical condition must be two distinct events, not necessarily in a causal relation. The cause of a brain state in feeling pain is not necessarily the body. Feeling pain is a reaction and is truly attention-necessitated.

Perception or its cause

If there is a good reason for something to exist independently of another and be separate from it, it will not be difficult for us to test many mental items to determine whether there are two distinct processes in perceiving a physical condition and reacting to it. For instance, in perception, leaving aside the question of whether sense-data are outside us, we can determine whether seeing and sensing data are two separate things. You may say that in the process of sensing, sense-data (in the rawest sense without cognition) are registered in our retina. If I look out the window, there is no reason for me to think that all the available 'sense-data' in the field in front would not be available to me to see if I choose to do so. Yet, there are many items not in my immediate attention and are not 'seen', so to speak, unless I draw my attention to them. Therefore, it would not be safe to say that I will (as opposed to can) always see whatever there is in front of me; seeing as a cognitive progress must be distinct from merely sensing sense-data. This is an argument against the causal theory of perception in that there is no necessary connection between the causation of data and seeing them. In seeing, there is a positive and intuitive process (other may call it willing) separated from the causation of sense-data. Again perceiving is also attention-necessitated. In this case sensing is a happening (stimulus) and seeing is a reaction that is from within.

Being stimulated is not followed by an automatic awareness and more significantly, by our immediate response. A response must exist with or without a manifestation of a reaction in order that there is a root to a reaction not found in the stimulus. Also, for a movement of the living without an external cause, a response must come from within. Since when an attention is drawn to the condition of the body a pain is felt and since the condition of the body may not always induce pain, it may be suggested that the attention carries a reactionary awareness which is instantaneous. It is this attention and awareness that are a necessary link between a bodily condition and a response (of pain).

The response to physical conditions

Having cut the necessary causal link to cognitive (mental) perception, I shall introduce a notion of response. By introducing the notion of 'response' connected to a physical condition, we can rule out that a response can be seen as an effect in a pure physical causality without presupposing some extra-physical causes. Movements of the living or behaviours with cognitive content are not causal responses to physical conditions or the environment, but the consequents of these responses, or their reactions. A 'response' is in this sense the inner happening 'reacting' to physical conditions in ourselves without any outward manifestation such as a movement. I am also aware of the happenings as non-physical reactions to physical conditions. In our awareness, these responses are not observable as outward manifestations of the physical, but directly experienced. But if they are followed by physical manifestations, such as behaviours, then these inner responses and physical conditions connected to them will be understood in terms of behaviours. Adding to this, their public understanding would have assumed a presupposition that our natures are similar if not the same. If we assume that we have the same inner responses to the same physical conditions, our respective reactions in behaviours conditioned by these responses can be objectively judged by reference to the physical conditions conducive to our behaviours.

Every movement, if it is considered as a part of reality, must be conceived of as being related to all else. Since we have said that movements of the living have no physical cause we cannot conceive them as a part of all else in this causal sense. Instead we conceive of it as a manifestation of a response to things other than itself. It is not a causal response or the manifestation of it. That every living thing responses to things outside itself is a connection that enables biological movements to be conceived as a part of all else in a whole reality. This is perhaps the link which philosophers had sought for a long time even if they had conceived it as a causal link necessary to explain the interaction between the mind and the physical. Whereas their causal link is usually taken as 'causing from the outside', but a response is an inward process looking outwards that can only be put down as the nature of the living. As I have discussed, even perception has an response in its attention that is beyond what the physical causal laws can explain.

We may need cognition to consider a physical reaction to our responses, but I cannot say that my inner responses to physical conditions need another level of cognitive judgement since they are in awareness. That is to say, our inner responses to conditions are not subject to our will, our choice, our reasoning or our contemplation. These responses are immediate and determined. If one asks what reality there is to determine these inner responses to physical conditions, my answer will be the postulation of a thing that I call human nature. It must not be taken to mean that human nature should be all non-physical, or that these responses and our reactions thereafter can exist without the physical.

An attention itself to a physical condition cannot create a response, just as seeing a stone will not invoke my appetite; there is more to it in the attention itself that is necessarily associated with a natural response. A response cannot be physical since a causal link has now been cut. This non-physical happening in response to physical conditions must be a determined nature, even if our reactions to this response may be cognitive. And if this response is physiologically caused, it cannot be conduced necessarily by a body condition for the lack of awareness.

A non-Cartesian dualism

The disembodied mind in the Cartesian dualism lacks an existential origin for its disembodied mental activities; for without the physical, how can we feel, eat or arguably think? Or without human nature, how can we response to the physical? The lack of causal connection between the physical and the mental will not destroy the conception of dualism (perhaps not of the Cartesian type), since it is a matter of fact that living things have bodies as well as movements without observable causes. The absence of the Newtonian theory of gravity has not stopped men from believing for centuries that apples do fall from trees. Dualism in this sense is not so much about two separate and distinct substances, the body and the mind, but about the body itself being a living object. Thus a duality in this metaphysical reality must be a reasonable presupposition. This is a duality of the living and the non-living; of biology and physics and of all things judged to be extra-physical and with values, and things that are not. Things of no value and things merely physical are not things men can understand easily. Men understand things in the connection to other things and ultimately their nature. We see tables but not a collection of atoms in a particular shape or form, in space and time.

Human nature and its responses to physical conditions

Consider the mental item of pain. I can say that pain is a response in our awareness, or an urge to respond, to get-rid-of, or to avoid the possible damage to my body (a physical condition). Not only an urge of the unpleasant, pain is an urge that springs from an 'alarm' to preserve the body, to protect it against destruction. It may not necessarily relate to a cognition stage in the face of such a precipice; for this is only an alarm to danger, a nature in us to response to a physical condition we are in. If we do not see the body harmed, we may not feel pain; we may have a sensation, but we may not have a reaction to it. In the awareness of pain, we are responding to this sensation. Hence the response is not caused by sensations or any physical stimuli, but instigated by our nature through awareness. In a sense feeling is a kind of response to the physical conditions.

Although a physical condition may not always bring about the same response, a pain-response will always retain characteristics, as being unpleasant, loathing, or excitable and so on. Thus a response though connected to a physical condition, is indeterminable without a reference to a physical condition from which they may arise. A response to a physical condition and the condition itself are separate things. If our nature does not supply us with a response to possible physical damage, I can imagine that losing a limb or finger will be a casual matter without an alarm or flinching. I can understand your feeling pain, if I see your wound; and perhaps I understand more if I also behave the same way as you do with the same wound. Perhaps, if there is no wound, your pain may be a fake unless I believe your behaviours are true response to the pain felt by you. The existence of pain is not the physical condition itself or in it, but in an intuitive response to a physical condition, and others' pain is understood using an analogy grounded on a common humanity. This analogy is not arbitrary if there is a presupposed and commonly shared nature. This is pain in the public sense; in the case of pain within our awareness, it is simply incorrigible through experience. Its existence is not of our choice; it is an aspect of our nature that is immediately brought about in the recognition of a physical condition. I consider this as the non-physical aspect of my being in being alive and responding to physical conditions.

Other mental items such as anger, fright or hunger, can be all seen in the same way as pain. Human nature endows us with a disposition, an impetus if you like, to respond to the physical. And the cause of the physical is distinct from the cause of its responses. How we react to these responses depend on our interpretation or evaluation. Many philosophers, such as Thomas Hobbes think the initial supply of stimuli from outside cause our feelings. If that is so, it cannot explain the causation of non-stimulated mental experience we have, let alone why living things can move with a purpose and intention that cannot exist prior to their fulfilment and in terms of a purposeless stimulus. A physical stimulus and a mental reaction to it are two separate things; and they cannot be identical or be each other's physical cause and effect at the same time. Something can respond to the physical and initiate indeterminable actions, and this reality must be acknowledged. This reality is human nature. Chemical reactions are physically caused; their causes are tangible in prior events. This is not a case of responses from human nature the necessity of which is not in the physical conditions.

In awareness, pains and other feelings cannot be described like we describe physical things with colours, shapes and places. They can only be referenced through physical conditions and our nature. They cannot be described except through physical conditions. These non-verbal existents in awareness are the non-physical. They are experienced and unspeakable, and we refer to them by the physical representation of our reactions to conditions. Therefore, to know pain or a feeling is to experience it. But to 'know' of others' pains or feelings, we must have our own experience of them in our responses to physical conditions associated with them. Thus the cognition of the mental cannot be the same as the cognition of the physical.

Criterion for being private and mental, and ownership

Whatever is said of being mental, from the first-person point of view, cannot be based on its being private and inaccessible, even if it is the case. For the existence of a mind presupposes privacy and inaccessibility. If there is another mind in a physical thing, its existential confirmation does not rely on knowing it through private, perceptual data, whatever metaphysical reality there is about these perceptual data. The idea that, precisely because we cannot have direct knowledge of another mind through the physical, we cannot know its existence through physical data alone, is a double-edged blade cutting both ways. That we cannot know another mind through the physical, cannot prove or disprove its existence in whatever conceivable form. So if we cannot 'see' the mind, we cannot say it does not exist, any more than we can say it exists. And knowing (instead of perceiving) another mind depends on what cognitive input I can experience, which does not come from the perceptual knowledge of the physical, since there is nothing in the physical to give us an intimate knowledge of another mind.

If there is an input not known through the knowledge of the physical, this input (not perceptual experiences) must be found nowhere but within its being conceived. If conceiving can be non-perceptual, it is not identical with any physical thing perceived. For even if a chair is said to be a bundle of sense-data indistinguishable from the sense-data acquainted, epistemologically, a chair is distinct from these sense-data, since we call it a chair and not a bundle of colours. Here, because of this distinction there is one thing, which is conceiving another that is being conceived of, otherwise how can we explain the epistemological content of the physical is such a variety? Conceiving, as a type of experience cannot be the same as the conceived; for if it is, there will be no sense in something else being conceived of, or even perceived. Note that I am not making a distinction between a conceiver and the concept. If conceiving lies nowhere else and if the physical is less than what is conceived of, not only has conceiving no existential origin, but has no ownership too (that is to say, nothing is doing the conceiving). There is then no sense for it in being private or inaccessible. Being 'private or inaccessible' now is not so much a relation between two or more minds, but a unique phenomenon, in that there is nothing to claim an association with it, or a possession of it, except itself.

Conceiving is an act to determine existence. If conceiving is not the conceived, the conceived does not owe its existence to itself or to its being conceived of. If conceiving is so peculiar, only a presupposition of an owner, can make it ontological acceptable. It is only because there is a presupposed ownership, in the absence of everything else, that conceiving, and therefore the conceived, can be private and inaccessible. This is one way to explain 'privacy'. On the other hand, privacy has a sense of 'being private with exclusiveness', and in this 'privacy' to the 'exclusion of something else', there is a presupposition that not only something is excluded, but also there is something from which others are excluded. Unless we explain the sense of 'privacy' not in terms of an implied exclusion, there is nothing else we can infer from it. Very little metaphysically can be said of an analytic sense in something being presupposed. This leaves the only thing outside conceiving itself, and that is its ownership.

Why does conceiving or the feeling of anger or joy, need a owner? What is it meant for these things to be owned? If something is dependent on something else for its existence, it can be said it is owned. An object can be said to own its extension. But conceiving or feeling is not a thing that can be imagined without a content, a content conceived of or a content felt. Without content, conceiving, feeling or even thinking cannot exist. In this sense, we can say that ownership is also a supply of this content. By saying something is owned, we mean that it has a content the source of which is in something else.

Feeling angry has a source not in the feeling itself, but in our nature. The content of conceiving, feeling or thinking is not in things physical, nor anywhere else except its owner. To say that these items are owned, is to say that they cannot exist on their own without a relation (therefore content) to something that gives them the content. If feeling or thinking is all but generality, it cannot be public without privacy since public understanding rests on private experience of a similar source; therefore anything general has no privacy and inaccessibility. Feeling or thinking generally without specific content is inconceivable in that we cannot begin to imagine what thinking or feeling is like without specific cases. Thus the understanding and the awareness of feeling or thinking must also affirm a relation to an ownership of something. To call this thing a mind is to beg the existential question of what it is as an existent or entity. This we cannot do. I shall call this ownership a mental or non-physical aspect, that is implicit in awareness and understanding. Awareness is unique so that we cannot imagine another kind of it. It is therefore also private in this sense. When we talk about the mind, we are talking about these mental aspects that are extra-physical and presupposed by determination and understanding. I cannot assume that accessibility has a sense in being open to another awareness, since awareness is unique and singular. No imagination can possibly conceive of an alternative awareness.

This dualism is incompatible with the Cartesian dualism

To explore the peculiar aspect of conceiving things not associated with the physical further, we turn to another mental item of 'thought' itself. This item is important because there is a sense that thoughts are different from feelings and sensations. Descartes thinks that feelings and sensations are physical, and have to do with the body; hence he thinks that a purely mental self is a thinking thing without extension and other physical aspects. Descartes must have thought that the mind, in his *Cogito*, can contemplate physical items of feelings and sensations. Descartes does not include all items ordinarily recognized as mental, in the essential content of the mind. He chooses thoughts and thoughts alone to be the constituents of the mind. He thinks that feelings and sensations are modes of thoughts without which they would not exist (*Sixth Meditation*). Obviously, Descartes does not think that the reason that they are in consciousness is important to determine what the mental is. He thinks that only thinking is the essence of its being; that as feelings and sensations depend on the body, they cannot be mental. Independence is the Cartesian criterion in determining what the mental is, hence he thinks that the mind and body are two totally independent substances. By this criterion, our dualism in which the living incorporates both the physical and the non-causal movements, and various extra-physical items that explain them, cannot be said to be the same.

In Descartes' scheme, there is thinking, the thing that thinks, as well as thoughts. Certainly we can subsume thinking under a thinking thing because a thing that thinks implies such. What is the constitution of the Cartesian mind? Is it the thoughts or thinking itself? Or both? If a thought needs to be thought of, then a thought is dependent of thinking. If thinking is nothing without a thought, then thinking is again dependent of thoughts. To be a Cartesian mind, it must consist of both thinking and thoughts, but not thinking alone. Can these two mental items, thinking and thoughts (both unextended) be independent of each other? To say that a mind is a thinking thing is to say nothing about what a mind is; indeed it is not even possible to conceive of a mind thinking without thoughts. Thinking without thoughts is not conceivable and the separation of thinking from thoughts is not credible. Therefore the Cartesian mind, cannot exist without thoughts. If feelings and sensings are not thoughts, the Cartesian mind must belong to those who believe that they can think generally but not particularly. No wonder he claims that animals are mindless automatons.

Thoughts are very curious things. For a start, there is no thinking without them. But Descartes thinks that this is possible, so it is thinking that constitutes a mind and not the thoughts. But how can thinking alone be the attribute of a substance (the mind), without thoughts themselves? Thinking and thoughts are not a duality in the Cartesian sense. Thoughts are non-extended; the physical objects are extended; this is where the Cartesian duality lies, and this is a duality between the physical and thoughts, and not between thinking and thoughts. If thoughts and thinking are inseparable, it may help Descartes establish the Cartesian duality, but as it is, it does not help in questioning whether there can be pure thinking without content. Thinking of thinking can be a content idea if thinking and thoughts are one and the same. This can now be posed as whether there can be a 'thought about a thought', leaving out thinking altogether, only if thinking but thinking may not imply thoughts in Descartes' sense. This is not our kind of dualism.

Distinguishing awareness from thinking

By rejecting the existence of thinking without thoughts I can say that I am aware of a thought, or thinking about a thought. Will this not be a thought itself? If it is, can we say our awareness of feelings and sensibility is a thought too? If not, what makes them so different? If every happening in our consciousness is a thought, feelings and sensibility must also be the content of thinking. Ordinarily, when I say 'I feel a pain', I do not say that I am thinking of pain, but that I am aware of pain. In my awareness of pain, I am instinctive in my response so that there is no content in this awareness relating to belief, truth, falsehood or inference. Whereas ordinarily I too associate thoughts with these reflective notions. The same can be said of the awareness of sensual-data. The idea that sensibility is the incorrigibly given, is not the idea that there is a secondary reflection on this incorrigibility by applying judgement and belief, but that the impact of the given sensibility is so instinctive as to render such contemplation redundant. This is not to say that we cannot have secondary thoughts about our awareness. Awareness may be distinct from thinking because awareness can exist without content whereas thinking cannot. There is also an earlier argument for this distinction. Perhaps we may confuse awareness with thinking. What is being aware is a response or an instinctive disposition, but what is thought of is the contemplation of relations.

The possibility of denying awareness or thinking

Awareness in this epistemological sense is distinct from thinking. In awareness, I have no reason to rule out an attention to thoughts, any more than I can rule out the existence of the thinking of thinking thoughts itself. Granted this distinction, can we deny thinking without admitting that this denial is thinking itself? If there is awareness over and above thinking, perhaps thinking of thinking is the awareness of thinking. In this sense, an awareness of the denial of thinking, is an awareness of the state of the mental, and not the thinking of this denial. All this depends on whether the argument on the distinction holds good. In proposing that we cannot doubt our thoughts (thinking, in the Cartesian sense), has Descartes missed out this possible distinction between awareness and thinking itself? When I say to someone, 'I am thinking', someone asks me 'What are you thinking?'; I say, 'I do not know'. If thinking needs a content, a thought, and if I cannot answer the question, I either do not know the content, in which case, I was not thinking at the time (it is hard to admit that this is the case); or I know of the content which I was reluctant to tell. In the Cartesian sense, a doubt about thinking is a thought about the doubt about thoughts, in that case we have the content of thinking or have thinking itself as its content. But if we do not know of the content of thinking we have doubted, we are not doubting a 'thought', but the thinking itself, and this doubting is now a secondary thinking apart. This seems to be an open invitation to a vicious circle. And it seems to exhibit a counter-factual here because ordinarily we do not think that thinking of thinking is itself a secondary thinking, for the lack of a thinking content. A statement of 'I do not know what I am thinking' is a probable answer.

This problem can be resolved by separating awareness from thinking. We can say that the awareness of thinking is instinctive when there is a happening in 'consciousness'. Thinking or doubting our thinking is an awareness. Thinking needs an awareness; to deny thinking is to deny awareness which is not possible since awareness is not subjected to our will. To deny thinking is possible if we do not deny its awareness. I cannot be thinking if there is no content, but I cannot fail to be aware if its denial in turn needs an awareness. In another way we say that to doubt our thinking is itself an awareness. This may not necessarily be thinking. Whether we believe that 'doubting' involves judgement that may only apply to thinking and not awareness, there can be no thinking without an awareness. The Cartesian premiss that doubting a thought is itself a thought, is not an analytical truth, but an 'empirical' truth since doubting is an experience itself. Furthermore, the content of awareness can be non-epistemological in the same way the content of sensibility is; they are both instinctive. However, a thought is epistemological if judgement is epistemological by definition, therefore its content is also epistemological. If so, the denial of a thought can either be a denial of its epistemological content or a denial of its existence. In the former, the denial is possible if its non-existence is not implicit; in the latter the denial of its existence is not within our power, since a thought comes with an awareness.

Consequently, when we say that we cannot doubt the existence of thoughts, we should mean that we cannot doubt the existence of an awareness (of thoughts or whatever happening there is). It is not so much because doubting its existence is a thought itself, but because doubting an awareness needs an awareness itself. Awareness is a state of being and its content may not necessarily be anything specific. Hence unlike thinking, it can subsist without a specific content. Awareness cannot be denied not only because a denial is an awareness, but also because reasoning itself cannot deny it. When all my sensory inputs are deprived and I have nothing in particular to think of, my awareness is the receptive attention in parts of my body called upon even without a specific input of sensory data. It is my belief that our awareness, thoughts and feelings are all distinguishable in this way. Doubting implies the understanding of something, i.e. a thought. Doubting is reasoning about something and therefore more than one thing in itself. Doubting must have a content too. Awareness is instinctive, not reasoning, hence what can be denied is what is reasoned, but not the awareness itself. Every time we think, we are aware that we think, instinctively and not reflectively. The separation of awareness from thinking provides a metaphysical ground for an instinctiveness to establish a duality to explain a non-causal response in the mental. It is claimed therefore that every mental item has an awareness, an ownership and privacy. But whether we can say that 'I' or the mind, is awareness itself, is another matter altogether.

Awareness is the first step towards an epistemological reality and freewill

Since I do not make a metaphysical distinction between feelings, sensibility on the one hand, and thoughts on the other, I do not see an importance in them being either spatial or non-spatial.

'Mental' states, physical or not, are mainly represented in perceiving, conceiving (thinking) or feeling. Each of these, if not regarded as a responsive reaction, has its own response for it to be more than causally induced. Perceiving has a selecting attention; conceiving has a disposition to believe; feeling has a tendency to act. It is these responses and their potentiality that explain movements of the living as reality outside observable causes. ('Observable' is in the normal sense of the word.) But every response is in awareness, since the physicality of these states is contentious precisely because they are supposed to be states of consciousness and not just physical events.

However, it is not to say that the awareness of feelings, sensibility or thinking may not be spatial in some sense. In considering a brain state, we can say that in every brain state, there is an awareness of it, not in the sense of seeing synapses from the outside.

Awareness in this case is the first connection between the physical and the non-physical. Whether a state of sensibility, thinking or feeling is physical or not, if a response to them is causally distinct, the awareness of a response must be causally distinct. In this sense awareness can be considered as a mental state since it is causally distinct from a 'physical state'. If physicalism can safely say that feeling, imagery and thinking are products of the brain states, brain states cannot explain a secondary awareness of these feeling, imagery, thinking or even awareness itself, if there is no secondary awareness. If I am right, there are two physical states to explain a dualism of awareness and its content.

Since there is a difference between having a stimulus and having an awareness of it, in having a stimulus under the physical law of causality one cannot causally explain the existence of awareness. Examples have been given in the case of people not necessarily feeling pain when physically hurt, or 'seeing' things which are not physically there. There still remains the possibility that awareness can remain a biological state, albeit without a causal explanation in the non-biological causality. In the case of private experience, the awareness of what there is in our consciousness is clear and instinctive. Thus awareness is the first step towards an epistemological reality from a metaphysical reality that, in the absence of relations and values, is of little or nothing to talk about. From the viewpoint of physical behaviourism, awareness is something not seen as the physical, but it must be implicit in order to make sense of the distinction between behaviours and movements. Living things react to the physical conditions instinctively and variably. It is instinctive because it presupposes a nature of the thing. It is variable because cognitive process is the only explanation and because not every stimulus always produces the same reaction from a beast, whereas the physical causal law would have suggested otherwise. To understand this variety in these reactions, we can only draw on our own cognitive nature to explain other cases. Awareness of a 'physical condition' is a necessity to trigger off a natural and spontaneous response to this condition. Though human nature provides us with a deterministic inevitability in our responses to physical conditions, reactions are cognitive that provide us with the sense of freewill.

At this juncture, some may suggest that a biological state of response can be induced by chemical reaction within the brain, even if awareness cannot be conceived of to be so. Again this is the epistemological versus the metaphysical reality. If a biological state is produced by chemicals, it cannot explain a preference or aversion to this state in our consciousness. This is to say that if chemicals can produce immense 'pleasure' or 'pain' in the brain, what chemical state will be produced to conceive of it as a determinable preference or not just a preference? A chemical state is a physical state and will remain a physical state just as corrosive acid on a stone provokes no reaction from the stone. A drug can produce a biological state, but never a reaction. A reaction is not a part of this physical causal chain. It is also because a response is spontaneous that we may regard both the response and its physical state as one and the same. This cannot be so if physical causality is questioned and a separation of response from the physical state is implicit through the distinction made between the living and the non-living. In all these, the awareness of and therefore the response to the physical are a precondition to all reactions to the physical conditions. Without this implicit understanding, movements cannot be taken as behaviours. The will is the slave to our nature but cognitive in the interpretation of this nature. It is basically rigid and epistemologically varied.

If there is a mental state to interpret the content of the perceived physical world which physicalism sees no need to postulate, there is a state of awareness any brain state alone cannot explain. For interpretation is epistemological and not physical. It is a truism that all things physical need to be interpreted (with relations or values), and an interpreted reality is an epistemological reality that pure physicalism cannot hope to explain. If the physical can produce a separate state of awareness to accompany each mental state of perceiving, it will do so as a matter of course under the law of causality. If in the case where there is no awareness, this causality will break down and will not explain why an awareness may not be found when a physical condition exists to allow a perception and its accompanying awareness. This is the case of not being able to see everything in front of us which is in principle perceivable.

Sensing and sense-data

I do not think that the argument between physicalism and mentalism can ever be settled, if there is no acknowledgement of an epistemological reality. In every phenomenon classified as mental, there is a duality for its existence in its awareness; there is no physical manifestation to substitute awareness since it is not the phenomenon itself. All these phenomena, such as thought, feeling, pain, sensibility or imagery, owe their existence to awareness; and whether they are identical with physical states, will not stop them from having a duality in a response. These phenomena owe their existence not to the physical but to awareness, and in this sense they are mental.

Similarly one may also argue that the physical is mental if all things physical is sensed in awareness. Of course this is the main philosophical debate of whether sense-data are mental or not. The crucial difference here is in the separation of sensing from its awareness in a duality. Whether sensed data are identical with sensing or whether sense-data are in the physical world or in our awareness, is at the heart of the debate between those thinking that the world is materialistic and those thinking otherwise. The claim that anything in awareness is mental, is compatible with dualism or any monistic idealism. If we accept that sensibility is different from sense-data, we are accepting a kind of dualism anyway. Or, if sense-data are not in the physical things perceived, their separation from awareness will mean an epistemological dualism and nothing more. This separation will allow sensed data to be capable of being aware without implying that these sensed data are in awareness or in the physicality of things. This way, metaphysical reality can be either dualistic, or monistic in this non-physical sense. But any dualism would be incompatible with a world wholly materialistic where awareness and what is in awareness are exclusively physical. There can be no dualism in physicalism but there can be a dualism, an epistemological dualism, in idealism.

Thoughts and its ontological origin

What a thought is, is difficult to say. Generally, we speak of a thought in terms of its linguistic representation, which cannot be identical with the thought itself. For if it is, how can we explain our mistakes in expressing our thoughts? If expressions are interpreted thoughts that allow mistakes in their interpretation, do we need a secondary thought process to make such interpretation? If so, how is an original thought manifested in order for an understanding to be formed for interpretation? There cannot be another thought for an interpretation of this expression, at a second level. There is one Wittgenstein opinion I will use positively. This is the case where he refers to thinking in a chess game: when a person in a split second realizes and understands a move, he exclaims. From not realizing to realizing, it may only be a short moment, but how we can formulate a linguistic expression of this thought realization in such a split second is beyond my own experience since chess is a very complex game. Yet, it cannot be denied that words and language do help our thinking, even if they are not identical.

What a thought is may not be important since we all experience it. If linguistic expressions are considered as physical and causally formed, a thought that is not identical with a linguistic expression, cannot have a causal origin in the physical that is responsible for the formulation of a linguistic expression dictated by the affairs of the world.

If thoughts are considered as not spatial, in what sense are they not spatial? If things thought of are spatial, would it make thinking itself spatial? Are perceptual judgements thoughts? If they are, in what sense they are non-spatial? Descartes' idea of thoughts being non-spatial has more of a sense in being intangible than not-in-space, and we can say that energy, force or power in things is intangible, and therefore non-spatial. This makes the demarcation between the spatial world and the non-spatial mind more precarious.

If thoughts have any metaphysical significance, we must account for their origins as we account for the origins of all existents. It is this origin of thought, which cannot be accounted for in the same way the origin of movement in a living thing cannot be accounted for by the mere physicality of nature, that brings about our conception of an alternative, non-physical reality. Terms like 'force', 'power' are such conceptions, not because we can conceive of these things without physical objects, but precisely because physical description is not sufficient. We may have perceptual content in our thought, but perceptual content is not responsible for the origin of thoughts; for having thoughts, with or without perceptual content, is having more than the awareness of an 'object' of thought including its perceptual content. As I earlier have proposed, notions such as truth, entailment, belief or falsehood are also involved in thinking, if not responses to it. If we accept that these notions are reality outside us, we must somehow explain them in terms of the physical outside us, to sustain our claim that these notions are causally linked, even if they are not identical with some physical events. But what is outside us, if it is not the physical world; and what else is there apart from physical things, even if they are beings independent of being conceived?

Hence there comes the notorious term called 'facts'; are facts the interpreted reality of the outside or just reality uninterpreted? If truth is about something corresponding to facts, who makes such judgement of correspondence? If the truth of something is in its correspondence with the physical, can we find a physical event that is identical with the assessment of such correspondence, as well as the conceived 'facts' too? Even if we can find it, how and why does the physical nature establish such correspondence? If nature presents to us only its physicality in our observation, nature is all but sense-data without judgement, if sense-data are non-judgemental and non-relational. Under these circumstances, it is not at all clear whether data can be understood, let alone conceived under a causal law. To judge a truth or correspondence between the physical world and facts, even if they are all physical, we can only understand it properly if it has a non-physical dimension, because understanding is this dimension. The ontological origin of this non-physical dimension lies nowhere but in the exposition of the metaphysical reality; without acknowledging this, nothing physical can be understood, let alone conceived of. To say that there is an origin, or a 'cause' assimilating a physical cause, to explain the ontological status of things like thoughts, is to say that there is a physical purpose served by thoughts in the judgement of truth, falsehood, and so on. The justification of this cannot be found in the physical, but in our own personal experience. Therefore, if a physicalist or scientist who does not accept that we see more in things than their mere physicality, he or she must ask him or herself a question: in an all-physical world, is there no need for a sense of truth, falsehood or the like and if so, how can a mere physicality account for it? If we rejects this, what physicality of the world accounts for our judgement? Scientists are human too no matter how they may reject this realm of epistemological reality; for epistemological reality is not something you can leave aside in observing a metaphysical reality. To look for the origin or purpose of thoughts, we may uncover the purpose of each thought, analysing it to a satisfactory end; that is to say, we shall uncover why we think about certain things, and where the conclusion of thoughts can lead. To say that thoughts have conclusions in themselves is to say that thoughts, akin to physical events, are linked in a chain just as physical events are taken as a train of events. Each thought is a thought because there is another distinct thought. Thoughts are associated by their content, and eventually there will be an end to a chain of thoughts. In the physical world it is time that links events, but what thing physical can link thoughts to thoughts?

Thoughts are to serve beliefs and therefore actions

It may not be true that every conclusion is followed by a belief or a state of believing, for thoughts and beliefs are intertwined. Both need each other and both can be each other's reason and consequence. In a way, thinking is a process and believing is a state, so that the ultimate question of why we think, is the question of why we have beliefs thought out, confirmed or unconfirmed by thinking. A state of believing may be taken as a physical state, if we do not accept that believing is mental. It will be fair to say that thinking is to serve our beliefs, without which there can be no thinking necessary. If a state of believing is a state of disposition or a disposition to contemplate actions, what is a belief for, if it is not to serve our actions and satisfaction? We act with a subjective certainty, an eye for success (to confirm our belief), and with a subjective satisfaction in our interaction with the physical conditions that we are given. One must not think that the interaction with a physical condition is all about survival, nourishing and comfort. There are many peculiar requirements from men beyond these basic needs, such as vanity, power or a thirst for knowledge.

Again, without the awareness of these needs in human nature, I will venture to say there will be no need for men to think. Thinking is not necessitated by the rationality of men any more than actions are under the necessitation of rationality. Therefore the origin of thoughts must lie in men's nature and beliefs and is part of the process of this nature to propagate itself through movements that are called actions. The nature of men is non-physical in the sense that their movements cannot be physically explained conclusively; hence a thought's origin lies in this non-physical nature of men, even if it can be argued that there is a brain state for every thought. For we are in a quest for a response to a physical condition, therefore a belief. Even if a belief is a physical state, a response (not a movement reacting) to it cannot be a physical state.

Contrasting thoughts from sensibility

In contrast to sensibility (not thinking of sensibility itself), thoughts are not passive in the way sensibility is, as the given. Our choice in what we see, except paying selective attention to what we see, does not really exist. Hence the epistemological incorrigibility in sensibility exists not because the given cannot be doubted, but that there is no sense in doubting anything that is given to us in our sensibility. Doubts arise when subjective judgements are a matter of a corrigible or incorrigible choice. Men are not born to recognize the incorrigibility of '2 + 2 = 4'. We accept it with a reason and this reason comes from nowhere except in thoughts within us, even if we think it is objective. Thoughts are not passive but active in that men search for a solid permanency upon which they base their beliefs for actions and satisfaction. Therefore, if thoughts are considered as physical (brain) states, they will not be active, but passive, in the sense that physical stimuli from outside cannot account for their purposes or origin that are non-physical. To understand actions as opposed to movements (the non-living), we can only draw on our intimate experience and understand them in terms of these mental notions such as feelings, truth, falsehood, needs and values. Certainly stimuli can induce physical actions of the involuntary type, but if so, how can humankind have a sense of epistemological reality, let alone a sense of purpose beyond involuntary movements? Where lies the reality of men's contemplation and judgement?

Awareness that binds all mental items; awareness in others

Speaking of a mind or two minds, of mental substance, or of the inside or outside of a mind, there invariably is an implication or assumption that a mind is an entity with a boundary. This boundary contains all that is mental such as feeling, thinking or sensation, separate from what is outside itself. Thinking this way, there is no criterion to bind these mental items together, and to confine them within a boundary. One way to speak of mental items in this way is the neo-Cartesian postulation of something that 'owns' these items, which are, of course, its attributes. Inevitably, this something must have some connection with the self, just as Descartes will say that 'I' is this thing that thinks (of these things). In the idea that there is nothing left if all sensible qualities are taken away, this postulated 'mind' will suffer the same fate if all mental items are taken out. Therefore, accepting the existence of mental items as having a non-physical aspect, is not the same as accepting that there is something underlying all these mental items. Thus if all mental items are non-physical, it will not follow that there is a mind that contains these things that are non-physical; for if everything is taken away, the existence of the mind will also be taken away. This is of course counter-intuitive since we ordinarily believe that mental items belong to something through a totality of inaccessible private experience. Without being counter-intuitive, I must reject the existence of the mind as a substance, or as a 'container' that holds all mental items, and seek an explanation elsewhere, of this belonging.

To submit my being as an existent only to the manifestation of mental items, is not always satisfactory since I cannot abandon the physical aspects of the body in the conception of all things mental. We cannot instinctively ignore the possibility of the destruction of the body, by thinking that all our mental items have nothing to do with its possible destruction. We cannot say our body is not the self, for a possible disembodied self cannot explain perception or pain which are body-dependent during this embodied existence.

In considering all items mental, I must remind myself of an aspect that is common to all of them. This is the aspect of being aware. As all mental items owe their existence to being aware, awareness is their mutual association. Awareness is private and unique; I cannot imagine or conceive of another alternative, since awareness is all there is to propagate any existence. In the case of the possible existence of the physical world independent of sensibility, awareness supports the sensibility through which the physical world exists as being seen or contemplated. In the case of the existence of the mental items, they depend totally on it. Awareness is in a sense what we may call consciousness. Since we do not know awareness or consciousness outside ourselves, we do not say of things that they are conscious, but that they are alive. Consciousness is private and cannot be attributed to things. I have no experience of others' consciousness to be certain that other things have the same state of awareness as I have. The sense of being alive must be distinguished from being conscious, to avoid confusion in my way of using this term.

The state of awareness

I like to think that there is a pure awareness, perhaps distinct from the thinking of thinking that cannot exist without content, and quite definitely distinct from that of perceiving data. The latter may suggest an awareness being physically caused by sense-data taken as a physical cause. If I am in a sensory-deprived environment, I cannot say that I am not in a state of awareness for the lack of sensory stimulation; I can certainly 'sense' my own body in a state of receptivity ready for anything with which it comes into contact. This awareness is an awareness pure and without stimuli, quite different from the awareness of data, and perhaps of thought-content. Can we say that this awareness is thinking with the self with awareness as its content? Certainly we can, but for many, thinking is thinking with reasons and beliefs; this marks it out from awareness itself, but awareness is none of these. I shall call this pure awareness a state of awareness. This state of awareness must precede thinking of thinking and perceiving. This is a state of being alive from the point of consciousness, without which there can be no perceptual awareness, no awareness of thought content, or anything else. I doubt very much that if we are in a deep coma or unconsciousness (not in a state of awareness), there could even be a question of thinking of thinking, let alone existence. And it is not an exaggeration to say that we come in and out of existence, for the lack of a continuity in consciousness, only to construct a continual existence by the subsumption of all experiences of the past and present into a consistent whole. I exist because I am in a state of awareness.

The mind is indicative, not a substantive entity

Still, if awareness binds all things mental, there is no reason for us to think that this awareness alone is somehow the whole mind. A mind is not so much a definitive singularity to contain or to exhibit all items mental, but an indication of the non-physical and the living. Awareness binds these items together to give a sense of belonging, because in awareness, a relation among mental items exists. If I am aware of pain and if I am also aware of a thought and a bundle of connecting perceptual sensibles, an association among them exists in their mutual awareness, in judgements and in time and space. But such an association does not or may not exist in the mental items if they are being known independently of one another. If I have been punched in the eye and I feel pain, there is nothing in the punching, or in the eye that can suggest that punching the eye and the pain are associated. This is to say, that if a pain I am aware of is not associated with these perceptual data, there is nothing to connect all the mental items together as one conceptual phenomenon; then these items are unconnected without unity or belonging. Thus a single mental item, if it is linked to other mental items in awareness, will be in unity by association. Beyond this awareness, a mental item is not understood in the context of a whole experience.

The brain and the mind

Conceiving a connection among mental items and having an awareness of this connection are the unification of mental items under a single or whole experience. It is not surprising that we commonly think of mental items as existing within a thing or substance. The realization of a close connection between brain activities and mental items may also give us the idea that all conscious items are identical with the happenings within this physical (albeit biological or living) thing called the brain. Even in the presence of corresponding physical happenings in other parts of the body, we are hesitant to claim that these states are identical with those mental items. The idea that a mind 'resides' within a physical boundary of the brain cannot conveniently be taken for it to establish a physical stage on which the brain is the cause of all conscious items. It is not only because the activities of the brain have a cause not accountable by its physicality, but also because the stimulated 'action' is not only on the brain, but on other parts too. Unless we can reasonably account for the awareness of brain states with a purely physical explanation of a response, and not on an epistemological footing, we can only consider the brain as something physical upon which an awareness depends, just it largely depends on the other parts of the body.

But for this dependency, an ontological identity between the brain and awareness cannot be readily assumed, though one may say that electrical discharges among water droplets, and the manifestation of a flash of lightning with a thundering noise, are two epistemological aspects of the same thing. This is usually taken as an analogy between brain activity and mental phenomena being two aspects of the same thing. But to say that is to ignore an important metaphysical aspect accompanying all mental aspects. This is the lack of a physical cause in the physical movements (or changes) of a living thing (the brain), and the existence of responses. Thunder and lightning are not responses to whatever state water droplets are in, because thunder and lightning are rigid, causally 'necessary' or permanent manifestations whereas responses are varied, non-veridical and judgemental which put paid to the validity of this causal law. Still thunder and lightning are interpreted phenomena that cannot be metaphysical in reality. If so, why should there be a different reality?

Brain activity has no physical cause outside itself in a chain of physical events, any more than my jumping up in the air has a physical cause outside my body. A gust of wind can certainly raise an organic arm, just as electrical impulses can induce movements in this arm, or activities in a brain, but such physical explanations are not always adequate enough to explain a causality in movements of the living. An arm can resist the wind that attempts to raise it. The signs we look for, in making a claim of physical-mental identity, are in movements and changes, hence physicalism does not say a brain is identical with a mind, but only that a brain state (movements inside a brain) is identical with a mental state. Therefore in saying that mental items have all those physical, causal aspects, we also say that they are not merely epistemological, but also metaphysical as well. But why? Consequently, seeing lightning in colour and not in abstract entities (such as electrons) must be explained by an epistemological reality. All things mental come from this epistemological reality. Science cannot ignore an epistemological view of the physical things no matter how advanced its technology becomes, for it is colours and sensibles that are the main content of its investigations; without epistemological reality, there is no science. It is the epistemological reality that constitutes relations and without relations the investigation by science is nothing. A scientist who does not explain his observation is no scientist at all.

The mind and reality

By rejecting the brain as identical with the mind, I am not saying that there is a thing called the mind that dwells in no space, somewhere yet unknown. The mind is nothing but the associated sum total of all the aspects that are the non-physical, dependent on the physical. The mind is nowhere because we cannot point to it except through the non-physical. The mind is epistemological. In the awareness of the non-physical happenings, we say there is a mind; we have no more sense in pointing to a centre of all these happenings bound together by a common awareness in a unity of experience, than the sense of an entity. The mind is everywhere in the awareness of all things and of the body - a body that is alive, so that every awareness of a sensation and movement, is not only explainable by the physicality of the body, but by all aspects in a unity of experience. This is what I mean by being non-physical, or mental. Other physical movements of the body not within this awareness and unity are movements, not behaviours. An awareness of our own movements includes their being associated with other mental items in the same awareness. An awareness of a sensation without such a connection lacks a unity with other mental items, and thus lacks the sense of response and personal identity. A heart-beat is not in our awareness and in this unity. It is probable that the judgement of a unity presupposes awareness, but awareness of this may not presuppose a unity. I may feel the heart-beat or a spasm of a muscle, but if its association within my experience is only with the body and not with items such as joy or pain or pleasure, they are only physical. There is a lack of response. In sensing, a sensation is nothing without a cognitive judgement as to its associated experience. Hence a particular colour is mental in the awareness of this sensation, but a sensation is a mere happening indescribable; and that may be physical. I think there is a difference between the awareness of heart-beats as a sensation and its awareness in association with other mental items, manifested either as rhythms or as pain. The unspeakable former may be physical, but the latter is mental in this sense. The sensing of sense-data and awareness of them in a cognitive reality, are two separate things. Thus this philosophy is not a total rejection of an external realism. External realism is not only the unknowable, but unspeakable.

As soon as we start to think or speak of it, we open the door to an epistemological reality that may or may not be subjective. The mental is inside this doorway and the physical has no causal link to it. Humankind and the animal kingdom act because they are mental beings that interact with the physical rather than submerging wholly under it.

Rejection of a causality for the mental

The mind, being the sum total of the non-physical happenings in awareness, is not a substance and anything physical, other than what there is in our awareness. In this sense, there is no need to explain a causal connection and interaction between the physical and non-physical. This is so because the existence of the non-physical does not owe an explanation to the existence of the physical through a causal connection. Many dualisms in history were criticized for the lack of a causal connection, because it was considered that the mind must act upon the physical. But, for me, the mind reacts to the physical rather than being acted upon by the physical. It must be seen that there are two causal connections here if we reject that physical causality applies to all things. There is the cause of the physical upon the mental and the cause of the mental reacting to the physical. The rejection of the existence of one does not entail the rejection that of the other.

We see that the biological sector of the physical world has in itself, a non-causal aspect in its movements. Whether there is a cause of the physical upon the non-physical centres on whether there is an empirical possibility for the non-living to become alive, if we can pose the question correctly. It is a matter of fact in the nature of things that living things do move without a physical (external) cause. It is not a matter of whether we can prove that living things can move without a physical (external) cause, since this is the state of affairs of the world. To find a cause of life is not a matter of proving nature is right or wrong, but a matter of seeing whether our interpretation of nature is true or false. Thus, the cause of the physical upon the mental is rejected. As we have made a distinction between two ways of causality, the rejection of the physical causing the non-physical does not mean that we can reject the 'cause' of the mental upon the physical. The latter cannot be understood from the physical, but understood from within our experience called mental.

One may be concerned that all these mental happenings, if not rooted on something permanent and substantial, something will descend into a kind of phenomenalism. Thus, there is something missing in all these mental items.

9.2 The mind and the self

The body is indispensable to the self

Referring to the unity of these mental happenings as the mind, is not the same as referring to this unity as a self. Descartes thinks that, from the existence of thinking, we can adequately infer the existence of the self as something that is responsible for thinking. Apart from the reasons I proposed earlier to reject such an inference, there is also the reason that the self we ordinarily speak of is more than the mental content of thoughts in the Cartesian sense. Descartes sees that the body is merely physical, and to sustain the mental as being independent of the physical, he must of course reject any connection between the body and the mental content. Yet, Descartes does not see the importance in making a distinction between the living and the non-living, which can metaphysically imply a non-physical reality in all living things. To accept the dependence of mental items on the physical body, one must also acknowledge the importance of the body in this respect. In this association, even if the self is only the mind in the Cartesian sense, it will make no sense to leave out the body on which mental content depends.

Ordinarily speaking, we do regard our body to be part of our self-identity. With this acknowledgement, all the items Descartes discards as being physical or bodily, will come into reckoning in this self-identity. All feelings, pains and sensations to which my bodily movements are associated, are part of the 'I', and that cannot be doubted.

The self of the present presupposes all past selves

Self-identity is not about how the past 'I', the 'I' in my memory, or the changing 'I', can be seen as identical to the one and only 'I' of the present. As I have argued before, the past 'I', the 'I' in my memory or the changing 'I', presupposes two separate existents that cannot be logically reduced into one or into the existence of another, without making this deductive argument circular. And yet it is the presupposition of the mind that can really make sense of self-identity. I have examined this topic at length[19] I shall not get into the argument here in depth. Self-identity is self-evident if the self is known or determined. Through a sense of belonging, uniqueness (privacy) and unity, all epistemological selves (the past, changing selves) are presupposed in the knowledge of the present self, if all the mental items are to be understood as they are. Understanding mental items of the present, the past and the changed items that constitute the being of these selves, is indispensable to this knowledge, so that if the past and the changed mental items are not part of this unity of experience, we can no longer understand the self of the present.

Self-identity apart, the self cannot be known like tables and chairs. For if it is so, knowledge of the self through space and time will not deal with mental items that are the important constitution of a self. However, in the metaphysical exposition of the non-physical element, that is, the distinction of the living from the rest, one aspect of the self is in this manifestation, i.e. being alive. We act rather than move. Not only that, we act with purposes and intentions that are in association with other mental happenings. This association is an awareness of our actions belonging to the self. The self is a sum total of all the mental, the physical in awareness in a unique association through a metaphysical necessity in their understanding. Again this I have argued elsewhere.[20]

The conception of the 'I' is not all about mental items; it involves a duality of the mental and 'physical'. Again, the 'I' must involve the body, for without the body, there can be no execution of actions and no perception. Many human feelings are bodily related, especially the instinct in the awareness of the possible destruction of the body, of death, of hunger, pain and discomfort, even if the physical alone cannot explain their existence. In this sense, human nature provides the content of my being as a source of response to and for all these feelings and values. In this sense, the accountability for the existence of mental items such as feelings, may not need to be found in physical stimuli from outside.

Human nature is that which is responsible for all our responses to physical conditions.

Persons and understanding persons

Since the understanding of things is always the understanding of a generality (as opposed to an identity of a thing), our understanding of others' existence has the same physical and mental senses. The particularity of another person is confirmed or unconfirmed in the same way that the particularity of an object is confirmed or unconfirmed. But the term 'person' must involve more than this object physicality; this is the 'person' in an extra-physical sense. A living person is a thing that has actions and behaviours which cannot be taken as movements of his or her body. Thus, metaphysically speaking, what we can know of a person is more than what we can know about his physical movements. Knowing a person is knowing their behaviours without causes in their responses to conditions. Epistemologically speaking, I do not share others' awareness, and therefore nothing about others' mental items is known to me. But this is not a lost cause, for we can compare our own response and reaction to similar physical conditions with that of others. If this is an understanding that underlines all reactions, there is a presupposition of a sameness or similarity in human nature.

Consequently, each of us understand others' mental items in terms of our own, and our agreement on this content signifies a similarity of our reactions to the same physical conditions. Without such a presumption, the similarity of reactions to the same conditions cannot be explained. In saying that we react similarly to the same conditions, I am not saying that there is no cognitive or interpretational differences. But our intellect will tell us that the underlying purposes in these reactions are the same. All men will eat fish when they are extremely hungry, even if they do not do so normally. The similarity in our reactions to the same condition is more pronounced when the threat or the discomfort of these conditions is more extreme. Knowing others is a reflection on ourselves and of our nature, in values which must fundamentally share in the same thing. It is certainly true that defining a mind or a self presupposes its identity and thus we must define first a person or a self before thinking of its identity. A logical identity may well be superseded by such a determination of the self.

The same person

The criterion for determining the sameness of a person through spatio-temporal continuum from a third party's standpoint, is not different from that demanded of the identity of a physical object. This was discussed earlier, when considering the uniqueness of space (see pp. 139-144). For every body in a space is uniquely a particular. But from a subjective, personal and private standpoint, the particularity of a person is a totally different matter altogether, since we are not talking about stones and chairs that have no behaviours but movements. Unfortunately, we are all beings whose consciousness is not without breaks and limits, and that poses a problem if the identity of a person strictly needs a continuity in awareness without breaks. This can be overcome by examining the nature of our experience, inner or perceptual. Our experience, as I explained before, is impossible to be understood, if it is not taken as a whole with the past, because every bit of experience of the present is presupposing and in turn presupposed by the past; as is our expectation. As I have argued before, identity is far removed from a process of positing two entities to find their common qualities. It is a process of recognition and understanding through the past. This, again, is true of the way universals work in our conceptual understanding of things, by placing universals in an epistemological reality. A break of consciousness will not matter if the awakened affairs fit in well with everything past and future.

We can certainly conceive of others' identities likewise. My recognition of a person as the same person throughout a period of time depends on my own experience of him or her in a whole, coherent unity. But this is by no means an absolutely incorrigible knowledge. My faith in the coherency of my experience of another person coupled with the coherency of events in nature, makes it highly improbable that a person is not the same if there is a vast amount of experience about him or her that conforms with every bit of my present knowledge without inconsistency. Therefore it is not the unity of persons through temporal stages that makes a person's identity, rather, it is the unity of my experience that confers a unity of temporal persons.

Ownership of experience

Hume thinks that experience (he called it sense impressions) is separate bits and bundles unsupported and unconnected. This I think is erroneous because understanding experience is not intuitive but reflective, albeit instantaneous. The connection and support among impressions is not a matter for perception, but a matter for the understanding. The understanding of the present is presupposed by the past in memory. This makes a good case for establishing a 'belonging' or ownership of immediate experience by linking it through understanding to the whole store of one's experience. The other uniting factor I have also argued before is the awareness itself, of all things mental. Awareness is a unique thing and there can be no demonstration or imagination for the existence of two or more awarenesses at any one time. The uniqueness in spaces can also provide a uniqueness in perceptual experience. In this case, the sense of belonging and being private must also exist in awareness. Even if we can imagine that body transplants can recreate a new awareness, we must first recreate a memory that is consistent with the 'new' awareness. To create memory we must create facts. Otherwise, we may question whether such recreated awareness is the same awareness as before.

What is a person?

As to the concept of 'person', it must be said that this word is used normally to refer to humans. Since the conceptual difficulty in sustaining the incorrigible existence of a person in being more than a physical object erects a barrier to the perception of him or her as an analogy to ourselves known by direct experience, our defining criterion for another person as a self-willing agent with similar nature, is hampered. What is a person that has a will and all the mental content assimilating those that we have ourselves? To begin this defining process, we start with a separation of the living from the non-living by the criterion of movements without external causes. Within this kingdom of the living, the common characteristic of all its members is that of moving without external causes. We can 'understand' a plant that can die since the same sense of dying applies to all living things. We can understand all living things by this common characteristic, and hence understanding their reactions to the physical condition that prohibits life. We may not grow a tall stem, as a tree does, to fulfil life, nor may we have to eat a rat to understand a cat's reaction to the prohibiting condition of life. We only need to understand that a tree needs nourishment as much as cats or we do. When we will come to the separation of the animals from plants, we appeal to our observation of their respective reactions to physical conditions too.

We can understand more about animals than plants, because there are animal movements (reactions) understandable in terms of our own nature, which may not exist in plants. If there is a physical limitation in plants that marks them apart from animals, we must accept that this is the nature of things. That a plant has no locomotion (generally) to escape or to hunt, is the limit of our understanding of their reactions.

Next, in the animal kingdom, we understand each species also according to the understanding of their reactions to environment as compared to ours. Insofar as those reactions that we can honestly say we understand, are concerned, we identify a common, specific aspect of nature shared between them and us. The more aspects we can understand about a particular species of animals, the more we consider them to be closer to us in nature. Animals may not have vanity exhibited by some human reactions; that is why I understand humans more if I understand vanity. Thus there are animals (dogs or monkeys) closer to us and animals farther apart (earthworms for instance) from us. We mark animals out from human beings not essentially by physical appearances; we even call other humans animals too.

Our nature is markedly different from that of animals in aspects, which are farther away from our understanding. There are human reactions to conditions that are not found in monkeys or lions.

Reactions, it must be said, are not always about an instantaneous movement reacting to something; it may be a delayed and cognitive chain of actions, even though an instant reaction can demonstrate one's nature more than a cognitive and considered reaction can. Thus, it will be very human of monkeys to gather round a single individual to hear it singing in a monkey opera. Similarly, instinctive reactions in animals can exhibit more about the nature of the species than anything else. Thus, our instinctive reactions are rarely seen because of our cognitive capability to hide our reactions and, therefore, our nature. This creates a barrier to understanding of humans in general. But these cognitive interferences (or what I may call the cognitive interpretations of nature) will be less pronounced or even absent, when men are crudely exposed to their bare, extreme nature. In the face of immediate death, the cognitive choice of a man's reaction to a situation is close to nothing, and the instinctive reaction he has in himself will surely surface and take over.

Finally, among humans, we can understand more of others' actions and instinctive reactions because our natures are closely similar if not the same. Our close recognition of others' reactions and that of our own shows how close we are in our nature that we may have in common. Hence, our understanding of our fellow beings is far richer than our understanding of other animals. It is in the same way we share a common nature with plants in being alive, that we can understand human and plant growth; human hunting and the nutrition movements of plants; human digestion and photosynthesis in plants. If we strip this understanding of our inevitable determination, from the understanding of plants' movements, there really is nothing else. Or if we strip away the assumption of this similarity in our natures, there will be nothing remaining for understanding other humans. Science is satisfied that it understands what photosynthesis is, precisely because it understands it in terms of life and nourishment and nothing else.

A person, generally speaking, is a term said of another being understood in terms of ourselves. Many have called their dogs persons. Another person is about having affinity to ourselves. The most affinitive beings to us all are inevitably our fellow humans, not least because other humans resemble us more than animals. It would be absurd to say a monkey is a person if we can point out the aspects that appear to have something in common with ourselves. Still, it is not unkind to say that monkeys are not persons, if we refer to those aspects of human nature that we do not share with them. A person is an object that has more than its physicality. A person is judged by its movements without external causes, therefore behaviours. A person is a living thing, first and foremost. There is a diversity in conceiving of these non-physical aspects of living things. This is why men classify the living world in terms of what they may call, intelligence, which is actually nothing more than their prejudice against what they think is outside their nature. For some think that men are marked out from the beasts by their intelligence. But they will hesitate to acknowledge it when their closest relations are born with feeble minds. Within the human race, a nation or community, man will continue to classify persons according to their affinity to him, which explains why we have secular communities within communities. Thus the term 'person' is a very indefinite term depending on the aspects we choose to understand a person. Chimpanzees are certainly persons, if we can establish a good understanding of their behaviours.

The importance of the mental

The reality of the non-physical or the mental is important to any humanist, because no matter how one fails to argue against the exclusive existence of a material world of cold necessity, or the reality of a material order to which men may be forced to conform, one can always bring out the non-physical aspect of this material world, as nature's facts misconceived by materialism. This aspect of nature is the living, the epistemological reality that exists only in humanity. Certainly our slogan is that there is nature and there is also human nature. Of course, there is the danger in the creation of an absolute rational order without a physical-world order, through human rationality. This is the reality of thoughts in a so-called epistemological necessity; and men can easily subject others to conform to this 'orderly' reality of the rationale. However, rationality is by no means as indisputable as nature's physical necessity. If there is a necessity for an order, either through the law of physical nature or through an absolute rationale, humankind, being part of either of these contentious realities, can certainly be asked to submit itself to these realities, and to have humankind's own nature buried beneath. A humanist must resist this and bring about the reality in the nature of men either in addition to or in replacement of these two contentious necessities. The next two parts of this book serve to argue for these points.

PART V

SCIENTIFIC AND PERCEPTUAL REALITY

10. Scientific reality

10.1 Why should there be a scientific reality?

Scientific reality is not empirical reality

There is a generally conceived idea that science is all about observing objects and events and that its knowledge is based on a knowledge called inductive knowledge by supposing a degree of 'certainty' inferred from a sheer number of repetitions of observed events. By this idea, one would have thought that the reality constructed by science is a reality of sense-data, of seeing and of the working of things, in other words, an empirical reality. This is far from the truth. For, over and above the need for observations, there are hypothesis and theorizing in the scientific inference from observations. Thus the reality postulated by science is not mainly, or at all, about empirical reality, but a reality centred on hypotheses and inferences drawn from observations and induction. There is a big difference between a reality based on observations on the one hand, and a reality based on inferences, induction and hypotheses. If this difference is not observed, then, one may be misled into thinking that an inferred and hypothesized reality, started out as observation, can end up as an empirical reality.

What kind of reality does science give us? It must be kind to say that empirical data must first be interpreted, and interpretations must be done with certain principles in hypothesizing and generalizing. These principles are the tools that tell us what reality there is by subsuming empirical data under these principles. Therefore a conclusion on the data is not the same as the conclusion or the interpretation of the data. One cannot avoid this cognitive processing of data, anymore than one can avoid the questions on the understanding of these data. Hence, there is an understanding of a scientific reality as well as a 'data reality' that is not scientifically interpreted. A scientific reality is a reality that is understood according to those principles, and not a reality rich in raw sense-data. It must also be kind to say that human sensory limitation restricts what empirical data can be collected without other aids. But what amounts to empirical data that are aided, is also a question about the interpretation of data, and not about raw data incorrigible as they are. Consequently, I conclude that scientific reality is not empirical reality.

10.2 The interpretation of empirical data

Scientific reality

It is not that we have not known, throughout history, that apples fall down from a height. The reality that apples always fall down from a tree is an empirical reality restricted to that given by sense-data. The reality that there is a law of gravity governing all extended things, is a scientific reality. The reality that light is waves of something, or just waves themselves, or tiny things called photons, is a scientific reality that is miles away from the empirical reality which says that light is colours and brightness. The reality that matter is made of tiny indivisible things, or that matter is all tiny capsules of energy, or that matter is motions of tiny things around something else, is a reality of science, not empirical, for neither do we see these so-called 'things' or can we conceive of them in terms of our ordinary, daily empirical experience.

Recent philosophy dares not tread into the scientific world except 'to flirt' with the basis of induction, even though philosophers are definitely passionate about what reality there is. There is an acceptance that scientific reality, given time for science to excel, will give a true reality that our senses cannot know, and this is not a reality that philosophical investigations can serve with any purpose. Perhaps some may think that the purpose of philosophy is better served by seeing it as a branch of science. The reputation of science in giving us a reality over the above sensibility, is based on practical successes. We can say, 'whatever works must be real'. This is a very seductive idea. With a generalization and the conjecture from repetitions, we project and predict events in conformity with this generalization, so that whatever happens accordingly will confirm, as they say, the usefulness of this generality. 'All ravens are black' is a generalization from all instances of observed ravens. But scientific reality is not just about this generalization of instances; many scientific statements about reality are conceived of under different principles that are more than generalization.

The origin of human species consumed by the principle of evolution is one example. The empirical evidence that serves the idea that different animal species evolved from one singular source is far from a straightforward generalization of observable instances, albeit only fossilized instances. Within all the conceptual claims of evolution, there are many assumptions and principles that convert our observed data into such a theory. For instance, that all lives need to adapt to its environment, is a principle. The idea that genetic materials of the body have a close connection with the growth and characteristics of the body, is a generalization of observed instances, but that a genetic material can somehow 'decide' these characteristic is an assumed principle that there is a purpose in this genetic decision in an idea that if something has a purpose it must have a will for this purpose. Without this, genetic materials have no more a close causal association with bodily characteristics than an association which food has with bodily fat. Thus the reality of genetic materials in being 'responsible' for bodily characteristics cannot be confused with the reality that these characteristics have an assumed purpose towards an end, whether it is an environmental adaptation, or an assumed biological excellence.

The reality of cosmic bodies and space is another example. That the sun moves around us (the earth) has been our belief for thousands of years, and our empirical reality, since we have observed the sun from the earth. With the advance of mathematics, the scientific reality had been that it was the earth that moves around the sun; and in light of the principle of relativity, this reality can be seen either way depending on the frame of reference. Still these three interpretations of empirical reality are not irreconcilable, just as the observation of an elliptical shape of a table is not irreconcilable with the reality of the table being round. No one will say that I am mad if I say that the sun goes round me and therefore round the earth, because I can isolate the principles that can explain all different interpreted realities. Many think that scientific reality is real because it works; it is not a matter that the scientifically interpreted reality is veridical, but a matter of the true reality that is veridical. Leaving these more basic examples aside, we can see the problem is more profound when we look at the more complex reality at the macro-cosmetic level or the micro material level.

Interpretation of nature

The human limitation in seeing beyond the sensibles, leaves a reality to be constructed out of mathematics and interpretations. How good these interpretations and mathematics are, will decide how believable this scientific reality is. For example, scientific data of a distant star are no more than the interpretation of movements using detecting instruments supposed to be caused by the light from the star; and that is only an interpretation of data no more empirical than fossils in the rocks telling what past was. Science can establish a 'principle' in saying that there is a definite pattern of light waves of a thing receding to a distance from us, and if such a pattern is 'observed' in space of a cosmic object, science will conclude that this object must be receding to a distance from us. Thus the reality in space of a stellar object receding from us is not empirical in the ordinary sense, but conjectured with principles that may or may not be sound, and from data construed with principles that may or may not be sound. A 'black hole' in outer space, or a 'quark' or 'proton' in inner space, is the content of a reality that is constructed out of interpretations. The important thing to say about such reality as to its true veridicality, is not about whether something can be predicted to work in accordance with this interpreted reality, but whether such reality can logically entail such predicted happening. For an interpretation of nature cannot interfere with nature, which dictates what happens. If an interpretation of nature is wrong, it does not necessarily bring about a cessation of nature's events that happen to be explained this way. For example, if I interpret the sub-atomic reality of 'particles' as a world of miniature angels that has the will and enormous power to create enormous explosion under certain conditions, an atomic explosion can be said to be a confirmation of my interpretation of such reality. This is an extreme example designed not to suggest that scientific interpretations are as absurd as this is. The point is to show that interpretations cannot always be confirmed by events that they are supposed to predict, for interpretation can never be reality itself, in the same way that redness cannot be confirmed or unconfirmed either. This leads to the question as to how interpretations (good interpretations) can have (instead of must have) such close relation with reality. In this sense, scientific reality, in having the need to interpret empirical data, is not empirical reality.

10.3 Mathematics and relation

Mathematical truth is not empirical truth

One of the most common ways to construct scientific reality is by mathematics, which also involves principles. For men cannot really 'see' the motions of planets or stars; nor can he see phenomena in microscopic parts. As a result, much of scientific reality is interpreted with the aid of mathematics. A tiny dot of light in the sky, according to science, is a huge thing thousands of billions of miles away. This reality is not an empirical reality, but a scientific reality of mathematics. It may well be true if the principle is sound. But science goes beyond this and can postulate entities with physical features that are merely mathematical entities and nothing more. A reality aided by and understood through mathematics is a reality seen to be more reliable because most people think that conclusions from mathematical deductions are necessarily true. Mathematical truth is a truth about relations, while physical reality is not so. This opens up a question not only of the reliability of mathematic deduction as an instrument of truth, but also of the relation between reality and mathematics. It is not a matter of whether a necessary truth in mathematics can be carried over to the veridicality of reality, but a matter of how such necessary truth can be related to the truth of an empirical but interpreted reality. For instance, given the truth in '2 and 2 is 4', how can this truth be the evidence for a physical reality that has nothing to do with '2 and 2 is 4'? Thus in any interpretation of scientific reality using mathematics, and even if all deductions are scrutinized to be true, the mathematical principles and the reality they are supposed to explain, must be established quite separately.

Mathematics and empirical reality

What is mathematics about? Mathematics cannot show us metaphysical reality or an epistemological necessity, for it is only the representation of relations. Some say that mathematics is a kind of knowledge that is totally independent of empirical consideration. This idea does not only suggest that the origin of mathematical knowledge lies outside empirical experience, but also that mathematical principles have nothing whatsoever to do with empirical reality in any way. But what significance has mathematics in the scheme of human understanding given the fact that humankind is constantly preoccupied with it? When we discard all the empirical content in our mind and try to imagine mathematics in all its numbers, calculations and inferences, what are we thinking of? All mathematics copies the relations of the world or its is relational within itself through definitions.

10.4 Numbers and relations

Numbers and reality

The idea that numbers and mathematics are a special kind of reality or part of our world-reality, is not new. Mere observational knowledge, or interpretation restricted to the observable, cannot introduce to us or assure us of a reality that modern physical science would have us believe. Unquestionably, numbers and mathematics play an important part in this scientific reality. Pythagoras or the Pythagoreans (about 532 BC) believed that 'things were constructed of 'numbers'. What they actually meant was that there was an importance in mathematics and numbers in the construction of the relation of things or in the understanding of them. Thus when the idea of a reality constructed of numbers, is taken so seriously, the Pythagoreans are seen as a religious cult in a modern-day view. And if my interpretation of Plato's philosophy is correct, he believes that numbers have an ontological basis far more secure than sensibility because mathematics are the knowledge of reason rather than a perceptual understanding or an intuition. Thus he believes that numbers have a realm of reality similar to that of his Forms. In the history of ideas, a reality founded on reasoning rather than experience is helped by the deductive reasoning that logic or mathematics are supposed to offer.

Whether or not scientific reality is a reality of the observed or a reality constructed out of mathematics, is difficult to say; and this reality depends on what our views on numbers and mathematics are. That scientific reality is not empirical, is based on the idea that many scientific existents (such as black holes, quarks, and so on) are not observed entities but mathematical realism.

What are numbers?

Let me take a reluctant diversion into numbers and mathematics: '1', or unity, is seen, in my view, as the first entity upon which all other numbers are founded. For if there is no unity, 2 cannot exist. There is a definite relation between 1 and 2 by which 2 is understood, but not vice versa. The idea in '2', that there are two '1s', appears to beg the question as to where this concept of 'two' comes from, if it is not seen as a circularity without something that explains what '2' is, independently of '1'.

To answer this question, I will have to plunge into the chasm between two ideologies, each providing a different answer. On the one side, for this two-of-1 concept to be independent of '1' itself, some will say that this knowledge is innate or born within us. I cannot see how this proposition can actually be refuted, unless this refutation comes with a divine authority. It leaves me only an option to explain the possibility from the other side of this chasm, and to convince myself if my reasoning is credible. From this viewpoint, I see no reason to think of mathematics as an innate knowledge supporting a reality of an innate kind. At this point, I must emphasize that believing that our reality is a reality of the sensible, may not necessarily entail that this sensible reality is an all-physical reality.

I return to my earlier assertion that the concept of a unity (oneness) is a mind-defined limitation with boundary and parameter, of definite sensible quality or mental content. By 'boundary' I do not mean just a physical or spatial boundary itself. It is a 'boundary' of limitation or a confinement of content. Within the confine of a mind-made boundary or parameter, that can define oneness, there may also be sub-boundaries and sub-parameters, each of which also defines a unity or '1'. Therefore the boundaries and sub-boundaries in this defining must have a relation, if sub-boundaries are seen within another larger boundary. Perhaps the nature of the mind is empowered only to concentrate on one particular inclusiveness or another inclusiveness of a higher grouping, at one particular moment. This is an explanation of our nature, rather than the explanation of the concept of '2'. In this way, and within a unity, we have sub-boundaries, which, if seen within a unity, must be its parts. Parts are units too, each with its own sub-boundary and sub-parameter. The nature of the mind, if applied to sensible things, will offer us individual objects through boundaries (including spatial boundaries), and their parts within sub-boundaries. For if the mind does not make demarcations, or confine its attention by demarcating, there can be no individuals and the concept of oneness. This representation of oneness can be conceived with content, but not necessarily the content of sensible qualities. This is the necessary condition to invoke this special nature of the mind in defining and conceiving inclusiveness. Therefore this defining must precede the individuation. Consequently, I shall say that defining an inclusiveness is the concept of oneness expressible independently of sensible qualities.

Within a unity or 1, we have fractions and divisions, each of which has its sub-divisions. There is no need to conceive of 'two' independently of 'one'. And the conception of 'two' is the conception of the division within oneness. There is no separate concept of 'two'. Since, within a unity, we can conceive of a part within this inclusiveness or boundary, we can also conceive of another part with another inclusiveness or another boundary, and so on to infinity. And infinity is very much an act of the mind rather than a reality conceived of in terms of it.

Numbers and counting numbers

So far, we have individuals of conceptual oneness, and sub-individuals within each of them; we have not yet dealt with 'why-one-and-one-make-two'. But again, at this point after establishing what '1' is, '2', '3', '4' or '5' will naturally be the higher groupings of those sub-individuals that come before it. And, I shall rely on the power to define an inclusiveness of the mind to go further from this conceptual oneness. If the mind can see, at first, something with an inclusive boundary, as well as focus on a sub-unity within this inclusive boundary, it is not unreasonable to see that the mind must be able to define sub-inclusiveness and set sub-boundaries of more than one sub-individual. If reality has numerous individuals unconnected, such defining power can certainly embrace several individuals, and 'define' them as one, thus setting an attention to a grouping of individuals, or deselecting a boundary to 'redefine' it in another way. In this sense, all numbers are derivative from oneness and are related.

The concept of 'two' is one grouping (of a higher order) of one division or individuation within a boundary set. This leaves us with counting, or identifying that there are 'two' sub-individuals within a group of one. Counting itself or identifying a quantity must be an empirical knowledge in my view. It has been said that in the 'primitive' days of humankind, when a shepherd wanted to know whether the same number of sheep had returned from grazing, he used objects, such as straws, taking one straw to represent one sheep each time it passed through the gate. This was supposed to be a 'primitive' method of counting. But how could he count the straws, let alone have the concept of numbers, even if he can claim an equivalence between the quantities of straws and sheep?

I do not think that there is any serious or reasonable

challenge to the notion that counting by identifying 'one' in a sameness in quantity among objects is as intuitive as seeing colour itself. Though one can say that an equivalence in quantity cannot determine or count '2', '3' or '4', since there is only a quantity of sameness. Counting needs an exclusiveness to a unit to determine what is 'more-than-one'. But that a group includes one division making therefore 'two' individuals, is not so difficult to see, if we know what oneness is and if we can count one. Therefore one division within a 'one' is the concept of two, which depends only on the knowledge of oneness. Still within this oneness, each sub-division will also be one and countable as one. Counting needs memory certainly, and the mind's power of memory is not unlimited; hence the shepherd used straws to help his counting. It was not at all certain whether he needed straws at all if his flock only numbered only two or three. If we take out an individual one by one from a group (of one), do we need to have resort to the preconception of two-of-one, three-of-one or four-of-one to be able to count? It seems that as soon as I have said, 'this is one and that is one', immediately I am compelled to say there are 'two' instances in counting. But this 'two' is only a label to refer to this counting and is not necessarily a preconception of what 'two' is. The case remains even if I can count objects in physical space. Whether we need the preconception of two-of-one or three-of-one, to recognize the sameness and difference among countable quantitative groups like 1; (1,1); (1,1,1); (1,1,1,1); (1,1,1,1,1) or (1,1,1,1,1,1), I am far from certain. And I am loath to think that our mind cannot intuitively see the differences among these groups quantitatively, given that we can define 'two' as one division within one in a relation.

If we can intuitively see these quantitative differences then, numbers with the exception of '1', are really names labelling groupings of the same individuals ('1'), and thus constituting the understanding of the meaning thereof, without having to say that any recognition of these groupings presupposes a prior understanding of them. That is to say '2' or 'two' is only a name to label (1, 1) grouping without admitting that understanding (1,1) as a group presupposes the understating of '2' or 'two'. Practical experience with objects in these quantitative groupings will of course create a familiarity between numbers and quantities; for the boundary of oneness can dissipate from awareness, if counting objects in practical experience becomes a habit and intuitive. In another sense, if we can recognize the quantity of one taken away from a group, leaving another distinct oneness within that group, we have another definition of 'two-ness', if there is a relation and distinction recognized between the former group of '1 and 1', and the latter group of '1-left-behind'. This distinction is certainly possible if memory is to serve us. We are not saying here that taking away one and leaving one behind, from two associated groupings, is presupposed by the concept of 'two-ness', but that this 'one-gone-and-one-left' concept is another definition of 'two-ness'. In the same way, we can say that in a quantitative group of 'one-gone-and-two-left', we do not need a prior concept of 'three-ness' to decide it. This quantitative concept is the concept of 'three-ness', having included the definition of 'two-ness' as defined by 'one-gone-and-one-left'. And indeed, if our memory permits, the terms 'four', 'five', and so on, are very much understood in the same way, through quantitative cognition (as opposed to numerical cognition) in our empirical experience.

Numbers are relations

If I have succeeded in explaining the concepts of all numbers (except the unity) in terms of oneness itself, numbers are the extension of a quantitative relation to oneness in their most basic conception. Since numbers are relational groupings by the mind in marking out the individuals within larger groupings, the groupings can be conceived of in many ways. For instance,

24 is 23+1 or 22+2 or 22+1+1 or (2+4)+10+8 and so on. In this sense, all numbers are expressions of different levels of relations, or relations of relations, of quantities originated from oneness itself. Therefore, every number except '1', is expressible in at least one relation and that is a relation to '1', as well as in many relations with other groupings of '1', by adding to any grouping, or subtracting from it, a unity determined by the mind. Likewise, multiplication and division are no more than symbols of a secondary relation among numbers. I say a secondary relation in the spirit of an example such as this: if 9 is stated as a relation to 1, in (1,1,1,1,1,1,1,1,1), then its relation with (9,9,9,9) is a secondary relation in that the grouping of '9' and have sub-groups that signify the former quantitative relation with '1'. Such relations can be piled upon one another indefinitely, as far as the mind can comprehend. In mathematics, relations or relations constituted by group relations are sometimes symbolized for simplicity, so that they are seen as remote from the original representation. Mathematical methods are deductive so that original relations are maintained throughout. The remoteness of symbols for a multitude of relations in mathematics from the first postulation, must render a scientific reality based on mathematical representation difficult to understand and explain.

Other mathematical relations

In all, pure mathematics is a study of relations that can be traced back to oneness itself, and, on its own, there is no metaphysical reality in it. I will not here get into the epistemological bases of mathematical deductions, save an insight into a reality constructed from mathematics. Certainly among all these representations of relations in numbers other relations are introduced that are not based on the original oneness; for instance, geometrical relations (such as the Pythagoras theorem). Here we are importing into the relation of numbers, relations obtained from and related to the physical world. The Pythagoras theorem is about the relations among three side of a type of triangles in general. This relation is not a pure relation of numbers for us to say $A^2 \times B^2 = C^2$ is true, unless we bring up its representation: that A, B and C are the sides of a right-angled triangle and C is its hypotenuse. This is to say the truth in the relation of $A^2 \times B^2 = C^2$ lies not in the set-equation itself, but in the relation of something they represent. In the same way, the relation between the circumference and the diameter of circle or the relation between all angles and sides of triangle are introduced into this relation. As a result, we look upon geometry and mathematics as a discipline of knowledge not only of the relation of numbers, but of other things. We shall leave out the argument of whether geometrical objects are ideal objects or sensible objects, since I have discussed the similar problems involving straight lines.

There is one more aspect that makes the mathematics of these relations possible. It is the consistency in these particular relations (as opposed to the relations of consistency). The relations between the sides of triangles, and between the circumferences and diameters of circles, are assumed or judged to be constant at all times, before they can be asserted as rules for deductive calculations. A graph to show a relation between two sets of numbers is a physical representation of a relation, not of numbers themselves, but of relations imported and represented by these numbers. For there is no relation among symbols, other than a relation among what they represent. Still when mathematicians describe relations by reference to the spatial relations among the points on a graph, they are not introducing a relation to establish the positions of various points on this graph, but a relation that these numbers represent outside the graph by using a 'mathematical language' (the graph) to explain the same. For example, the growth of a plant in length can be represented by a relation to time durations and also represented by numbers. This is a relation between growth and time quantified by numbers in a secondary numerical relations. Again, it is the constancy in that relation that makes this interpretation possible. An army decoding an enemy's telegraphic messages relies on an assumed consistency in the use of alphabet - a constancy of relations of the alphabet. It can only be successful if the mathematical probe.for a consistency in this relation within the alphabet is successful.

Mathematical relations confer no reality; constancy of relations of reality underpins mathematics

By representing relations of things, being constant in themselves, mathematics may certainly represent reality, only a relational reality but not reality itself. But such represented, relational reality must assume sensible input without which relations remain a projection of our imagination. For example, if I say: there is a thing with a centre, passing through which is a line that ends at two points on its circumference; and this line always has a constant ratio to the length of the circumference, what reality can it represent to me? It is not at all certain whether it is because something is a circle that it has a constant relation between its circumference and its diameter, or whether it is because something's circumference and diameter have a constant relation that it is a circle. For if the latter is true, then that a thing is a circle, depends on whether a quantity of constancy (the π) can be found. As we know that this ratio is infinitely indivisible, and can never be found as a 'real' number, therefore a 'circle' which has a circumference of 3.1416 times its diameter is a more perfect circle than another which has a circumference of 3.14 times its diameter without being a determinate reality. A circle is not defined by a particular constancy and constancy is a measure of certain circular things. It has been said that a perfect circle in the sensible world does not exist and that perfection is only found in mathematics. By this demonstration, mathematics and geometry cannot deliver us with a perfect circle either since the ratio between the circumference and the diameter is indefinitely indeterminable; the more precise number we use to determine this relation, the more 'perfect' a circle will be; and this 'perfection' is in the pursuit of a circular perfection towards infinity. In this sense, the mathematical representation of the world is not a reality underpinned by mathematics, but a representation of the world through the assertion of a constancy of relations. Many constant relations are associated with sensible things and these we may understand, but those entities constructed out of pure relations represented by mathematical symbols or equations, are more difficult for us to understand. Mathematical symbols are nothing but a shorthand for complex deductive equations representing relations. Space-time and 'black holes' are examples of these symbols that have transcended from relations into a scientific reality.

Mathematical relations and reality

If the former is true, that is, the relation between diameters and circumferences is constant because it is that of ideal circles, we have to determine what a perfect circle is without having to rely on this particular relation. It is very conceivable to think that men can certainly know what a circle is without knowing the relation between its circumference and its diameter, just as we can see a 'perfectly' straight line without having a preconceived notion of straightness. This I have argued before. For a man's mind and perceptual faculty are not a construct so perfect as to perceive straight lines without minor and unseen blemishes that a seemingly straight line must have. Men do not have x-ray vision or electronic eyes. In this way, positing an 'ideal' circle without determining the absolute relation between its circumference and diameter is not proposing a reality independently of sensibility. The curiosity as to why a circle has a constant (as opposed to definite) relation among its parts, lies in the mystery of reality that is in the nature-given sensibility conceived of by men, and not in conceiving a circle independently of it. Thus mathematics or similar disciplines are all about relations only, relations that can only give us a sense of reality in things subsumed under them, so that this relational reality is seen and conceived of as a totality of a world experience.

Therefore, relations themselves do not have a particular importance in reality, but their constancy or consistency does. For example, the progression of numbers can be represented by points in space, or the progression of time by a movement of constant speed in one direction. The addition and the division of numbers into fractions, can be represented spatially by a diagram. Success in understanding a relation through different forms of representation, suggests that we understand the relation among numbers in the same way we understand the representation of space and time, without having to say that space and time are numbers or their relations. It is therefore the constancy and not the form of a relation that is important in our sense of reality and in our understanding. For the similarity between spatial progression and numerical progression, suggests a constancy more than a mere form of relation.

Take another example in the blackness among all ravens. What brings this phenomenon to our attention is the inductivity, and not the blackness itself; just as it must have been the induction in 'all-bodies-fall-downwards' that has captivated Isaac Newton to inspire his theory of gravitation. For without this sense of constancy or consistency derived from relations, that this raven, that raven, and all those ravens are all black cannot be seen as a peculiar reality at all. Without this constancy, all ravens are black is a mere relation, and I will not expect all ravens to be black. There is a difference between seeing repeated association and seeing a constant relation, and it is the latter that gives us a sense of reality by associating something with a totality of reality. Certainly a constancy of relations is not a relation itself, but a condition of judgement of reality the identity of which lies within us. To see a constant relation is to see a reality, a human reality, if you like.

10.5 Relational reality in mathematics

Relations, among things, are peculiar because the mind can conceive of them without having constantly referred to the things upon which their existence depends. We can refer to numeric relations quite independently of things, since these relations are conceptual. Thus there are those who think that concrete individuals owe their existence to these relations rather than the opposite, because they think that all relations are analogous to numeric relations. This aspect we have discussed in the problem of universals. If we consider this carefully, it will appear that this is not whether the particularity of a relation can be conceived of without individual things, but whether the constancy and the generality of relations that can be conceived of independently of things.

When I say of 'a horse' or 'one horse', the quantitative relation of a horse as one or many parts, is not a relation that can stand independently from the sensibles and still retain a horseness quality. Certainly the sense in 'a horse' is more about a reality than about the concept of 'a' or oneness, which on its own says nothing of that reality, but a quantity. A relation is about two or more things, otherwise an instance of a relation cannot be established. When I see lightning and thunder the first time, I would not see a relation until and unless a consistency can establish for me a 'habitual' association. This is not to say that a relation can presuppose its own existence. For if it were so, as David Hume has pointed out, the question of the observability of a causal process, for instance, would be answerable in terms of a predetermined concept of causality.

Thus a relation is only possible if it is seen with sensible things in a whole scheme of reality. Having accepted that relations have a sense of reality to which all real things transcending their mere sensibilities, are attached, I do not accept that it will follow that these relations are necessarily a part of reality, as opposed to being the process of judgement about reality. If this reality constructed out of relations is seen to be erroneous, it is our own judgement that are at fault. A 'horse' in reality is always a fulsome unity, and never half or double. A reality of relation is about constancy, and never about definitive quantity and quality in general. Without relations, we can no more see a horse as a running particular than see many legs, a torso and manes moving in space, unconnected. The parts of a horse in a constant relations give us its wholeness in reality, as well as the conception of the parts as individuals. But relations without the sensibles (horseness or grass-eating) are purely conceptual, binding the sensibles together, and are not in reality themselves.

Scientific, mathematical entitles are not part of reality

Consistency or constancy of association in things enables us to think of this association separately, correctly or incorrectly. For instance, gravity is a relation that is conceivable by assuming an inductive generality as a 'law of nature' to sustain the relation. In the true Humean test of observability, we cannot find anything in our sense experience that explains this relation, except our conception of a constancy of this relation. In short, a relation is not an observed thing, but observed of things. As we can conceive of relations independently, and if the sense of reality has its link to all relations, relations are considered by many as entities, 'seen' to be real by subsuming them under terms or by assigning an unobservable reality to relations. Indeed, this is not new. To subsume reality under relations only, is rarely noticeable. For example, a picture can be seen as a duck or a rabbit within our permissible interpretations under different relations. Here, we have a sense of reality that things are not so much dots of colours and shades, but relational to all things in a totality of experience. To do so is to ignore the bland reality that affords all sensible things identities and individuations. Much scientific realism is based purely on relations offered by mathematics without consideration of the sensibles. 'Black holes' and sub-atomic entities are things constructed from relations by science, and their reality is as good as their relations conceived to other things. To say that space can bend, or light is made of photons, is to say of a group of relations, constant relations perhaps.

With the exception of numeric relations, a relation of the sensibles may not be understood and conceived of without the sensibles available for conceiving it. But a pure relation of relations which have no connection to sensible cannot be understood since the understanding of a relation is through its connection to sensibles. Thus we have symbols to represent complex relations and we find it hard to understand mathematical symbols that are relations of relations. I do not need symbols to recognize or imagine a simple relation such as redness (not the incognitive sensation) itself. Relations are only relations of particulars, conceived of in reality. A relation is an association of certain sensible things, and it makes it difficult for the mind to determine one relation on top of another. But a relation cannot be a relation of the same relation, and if a relation is a relation of another relation, and not of particulars, a reality in an infinite regress will surely follow.

If space is seen as a relation, and since it has no properties itself, its reality is rooted to things that exhibit this relation. It makes no sense to say that space can be 'bent'. What science means by this space-bending is that the assumed peculiarity in the speed of light being constant under all circumstances, cannot be reconciled with the original notion of space (distance) so determined by the relation between the time taken for a thing to move in one direction, then this 'bent space' is an entity constructed out of mathematical necessity and relations. Indeed so is the entity called space-time (as opposed to space and time). The speed of light, if it is constant under all circumstances, creates an anomaly contrary to our normal, relational conception of space and time and this anomaly can only be explained in terms of other assumed relations that may not be true. Whether this is all true or not, there cannot be any doubt that a scientific reality constructed out of relations, mathematical or otherwise, has a sense of reality for us all, only through a constancy. And this relational reality is not something that is independent of the mind, for relations are judgements. But, scientific reality is conditional to our understanding these relations, and without relations conceived through sensible things in a whole experience, there will be no identity, no particularity, and no understanding within sensibility. There are many relations proclaimed by science that ordinary men do not understand, and whether this proclaimed reality constructed out of mathematical relations is a true reality, depends on whether these relations can be subsumed under a singular world experience. In this sense, I cannot even imagine how to conceive of the existence of a 'black hole' in space, if all the properties of this entity are inconsistent with my world experience.

When I see or hear something, later to be judged as a phantom percept, the ontological question is not whether my 'experience' of this thing exists or not, but whether it is real. If this is so, there must be a separation between existence and reality, as things that exist may not be real (but not that things real may not exist). This I have argued in depth in the early part of this book. If the ontological basis for existence is our sensibility, then the reality of existents so separated, must involve more than sensibility, and this lies in a constancy of relation with the rest of the whole. A thing owes its existence to being conceived or perceived, but owes its reality to its relations to other things. Indeed the identity of a thing is a process of relation-seeking by the mind. A sound heard is more real if there is a relation between itself and the movement in the eardrums and vibrations in a loudspeaker. This relational reality will come to the fore, when we demand to know the situation instead of particular instances in a perceptual reality. This is common sense, and overall scientific reality is not a reality for the elite, since the world is a public reality. Theoretical science has less claim to a true reality than practical science that takes up the demonstration of these relations. Even so, a practical demonstration is no guarantee to a true interpretation of nature. A man who tells me that it is an angel who ignites an atomic bomb, finds no sympathy in my belief; but when an atomic bomb explodes, he will say, 'I told you so'.

The reality for a humanist must be that which takes into account the peculiar way a mind conceives relations among things, and not only the reality that science tells us as composed of all things physical and material. Even if the universe is nothing but physical and material, there is still an extra-physical dimension by which this universe is conceived to be constantly relational and above all, alive in part. Without the conception of relations over and above the mere physical, there can be no scientific reality, let alone science. Should a humanist accept a universe of an all-physical causality, he must have left himself out from the world of the living. In a scientific world, we are told that rainbows are movements of electrons at different level of 'excitement'; sounds are waves of air and vibration of ear-drums; or colours are mere different spectrums of light in an emission of energy. All these are very well except that, for them to have a reality in our world, they must be associated with, and seen to explain, human experience in terms of relations within a totality of our experience, otherwise they have no sense in the scheme of human reality. Is there a separate reality apart from human reality, or is there a metaphysical reality without a epistemological reality?

11. Perceptual Reality

11.1 Perception and beyond

Should there be more than what is perceived?

The profound implication of Bishop Berkeley's philosophy of the sensibility has had much influence on the contemporary investigation of perception. Perception is important not least because reality is generally considered to be seen or sensed first and foremost. Berkeley's arguments that primary qualities such as solidity or extension cannot exist without other secondary qualities, allow him to draw the conclusion about the nature of sensibility in being mental, or mind-dependent or matter-independent. To speak of a perceptual reality, we can hardly escape Berkeley's legacy. We notice that by saying that primary qualities are dependent of secondary qualities, we are in fact entering into the realm of relations. And this is not all new; as I have examined earlier, much of scientific reality is all but relational, or constructed out of relations.

Thus, John Locke, Kant and many others have the eerie belief that there is more than what is perceived by the senses. Locke's idea that there is a substratum underlying all sensibility even though we know not of it, and Kant's idea that there are things-in-themselves, are the never-go-away expectation of reality to transcend our senses. This is not a mere philosophical expectation, but, as many may agree, also a common-sense expectation.

There is a sense that our sensibility is somehow responsible for something outside our minds. Berkeley thinks that such reality is beyond the senses and is dependent on the perception from a higher and divine authority. There are the causal theorists who think that objects can cause or be responsible for our sensibility, not to mention those scientists who believe in a reality not seen by the senses. The reality of science in all its sound waves, light waves, photons, atoms, electrons, quarks, temperatures or gravitation, is beyond our humble sensibility. Yet, I can hardly say that electricity does not exist because I do not see it. Electricity on the whole is not a separate entity outside a medium through which it is conducted, but an expression of motions or activities of postulated entities called 'particles' or 'pockets of energy' contained in a medium. This is a reality constructed of relations. No sane person will put a finger into a power point because he or she does not see any activity in the metal of the power point. Such is the power that relational reality has on our practical life, that we can hardly ignore it without having to suffer the consequences. However, a relational reality is not always a product of modern science; for the nature of things has been with us since the beginning of time. A relational reality is not solely explainable in terms of our sensibility. Even if we accept that objects of perception are no more than mere sensibility, there is still a case to answer as regards the nature of this sensibility. If we call sensibles sense-data, it is not certain whether sense-data are inside or outside our mind, conceptual or intuitive. Whether sense-data are conceptual or intuitive is difficult to say.. Many philosophers since Berkeley have conceived a crucial nature in perceptual sensibility, in that sensibility is the given and not 'manufactured' by the mind. Some say that objects are permanent possibilities of perception. All these are again relational claims beyond sense-data.

The security of our common sense, if perceptual reality is anything to go by, does not perish in a blatant rejection of a conceptual void beyond sensibility. For instance, David Hume's example of a double vision caused by fingers pressing on the eye-balls, giving a 'distorted' perceptual reality, is not something one can refute by examining sense-data. Since a veridical perceptual reality can be restored from a double vision, and since there are comparable visions before and after this double vision, there is a possibility of establishing a relation among them all. It is through this relation that common sense and perceptual reality are rescued from the savagery of reason. But, then, can there be common sense without reasoning? Common sense is a notion that many philosophers think, needs no elucidation, but one person's common sense is another's joke. The situation of this term within philosophy is in a sorry state of affairs.

11.2 Causation and perception

An epistemological gap

The causal theory of perception is seen as a scientific way of looking at the whole mechanism of perception, so that the explanation of the percepts, conditions, light and distance are seen as a whole scheme explaining how the perception of objects can take place. In the path of light 'from' the surface of objects to the lens of the eye, ending in the retina, the sense receptor, such description of perception is a common-sense belief in most of us, who have been exposed to some scientific education. Just as science has taken them for granted, percepts are scientifically crude with all their perceived dots of sense-data in their most rudimentary rawness, and yet, are sublime enough to express them to be things of functions, and of beauty; the epistemological gap between crude data and sentient things is ignored, hoping psychology can supply an answer. Without first examining this gap, we should see whether such causal connection is possible.

Causality of perception is impossible

Perceptual causality has been lamented by many including Wittgenstein, the father of what I call modern-day 'college philosophy', because it presupposes the existence of a cause, i.e. the percepts. Wittgenstein compares it to climbing up a roof with a ladder, throwing it away and then claiming success in reaching the roof without a ladder. Other causal relations among events are less problematic because both the cause and effect are observable phenomena as events, even if the process of causation is not seen. But when it comes to the question of causality in observation itself, such an epistemological priority of the cause cannot be granted. For we are here trying to establish a causation from the effect (the retinal stimuli and perceptual judgements) to the cause itself which in turn depends logically and epistemologically on the effect and nothing else. In the earlier part of this book and elsewhere,[24] I have made a distinction between metaphysical priority and epistemological priority among many concepts including causality itself. Perhaps the Wittgensteinian objection is only an epistemological problem and not a metaphysical problem. Nonetheless, this logical gap provides an insurmountable difficulty for claiming a causal link between percepts and sensory stimuli, let alone between a stimulus and a sensation.

Another epistemological challenge to any causal theory is this: a causal link between percepts and seeing is always a necessity, since causality means that a cause is always followed by its effect. My eyes are passive receptors of data from a visual field in front, and every bit of light and colour from whatever object there is in the visual field, will invariably cause every bit of stimulus in my receptors. If the existence of every stimulus automatically means the existence of seeing something, we will see every bit of our visual field, since causation has no discrimination. But perceptual reality is not like this. We see something because we focus our attention on this or that thing. Of the things on which our focus of attention is not trained, there will be no seeing. If one argues that a perceptual causation will provide a possible and not a necessary perception, then, it must be admitted that this possibility is a matter of choice rather than a necessity. Still, why should causality be a possibility as regards effect? Therefore the active nature in perception must rule out a necessary connection between a percept and sensing, that is vital to perceptual causality.

The science of causation can best provide a causal link to establish a stimulus. This stimulus, taken from a logical viewpoint, is no more than a disturbance caused by 'particles' or 'spots of energy' reflected from a percept. They are not the percept itself. What we see is light. Is light reflected from an object or its surface, identical with the object or its surface? Unless science can explain such disturbance in terms of an object seen or in terms of its representation, this gap is still wide open. One may say that one cannot simply explain the electrical charges among water droplets in terms of the perception of a colourful rainbow. But it is precisely that electrical charges, which may be identical with colour or light, are still percepts before perception, i.e. the cause; whereas the identity of their effects, being stimuli on the retina and being colour sensations are totally different things. In perception, we are not claiming only that the percepts cause sensory stimuli, but also that these stimuli are at least a representation of the cause in order for the cause to be seen as a percept and as a sensation. What kind of identity can science propose? At best causation can explain the existence of stimuli, but never the identity of the stimuli that are variable. These invariables are identities through human values in the broadest sense. Reality, as I have argued, is not a singular facet; be it a subjective perceptual experience or an objective rationale, or both. Hence causality of perception is impossible.

Another misconception of causality, in my opinion, is the idea that static objects, large and small, can be a cause. But causality is about causes and effects all being events, not static objects. If there is no motion of light, there is no perception of colours. Also, the idea that the whole universe is made of things and events glued together in temporal succession by causality, is conceived of by many to be something that can explain all and sundry. This causality cannot explain the cause of the movements in living things, and it cannot explain perception in the same way if perception is taken as an active motion in a living body.

Causality is a complex subject that needs a separate book for its elucidation.[24] Basically, in my view, causality involves events and not static objects. In the case of gravitation, it primarily involves movement of another object towards the cause (another body); but without the movement of the effect, there will be no manifestation of gravitation. Causality is about something moving something, or something changing something, like Aristotle's movers and a prime mover in his days. Causality is a process that explains the existence of an effect, but not the identity of any two things, let alone the identity of the cause and effect being the same thing seen. Causality is not a process that can explain why an effect (the percept) is the same as the object we see, or why it can represent, resemble, be an image of, something claimed to be the cause; it is a process that can explain changes and movements only. If the stimuli on the retina are mere motions and changes, then this causal process may plausibly explain it. But having retinal movements and stimuli are far from having the event of 'seeing'. There are no perceptual and representational relations between the earth and a falling apple even if there is a causal relation in gravity.

That a causal connection is about movements and changes only, can be further affirmed by the failure in many sundry and minor arguments for perceptual causality. For instance, when we see a table, we only see a part of the table, and there can be no causal link to other parts unseen in a three dimensionally implicated reality. Hence if the causal theory is true, our reality is composed of everything partially seen. Or are we seeing the surface of an object, instead of the reflected light only? And if the origin of a causal process is in what we see, then the origin of the light beam reflected from an object should lie in the sun or a distant star. Thus to say that sense-data originate from their cause, that is, the object seen, is to say that causality can provide more than explanation of movements and changes. And this is not causality in the ordinary sense.

There is a way to claim that sense-data, though not inherent in physical things themselves, represent certain properties of these things, perhaps in their natural disposition. Thus a red ribbon has a property to manifest a sensation of redness in us, or the redness of an apple representing its state of ripeness and so on. This theory does not have the defects in the causal claim that I have criticized before, because it maintains the claim of a causal connection in respect of dispositional qualities and not perceptual details. But the origin of the details of sense-data have to be explained, if not outside a causal connection. For we do not, as a matter of fact, perceive dispositional properties, but sensibility. Dispositional properties are inferences from sense-data, the relational reality as I have argued before. Redness itself cannot give rise to the idea of ripeness, even in fruits, nor can the idea of hotness, in the state of a piece of metal. As I have examined in the chapter dealing with universals, natural properties are not known from sensibility, but from relations conceived. This is the situation of John Locke when he advocates the existence of something-we-do-not-know-what. This is not a situation with which I have no sympathy; for the idea of a relational consistency proposed in this book is an acknowledgement of this sense of reality. This is only one aspect of reality, and the other I have maintained is the value-indicative aspect of reality in cognitive interpretation; this is as the idealistic aspect of reality. Without this idealistic and interpreted aspect, reality is nothingness in itself.

11.3. Veridical perception and beings

The conditions for veridical perceiving

To claim that what we see is veridical has many problems. If something is seen by more than one sentient being who have different sensory organs, not to mention privacy and inaccessibility, to interpret them, a public veridical verification is doomed to fail from the start. Still there remains a sense that not all we see is veridical, considering only our own description of it. For instance, in an earlier example taken, seeing a circular coin (a perceptual judgement) is compared to the actual sense-data of the coin which are really elliptical. Similarly, a straight stick is seen bent through the medium of water. Even in common sense, sense-data are not always taken to be the reality of things. Many may think, in complete contrast to this, that the immediacy of sense-data belong to the surface of objects. Thus the redness seen is on the surface of the book (in space) and not in my mind. And what about perceptual agreements among us? Someone kicking a football towards me, must have perceived a percept to which I can react with my own perception of the same, so that my judgement on the timing and spatial position of the ball are in total harmony with his. Then too, we will have a sense that things continue to exist without being seen and that things can react among themselves independently of the sense-data, from within or from without (depending on your view).

All these suggest all the same, a dilemma facing our judgements of perceptual reality: our perceptual judgements cry out for a reality beyond the sensibility, and yet our sensibility constantly reminds us that there is really nothing else beyond itself. I do not think that one's beliefs would become a philosophy of materialism or realism, if one accepts that the perception has more to it than merely gathering sense-data. In this metaphysics, there is no claim for an existent independent of perceptual sensibility; rather, there is an examination of the nature of sensibility, in its relational consistency among other claims. The acceptance of sensibility as 'the given' in the nature of things, is vital in our investigation into the sense of reality based on sensibility itself; this is not to say that sensibility is caused by things outside our mind, or belongs to something else. That things are seen with sensibility and by sensibility, is an acknowledgement of the importance of the human factor governing a perceptual reality associated with human actions. The objective sense of a reality through sensibility is a fatalism for man, not of his own making. And yet this reality also accords his interpretations within the parameters set out by nature itself. Man's limitation in his biological make-up is certainly nature's limitation. As I have expounded, a relational consistency (as opposed to mere relations) is another.

Permanency and veridical sense in reality

When I sit in front of a book, I see all there is for me to convince myself that there is a book in front of me. When I look away from the book, out of the window, I ask myself: what grounds do I have to think that the book will not be there again if I turn my head around? I am quite happy with the idea that the book does not exist while I am looking out of the window. For this is an assertion of non-existence, very much in line with the definition of existence. To exist is to be perceived and conceived. But I cannot be certain that the book will still be there when I turn around. This idea is not just verbal. Surely I must have reasons for both of these dilemma. If there is a certainty that the book will be there when I turn around, it cannot be a logical certainty because whether I shall see the book again has nothing to do with the definition. Similarly, facts are contingent before their actuality, so that the book can be there contingently even if it does not 'exist' while I am looking out the window. If all facts are contingent why should I be certain that the book will be there when I turn around; and why should I have this expectation from a contingency? What would my reaction be if the book is not there? I may suspect that someone has sneaked in unnoticed and taken the book. Something else may explain this; explain, that is, within what I would regard as being convinced. When this criterion is applied, it is clear to me that my expectation of the book being there again, stems from what is believable and what is not believable within the repertoire of my experience. Of course, the book existed before I looked out of the window, might not necessarily be the same book seen when I turned around. The belief that they are the same cannot be deduced from perceptual content that lacks a existential continuity. Perceptual content has its sense of existence in the present and direct vividness.

When reflections are applied, we enter into reality - the reality in which the book exists. Our earlier slogan that reality is within existence will play a part to comfort the uneasy feeling in accepting the idea that there is no existence without perceiving or conceiving. For the claim that the book at a second glance is the same as that of the first glance and has continued to exist and survive to the second glance, is a matter of reality, leaving the notion of existence to the immediacy of perceptual experience, as a matter of its definition only. To get a sense of reality in objects seen before, in a continuity to the present, we shall see it as a whole, in which a constant relation with other things can be assumed or perhaps reasoned. If 'looking out the window' incorporates a knowledge that someone is present behind me moving everything around, I will be foolish to form an unshakeable belief that the book would be there when I look around. The relation of the book to the activities of a man is not something we can deduce from logic alone. Such relation comes with experience. What we can expect from any relation is what we can and have learned from experience enabling us to assume or reason that nothing will change without changes in other things. If I do not see a book when I turn around, knowing that there is nothing conceivable has changed, I will be very surprised. It is not that changes in things have strict rules, but that changes of things are constantly linked to changes in other things. It is not that changes in things can happen independently or dependently of other things, but that non-relational changes are never something I can contemplate without abandoning past experience given to me. Every change demands an explanation, which is a relational dependency having a sense of continuity for the existence of all things. Again this is an underlying consistency in all relations. This continuity is not so much a sense derived from seeing the thing identical with the former percept, as it is a sense derived from their relational constancy in the reality as a whole.

This relational permanency can supplant the sense of veridical perception of things. Our perception is not like taking a picture with a camera having a singular visual aspect in data received; it is laden with judgements that may not be conferring a perceptual content only. These 'extra-perceptual' judgements confer a relational constancy to the things seen, so that a reality is constructed with the comfort of reason. If judgements on reality are within a relational constancy among all things, any inconsistency within the relations will call for an investigation or re-examination of the whole or of the instances. For example, a round table can be seen as oblong or oval depending on a perceptual position. Many have questioned whether roundness of the table is the veridical shape, or what the real shape of the table is. This is very simple. Everything should be judged for its existential qualities in the context not only of a whole, but of its relations with everything else. A round table is round if it is viewed at a particular angle to its surface, or oval at a different angle. This is where the relational content comes in. It is a constant fact that anything seen two dimensionally as round, can be seen as oval three dimensionally. A table that is round is also oval given these conditions. But if a table seen as round at a particular angle to the surface, is also seen round at a different angle to its surface, this will certainly be an anomaly and not reality, since there is a lack of consistency in the relation. Seeing a table both as round and oval is a veridical perception if there is a constancy in the relational explanations to the difference. A carpenter called upon to make a round table will not be puzzled as to how to make it, for he knows that if he makes a round table seen to be round at a particular angle to its surface, it will look oval at another angle. And this thing possessing two 'curious' shapes (not at the same time) is a round table. So we call something round if it is seen circular at one angle, and oval at another angle; the choice of words, 'round' and 'oval' does not really matter in conferring it different aspects of reality, in a constant relation with each other.

This again brings to mind the earlier problem concerning primary and secondary qualities that have dogged philosophy for so long. Descartes used wax to demonstrate that melting wax changed its solidity and shapes but not its extension (a primary quality), which he thought must be the inherent reality of this substance. John Locke made the distinction between these two qualities to underline the reality of primary qualities in things-we-do-not-know-what. Primary properties such as extension or motion, are said to be inherent in things 'outside' sensibility. Bishop Berkeley in his infinite wisdom argued that since all primary qualities could not exist without secondary qualities, these two qualities must be indistinguishable. My proposed relational constancy is not a rejection of this Berkeleian non-distinction between primary and secondary qualities, but a constitution of reality through a relational constancy among qualities. In this way, the Berkeleian argument on this inseparability has neglected to examine the relations between primary and secondary qualities, beside their dependence. The source of these relations which also explains their dependence, is found in our nature. It is our nature to feel, to sense, to think and to judge with a purpose. So that hardness always comes with pain when struck by our fists or fingers, depending on our tolerance; hardness is not about a sense-datum (or the Berkeleian 'idea'), but about the relation between one group sense-data and another, closely associated not because they are so, but because of man's nature in perceiving them in relationship. That extension cannot exist without colours and shades, is not about that the reality of extension being distinct or not distinct from colours and shades, but about their constant association. For we have seen so far, distinction and independence alone cannot be part of reality. Together, extension and colours can offer us in a chunk rather than the singular aspects separated from the totality of reality. The unreality of matter argued by empirical idealism holds well because this unreality is built on bits and pieces of sensibility, which have no relations among themselves. A sense of realism from subjective sensibility comes not from individual datum or group of data, but from the relations among themselves in a constancy not necessarily imposed by the mind but conceived of by the mind.

The surface of a thing may feel smooth, but I may exclude from this smoothness the touch of hardness and impenetrability that are also sensibility. The relation between sight and sound, or between seeing a lion and hearing its roar, is not about these things being seen together, but being associated so that one sense can remind us of the other with a reason in a being of existence. The sight and sound of things have a relation in reality that is actively sought (by a mind), and the relation itself is not a passively given thing. The mind seeks reality for its ends, therefore it seeks relations of a thing with all else and consequently its understanding and determination. It is the underlying consistency that is passive in the sense that it is given to us. Seeing a lion and hearing its roar are a reality more vivid than seeing alone. The existence of a constancy of relations among things enables us to make assumptions and fill in the gaps of reality that we do not directly see. We do this when we claim to have perceived a whole cup, which is actually seen of one surface. This relational construct of reality serves us well with beliefs in the totality of the whole, over and above our sensibility. This is a far cry from the idea of reality that sense-data or sensibility are the given and not of our making. For if bits of sensibility are given to us separately, without connections, reality has no connection as a whole and the whole cannot be constructed from sensibility either. Such is the sense of reality that constructs all existents, including what we may conceive as substances.

Perceptual reality through relations

In the earlier example of the data of alphabets gathered from the enemies of war, these data look random only because the intelligence cannot understand them. But nothing for human understanding can be at random. To decode such 'random' data, the army must first find a internal pattern (a consistency) in how these symbols appear in an association among themselves. The internal pattern (consistency) gives a sense of understanding, therefore a reality in the random alphabets. For if reality is not to be understood, what else is there to be said of reality? The ultimate understanding through this consistency among the 'random' data, is value-imposed, in the same way we impose a value quantity on mathematical relations to give it a sense of qualitative reality. If we substitute A or B in (A = 1/2 B), with 'horse', 'tree', 'mile' or 'currency', we have an evaluated relation. The suitability of this within reality, is a matter of nature through our judgement with other relations. Thus the reality of a donkey is half the size of a horse (depending on which aspect we are referring to) lies not in the size itself, or the horse-ness, or donkey-ness, but in the consistent judgements of nature.

Sensing in space and the separation of sensing from reporting of sense-data

Apart from this relational reality, what more is there to sense-data? To answer this we must examine the nature of sense-data. If they are not mental, they are not epistemological; and when this link to understanding is cut, it will not be acceptable even if it is an assumption. Yet even when this epistemological aspect of reality is firmly established, sense-data may still be considered to be more than mental happenings.

The first aspect of perceptual experience must be the separation of immediate sensing from perceptual judgement itself. This claim is not mutually exclusive to the idea that perceptual experience is direct as well as immediate. By 'immediate', we only mean it in a temporal sense, rather than different stages or processes. Reality needs being reported, and its report, in spite of our assimilating it to an 'unreportable' reality, is inevitably subjectively or mentally (in the broadest sense) based. To claim that reality and reporting are one and the same thing, one must either be a materialist or an idealist, since they must be either solely materialistic or solely mentalistic, but cannot be both. This poses an extremely uncomfortable problem both for the materialists who think that there is a mental side to reality, and the idealists who think that there is a material side to the mind. Since this philosophy is a minimalist dualism, albeit only relational reality within a totality of experience, a separation between immediate sensing and perceptual judgement must be held. If immediate sensing is direct reporting of reality, there is no need to involve perceptual judgement itself.

If we allow, say, a sensation of colour to be the primary and basic human encounter with reality, we can hardly convince ourselves that there is no colour judgement of this sensation. A separation of primary sensing from cognitive sensing is not saying that seeing is separable from perceptual judgement, if seeing has any cognitive content. As my discussions on universals and reality have shown that every bit of experiential claim has a Platonic ghost (the Form), that casts doubts on a direct knowledge of an independent reality in the absence of judgements. A patch of red in front of me has my awareness of it, and therefore my perceptual judgement; yet, I can deny my judgement by imagining an alternative, or isolating my judgement from this sense impression, without being able to alter or erase the sense of a 'being' in the spatial position where this patch of red lies. This is the sense that sensing is sensing in space. This is a similar situation many philosophers have argued in their own ways, that there is a cause to sensing or a permanent possibility of sensing or an underlying substratum of sensing or impression, and so on. At this juncture, philosophies of reality depart from one another to take up their respective conjectures.

Just the reality of the mental exhibits itself in a duality in living things unexplained by physical causality, basic sensing of reality also exhibits such a duality, in that the 'physicality' originated from judgements of the mental, cannot explain its independence from sensing. In turn, a purely mental explanation cannot carry us to the land of a non-mental reality. When I close my eyes, I do not see the patch of red. But the reality (as opposed to the existence) of this colour patch lies not in my immediate sensing; for if sensing is what there is to confirm reality, it is only a matter of a simple analytical truth that, if something is not seen it does not exist. The reality of this colour patch lies in its relation with other instances of experience, and its permanency; therefore, the reality of this red patch in being seen and seen again after interludes, is judgemental. On the other hand, its sense of 'being' in space, is not explainable. Hence we say that a colour patch as a basic, perceptual impression, has a sense of duality in both not being a part of reality (but existence) (if we cannot explain its being without a relational totality), and being a part of reality (we can understand

and report it in a relational totality). There is no contradiction here since two positions are mutually exclusive so that sensing can be considered to be in either one of these positions, alternatively. In the former, it is an existent in awareness, albeit without judgement; and in the latter, it is more than an existent since it is also in reality by judgement. The difference here is between 'explaining a being' and 'explaining a reality in terms of a relational totality'. This is also the difference between '"being" not in reality' (dreaming or phantom experience) and '"being" in reality'. Incidentally 'being' here means existence, rather than the 'being' of the unseen reality, the type we explicated in our chapter on Bertrand Russell (see p. 3).

To explain something in terms of my own judgement and sensibility is to explain a being within myself or indeed my own being, and not anything else. My own sensibility with judgements can be a reality or may have a sense of reality. This is a curious sense of reality without independence, or of a being without a reality, but it is not impossible to imagine it. In dreams, the content has a being because it has happened in awareness, and since I cannot explain it in terms of my whole veridical sensibility (as my eyes are closed and sensing nothing), it has no reality. Nor can we say that it (the content) has no being (existence) in my awareness, in which case, it is not an independent being. As I have discussed in the beginning of this book, being is in being conceived, but being conceived is not always being in reality.

Thus a patch of red may have a reality outside its being perceived, but its being lies nowhere else but in sensing, or in fact it is the sensing itself. This sensing has no judgement (report). The duality in a combination of being and reality is not a tautology because they are not always inclusive of each other, and because their independence on each other is shown by the fact that reality is within being, but not vice versa. I suppose that immediate sensing is one of this kind, that is, a being outside reality. But what propagates a sense of being in things seen as independent, if a thing in-being is a being perceived or conceived?

When I see a patch of colour, can I refrain from all conceptual judgements of what it is and still see something? But if there is no judgement, what is it that is in front of me? Various philosophers have examined in detail perceptual content and find no substance of being. Why it is so has been explained before, but how it is so may be helpful if I can elaborate a little more. Traditionally, the lack of veridical correspondence between perceptual judgements and percepts is the real problem. But that is only a problem for reality, and certainly not about dependent existence in the sense I have portrayed it. A elliptical shape seen but judged as circular, is a prime example of lacking correspondence. But this is only a problem of reality since elliptical data are presupposed.

If seeing a patch of colour has nothing more than mere sensibility, there will be no distinction between seeing and dreaming, if the consideration for the reality is left out. When I make a ontological assertion of my sensibility, I cannot do so without presuming the existence of a self, that perceives and conceives with understanding.

Leaving aside how this comes about, which I have elaborated earlier in this book and in another,[21] we shall take it for granted that this is the case. To say that there is a being, not something in being (that is being perceived or conceived), is to make a contrast of beings between a presupposed self and a thing, a being. All our sensibility suggests to us that there is nothing in itself that supports such a distinction, therefore insofar as sensibility is concerned, any 'being' of sensibility is only an 'in-being'; and there is nothing to separate what is perceived from what is in-being-perceived.

Thus we need to make a distinction between perceiving and the self. Though all sensibility has a sense of being in the self, its duality makes it an item in reality or in existence, enabling us to consider it as a being outside the reference to the sensibility that deals with relational reality. Considering sensing as non-relational, thus dealing with only the existential aspects, is considering it as mere happenings, stimuli, or the unspeakable in awareness. The unspeakable awareness is a state of consciousness without judgement. Still we have more to this unspeakable awareness. We have space, for to sense is to sense in space. Space has no content to speak of, but a position that is self-evident if the self is a referential point. The thing that gives a sense of independence to all sensibilities, is space, and we sense things in space. This I have examined in detail before.

When I see a colour patch, I can conceive it as a colour sensation by judgement, but I can also sense this colour (redness for example) in space. A colour is something I may or may not need a word to express; I point to it, I look at it and I am aware of it. There is a difference between claiming that I have a sensation of a colour and claiming that I sense 'it' in a space. When I see a patch of colour in space, notwithstanding its vividness in reality, this spatial sense is a referential to myself as a point of reference, in space and nothing else. I cannot say that space and sensibility go hand-in-hand, in the same way Berkeley says that primary qualities go hand-in-hand with secondary qualities. This would suggest a possible mutual separation. Space is an indispensable part of sensibility itself. For we can certainly conceive or perceive the void without objects (sensibility), but sensibility is inconceivable or imperceivable without space. The inseparability of space from sensibility should give us a sense of outer sense in sensing. That all things existed are in space is not an absurd possibility, for even God's existence has always been exemplified by us in a spatial appearance. Whether this is our illusion ultimately, I do not know, and this is not a question concerning reality, but existence. In dreams, we may see things in space too. But dreams exist but are not real.

Sensing, therefore, is, in one way, the unspeakable existential awareness, in space, with an outer sense, with a sense of independence and without the consideration of reality. On the other side of this duality, it can also be a judgemental awareness of reality with content that is beyond sensing.

Outer sense by criteria of the self

A sense of existence outside gives us a reality for our interactions. Interactions are interactions with something other than ourselves. A sense of a being other-than-ourselves is the essence of the outer sense in space. Since all spaces (regions or positions) are only determinable by reference to a permanent point, i.e. the self, all positions in space are somewhere other than this reference point, i.e. the self. This is the outer sense in space. When we sense a colour patch, we do not have this sensibility inside us. It is a sensibility in space, in anywhere but a point of reference to all positions we know. And with this comes our dualism that a sensibility can be both a mental attribute in reality as well as outside us, in being, in space of course. I see the red surface of a teapot that is both my sensibility as well as my sensibility outside myself in space. It is both a being through sensing and reality through understanding. Thus the measure of the self as a perceptual reference point, is vital in marking existents apart from ourselves through space. Sensing on its own without the established existence of the self and space cannot offer an independent, ontological status to all things seen. Without the self, the location of position is impossible as a particular, and hence there will be no distinction or separation of an existent from the self. Without the self, and without this distinction, perceived sense-data of immediate vision cannot be conceived as belonging to the surface of the percept.

Perceptual agreements

In the case of a public reality in which many people see the same thing, there is no verification of a common perception. Without having to dwell on the difficulty in determining whether we do see the same thing, I think that a perceptual agreement is not an agreement on the sameness of our respective sense-data or sensation, but a mutual, ontological acknowledgement made possible by space, and relational consistency. It is an agreement on reality, but not on existence or perceptual content. Without common space or a region, each with a measurement of a subjective determinant, public agreement on things seen is unimaginable. There is also a touch of reality in the agreement on the constancy applied to relations among all things seen. This is an agreement about reality, and not existents.

The reality of things not perceived

When we consider that things may exist or continue to exist when not perceived, we have a metaphysical question of existence and not of reality, since there are no relations that can be established through cognitive judgements from perceptions. But by the criteria concerning what constitutes existence, argued in the first part of this book, things not perceived are not existents. To consider this counter-intuitive question of why we consider things to be existents without being perceived, the content of our perceptual experience used to determine a relational reality cannot help us. For when there is no perceptual content, there is nothing available for existential and reality judgements. This is a logical truth within the meaning of 'existence', or how it is defined.

The cause of such a counter-intuitive question is this. There is a possibility that relations can be conceived indirectly through the sense experience other than that derived from a postulated 'existent' not sensed, so as to infer an existent within reality through relations. For example, the science in Descartes' age says that the motions of cosmic objects have no causation through direct contact with bodies; hence it postulates the existence of ether as a 'substance' that 'swirls' unseen in space moving cosmic objects. Thus some may think that things not perceived can remain in reality, since our relational constancy within the totality of experience may guarantee their place in reality. This is not a consideration for existence, but reality, since we consider existence to be only a product of sensing and awareness. Also, in considering something that is outside sensing, there is an implication that whatever is outside us must be independent of being sensed and of the perceptual content. If there is a thing outside us, independent of our consciousness, it may be real but not perceived and will come into being if and when it is sensed, even though we may not know its existential content except its constant relations in reality. A chair I saw a minute ago without turning back my head to re-sense its existence, is such an example. A unicorn that cannot be sensed does not exist. Its reality depends on how credible the relations by which we conceive it, are. Thus the distinction between existent and reality is important, in order that we can see this difficult philosophical problem in different lights.

And we must bear in mind that a claim of existence is not always followed by a claim of reality, but not vice versa; since reality is within existence and not the other way round. A reality without sensing, therefore existence, as shown in the preceding paragraph, is an epistemological reality that can be refuted by cognitive arguments, in the absence of which it can at best be grounds for postulating a possible reality. A true and metaphysical reality must be capable of being confirmed by existence, i.e. sensing. Thus the chair seen a few minutes ago must be re-sensed to be confirmed as an item in a metaphysical reality. The sensing of data is not a subject for refutation, any more than a self is a subject of existential rejection. A claim of existence does not have more content than what sensibility there is, attributed to such existence, except the outer sense in space that is not sensed. A thing continues to exist unperceived is a reality and not an existence, determined through relations.

The unspeakable sensing

When I see a colour patch, I have no doubts that my sensibility is in space away from myself. In this basic sensing, I do not feel this colour sensation in myself in the same way I feel pains. Without a cognitive perceptual judgement of this colour in a shape, size or 'redness', it remains my sensibility. These two things are inseparable. Where the basic and primary sensing stops and my judgement begins, I can hardly say. Perhaps the basic and primary sensing ends in where a cognitive awareness begins. But then basic happenings must need awareness too. This is a difficult question for the mind, in having such an immediacy, so that awareness can never capture the beginning of its cognition. No matter how sensing comes about, we can safely say that at this minimal stage, a sensing must be the earliest awareness of which we can barely start to talk about it. Such an instance of perceiving moment and its sensation content must have a duality serving both the being (the outer sense) and reality (the relational sense of content and essence), both of which are separable and yet interdependent.

I sit down and see a tree in front of me; I can certainly imagine that I can get rid of all perceptual judgements I have about the tree, albeit with difficulty. Imagine that there are no green-ness, no leaf-ness, no shape-ness, no branch-ness, no size-ness and no other determinable judgements; I am sure this thing will remain in space because a sensation is a sensation irrespective of what and how we can call it or judge it to be. As long as we have sensed a perceptual happening, we cannot fail to see an existent even if we have failed in our determination. This is so if I can say that a judgement of greenness for instance, is only verbal and an understanding, and not an existential content which is the unspeakable.

Metaphysics of human content

Thus I have started off this book with the examination of existence and reality and almost ended it with the same. A metaphysics for humanism is a metaphysics of human content. Not only that, it is a metaphysics that puts human reality, and with that human experience, above the metaphysical reality of the dead world. It is not at all certain if men are here to serve a universe of materialistic order, or if this materialistic order is a conception of man through his nature and his needs to understand, therefore is here for him to interact with. I would prefer to think the latter is true. For all these terms such as 'reality', 'existence', 'order' and 'truth' are first and foremost humanistic terms; without us - humankind - they have absolutely no sense. We see this world with our evaluative eyes but we do not always admit it to be the case; for we want our values to be permanent as the sun and stars. Hence we would conduct our affairs by imitating the materialistic regularity of a misconceived universe to bring about a permanency of those values that we regard as a constituent of a materialistic nature, forgetting that we are an even more important part of it. This view of the universe based on some philosophical ideas is something I have sought to refute. A metaphysical reality in my philosophy is one constructed by humans with all their values they fail to see, in all the objectivity they think they have found. This myth must be exposed and I hope this book can help to do so convincingly. Lastly, we must briefly examine a reality constructed out of our reasoning. This I think requires a extra-human authority.

PART VI

THE RATIONAL REALITY

12. Arguments For A Reality From Reason

12.1. Reality of the categories and universals

Reality out of existence

Earlier, I mentioned a constructed reality, which did not depend on the existence of sensibility. This is the construction of a reality by logic or reason, seen as a construction that can go beyond our sense experience. In this reality, its construct is something that is also dependent on us even though all the metaphysical constituents of such reality are purely epistemological in their origin and determination. Some ancient Greek philosophies on reality advanced doctrines proposing that reality is the construct of mathematical entities (the Pythagoreans), or of the Forms (in the Platonic Forms they are more or less universals). Aristotle's reality is basically a union of 'matter' and forms, the latter of which gives the predication of a substance or its actuality. A particular horse has its being in the potentiality in 'matter' that substantiates its form, the horseness itself. Hence the typical Greek philosophical reality is never without the importance of universals in the construction of an reality of the intellect, outside sensibility.

The rational metaphysics of Aristotle in seeing the Form as an inseparable part of reality of the particulars, suggests that the Form is the end towards which every existent strives to fulfil. Hence a stone has more dominance in its material (substantive) content than in its formal content; and animals have more dominant formal content than that of a stone. Men are the highest existents in that their formal content almost overwhelms their substantive content.

Rationalistic metaphysics has the attraction to many in thinking that it is a metaphysics placing human content (the spiritual content) above all else. It is easy to think of the metaphysical systems of Plato, Kant or Hegel as systems of this kind, in which the ordinary notion of 'human spirit' is not buried beneath the reality of 'material substance'. The reality of 'human spirit' alone is not all humanity, if it is the reality of the pure intellect. For humanity with all its feelings and emotions, is more than a capacity to think, albeit coherently. It is the nature of man that is humanity of the inclusive reality. In a rationalistic metaphysic, human rationale, being objective is dubious in human nature, for we are only rational in the eyes of others. When it comes to the confirmation of this objectivity of our rationale, nature itself and humans themselves, cannot guarantee a universal agreement, not in the same way sense experience can. Every philosopher thinks his or her own rationale is impeccable. Thus a subjective rationale can be taken as objective, by the mere measure of popularity. Aristotle never adequately explains why higher things should strive towards a higher formal existence. Things are seen more dominant in their formal substance, only because this is how they are, in the nature of things, and not because of an Aristotelian rationale.

The fact that universals cannot be understood without, or be separated from, the particulars does not deter these types of rational philosophies. For it has been argued that these universals - these intellect constructs - are not existents, but beings that underline a reality only 'seen' by the application of our intellects. Therefore we have things that are, and yet do not exist. The early part of this book constructs a reality within existence, but not an existence within reality, and provides a coherent answer to the rational determination of the terms, 'reality' and 'being'. This problem probably bothered Plato; hence he asserted that Forms exist in a separate, third realm of reality, and provide his reason for getting out of the absurdity that things are, and yet do not exist (being sensed). Apart from this verbal realignment of the terms of 'existence' and 'being', a rationalistic reality has another problem. This is the problem of how these intellect-constructs can attach themselves or be attributed to particular things to form a permanent reality without arbitrariness. This unsubstantiated arbitrariness can show its face in many philosophical problems concerning attributing something to something else. David Hume's insight into the arbitrariness in attributing a causal relation to events, and attributing values to facts, is a prime example that stems from this. If arbitrariness is the rule of the day, the so-called Platonic 'third-man-argument' is a good example of this lacking of rationale in attributing a form to a particular thing, that leads to an infinite regress. In the Aristotelian and Lockean metaphysics, we see that if we take away all universals or sensibility from an object seen, we have nothing left 'underneath'. It is this nothingness that puzzles humanity.

Kant's rational reality

Then enters Kant into this battle of the intellect. Kant's universals are not the universals closely associated with the sensibles, as some may like to think. Kant's universals are those that are conditional to our possible sense experience. These universals too, are independent of experience, and are *a priori*. He thinks that we can only see appearances through these categories that are universal conditions of human knowledge (including perceptual knowledge). Seeing them within the problem I mentioned earlier, we consider these categories, being epistemological no doubt, as objective instead of subjective. But we are told that there are things that can be both subjective (in the sense of being epistemological) and yet objective (in the sense of having something categorical and conditional behind seeing). In this sense, something that is epistemological may no longer be said to be also subjective. But, in Kant's mind, these categories, or principles of reasoning, or universals, do not have to exist in a separate realm of reality or be independent, and can still remain a part in our epistemological faculty, which usually is subjective. Therefore in all things mental such as knowledge, understanding or perceptual judgement, we have both the objective and the subjective. The objective conditions all our judgements and our perception of reality. Still Kant will not go so far as to say that there is a reality outside this objective-subjective, rational construction. Thus Kant's metaphysics is a transcendental reality. The odd thing Kant introduced and called the thing-in-itself, is very much his common-sense conjecture, left out in the cold.

In a sense you can see that Kant's metaphysics is a reality of humanity which contains an objective rationale independent of other subjective frailty such as emotion and sensibility. In another sense, you can see that Kant's metaphysic, being exclusive of the importance of human emotion, is not a humanistic metaphysic. This depends on our view on this Kantian objectivity. What can we say of these categories? Are they mental or non-mental? Can we have an objectivity in our mental faculties? What reality and ontological status do these universals have, as conditions to construct a reality? Or are they a part of this reality?

The answers to all these can only be ambiguous due to the cleverness in using the term 'objective'. It can be said that, '2 + 2 = 4' or 'all triangles have three sides' will always exist whether we apply our reasoning or not. But it is not to say that this reasoning can have its 'being' without being in awareness or conceived, otherwise how are we to define 'being' without a conception of being? If objectivity is man's nature, I can agree. A cat may certainly not conceive of '2 - 2 = 4', or indeed not all humans can conceive of this notion. Thus it can only be an objectivity for a number (albeit large number) of humans and never be universal. Also its independence of awareness cannot be conceived. How are we to conceive it? If I conceive of '2+2=4', it must be in my mind; but has it been put there by some being? A rationalistic reality constructed by objective reasoning, attempts to give us this sense of a rationale being given to us. For instance, the existence of God, unseen, is constructed out of this objective reasoning the rules and order of which are given. This curious affair I must leave aside. In this way, when I use this word, 'objectivity', I shall use it in the sense of 'being given', incapable of being conceived in any other way than what is. That is the kind of rational reality under which humanity subserves, irrespective of other aspects of human nature. This is the reality to which we must object.

Rationalistic reality is necessarily monism

What do we mean when we say that universals are real? A particular horse is real. But is it real in virtue of its being a horse or being an object? Is its being real dependent more on its horseness or objectness, than anything else. If so what is this 'anything else'? If not, what is this horseness or objectness? If there is nothing else, to say that universals are real is to say that horseness or objectness is real, even though we do not see horseness or objectness, but see a particular horse or a particular object. If we say that horseness is not real, what can we say of the particular object with this horseness? The way to resolve this is not just to distinguish a being from existence relying on the sense of dependency. There is the possibility that we may have misconceived the whole idea about universals. To what extent is this misconception, I cannot tell. But an independent existence in reality of these universals, demands us to conceive this reality as a singularity; for plurality does not have a sense of independence.

Even some pluralistic, rational philosophies deploy the concept of 'modes' of substance in order to avoid this wrath. The reality in a final singularity is almost certainly a logical conclusion for any metaphysical philosophy postulating epistemological items, independent of our subjective sensibility. Just as we can see Plato's thoughts on universals moving towards a singular reality, we also see that Hegel and others come to the same conclusion. In Hegel, it is the Absolute; the idea itself that is self-explaining and self-subsisting. In Plato, it is the Good itself that suggests a perfection for everything to be as it is. In Spinoza, we have the final monistic nature of which everything else is its attributes. In Leibniz, we end up with multiple monads that are totally (and unsatisfactorily) unconnected among themselves. A monistic philosophy ultimately leads to a divine, singular reality in which humanity has no individuation and significance.

Rejection of logical priority, therefore logical independence

In saying that there are no universals without particulars, one would imagine that the existence of universals in the absence of sensibility will be all but dismissed. To rescue this, rationalistic philosophies will claim that there is a logical priority different from a temporal priority. They will say that universals are logically prior to sensible things. Thus the absence of sensible things cannot eradicate the existence of universals. May it at best be argued that there is a difference between logical priority and perceptual (or temporal) priority? We can say that if particulars exist prior to 'their' universals, it will follow that without particulars, there will be no universals attributed to them. However, if we say that there is a sense that something can be logically prior but temporally posterior to another, then we can say that universals can exist logically prior to their particulars without having to admit that this priority is subsumed under a temporal priority, making the earlier conclusion an inevitability. With logical priority we will have also a logical independence.

What exactly is a logical priority? All human thoughts are governed by a temporal order since one thought has to follow another, otherwise nothing is heard, seen and understood. Logical priority is a myth that I do not understand. If it is referring to logical steps in deduction, I cannot see how they are not in a temporal order. If it is referring to an abstract form of logical argument being a conditional mode of thinking, that is to say, an argument: 'all men are mortal; I am a man, therefore I am mortal' has the logical form of 'all As are B; C is A, therefore C is B' which is the mode of thinking the former argument, then, we shall examine it further. Even if our reasoning is always in this logical mode, there is still a temporal order in the understanding, from grasping the logical mode (the variables) to grasping the verbal (valued) argument. If understanding universals is analogous to understanding a logical mode, then it is an understanding with a temporal priority and no others. But when we see a horse (with this horseness together), should there be a mode that determines our way of seeing, analogous to a logical mode that may determine our way of reasoning? Logical modes are pure invention of the logicians which like a mathematical formula explicates rather than models our understanding. In a 'simple' and immediate perceptual judgement, there are certainly no elaborate, intellectual reflections like a logical argument with a logical mode of reasoning. To dismiss this convenient analogy between the logical priority in universals and logical forms, we again ask the same question: what logical priority is there relating to sensible universals. Logical priority, if it is not a conceptual priority, therefore a temporal priority, is no priority at all. Again, it can be argued that a logical priority is merely a logical separation as regards identity. But, a separation from what? There is nothing 'underneath' sensibility and/or perceptual universals. In considering the existence of universals, there is no sense in the notion of logical priority or logical independence, because there is nothing else to be prior to, and nothing else to be separated from. It seems that particulars and their universals are in the final analysis, either inseparable or nothing in dualistic opposites.

Earlier on, I have introduced a term, epistemological priority.

This is a term quite different from the so-called logical priority, since it is a temporal, conceptual priority, and not temporal, metaphysical priority. In this epistemological priority, one understands something prior to understanding something else, which, in reality, occurs in posterior to that which was understood first. The case of cause and effect is an example. Since there is no logical connection between a cause and an effect, except in their understanding, the use of epistemological priority, is more appropriate. Consequently, I cannot see any sense in the use of the word, 'priority', in a logical connection, without a temporal connection.

Independence as the core of the problems

It is unclear why Western philosophy has been obsessed with this notion of independence for so many generations. Perhaps it is a religion-inspired Utopia of the intellect to which we are inevitably drawn. Such a notion of independence, whether be it an independence of humanity or an absolute independence (if there is anything known without humanity), is a seed sown for the problems which inevitably confine Western philosophy to a long analysis of the two opposites: materialism and idealism; physicalism and mentalism. This notion of independence also prohibits the growth of philosophical dualism. For anything independent, that is not knowable, can be absolute in reality; but if so, how can an absolute reality be known by humanity? If God is such a reality, would it be defamatory to say that His existence depends on human conception? Indeed, many philosophical arguments for God's existence lie nowhere else but in the human conception of this idea.

Perhaps, this notion of independence is a science-inspired necessity. A scientific reality being a product of human conception is not appetizing to many. Yet, scientific materialism has no explanation for the human conception of mathematics, hypotheses and observational judgements, within the raw facts of materialism. On the other hand, the exaggerated excellence of human reasoning, which, as in the science of logic, is elevated so high in the hope that deductive reasoning can deliver an independent reality. Yet most logicians will agree that whatever conclusions may be drawn from vigorous deductive reasoning, they can only bring about what has already been contained in the meaning of previous axioms. There is nothing new coming out of any logical investigation, except a clearer conception of the meanings in the premisses. If there is any independent reality revealed through logic and our rationality, it is our nature given at birth. The reduction of the *a priori* content of the intellect to the mere conditions of judgements, is of no help to resolve this problem of independence. For God's existence still has to be deduced by us through our intellect, albeit given by Him, and so His existence is still dependent on the success of this intellectual pursuit. For some, it may not be seen that the very essence of existence is a humanistic term, which demands a human conception.

The lack of enthusiasm for an independent reality can explain why we are also reluctant to accept that there can be 'being' without a confirmation of existence through sensibility, or a reality not conceived through sensibility. The mere word-twisting and meaning-manipulating cannot do; soon or later we will return to the original question of what 'being' is. An existent not conceived through sensibility, is a hypothesized existent. The argument for the existence of the non-sensible and conceptual entities, starts from and rests firmly on the argument for the existence of universals. Once one is convinced, not only universals of the sensibles can rest in a pure conceptual reality without being the existents in the sensible world, but nothing short of conceptual contradiction in these ideas will reject them in rational philosophies.

Everything that is conceived of may or may not exist. In the end, it is all down to our definitions of existence, of being and of reality; for we can certainly define 'existence' and 'being' in terms of conception alone without incoherency. A definition may help to settle the ontological conception between two schools of thoughts, but it may not help the discovery of an independent reality. There is a saying that to deny the objectivity of universals is to deny the objectivity of stones. But if sensibility is mere appearance, how can universals give us a reality beyond appearance, since sensibility in its understanding is universal? But, we are considering universals as independent entities separated from particulars. If universals are the construct of the world, and since they are not in space or time, the world of such reality must be spaceless and timeless. If there is such reality by conception, let the *a priori* intellectuals show us how this reality is possible; and if we disagree, let no one say that we are irrational or that we are not endowed by God with the same *a priori* intellects that they possess. Things of the universe are not logical consequents of human logic, but consequents of human understanding that can be both fallible and incorrigibility. That we think in a logical mode, is a fantasy best demonstrated by an analogy to Kant's comparing it to a feather flying in a vacuum without air.

12.2. Nothingness, negation and reality

Hegelian reality argued from being or nothingness

Hegel's reality is a reality constructed out of logic, albeit his own dialectic logic, that is not totally divorced from deductive reasoning employed by syllogism. I am not concerned with how he deduces his metaphysical reality in a system based on three notions, the thesis, the anti-thesis and the synthesis. But let me examine his first premiss from which his rational, metaphysical system is derived. For surely, if one places so much importance in the deductive reasoning for the discovery of a metaphysical system, one's conclusion must be dismissed or accepted according to the strength of the first premiss from which one proceeds.

I think it was Spinoza who said that affirmation is negation, which effectively proposed that affirmation and negation are two sides of the same coin, so to speak. Hegel's first premiss is found in *'The Doctrine of Being' (Encyclopedia of the Philosophical Sciences, [1830] 1975: Part I, Chapter VII)*, in which the notions of being and nothingness come about as two opposing, but same concepts. In this 'being', it has the meaning of 'is' in an expression such as 'there is an apple'. He thinks that if all universals or predicates are removed from an existential expression, we are still left with 'there is...' that signifies the notion of being. We must at once take note that, initially this is the same position taken by Locke as the substratum underlining all sensibilities, or the same Aristotelian 'matter' that supports the Forms. The unacceptability of Locke's things-not-known, or of Aristotle's 'beings', is due to the contradiction involving knowing something that is nothing and therefore unknowable. However, Hegel's 'being' brings forth its contraries, i.e. there is the nothingness and a being, and attempts to say that they are one and the same.

As we have seen, from Spinoza and others, that negating a being has a logical effect of affirming the being. Since nothingness is a negated being, we can see that to understand nothingness, we must first understand being itself. That being entails nothingness is, in a way, quite obvious. But whether nothingness entails being is another matter. There emerges the ambiguity of nothingness itself: nothingness can mean the unconceived - that is beyond thought and imagination; nothingness can be implicit in the notion of being preceding nothingness itself in our understanding. If nothingness is the unconceived, there can be no entailment of being. If this 'nothingness' has an entailment in being, nothingness is not the first premiss of the Hegelian system, but posterior to 'being' itself since it is the negation of being that brings forth nothingness. So what is this Hegelian 'being', if it is not inferred from 'nothingness' which has no essence, and if it is the 'being' with an essence negated to becomes 'nothingness', and if it is a 'being' that retains no ontological status having all its properties stripped away? So where does 'being' come from?

How can we know the principle of being itself? Hegel thinks that all justification of Being as the first principle and as the first category, is the sign of independence. But being is in being conceived. So if we subtract all that is known (conceived), there is nothing left. He thinks being is the thing in itself after the subtraction of all universals. How do we conceive of such a being with nothing? We can conceive of the notion of nothingness, not as the inconceivable, but as the negation of being, an existent which is the opposite of nothingness. Of course this is an idea; equally true is an idea coming from mathematical deduction. To negate a number, say 3, we do not have zero, but -3, which in turn confirms the conception of 3 itself. In a mathematical negation, there are different meanings; the negation that means 'erasing all' or the negation that means a minus quantity. Still 'erasing all' should imply that there is something to be erased in the first place, that is the ontological affirmation by negation. If the Hegelian nothingness is such a notion, then being must originally have had something that is now erased, and this something conceived of prior to its eradication cannot be without a content. If this being is identical with nothing, where was the conceived existential content erased in the first place? Is it not the case that to arrive at the Hegelian first principle of two opposites (being and nothingness), there must be a conception of an essence now reduced to nothingness by negation?

Hegel has another idea. He thinks that this being is an indeterminate being, as opposed to a being that is determined. To him, a being that is determined will have essence as opposed to a being that is not. How can we imagine a being that is indeterminate? If Hegel seems to maintain that a being negated or deprived of its essence is nothing itself, would there be no difference between an indeterminate being and a determined being? That is of course a verbal confusion made credible. In this he proposes that Being is a thesis to which Nothingness is its anti-thesis and he thinks that they are both the same, so that he probably does not agree that nothingness is deducible from the understanding of being itself. His idea is that a pure being is an indeterminate being, and that being indeterminate, must be nothing, since there is no essence to determine what it is. Without professing to know Hegel's ideas well, I think he explains this dilemma by saying that to imagine the indeterminacy of being (not being itself), we have to introduce some indeterminate qualities which, since they are too not determined, are nothing. What he means by indeterminacy is a generality of the highest order. Something is so general that we cannot determine what it is except that it is a pure being. Here we have a universal of all universals. In a sense, the most general conception of general things is what he may call the indeterminate, but what I would call the unimaginable. Imagine 'colour', not a particular colour, just colour itself and we would have understood (or not understood) what Hegel means. This is the kind of indeterminacy he has in mind.

Here we return to the controversy of the Platonic universals. Can the mind imagine colour without imagining a particular colour? Can we imagine a being so general as to carry no content? Many will say, no. But that is not the point for the rationalist metaphysicists. The fact that we have a word, 'colour', which does not indicate its instances of particularity, will fuel the argument that there must be a thought or a conception of such generality referred to by this word, 'colour'. There is also a word called 'being' or a phrase 'there is'. This is a far cry from calling redness itself a universal, since it is a determinate quality. The same would apply to indeterminate essence. Hegel will say that there is a sense in conceiving essence as a universal essence without any particularity, or without determinate properties. At this frontier of knowledge, one has to decide whether one thinks that one can conceive in one's mind a generality of colour instead of a particular colour to decide what this concept or word, 'colour' really is. Of course, if we do not think that words are rigid references to all existents in reality, we can hardly agree that we can imagine an indeterminate colour in our mind.

Still it is not certain whether it is an indeterminate property that is negated from an indeterminate being, in which case the indeterminate property is nothing and nothing cannot be negated; or it is a determinate property that is negated prior to its negation, in which case nothing through negation entails a determinate being which must exist. If an indeterminate being is identical with nothing since indeterminacy is nothing, then how can nothing be negated and becomes itself?

Is an indeterminate 'being' also a being? Suppose there is no such a word 'being', can we conceive of such a concept, a concept that there is something not of anything in particular, but of nothing in content? I do not think that is possible. If it is a matter of logical separability between the concept in a word and our imagination, then we can see that Kant, in considering a separation of space from objects, has to use imagination to illustrate his point. His point being that we can imagine space without an object but not an object without space. This may be true, but the choice of argument by Kant is not just to rely on the curious notion of logical separability or priority. Hegel clearly does not think it necessary to show us how we can imagine a general colour without its particular instances. So he thinks that thinking of a being with indeterminate properties is possible. This is absurd, of course.

From being indeterminate, the Being becomes determinate in the synthesis of becoming, the final 'closing up' of the Hegelian 'triangle'. In this merging of the being (indeterminate) and nothingness, we have a determined being which implies a being of essence. Since Hegel thinks that his metaphysical system is the product of logical deduction, it must be noted that whatever can be deduced as a conclusion must first be contained in its premisses. If so, I would like to think that the emergency of essence from the synthesis of being and nothing in becoming must be in some way contained in this being.

If being and nothingness are the same, the coming from nothingness to being is the coming of one thing to the same thing; that any new essence can emerge from it is absurd. 'Becoming' is a temporal notion, as is the logical priority of universals, therefore, the Hegelian becoming is a sensible and temporal universal that has a time element and hence not a pure thought itself. If so, the synthesis of the thesis and anti-thesis is not a pure logical move, but a move that has a temporal element that is an empirical input. Of course, Hegel will reject this. Though one may say nothingness implies the negation of essence and therefore affirms a being, there is nothing in being and nothingness to imply the necessity of a unity or combination of two opposites, anymore than there is a implication of a passing from nothingness to a being of essence, or vice versa. Or does one dare say that the implication here is a synthetic input, as is the temporal sense in 'becoming'. It is all very well to say that becoming is a logical combination, but the mind cannot conceive of such unity as a necessity without a temporal notion. All things that exist may stay being and where is the necessity of something coming into being from nothing, or the necessity of something perishing? There is the ambiguity in an anti-thesis of a thesis. If an anti-thesis is a strict negation of the thesis, just as nothingness is of being, then other Hegelian anti-thesis cannot be seen as the same for the lack of logical entailment that may be contained in the meaning of being. For example, Hegel thinks that logic is the idea in itself and its anti-thesis, nature, is the idea in the other with spirit as its synthesis. In these, the anti-thesis of nature is not a straightforward negation of the original thesis, logic, the idea in itself. For the identities of a lower level of the thesis and its anti-thesis are without mutual inference, in the same way as nothingness and being can have no mutual inference without the input of another premiss.

Would the logical opposite for 'being' be 'non-being'? If so, this Hegelian nothingness must be a non-being, which is certainly not 'nothingness', or the 'inconceived'. In a logical sense, non-being is everything that is not being. To arrive at nothing, we start from a thing of being following a negation to obtain a nothing, and I am not sure that is a straightforward deduction. But if it is, 'nothingness' is implicit in being and not vice versa. If being and nothingness are two identical notions no matter how abstract they are, there must be a conception of this nothingness as a concept. Since a concept is as real as any universal, then these ideas of being and nothingness must be dependent in being conceived or thought of. In what sense are they absolute and independent? In what sense is nothingness or being, indeterminate and still a thought? If being or nothingness is identical with thinking a being or thinking nothingness itself, then thinking of a being is thinking of nothing too. If nothingness is unthinkable, then its anti-thesis of being is also unthinkable. Therefore being in term of nothingness must be unthinkable. If nothingness is the unconceived, its opposite must be also unconceived. If the Hegelian being is the conceived, then we are back to the Cartesian first principle. No matter how absurdly I can think, like the Cartesian principle, the Hegelian being is about thinking of 'something' not in particular, against which I have argued as absurd.

Since the original being and nothingness are indeterminate, and therefore nothing, nothing can be deduced from such a union. Or if the essence that emerges from the synthesis of being and nothing is an indeterminate essence, in which case it is still nothing; and if it will become a determinate essence, it needs an additional input of content to succeed. In other words, if being is nothing and indeterminate, what, which is originally in itself, can bring about its determination logically? Is 'indeterminacy' itself an essence of this being, if we allow the possibility of conceiving indeterminate essence in being? If it is, this being must surely have at least one essence in being indeterminate; therefore it cannot be nothing. Is this indeterminacy of being an essence, logically preceding the being, since all universals by which a particular is determined precede it logically and is independent of it? If so, the Hegelian first being is not the first premiss because its being depends on this indeterminate essence that must be the first Hegelian postulate. This is so, if being and essence are separable. As we have learned from the history of rational philosophies, a first principle of existence needs no explanation to justify its independence, let alone the metaphors and analogies Hegel hurls upon his readers to justify his Being. With the rejection of Hegel's first premiss, we must think carefully if the metaphysics that follow this premiss with all the Hegelian deductions are really about a true metaphysical reality.

Essence and being

Nothingness, in the sense of being void of all concepts, cannot imply a being. Perhaps the understanding of a being may imply nothingness by taking out all essences of a being. Nothingness, in the sense of having no essence, does not imply the sense of being, but is implied by it. But true nothingness is the inconceivable and there should be nothing coming out of it and nothing conceived. Whether a separation of being from essence is possible, logically or conceptually, raises the question of whether essence presupposes being, or being presupposes essence. Certainly essence is being itself and being is its essence. Any separation of the two is not only inadvisable, but impossible too. To deduce an essence from being begs the question concerning the substance of being, and that is an error repeated again and again in philosophy. Hegel is no different in this respect. Men will always perceive and conceive of this idea about a being beyond essence and no doubt such pursuit will go on.

Undoubtedly, the conception of an essence, whatever it is, gives rise to being, in an epistemological priority or in simultaneity. To maintain a being without essence or without prior essence, even if it is only a word, is beyond the mind's comprehension. If we step back from Hegel's seductive words and his seductive system, we will see that all the relations and categorical principles are supposed to be logically deduced from a single idea of being, hence it is very much a tautology, since everything has been contained in the original idea of being in order to allow these deductions. The unifying force of all things and their opposite is found nowhere in logical necessity, which seduces men into thinking that their wills too can be so subsumed under such a rationale for the benefit of logic, nature or God. Hegelian metaphysics is not a metaphysics for humanity, but for God and logic.

The implications that one might like to draw from Hegelian metaphysics is not what I wish to explore. As he claims to have discovered a philosophy to incorporate all historical theories, it is not difficult to see Hegel as an idealist, a materialist or both, depending on our interpretation. Of course, such a view could be very controversial. As a rationalistic idealism, Hegelian metaphysics cannot serve humankind as metaphysics for earthly humanity because of the 'spiritual' aspects. As I have explained before, all the consequents of rigid reasoning from universals cannot explain human actions. Reason cannot make us act. In as much as Hegelian metaphysics can be seen to have inspired

Marxism, it can also inspire totalitarian right-wing political views too; for if men see its philosophy as an insight into an underlying force of nature that governs historical and social progression, what role a single man should play in this reality is obvious. What this rationalistic metaphysics has ignored is that human nature, therefore humanity, consists of more than reasoning.

12.3. A reality of dependency

Independence and relations

In this last chapter, I shall sum up a metaphysics that is more or less a conclusion of all the argument and examination we have thus far conducted.

The search for an independent reality, not only independent of human knowledge, but of everything else concerning humanity, is an unsatisfactory affair. Not only is there a self-contradiction in being both independent and conceived, which is not easy, if not impossible, but also a reality that cannot be known. Within dependency metaphysics, we have the sense of an 'outside' reality through space; we have an 'objectivity' in motion through time; and above all we have a sense of reality through a constancy in relations.

Without humanity manifested from the understanding of the self, there can be no conception of independence and permanency, even if the universe will continue to exist without us. All senses of reality are necessarily the senses of dependency that afford us knowledge and relations. The sense of independence is very much misconceived in considering the self being outside it. This is impossible. As I have argued elsewhere, the self is not an existent through immediate perceptions, but a condition for all possible perceptions and conceptions, in which case the conception of the universe is truly and utterly confined to human nature, and within its limitation, naturally.

Universals and abstractions, raising their heads far away from the world of sensibility, are nothing but relations in a sense; relations conceived of by men, rightly or wrongly. Relations cannot be conceived of on their own without the particulars, which form a whole and coherent experience. Words cannot be rigid references to spatial objects in a definitive way, they are really references to relations, with a constancy in application. And in this sense, words and universals share the same epistemological origin, and it can be said that universals are verbal reality and nothing more. Relations are how men see things within a perceptual limitation, and, most importantly, as functional to their nature. This is about the evaluation of human values in our nature. This book does not elaborate too much along these lines, because much has been written.[22]

What I mean by evaluation is not only about aesthetic or moral evaluation. Feeling something hot is a feeling rooted to our nature. Hotness by feeling is not relative to other things, but the self. Other relations such as the expansion of mercury in a tube can do this. But hotness is a measure of human endurance, pain barrier found in human nature. In this sense, evaluative universals and sensible universals, are not relations 'floating in thin air', so to speak, but have an association with human nature, which I say, is 'objective'. Thus we can say that human nature is the 'objective' base that underlines all human experience. Seeing beautiful things is very much a human affair. Seeing a bed is evaluative and functional in terms of human wants; and so is seeing a door, a chair, a television and all things functional. Here human values and their evaluation are broad terms referring to things not contained in the basic percepts of our experience.

Identity in this metaphysics is not the identity of the indiscernibles, but the determinacy of being, which is what we can say of a thing. Objects and oneness are mind defined with spatial or conceptual parameters. This power of the mind also has its downside, since it also allow us to conceive of relations as objects through the limitation of content. Thoughts can only be thought of if they have conceptual parameters or limits in content, therefore, it is not inconceivable to think that words or numbers can refer to spatial objects through the limitation of content. We may see a red object and conceive of this 'red' relation as an entity through the limitation of conceptual content and extension and this may be the cause of misconception. Consequently, we may conceive many, if not all, relations as objects of the mind, through the similar limitation in extension we use for objects. It is not apparent to us that a universal reality can never be imagined on its own, or be epistemologically separated from physical objects. The argument of whether they are independent is a matter of how we define reality, existence and being. We can certainly define them in a way in order to justify the existence of relations in an independent reality. This brings us back to the original proposal that reality is not and cannot be independent, and still relational. If I can define 'reality', 'existence' or 'being' relying only on spatio-temporal experience, then I may not be able to say that things have no being outside sensibility. But I can say that the reality outside sensibility lies in a relation not concerning anything else but another reality, that is the reality of human nature.

Still, the sense of reality being independent of me will not go away. When I, in full consciousness, see all things in front of me with sunshine in my wide-open eyes, the reality seen is an unspoken one; and how can I speak of colours except by pointing to things of colours? How can I speak of my sensation? No sooner have I spoken of it, it will be a generality. When I see a table in front of me, the very fact that determines it as a table, immediately puts it into a relational reality. Be it a colour, a shade or feeling I can speak of, I am setting a parameter for relations, therefore giving it a dependency in this reality. But the unspoken and unjudged reality is so real to me that I can sense, feel and smell it. I cannot confirm or unconfirm, determine and identify these things without using relations of my own sensibility. If I am deaf and dumb, and can say no words of this reality, I still cannot get away from my senses-judgements of this reality. I see a green leaf in a certain shape, and think of all the determinable qualities, but can this be a reality without my descriptions? If I were to erase all words, all descriptions, all relations and all judgements, will there be nothing left? Not so, if my sensibility is not words, not descriptions, relations or judgements. But what is sensibility, if it is not all these?

Seeing a green thing, is not dependent on how I put words to it. I may call it red, blue or yellow; but I cannot get rid of this sensing. Words, with them come our perceptual judgements, relations, universals, sensibility and all the rest, are not the things I see. The difficulty is this: without words and thoughts of the percept, there is nothing to describe reality. But there is still this unspoken reality. How am I to report my perceptual reality? It is not as if it is not there, if I do not apply words and concepts to it. The 'green' thing I see is beyond words and thoughts. Hence I am convinced that these words are not a direct identity to the things I see, but to my perceptual moment that is multifaceted. We see reality by putting it into a net-work of relations of the past and present.

What is a sensed reality without cognitive content? Sensing is certainly there, even if we can imagine that all sensibility (cognitive) and judgements are withdrawn. For I cannot say that without perceptual judgements, I will not have unspoken perceptual sensations. We cannot say that after stripping all cognitive sensibility we will be left with pure relations in reality. But we will certainly be left with the unspoken reality. A sensation and its description or categorization, are obviously two things. For if its description or categorization is wrong, the existence of the non-descriptive sensibility will still remain. That there is a thing in front of me cannot be doubted, for it is its descriptive mode that can be corrigible or incorrigible, veridical or non-veridical. That what I see as oval should have been circular, is a dispute of relations and not of reality. A non-descriptive sensation is a sensing, whereas its description is a relation. But I am not saying that there is a non-descriptive reality over and above a descriptive one. A non-descriptive reality is a reality of immediate sensing. I am sure this situation must have been thought through when philosophers have contemplated their descriptive reality. An independent reality is the one that is not understood, non-relational, and unspoken. Unfortunately, humanity is such that the immediacy of understanding prevents such imagination, so that we can see trees, tables, chairs and everything else within a framework of understanding in all their functions, feelings and descriptive sensations. This is the sense of the non-descriptive reality which will immediately become a descriptive reality as soon as it is understood. External reality is not understood and therefore has no place in human reality.

Non-empirical relations

Since all relations within a consistent framework link everything within a whole experience to everything else, it is not beyond imagination that we can postulate an ontological possibility, pointing to an existent by reference to these relations. There is no false sense of reality when a particular man, but not a women or a dog, is being sought for a crime by general (relational) descriptions alone. Though this is rather simplistic, the sense of reality in an ontological postulation is not totally without foundation. Using this yardstick, we can say that the existence of all things is firmly fixed in this system of relations and experience. Therefore the postulation of an unseen being may not at all be irrational, if this postulation is within a whole experience, so that a definite identity can be found.

A rational reality is built on generality upon generality since there is an idea that many relations are non-empirical or not sense-related. Can a reality be constructed out of these piled-up relations? If we look at conceptual relations, which the Greeks or perhaps Kant regard as *a priori* relations, certainty, totality, plurality, unity or singularity for that matter, are all implicit relations among themselves. There is no plurality without unity or singularity; no singularity without plurality; no totality without plurality or singularity; no singularity without totality and so on. What subsumes them under the concept of quantity is this implicitness. In the sense the meaning of a class cannot exist without its sub-classes or those particulars made up the sub-classes. Thus the concept of quantity cannot possibly be conceived of without totality, plurality, unity or singularity. If there is always a generality of sub-generalities where will this non-empirical generalization of relations end, if it is not in the threshold of sensibility? As we see that a class owes its existence to its sub-classes, tracing back through this chain of classes and sub-classes will take us finally to the 'basic classes'; for instance, redness itself, as a sub-class of colour, will explain all its higher generality.

Extra-empirical relations lie in the act of the mind and in its understanding of particulars. The notion of oneness or unity, I hope, will explain the origin of 'quantity' and its sub-classes. The act of the mind sets boundaries for sensibles and limitation for a 'unity' and hence plurality. If this is correct, the concept of quantity is not a relation of relations outside sensible relations in its origin. Infinity and limitation too are subsumed under this 'quality', so that we cannot conceive of a unity or oneness without also conceiving plurality (divisibility). A plurality not limited is infinity. Similarly, the void as a unity cannot be conceived by the mind, in the same way it cannot conceive of infinity. Contrary to Kant, I do not think limitation is a quality, but a quantity. The rationalist idea is that these concepts of quantity are concepts conditioning our reasoning and conceiving reality; this is a philosophy imposing conceptual rigidity that is only explainable by the idea that knowledge is given rather than learned.

Whether these non-empirical concepts, such as the concept of quantity, are indispensable to the conception of a reality, is all but irrelevant if it is accepted that they are created by the mind. Such a reality will be a construct of the mind, in comparison to a reality constructed out of given sensibility. This is up to our intellectual choice to believe one or the other. Quantity certainly exists in the company of sensible particulars, or nothing can be seen in particularity and in plurality.

The antinomy of something is a 'relation' on which the logical construction of reality can depend. The word 'relation' here is a Kantian term, and not the terms I have used to suggest that all universals are relations. It is the act of the mind that produces antinomies in the act of setting limitation producing oneness and plurality. In this, antinomies are conceived as the failure in such an act. This also applies to the opposites in limitation or infinity, since the mind in exercising conceptual limitation to define a unity, cannot conceive of indefiniteness, or infinity. The mind creates but cannot determine infinity. For in every act of the mind in the organization of sensibles, there is the inconceivable in the failure of this organization. A mind that cannot organize content, does not understand. Consequently, antinomies are within the possibility of the mind's creation, not reality. They may not be objective concepts independent of sensibility. To conceive of all these non-empirical categories, we must first rely on the concept of 'opposite' or 'contrary'. If so, these categories are not as basic in this sense.

Explaining substance and categories

In considering whether every composite substance is or is not made of simple parts, I see that the act of limitation also plays a part in this basic problem. Indivisibility should be conceived as a failure to set limitations within a unity and not the nature of substance. A part within a unity is within limitation. That which can be limited has a content and every content is divisible. This explains why substance can be conceived as having and not having parts. In considering a unity, the mind cannot conceive an alternative to setting limits. This failure prevents the conception of a unity outside limitation itself. Since unity is by limitation, a simple oneness that is indivisible is a concept both outside limitation and within limitation, which is not conceivable. Therefore a substance both as one and indivisible is inconceivable.

The substantive categories, be they qualitative, relational or of modality, are arbitrary in their grouping, if they are seen in a different light. For example, if limitation is seen in terms of the limitation of quantity, it should be regarded as a sub-class of quantity, instead of quality. It is so because there is another aspect being invoked. If the sub-classes of a group are seen as the products of an understanding of antinomies, then, of course, they are necessarily the sub-classes conceived of under the antinomy of each group. But it is not inconceivable to see them as individual and unrelated, and not in related groupings.

To deduce sub-categories from a single category is to say that the understanding of the first depends on the understanding of the sub-group. The reverse position is not true. A sub-group concept cannot be deduced from its main group concept, since it has already been presupposed. In this sense, it is more likely that the conception, and therefore the existence, of a category depends on its sub-categories. To deduce a sub-category from a higher order is to misconceive the origin that contains the meaning shared by the category and its sub-category. If there is any independent category, it cannot be known. Still it cannot be denied that categories are existentially dependent on thoughts and the mind. If not, why do all things, seen in a reality, have relations with everything else? Why are these relations conceptualized into an objectivity reality, ontologically separated from, and prior to a sensible reality? The answers to these questions will mark a humanistic metaphysics from a rationalistic metaphysics in which human nature, conceived to be the source of our actions and behaviours, has no part. In a humanist metaphysic, it is the human mind that creates values, and see more than what there is in the sensible world. In a humanist metaphysics, the extra-empirical content is human content, derived from a nature separated from the non-living world.

Thus, if all these categories, such a reality, negation, substance, causality, possibility, existence and necessity, are to be examined in details, their grouping depends on how we understand these terms. How we understand these terms is by no means as clear-cut as '2 + 2 = 4'. The categories of negation, substance, existence and being have all been examined in details in their metaphysical connections. It remains for us to decide whether they are a fundamental, and the *a priori* core of transcendental knowledge, objective as well as necessary in conceiving a rational reality.

Causal relation is important to the argument for any viewpoint of our metaphysical reality. This subject is dealt with in a separate book.[24] The gist of the claim is that the 'perceived' necessity in causality, lies nowhere except in the scheme of our description of events. In my view, the necessity in causality is an analytical necessary. Thus if this is true, cause and effect are taken out from a necessary and objective connection between events. They are not regarded as a given *a priori* knowledge being independent of or conditional to, our understanding of nature.

Possibility, necessity and contingency are firmly in our epistemological make-up. Whether or not they are necessary conditions in conceiving reality, is debatable. In a sense, whether reality is necessary, possible or contingent is very much a question of whether the world is real in terms of being permanent and independent, or mere phenomenal (appearances), or whether we only conceive of this reality as an objective necessity. The necessity in this conception of reality is not an immediate and self-evident intuition, otherwise, what is the point in reasoning? Things are; only men can conceive of them as necessary, contingent or possible.

END NOTES

[1] Leung, S.K., 2000. *Nature of The Self*. London: Empiricus Books.
[2] Leung, S.K., 2000. *Nature of The Self*. London: Empiricus Books.
[3] Hamlyn, D.W., 1984. *Metaphysics*. Cambridge: Cambridge University Press, ch.3, p.58.
[4] Berkeley, G., 1998. *A Treatise Concerning the Principles of Human Knowledge,* ed. J. Dancy. Oxford: Oxford University Press.
[5] Bradley, F.H., 1969. *Appearance And Reality: a metaphysical essay.* Oxford: Oxford University Press, chapter 4.
[6] Leung, S.K., 2000. *Nature of The Self*. London: Empiricus Books.
[7] Leung, S.K., 2000. *Nature of The Self*. London: Empiricus Books.
[8] Bergson, H., 1913. *An Introduction to Metaphysics*, trans. T.E. Hulme. London: Macmillan.
[9] Leung, S.K., 2000. *Nature of The Self*. London: Empiricus Books.
[10] Leung, S.K., 2000. *Nature of The Self*. London: Empiricus Books.
[11] Kant, I., 1929. Transcendental aesthetics. in *Critique of Pure Reason*, trans. N. K. Smith. London: Macmillan, 2 (4).
[12] Russell, B., 1979. *History of Western Philosophy, and its Connection with Political and Social Circumstances from the earliest times to the present day*. 2nd ed. London: Allen and Unwin, p.459.
[13] Russell, B., 1979. *History of Western philosophy, and its Connection with Political and Social Circumstances from the Earliest Times to the Present Day*. 2nd ed. London: Allen and Unwin, p.688.
[14] Russell, B., 1998. *The Problems of Philosophy*. 2nd ed. Oxford: Oxford University Press, p.51.
[15] Russell, B., 1998. *The Problems of Philosophy*. 2nd ed. Oxford:

Oxford University Press, p.56.
[16.] Mill, J. S., 1973-74. *A System of Logic, ratiocinative and inductive*, ed. J.M. Robson (Collected works of John Stuart Mill, vols. 7-8). London: Routledge and Kegan Paul, Bk 1, chapter 3, 5, 8.
[17.] Locke, D., 1968. *Myself and Others: A study in our knowledge of minds*. Oxford. Clarendon Press, p.10.
[18.] Hamlyn, D.W., 1984. *Metaphysics*. Cambridge: Cambridge University Press, p.173.
[19.] Leung, S.K., 2000. *Nature of The Self*. London: Empiricus Books.
[20.] Leung, S.K., 2000. *Nature of The Self*. London: Empiricus Books.
[21.] Leung, S.K., 2000. *Nature of The Self*. London: Empiricus Books.
[22.] Leung, S.K., 2000. *Nature of The Self*. London: Empiricus Books.
[22.] Heidegger *Being and Time* (translated by Macguarrie and Robinson), Oxford University Press 1967.
[23.] *Language and Meaning in Human Perspective*, Empiricus Books, 2001.
[24.] *Causation and Causality - two mirrors of a cause*, Empiricus Books, 2001.

BIBLIOGRAPHY

Bergson, H., 1913. *An introduction to metaphysics*, trans. T.E. Hulme. London: Macmillan.

Berkeley, G., 1998. *A treatise concerning the principles of human knowledge*, ed. J. Dancy. Oxford: Oxford University Press.

Bradley, F.H., 1969. *Appearance and reality: a metaphysical essay*. Oxford: Oxford University Press.

Hamlyn, D.W., 1984. *Metaphysics*. Cambridge: Cambridge University Press.

Heidegger, M., 1967. *Being and time*, trans. J. Macquarrie & E. Robinson. Oxford: Blackwell.

Kant, I., 1929. *Critique of pure reason*, trans. N. K. Smith. London: Macmillan.

Locke, D., 1968. *Myself and others: a study in our knowledge of minds*. Oxford. Clarendon Press.

McTaggart, J.M.E., 1927. *The nature of existence*, 2 vols. ed. C.D. Broad. Cambridge: Cambridge University Press.

Mill, J. S., 1973-74. *A system of logic, ratiocinative and inductive*, ed. J.M. Robson (Collected works of John Stuart Mill, vols. 7-8). London: Routledge and Kegan Paul.

Russell, B., 1979. *History of Western philosophy, and its connection with political and social circumstances from the earliest times to the present day*. 2nd ed. London: Allen and Unwin.

Russell, B., 1998. *The problems of philosophy*. 2nd ed. Oxford: Oxford University Press.

GWF Hegel, 1830, *The Doctrine of Being* (Encyclopedia of the Philosophical Sciences), Part I, Chapter VII, translated by W. Wallace, 1975 (Oxford University Press).

INDEX

Italics refer to titles